Contingent Lives

THE LEWIS HENRY MORGAN LECTURES / 1999

Presented at
The University of Rochester
Rochester, New York

CONTINGENT *Lives*

Fertility, Time, and Aging in West Africa

Ipas Resource Center

Caroline H. Bledsoe

with contributions by **Fatoumatta Banja**

Foreword by **Anthony T. Carter**

The University of Chicago Press
Chicago and London

Caroline H. Bledsoe is professor of anthropology at Northwestern University.

The University of Chicago Press, Chicago 60637
The University of Chicago Press, Ltd., London
© 2002 by The University of Chicago
All rights reserved. Published 2002
Printed in the United States of America

11 10 09 08 07 06 05 04 03 02   1 2 3 4 5
ISBN: 0-226-05851-4 (cloth)
ISBN: 0-226-05852-2 (paper)

Library of Congress Cataloging-in-Publication Data

Bledsoe, Caroline H.
    Contingent lives : fertility, time, and aging in West Africa /
Caroline H. Bledsoe with contributions by Fatoumatta Banja ;
foreword by Anthony T. Carter.
        p.   cm. — (The Lewis Henry Morgan lectures ; 1999)
    Includes bibliographical references and index.
    ISBN 0-226-05851-4 (cloth : alk. paper) —
    ISBN 0-226-05852-2 (pbk : alk. paper)
        1. Birth control—Gambia.   2. Family size—Gambia.   3. Fertility,
    Human—Social aspects—Gambia.   I. Banja, Fatoumatta.   II. Title.
    III. Series.

HQ766.5.G25 B54 2002
363.9′6′096651—dc21
                                                            2001051050

♾ The paper used in this publication meets the minimum requirements of
the American National Standard for Information Sciences—Permanence of
Paper for Printed Library Materials, ANSI Z39.48-1992.

To Robin, Kara, and Modou-Lamin, and to the memory of Tijan
(October 1991–September 1997)

CONTENTS

FOREWORD

Caroline Bledsoe delivered the Lewis Henry Morgan Lectures on which this book is based at the University of Rochester in October 1999. They were the thirty-seventh in a series offered annually to the public and to students and faculty at the University of Rochester by the Department of Anthropology. The thirty-eighth lectures were delivered in October 2000 by Ulf Hannerz. The thirty-ninth were presented by Lila Abu-Lughod in 2001. Deborah Gewertz and Frederick Errington will give the fortieth Morgan Lectures in 2002.

The lectures honor Lewis Henry Morgan. In addition to playing a signal role in the creation of modern anthropology, Morgan was a prominent Rochester attorney. He never found it necessary to accept a formal academic position, but he was a benefactor of the University of Rochester from its beginning. At the end of his life, he left the university money for a women's college as well as his manuscripts and library.

In recent years the Department of Anthropology has sought out Morgan Lecturers whose work is of interest to a broad range of disciplines in the social sciences and the humanities. We intend to remain firmly situated in anthropology and to provide a forum for rich ethnographic description, but we also want to explore the shape of conversations across disciplinary boundaries and the ways in which anthropology acts as interlocutor in such conversations.

Caroline Bledsoe's Morgan Lectures are admirably suited to advance this project. *Contingent Lives* grows out of Bledsoe's involvement in a major study of birth intervals carried out in The Gambia, West Africa, under the auspices of the British Medical Research Council and the Gambian Ministry of Health. The project was distinguished by an unusual degree of cooperation between senior scholars in anthropology and demography. Her rich and provocative argument is a formative contribution to an ongoing conversation concerning the relationship between these two disciplines.

Contingent Lives turns on two pivotal moments in the Gambian birth intervals project. One was the realization that Gambian women were using modern, Western contraceptives in unexpected ways. Conventional wisdom in family planning programs suggested that in poor, less-developed countries such as The Gambia the first women to use modern contraception would be younger women with more education. It was not anticipated that many, even of these women, would use contraceptives to terminate childbearing, but it was hoped that they would use them to space children. As it turned out, however, Gambian women conformed to neither expectation. Modern contraceptives were used most frequently by older women with very little, if any, education. And they were used only infrequently and briefly to space children and thus protect the health of a child recently born alive and that of a next, anticipated child. Contrary to all expectations, Gambian women were especially likely to use modern contraceptives to "rest" and recuperate following a reproductive mishap—a miscarriage or stillbirth or the death of a child born alive—even though this appeared to reduce the time available to a woman to have children that she (and her husband) badly wanted. (This is discussed chapters 5 and 6.)

The other pivotal moment provided a fresh, culturally informed perspective. As Bledsoe struggled to make sense of the unanticipated findings concerning contraceptive use, Fatoumatta Banja, her Gambian collaborator, produced a sketch of a fertility survey as "an African woman might write it." (This is mentioned in chapter 5 and discussed at greater length in chapter 8.) The standard Western fertility survey now focuses on a woman's live births and their subsequent survival through childhood; it is organized chronologically. Banja's sketch pointed toward a very different survey instrument. It is not organized around notions of time, but instead treats women as social beings and produces a moral accounting of the bodily sacrifices they make in the performance of their conjugal duties.

Around these critical moments, Bledsoe skillfully weaves two powerful and provocative arguments. One concerns high fertility. The other focuses on ideas about time, aging, and morality.

High fertility refers to something quite remote from the experience of most readers of this volume. In population studies the term has been used to describe populations in which the average woman has as few as 4.1 live births or as many as 8.9. Such fertility commonly has been seen as a "natural" phenomenon. That is to say, it is thought to occur willy-nilly where women (and men) do nothing to limit childbearing when they reach a desired family size; where, indeed, women (and men) have no notion that limiting childbearing is possible or desirable. From this perspective, then, the actual level of completed fertility is a consequence of customs governing age at marriage, the duration of breastfeeding, postpartum abstinence from coitus, and so forth.

Against this conventional view Bledsoe presents a strikingly different and utterly persuasive account. The high fertility of Gambian women is not something that happens more or less automatically because they do nothing to prevent it. Quite the contrary. As Bledsoe shows us, it is a skilled accomplishment brought off through the active management by women (and their husbands) of their health, sexuality, and marriages. This management is embedded in and given meaning by distinctive West African concepts of bodily resources, aging, and conjugal responsibility.

Bledsoe offers a brilliant analysis of the management of reproductivity in the West African context, but she does not leave it at that. She also squarely faces the possibility that her Gambian interlocutors have insights into key features of human experience to which our own common sense and scientific constructs blind us. Here her argument concerns ideas about time and aging, or senescence. Key concepts in demography and reproductive biology treat the number of children a woman can produce as a fairly straightforward linear function of time. The capacity to reproduce begins with menarche, increases fairly rapidly, declines gradually, and ends at menopause. Senescence is driven by the calendar or one's "biological clock." Fertility is a function of one's use of time. The more time during the reproductive period that is lost or blocked as a result of delays in marriage or remarriage, breastfeeding, contraception, and abortion, the lower the rate of fertility.

Bledsoe argues that this apperception of time is embedded in contemporary Western common sense and recurs widely in other social and biological sciences, including anthropology. It is sustained in part by our very high levels of life expectancy at birth and very low levels of fertility and maternal mortality. Experiencing very different patterns of morbidity and mortality and with very different ideas about the management of their reproductive capacities, Gambian women (and, in some circumstances, men) have it more nearly right, as did many of our own forebears only a few generations ago (see chapter 9). Our lives—the lives of men as well as women and not just our reproductive lives—do not unfold as a simple response to the passage of time, but are contingent on unpredictable events and turnings. Since we are social beings, these contingencies include the doings of others. The management of our lives is all the more a moral accomplishment.

Both arguments are constructed in part through the use of a striking and powerful methodological innovation. Standard statistical analyses of quantitative data sets are designed to discern overall trends and patterns. And they are largely divorced from the situated statements of informants. Working with Epi Info, an epidemiological data entry program developed by the Centers for Disease Control, Bledsoe has developed a way to use survey data in a sharply contrasting manner. She uses the data-checking capacities of Epi Info to ask novel and unanticipated questions about groups and individuals, and especially about those actions that stand out against larger patterns. And she uses the text storage capacities of the program to listen to the voices of particular persons. In effect, she is able to turn survey respondents into ethnographic informants. The trick points to a path that many ethnographers—sociologists as well as anthropologists—will want to explore.

Earlier, I observed that *Contingent Lives* is a formative contribution to the ongoing conversation between anthropology and demography. As early as 1968, writing in *New Society*, Allan Macfarlane urged anthropologists to concern themselves with the dramatic changes in fertility, mortality, and population growth then taking place in the developing world. Nevertheless, from the contributions of Meyer Fortes, Audrey Richards, and Priscilla Reining in Frank Lorimer's 1958 volume *Culture and Human Fertility*, to John Caldwell's call for the incorporation of micro-level, anthropological approaches in demographic investigations, the impetus for collaboration between anthropology and demography has come from demographers. The result is what generally has been called anthropological demography. Paralleling Dell Hymes's distinction between anthropological linguistics and linguistic anthropology, this is anthropology in the context of demography. The problems around which research is organized derive from population studies and center on the determinants of mortality and fertility decline in aggregate populations. The theory comes largely from sociology and economics. More often than not, anthropology's contribution is limited to ethnographic methods. Though there are important exceptions, the key concept of culture generally is confined to the margins, appearing most frequently as a residual factor to account for some unexplained statistical variation and, as Eugene Hammel has observed, in a form long abandoned by anthropologists.

Bledsoe takes a large step toward what might be called demographic anthropology, demography in the context of anthropology. Demographic anthropology might be conceived of as the study of vital processes—processes involved in birth and death—as cultural resources and of the management of vital processes as cultural practices. Reciprocating demography's interest in anthropology, *Contingent Lives* shows us how close attention to the enormous bodies of quantitative data produced by demography may help us identify and understand underlying cultural conceptions. Bledsoe's work also convincingly demonstrates that vital processes, like other cultural resources, mediate among human beings; not merely ends in themselves, birth and death also serve as means through which other ends are attained. Similarly, the cultural practices through which people—Western population scientists as much as ordinary Gambian women and men—manage vital processes cannot be reduced either to exogenous material conditions or to abstract, universal rationality. Rather, they are among the historically constructed means that people use to represent and invoke their social and cultural order for personal and collective ends.

Anthony T. Carter
Editor, The Lewis Henry Morgan Lectures

This book, which builds on a 1992–95 field study in rural Gambia, presents some highly disparate views of the processes that we call reproduction and aging. It asks how we choose, from our vast cultural, historical, and scientific repertoires, certain lenses through which to understand these processes. How do we decide what to bring to the foreground and what to relegate to the background? What do we hold constant? Under what conditions do we shift to one or another frame? How, in short, do we handle the pieces of science available to us? It concludes that our filters and the ways we choose them are in one way or another extrapolations of our own times and concerns. Yet what is so remarkable is how readily, almost irrespective of our disciplinary or political sympathies, we can take these frames at face value and overlook the stark empirical contradictions they may pose. It is thus the pursuit of my own culture's logic, as much as that of Africa, toward which the book is directed.

The book contains several notable features. One is some apparent redundancy in the descriptions of fertility. For this, I ask the reader to bear with me. It is not needless repetition but an attempt to force a confrontation between different perspectives on a single set of phenomena. The book's scope is wide, and I run a line of argument down a slippery path. I expect that some readers will feel as confused as I am at times about where empirical reality lies. The results, however, appear to hold in ways that go against the grain of much current scientific practice, so my aim is to keep potential defectors on board as long as possible.

A second notable feature of the text is its effort to draw on a wide scholarship: sociocultural anthropology, demography, history, obstetrics, gerontology, reproductive biology, gender studies, and the history and culture of science. It ranges so far afield because the pieces of the subjects of reproduction and aging, as we have come to understand them, have been strewn throughout so many disciplinary storage bins. Indeed, understandings of much of the empirical material lies at the edge of tremendously technical subjects. Here, I am on thin ice. However, a number of people who know these subjects well have generously read chapters or papers and given me the benefit of their expertise.

This brings me to the book's third distinctive feature, and one that makes for highly unconventional anthropology: its methods. Although I had worked intensively on two projects in Africa (one in Liberia and the other in Sierra Leone), I had never worked in The Gambia. Mid-career demands of job and family limited my total field time to about eight trips of no more than three weeks apiece, much of it spent in a computer room in an upcountry field station. There, I tried to analyze the returns of surveys and smaller projects that had been conducted in my absence, asked follow-up questions of the fieldworkers, and wrote what I hoped would be improved interview protocols to be administered after I left. On top of all this were all the logistic demands of fieldwork: helping arrange for supplies and for transport for field workers, trying to help keep an eye on the budgets, communicating with sponsoring agencies, and so on.

In the midst of all this, I tried to do some of what resembled anthropology as my discipline has conventionally taught it. This included recording observations, conducting intensive interviews and case studies, doing textual analyses, and collecting field notes to try to piece together disparate bits of logic as the project unfolded. Whenever possible, I elicited local exegesis and analyzed key words to expand understanding, unearth interesting cases, resolve apparent inconsistencies, and elicit people's interpretations of the evolving results. All were elements of iterative efforts to probe the inconsistencies and interesting stories underlying the numerically coded responses in order to move the analysis forward. But I had almost no time to engage in in-depth interviews with anyone other than people who were educated, English-speaking, and (indeed) closely tied to the project or the world of family planning and health. I did spend enormous amounts of time in the United States puzzling over the materials that I took home or that were sent to me, and preparing for the next trip. And I tried to stay in touch by phone or fax for questions about new directions to take and to try to help handle problems. But my ability to engage in the sustained, hands-on field-work that anthropologists take as their trademark was highly constrained by having such brief spurts of time in the country, and my negligible skills in Mandinka remained a serious handicap throughout. Constraints like these sometimes make the social relations described in the book sound schematic.

As a result of these constraints of time and logistics, the book contains a paradoxical package of methodologies. The Gambian study was conducted largely by means of surveys, a social science method that has been the primary source of inspiration for none of the great classics in sociocultural anthropology. Of course, the term *surveys* can cover a wide ground; much can be accomplished with astute research assistants. Much can also be done irrespective of the manner in which the material collected is encoded. Many contemporary anthropologists who work at the edges of disciplines such as demography are seeking to break the barriers between the use of numbers and the cultural enterprise. Yet there are many ways to use numbers and many ways to align them with other forms of information. Although surveys are usually referred to as "quantitative" data and interviews as "qualitative," I attempted to combine both genres in every possible manner. One of the most graphic examples is the fact that many of the surveys contained open-ended commentary in which individuals explained their answers to key questions. Another was that the open-ended interviews as well as cultural analyses had a mutually informing relation to the surveys, and each survey's questions improved as a sense of the cultural terrain grew. Indeed, I began to treat numbers less as quantitative data than as cultural thought pieces. I found myself spending enormous amounts of time attempting to find ways to make survey numbers "talk" by sorting and scrutinizing them—"trawling" or even "crawling" through them would be better ways to describe the technique—in ways that might bring out the meanings they might encode (see chapter 5). In all this, a small quantitative data entry and statistical analysis program called Epi Info played a major role. By attempting to wring cultural insights from surveys and numbers, I found that it is possible to transform what appear to be universally standardized and quantified categories of demographic studies into persons embedded in a complex moral economy of social relations.

In sum, if my demography was unorthodox, my anthropology was even more so. In fact, it hardly qualified as sociocultural anthropological field-work in any conventional sense at all. Chapter 5 will pick up on the draw-backs of these methodological idiosyncrasies but their also quite unexpected advantages. Because the structure of the book reflects the discovery mode in which the pieces of logic unfolded, I allow the descriptions of the methodologies to unfold as well, to show how new discoveries constantly led to the need for new methods.

Nor was I able to investigate some critical areas of life in depth. Given the time constraints, marriage, child health, birth intervals, and contraception drew much attention. Politics and economics above the level of the compound drew little. Indeed, the study omits much of the sense of political, economic, and ethnic upheaval of contemporary African life, with the result that my discussions of the role of time in Gambian women's lives sometimes seem oddly out of historical time. One of the oddest gaps, given the nature of the project, was that of sexuality, in the sense in which it is usually taken in today's humanistic and social science scholarship: of sensuality and physical expression. I had a fair amount of knowledge about these subjects from two prior field projects in West Africa. But the need to spend the precious in-country time concentrating on both the immediate puzzles at hand and on the logistics of the project made it difficult to get much direct information on these subjects in The Gambia.

Given the limitations posed by these conditions and many others, the contributions of Fatoumatta Banja, the Gambian study's project manager and a subsequent collaborator, were of major importance. Fatou, along with several other Gambians, read drafts of papers and made important suggestions and corrections. It was her cultural guidance that led to the synthesis that emerged out of what I initially saw as a growing morass of contradictions in the interview and survey results. I describe some key moments in the research, among which the most significant was an evening in early April 1994 (described in chapter 5), when the two of us finally identified the source of my confusion. Thereafter, Fatou and many other Gambians (and, in the United States, a number of African residents and visitors) helped me reframe, piece by piece, all my knowledge about reproduction and aging over the life course. All this occurred in an unending stream of follow-up questions, in subsequent trips to The Gambia and through fax and phone lines, all through the course of what became for me several years of cascading aftershocks. Therefore, although the voice in the text is mine, it is a guided voice. It is certainly a highly edited one. The book, however, is written as an anthropologist's experiential journey of discovery into her own cultural life-world of science and common sense. At the outset it is framed quite intentionally in the first-person plural referent of "we-in-the-West," and, even more narrowly, as one of those who writes from academia. The voice changes, however. It speaks at first through the frames I used initially to discuss reproduction and the life course, and gradually it changes into the voice by which I came to understand them quite differently. As the consciousness about this shift in perception settles in, largely over the course of chapter 6, the "we" in the narrative voice becomes a tool in the juxtapositional logic on which the book's analysis rests. Sometimes "we" refers to people raised in and oriented to the West, sometimes it refers to we Western anthropologists, and sometimes it refers to we the population-conscious West. In addition, "we" sometimes refers to a more inclusive group: we as either Gambians or Westerners, or even we as people in the most universal sense. In using this narrative device, I ask the reader not to let go of perspectives that seem to have been laid to rest but to retain them as vantage points, exploiting them for further insight.

The book strongly reflects as well collaborations with several individuals, to each of whom I am uniquely and impossibly indebted and from whom my ideas have unabashedly drawn and benefited. I acknowledge first with immense gratitude Allan Hill, my co-principal investigator in the 1992–95 Gambian study. The study would not have occurred without his contributions or without his established base in the country, including the census he painstakingly helped set up and maintain. His visits to the country were more frequent than mine, and to him fell most of the logistical tasks of motorcycle purchase, field worker recruitment, and budget management. I acknowledge as well Anthony Carter, Jane Guyer, and William Hanks, who helped move the book far beyond its beginnings. These individuals will find so many of their insights and clarifications strewn throughout that it would be both tedious and embarrassing to cite them all.

For additional help and insights at various points in the project, I am grateful to the field workers, interviewers, and villagers in the Farafenni study area. It is impossible, however, to name all who helped. Just some are Umberto d'Alessandro, Karen Andes, Gillian Bentley, Kabir Cham, Barney Cohen, Ann-Zofie Duvander, Melville George, Brian Greenwood, K. O. Jaiteh, Momodou Jasseh, Dauda Joof, Patricia Langerock, Elise Levin, Matthew Lockwood, Reuben M'Boge, Sangeetha Madhavan, Kristin Mann, Tanya Marchant, Linda Martin, Susan McKinnon, Geoffrey McNicoll, William Murphy, Allieu N'Dow, Mark Nichter, Jay Olshansky, Alberto Palloni, Elizabeth Poskitt, Erica Reischer, Gigi Santow, Balla Silla, Heidi Skramstag, Bintou Sousou, Johanne Sundby, Adam Thiam, Marta Tienda, Linda Waite, Susan Watkins, Patricia Woollcott, and the anonymous reviewers for the University of Chicago Press. I am grateful to

Shobha Shagle for help with the demographic and health surveys and with some of the statistical analysis in chapter 7, to Jennifer Van Dahm for help with the bibliography, and to David Brent, Jennifer Gowins, and Christine Schwab at the University of Chicago Press.

I owe enormous thanks to members of the Department of Anthropology at the University of Rochester for inviting me to give the Morgan Lectures in October 1999 and for the generosities of time and hospitality they provided. Their extraordinarily careful reading and exceptional insights, together with those of the discussants (Kamran Asdar Ali, Anthony T. Carter, A. Stacie Colwell, Linda Layne, Mark Montgomery, and Ellen Ross), have provided key guidance in revising the book.

For their generous support for various phases of the project from which most of the study's materials were drawn and for time and resources to reflect on the findings, I thank the Gambian Medical and Health Department of the Gambian Ministry of Health, the Gambian Central Statistics Department, the Gambian National Population Commission, the British Medical Research Council, Harvard University, the University of Chicago, and Northwestern University. I also thank the Rockefeller, Mellon, and John Simon Guggenheim Foundations.

Portions of the book draw on previous papers co-authored with Allan Hill, Fatoumatta Banja, Jane Guyer, William Hanks, Patricia Langerock, Umberto d'Alessandro, Barthélémy Kuate Defo, and Shobha Shagle. I alone, however, am responsible for the present contents and interpretations.

All names of individual respondents in the study are pseudonyms.

CHAPTER I

Introduction

Kaddy Seesay, a thirty-year-old remarried divorcee, happened to fall into a sample of women interviewed every month for fifteen months, during a 1992–95 research project on contraception and birth intervals in rural Gambia. In this West African population whose people intensely desire children, Kaddy had undergone four pregnancies. Three were with her first husband. The first, a daughter who died before age three, was followed by two stillbirths. At this point Kaddy's marriage ended, very likely a consequence of her failure to produce children for her husband. Remarrying as the marginal second wife of a man already married to a younger woman with three children, Kaddy became pregnant for the fourth time and bore a son for her new husband. The monthly surveys began when her baby, still breastfeeding, was about seventeen months old. Four months later, this child died. Left in a precarious marriage with no children to support her in later life, Kaddy, still expressing a resolute desire for more children, did the last thing we might expect. She began a long course of Depo Provera injections.

This example presents three apparent anomalies. It shows high-technology Western contraceptives out of place: being put to use far from where they were manufactured, in a country whose uneducated rural inhabitants appear to have ideas about reproduction radically different from those in the West. It also shows contraceptive use out of time: used at a point in time and for a duration in which efforts to space children safely can hardly characterize the motive. Finally, it reveals contraceptive use in an unlikely social context, one in which a woman's future conjugal life seems to hang in the balance on the basis of her ability to produce children. It is small wonder that by the fourteenth month of the survey, Kaddy commented, "I am suffering in my marriage."

An outsider's first reaction might be to attribute Kaddy's contraceptive behavior to "noise," or data error. In a 1992 baseline survey of 2,980 women in the study area who had ever been pregnant, only 27 were found to be using Western contraception after what might best be called a reproductive "mishap." That is, their last pregnancy ended in a miscarriage, a stillbirth, or the death of a young child.[1] This was less than 1 percent of all the women in the entire survey: scarcely worth reporting, according to most statistical conventions. Yet Kaddy's case, as startling as it may sound to the Western ear, is not unusual for women in such situations. Of the 150 women in this survey who were using any form of Western contraception, 18 percent were doing so after a reproductive mishap—nearly four times as many as the number of users in the total population (5 percent). This finding is all the more surprising since, in a population whose members value high fertility, no one in Kaddy's circumstances should be using contraceptives, at least according to the conventions by which fertility in Africa is usually analyzed. And if this were not enough, many of the women had not only had a recent reproductive mishap; they had had a history of them. Finally, whereas population studies of Africa have assumed women who use contraceptives to be those with "modern" characteristics, the wave of the fertility-reduction future, only 3 percent of the women in the 1992 survey had ever attended school (almost no one over the age of thirty-five), and all were living in poor, rural conditions where high fertility is a life goal for everyone.[2]

These findings on contraception following a reproductive mishap, with little apparent regard for its temporal penalties for fertility, fly in the face of every demographic theory that has been advanced to explain fertility behaviors in places such as Africa. They seem to reflect efforts to reduce or "control" numbers of children under circumstances in which the economic gains of fertility vastly outweigh their costs and where a target family size can hardly have been reached. They certainly reflect circumstances that

1. Leaving aside sterilization, which might imply a volitional character somewhat different from that of the other Western methods, the percentage of users following a reproductive mishap was sixteen.

2. I use the phrase *high fertility* in part to avoid the term *natural fertility,* a phrase I discuss in more detail in chapter 2. However, African fertility rates of six or seven live births are far below a woman's potential fertility.

were overlooked in the project's earlier focus on child spacing as the motive for contraceptive use (Bledsoe et al. 1994): there *is* no child to space. Such observations make little sense in a population so desirous of children. Since these women value high fertility, such extraordinary anomalies pose significant challenges to prevailing views of reproduction and the course of physical life. It is at the extreme edges, where the logic looms so improbable, that a theory is put to its greatest test. Tiny numbers like these, as well as a whole series of anomalies that the Gambian material brings to light, have implications that have eluded not only demographers but anthropologists as well.

Durkheim long ago lent insight into the potential significance that cases such as Kaddy Seesay's represent. In *Suicide* (1951), he pointed out that apparent aberrations should not necessarily be regarded as separate from the rest of the population. Rather, they may be extreme manifestations of the entire shape of "normality" in a particular society, an observation that Rose (1992) develops in his discussion of the tail of the distribution in epidemiological studies.[3] If we take seriously the cases of women using contraception after mishaps, they also are an integral part of the population in some critical way that highlights what normality is like. But what kind of normality can they be reflecting? Examining a wide array of empirical findings, I contend that, in attempting to force the course of physical life (that is, its pathway of growth and development over the life span) through filters of linear time, we have looked through distorted lenses at the dynamics of high fertility in Africa, if not those of other times and places.

In this book I examine two disparate views of female reproductive capacity and aging. After describing a view that I call "linear," based on a countdown to menopause and senescence, I re-describe these phenomena according to what I call a "contingency" view. In this latter vision, the pace and character of the decline of reproductive capacity are outcomes of the cumulative physical tolls that women experience, tolls that age them or wear them out. Reproductive capacity is measured not by an abstract, universal, and naturalized time line of physical decline but by individuated experiences of cumulative wearing, traumatic events. The process of decline is seen as a function of the actions one takes and the social resources one can muster to mitigate the effects of injurious events. Thus, in attempting to avoid the wearing effects of multiple traumatic pregnancies that would attenuate her future capacity to reproduce, Kaddy Seesay, like many other

---

3. I use the examples of Durkheim and Rose with an important qualification: they do not point us in the direction of the analyst's cultural perceptions, the theme of this book.

women in her predicament, sought out Depo Provera not to limit her fertility but to regain her strength. But the differences between the two overall descriptions of life are immense. Perhaps most striking are the descriptions of senescence. In the first depiction, the pace and character of aging are chronological inevitabilities; in the second, they are products of social action.

The possibility that an apparently exotic set of facts is a more comprehensive account of the body's workings than the science we typically utilize in our writings and envision in our lives is a provocative one. What most interests me about these sets of observations, however, is how such apparently straightforward biological phenomena as reproduction and aging can be perceived in such utterly different ways. What soon becomes clear is that different phenomena can be deceptively commensurate. They may be overlapping and intertranslatable. But they are not necessarily identical. In fact, the more similar two perspectives appear to be, and the more they share vocabularies, the greater our chances of falling into traps of commensurability. Shrouded by layers of naturalized common sense, the multiple perceptual frames from which our science springs can follow the same track for quite a long way without our noticing how different they actually are. In the case of reproduction and aging, I believe, the vision of chronological "time in the body," on the basis of which we typically analyze fertility and aging, is deceptively commensurate with bodily temporalities that are more contingent in nature. As a result, scientists who study the course of physical life persuade themselves that they can assimilate information to a certain framework. Yet when the empirical baselines of time, place, and circumstance shift rapidly, views of "normality" change, and the conditions that shaped the original conclusions are quickly lost to view. We all entertain both the contingency and the linear models. We interweave their elements in different blends and in different contexts. I sketch below some of the tensions between universalisms and local specificities raised by this phenomenon of the disappearing baseline. The Gambian view, however, brings to the center what Western academic practice sets at the margin. It asks what the world looks like when contingency, and not linear time, is the cornerstone of physical experience.

The data for the book come largely from the 1992–95 project on contraception and birth intervals in rural Gambia. However, the book draws also on my prior field research in Liberia and Sierra Leone and from some brief field and library research on American and European counterpoints to the African findings.

Structuring the Problem

The possibility that high fertility is a social achievement rather than an accident of nature has indisputable appeal for sociocultural anthropology.[4] I document some of the anthropological riches the subject brings to light. Contraception, on the other hand, has hardly drawn the interest in anthropology that it has for demography, a field for which the rate of reproduction in a population is the point of analytical departure. Yet the latter half of the twentieth century saw a dramatic escalation in the use of what are commonly called "modern" contraceptives throughout the developing world.[5] Women in Latin America, Asia, Africa, and the Middle East are now using contraceptives in numbers that our discipline would hardly have predicted even two decades ago. But although increasing proportions of the world's women are turning to these contraceptives, little anthropological attention has been devoted to how people may be configuring them to their reproductive and social lives.[6]

Findings on contraception in rural Gambia provide a powerful discovery heuristic. Contraceptive use is a social activity in that it bespeaks relations with sexual partners and with a wider world of co-wives, in-laws, patrons, and ancestors. It also opens a window onto classical anthropological questions of time, aging, reproduction, and the body. In pointing to facets of their lives they seek to adjust, users are revealing by their contraceptive actions physical phenomena that our routinized perceptions miss. My interest in contraceptives thus lies not in their effects on fertility levels of the overall population,[7] the central issue in population studies. What interests me instead is why they are used. In rural Gambia, the principal reasons fall into two related categories. One is a woman's effort to manage reproductive life in ways that will secure her position in a social world dominated by her in-laws ("affines," in anthropology terminology). The other is her effort to bear all the children that God might give her by adjusting the timing and

4. For analyses of fertility as an achievement in very different contexts, see especially works on surrogate motherhood and the new reproductive technologies (e.g., Ragoné 1994; Franklin 1998).

5. I prefer the term *Western* to *modern*, since I dislike the assignation of "modernity" to things originating in Europe and the United States, excluding places elsewhere in the world. The term *Western* is itself far from problem-free, but it will have to suffice as a shorthand. The usual referents for contraceptives of this sort are various kinds of oral contraceptives (pills), Depo Provera, condoms, surgical sterilization, and the like.

6. For some notable exceptions, see Nichter 1989; Greenhalgh 1994; Morsy 1995; Asdar Ali 2000; Russell et al. 2000.

7. For such efforts, see Caldwell et al. 1992; Lockwood 1996; Mason 1997; B. Cohen 1998.

circumstances of her pregnancies. To any scholar attuned to the transformations in meaning in the global flows of ideas and technologies, it should not be surprising to hear that contraceptives are not always used in the way that the distributors intended. But the fact that they might be used for precisely the opposite reason is paradoxical, to say the least.

Demonstrating that high fertility is a social achievement and that contraceptives are seen as devices toward this end should be intrinsically interesting to anthropologists as cases of agency superseding what otherwise would appear to be uncontrolled biology or (alternatively) local cultural meanings superseding those of international population programs. Yet there is a more compelling reason why these themes should engage sociocultural anthropology. This reason has to do with the character of physical experience. This field has long had an ambivalent relation to universalizing models, especially those that seek to privilege biology over culture and social life. Margaret Mead's *Coming of Age in Samoa* (1928) argued strongly for the priority of environment in conditioning behavior and the mind, a position underscored by her mentor Franz Boas in his preface to the book and one that intensified in the latter half of the twentieth century. Even Meyer Fortes, who sometimes rubbed shoulders with demographers (for example, 1978), argued that although anthropology's sweep was broad, its limits with respect to biological questions were clear: "We must leave to physiology, genetics and demography the exact study of these determinants" (1958, 1; see also Sahlins 1976). In the wake of such reservations, the science of human biology has ebbed as a domain drawing central analytical interest in most of sociocultural anthropology.

Yet if we are to attempt a reclamation project, how should we proceed? Should we accept a "core driver" theory that privileges genes and biological forces as the underlying determinants of social life? In my view, we have all received basic genetic instructions to be human. Beyond this, there is so much room for tinkering that arguing for any hard-wired genetic contributions to social life would be misleading. What intrigues me instead is the tinkering itself: how we seek to make the biological social. Reproduction and the workings of the body are vital nexes around which social relationships are built. They are the objects of maneuver, exchange, valuation, construal—even play. Facts such as these make a strong case for designating human biology as legitimate, if not compelling, subject matter for sociocultural anthropology.

If I am to argue that the course of physical life offers pivotal subject matter to sociocultural anthropology, how should I structure this case? I would argue first that there are deep cracks in the core of contemporary Western knowledge that shape how all of us, whether we write from the universalizing sciences or from their humanistic critiques, collectively believe in certain naturalisms in the body. I would then point to a very different, even counterintuitive, interpretive frame in which physical life appears to operate: one in which social practice bears on physicality in ways that even the most resolute culturalists among us have not imagined. Such a possibility looms large in our handlings of facts concerning time and aging—specifically, the tendency to map aging onto the passage of time. This tendency has become deeply embedded in our early twenty-first-century middle class *habitus*, the taken-for-granted shroud of culture that guides our most minute perceptions and behaviors and in which social necessity is made to appear natural. The equation of age with aging (or senescence) shapes the way we write about the world. Yet it is so deeply embedded that, as Pierre Bourdieu (who most developed the notion of habitus) would predict, it is largely invisible to us.

Contemporary social science and humanities scholarship has shown convincingly that society symbolically inscribes bodies or tinkers with body form (for example, gaining or losing weight, building muscles, piercing, scarring, or tattooing the body). The Gambian findings, however, bring to light management efforts of an entirely different order. They reflect attempts to guide the physical trajectory of aging over the adult life course. What should most beckon to anthropology is the possibility that aging, like high fertility, is socially constituted to a degree that we have not apprehended. The possibilities that the process of physical aging is not tied to age, that time is not determinant of childbearing ability, and that aging is under social control in ways that we have not considered are highly counterintuitive to the academic common sense from which most of us write.

To address these issues the book takes two classical anthropological tacks. First, it lays out the logic of high fertility in a society very different from our own. Second, it deconstructs the concepts by which contemporary Western thought has conventionally viewed this logic. It does so to the point that the locally meaningful categories of experience, rather than scientific convention, increasingly dictate the analysis. Beyond this point, sociocultural anthropology has tended to hesitate, holding the exotic and the familiar firmly apart. This book takes an additional step. It takes findings that converge sharply around a certain set of facts that is very different from the one we usually employ. It recycles these findings *back* through Western science's own universalizing filters, to see how they stand up.

Alfred Gell, in his book on the anthropology of time (1992), acknowledges that his own theorizing about time draws examples largely from studies in geography and economics. By way of explanation, he points to a dearth of anthropological studies that attempt to integrate ethnographic groundedness with the conceptual flexibility that, in his view, is more evident in objectivist styles of analysis. Yet he argues that one should ideally attempt to exploit the tension between empirical and cultural or cognitive potentials that the analysis of time holds: the "analysis of collective representations of time must proceed along a broad front, continually charting the interplay between systemic factors, deriving from the spatio-temporal layout of the practical world, and the wide variety of symbolic constructs which agents deploy in the course of handling their affairs" (326). Gell's conviction that there is no fundamental contradiction between the aims of these endeavors points to "a huge, and so far unexploited, series of intellectual opportunities" (321).[8] It is just such an opportunity that this book attempts to seize. Starting from the empirical edges of fertility, time, and the life course[9] in a small West African country, it asks how we handle the pieces of science available to us.

Background of the Problem

Researchers from Western societies, where high fertility is receding slowly to a temporal and geographical vanishing point, face an increasing struggle to understand both the experience of high fertility and the modes of social life that are constituted around it. As most of the world settles into a steady pace of low or even below-replacement fertility, its citizens move ever farther away from the kind of personal engagement that would help them understand the dynamics of high fertility. In recent decades, moreover, population research in developing countries has focused almost exclusively on situations of, or possibilities for, fertility decline. Left aside are the dynamics of high fertility itself. Studies of high fertility are disappearing rapidly even from the international medical journals, whose articles now describe the predominant problems faced by older women as those of cancer, bone loss, and infertility.

---

8. See also Bourdieu (1990, 25–26) on phenomenology's tendency to confine itself to the taken-for-granted experience of the social world.

9. For just two of many excellent sources on aging and the life course, see Hareven 1994; Kertzer and Keith 1984.

Sub-Saharan Africa is a region where fertility rates have remained high and contraceptive use low. Demographic studies have characterized such situations as those governed by "natural fertility" (Henry 1961). Although abrasive to the anthropological ear, the term has been used simply to mean that because there is no desire to curtail numbers of children, fertility-relevant behaviors occur consistently across all birth intervals. As a result, there are, on the whole, regular intervals between births. Also implied, often, is an ignorance of, if not an aversion to, Western birth control technologies. Hence, whereas we can ask most Western women how many children they want and elicit a clear numerical response, Gambian women frequently respond, "Whatever God gives me" or "Ask my husband" (for a rich elaboration, see van de Walle 1992). Indeed, the testimonies of subfertile women suggest that they are far from happy with their divine allotment, whereas women who received a bounteous number probably would have liked even more. In populations such as this, where the demand for children appears to exceed the supply, the most obvious question is not the one that policy makers typically ask: "Why do they want so many children?" Rather, it is "Why don't they have more?"[10]

For high-fertility populations the conventional demographic answer to this question is expressed in units of a continuous linear duration that we call time. The units of time fertility analyses typically describe include age at first marriage, number of years in conjugal union, amount of time using effective contraceptives, and length of postpartum infecundable period (the duration during which a woman cannot conceive) and of birth intervals, all set against the countdown to menopause.[11] The following question thus arises: Given that African women want children so badly, why don't they produce more of them? The principal answer to this question is so taken for granted that it is seldom articulated: they run out of time. Indeed, two of our most strongly held tenets on these matters are that (1) time imposes the ultimate check on fertility by shutting down a woman's ability to conceive and that (2) pregnancy terminations that produce a living child are the key units of reproduction. Thus, the ability to conceive is seen as the essence of reproduction, and a woman's reproductivity—by which I mean her capac-

10. This question has inspired related demographic work in other societies whose fertility has remained high (e.g., Bongaarts and Potter 1983; Coale 1986). It has also been addressed in other ways in fields such as microeconomics, obstetrics, and reproductive biology.

11. I will use the term *menopause* to refer to the end of the menses although a pre-menopausal decline in fecundability may precede this event by several years.

ity to produce children—is framed in terms of the number of times she can conceive and bear a living child over a given span of time.[12]

The sense of time as the limit to reproductive capacity saturates our common sense. It pervades our lives and our science to such an extent that contraceptives are assumed to block off segments of time from a reproductive life span that is determined largely by genetic inheritance. In high-fertility populations, the logic that ensues seems to pit women against population planners on a temporal battleground. While women try to fit in as many births as time allows, population planners try to "protect" as much of this same reproductive time as possible through (for example) campaigns to raise the legal age at marriage or by supporting contraceptive programs to persuade women to delay, space, or stop childbearing.

As for rural Gambia, with its high fertility level, regular sequence of birth intervals, and meager numbers of current contraceptives users, it is tempting to concur with this depiction: women let biology and traditional norms run their course until time puts an end to their reproductive capacity. If we adopt the anthropological dictum of taking seriously what actors say, however, we confront a problem. Gambian women themselves do not necessarily see efforts to space births as limiting final family size. What is more, chronological age draws virtually no interest throughout rural sub-Saharan Africa, a fact to which generations of frustrated census takers and surveyors can attest. And whereas menopause is drawing unprecedented attention in the United States among educated baby boomers who have postponed parenthood, it is hardly discussed at all in The Gambia. The mystery, in sum, is why people who so intensely desire high fertility should display such profound indifference toward the passage of time. It is only when confronted with a jarring case like that of Kaddy Seesay—someone with such a pathetic reproductive history who appears to be blocking off significant portions of her fast-shrinking fecund life—that we realize that the entire picture makes no sense.

It is worth emphasizing that the project's initial focus on Western contraception in rural Gambia was itself almost a contradiction in terms. The ever-married women in the 1992–95 study's region had one of the highest total fertility rates in the world, 7.5 children. (The total fertility rate refers to all of the live children a woman would bear throughout her lifetime if

---

12. I use the term *reproductivity* to distinguish the ability to reproduce in general from demographic term *fecundability*, which refers to the probability of conception or capacity to conceive but which is often used more broadly to refer to the capacity to bear a child. My reasons for retaining tight control over this distinction will become clear later.

current levels of fertility continued to prevail.) They also had one of the lowest rates of contraceptive use. Only 10 percent were using any kind of contraceptive, including traditional (largely abstinence and an Islamic medicinal pouch called "juju"), and only 5 percent were using a Western method (mostly pills and the injectable Depo Provera), with a few cases of sterilization. The national rates, which included urban areas, were slightly higher (Republic of The Gambia 1993). The project was an oddity on another front as well: the participation of a sociocultural anthropologist. Most in this field would consider contraception to be one of the narrowest, most myopic of subjects. Tied to the applied, highly quantitative family planning world, it rips a tiny slice of human life out of a dense social and cultural matrix and casts a glaring light on an artificial, imported technology. But wrestling with this most unlikely anthropological subject, as seen through the lenses of both Western science and rural West Africans, suddenly brought to light a much broader set of findings that seemed to not only breach all demographic common sense for high fertility populations. It also unleashed streams of ideas for me on classical anthropological subjects of reproduction, marriage, time, and morality in a way that nothing before has done.

Many researchers associate the anthropological contribution to "harder" sciences such as economics, biology, or demography as complicating conventional views of the most appropriate entities to count by describing their meaning in context. Anthropology seldom ventures to solve an empirical problem in a harder science. This book attempts some of both. In the category of problem solving, it draws on various disciplines and a number of contemporary and historical sources, as well as the field materials from rural Gambia, in order to explain why rural African women are behaving in ways that would so clearly seem to undercut their attempts to achieve high fertility. In the category of complicating matters, the book points to a deceptive convergence between contemporary Western understandings of high fertility and those that have characterized other times and places. It contends that we have poorly understood the dynamics of high fertility. We have created the wrong human universal, one of linear decline and the physical life course, and relegated the right one, that of contingent physical decline, to the margin.[13] In doing so, we have overlooked very

---

13. Along different lines, see Martin's (1998) critique of biological research that maintains a mechanistic, linear vision of the body. In contrast, Martin argues, many nonscientists see change as nonlinear. The body is depicted in their models as a complex interacting system embedded in other complex systems, and all in constant change. Thus, small initial perturbations can lead to massive alterations in results.

different understandings of both physical experience and of the social life that may be constituted around it.

The most immediate application of these observations is to reproductive practices and aging in The Gambia. But they are equally applicable to our own academic common sense about these subjects. In a reflexive mode, we can ask how this sense is incorporated into our academic practices.[14] Doing so demands that we scrutinize some of the technical concepts that have been used to study fertility, with the expectation that they are the products of culturally specific categories that we have naturalized as universally applicable to reproduction and the body.[15] Equally important as objects for study, then, are the analytical gaps in other fields, including sociocultural anthropology itself.

Common Sense, Experience, and Social Practice

At its core, this book is about the dynamics of common sense about the body and its health: how, and under what circumstances, one version of "the obvious" comes to the fore, while others fade into peripheral vision. In particular, how do we create, remember, and forget ideas about normality in the childbearing body? Enormous amounts of scientific energy hinge on the assumption that there is a "normal" baseline of health. But is this the case? My contention is that it is not. I am not making an adaptational argument: that what is normal or healthy for one environment may be abnormal or unviable for another. Nor am I saying that humans have a genetic potential, although the environment determines how it will be expressed. I *am* making a set of perceptual arguments that ideas about the bodily "baseline" shift as health measures alter the human constitution, and that views of bodily reality continue to change when we shift the foreground and background. I am also arguing that the course of physical life is very much a function of social life: of relations among people in which bodily trajectories are contingent on each other. If these assertions are right, they would, among other things, undermine claims to be able to detect effects of particular factors on the body or its health.

14. Abu-Lughod's chapter in Riesman 1992 offers a useful exposition of the notion of reflexivity. The present book, however, is less oriented to questions of psychology than to those of empirical phenomena.

15. The present effort to relativize the life course parallels the work of Hanks (1996) in the domain of language; for example, "Meaning is historically [and contextually] specific, not subsumable under universals of grammar" (122). See also McKenna's (2000) challenge to current scientific views about the risks to babies who sleep with their mothers.

At the outset, then, we confront two puzzles. One is Gambian women's indifference to the passage of time in a society that strongly desires high fertility. The other is how our science handles its facts. Critical to both puzzles is the notion of common sense: the view that certain of our experiences seem so "natural" they scarcely bear mentioning. For wisdom on the notion of common sense, I turn to phenomenologically inspired works that routed subjective perceptions of the physical world and thought objects through the meaning structures of human experience (see especially Husserl 1964; Schutz 1973; Schutz and Luckmann 1973). Common sense, as it has been taken up in the social sciences and the humanities,[16] has come to be understood as unreflective belief about what is "natural." As Simmel (1971a, 6) observed,

[N]ature is the special way in which the mind assembles, orders, and shapes sense perceptions. These given perceptions of color, taste, tone, temperature, resistance, and smell pass through our consciousness in the accidental sequence of our subjective experience. In themselves, they are not yet nature. They instead become nature, and they do so through the activity of the mind which combines them into objects and series of objects, into substances and attributes, and into causal connections.

Although common sense is shared and overlapping among participants, it tends to be inscribed in certain social positions that are precipitates of circumstance or history (for example, Bourdieu 1984). It can be gained by Gambian women from direct experience. It can also be gained indirectly by Gambian men and contemporary Western women, who do not experience the rigors of reproduction in the way that contemporary Gambian women do. However common sense is acquired, it tends to take truth as self-evident. Because it is rarely singled out for thematic treatment, common sense is highly resilient to challenge. It trusts its schemes of reference to such an extent that action can be conducted by routine and recipe, not out of fully conscious awareness. Only when a starkly inconsistent experience is perceived might a realignment be required. At this point, other bits of knowledge that lie in peripheral vision can be seized from the vast stock of knowledge and put to highly pragmatic use (Schutz and Luckmann 1973, 36–40).
    The notion of common sense has been productive in anthropological

---

16. For some well-known applications in anthropology, see Geertz 1975; M. Strathern 1992a; contributions to Yanagisako and Delaney 1994.

works of many sorts. Geertz (1973, 137) demonstrated that what is moral or just behavior in ethics and religion is thought of as stemming from common sense. And Bourdieu (1977, 1990) built on the idea of common sense and practice for his work on the idea of habitus. Bourdieu's work has special relevance for this study, with its emphasis on the body's relation to the world. Becoming second nature, common sense knowledge is converted into motor schemes and body automatisms that become "pre-verbal" habits, or ways of acting (Bourdieu 1990, 68; see also Hanks 1996, 238). A critical point in the phenomenological position is that what we see as natural or commonsensical depends on our vantage point (Cooley 1902); hence, common sense exists in multiple versions. This means that the social order is not replicated mechanically. Those who possess common sense can elaborate it or erase it. Indeed, it contains some quite systematic distortions. Forces of power masked as culture are among the most important examples (see Foucault 1980 and Gramsci 1971 on related themes). Another key domain in which distortions occur is perceptions of time. The multiple social groups to which we belong (the family, the office, ritual), each with its own way of seeing time, may imbue us with multiple temporal perspectives whose inconsistencies we overlook. (See Evans-Pritchard 1940 and Halbwachs 1980 for some of the most significant statements.) The potential traps laid by common sense are intensified because our frames for viewing the world are deceptively commensurate with one another. Whether it is because contradictions are troublesome to solve, or because resolving them is unnecessary to our practical lives, we tend to allocate them, as Mauss (1973) observed, to the "miscellaneous" pile: to be sorted out, we perpetually promise ourselves, later.

With respect to the book's argument, the phenomenological baseline about common sense and experience runs in two directions. The first, directed at the Gambian material, examines the experience of reproduction and aging in a society with high fertility expectations.[17] The key theme here is common sense about the practices or techniques that produce certain kinds of spaces following births. Throughout the book, I describe various techniques, especially those with pregnancy prevention effects. Whether they are explicitly taught or inadvertently conveyed, they pervade understanding about how the body functions and how it should be managed.

---

17. In a review of Ross's 1993 book on reproduction among the working class in England at the turn of the century, Nord (1994) pointed out that the tolls of reproduction were experienced in intensely physical ways.

According to Castoriadis (1984, 231–35), the core meaning of the ancient Greek *techne* is learned practices (or techniques or tools) that effectively assemble, transform, and adjust available materials in an appropriate act, accomplishing or bringing to a full finish what nature cannot. In Plato, for example, techne is an activity considered to be voluntary but not necessarily derived from explicit knowledge. It may simply be an effective, standardized practice that has been handed down. In describing the techne, Castoriadis places particular emphasis on the use of what is already there; hence, the assembly and adjustment of existing materials. Contraceptives such as pills and Depo Provera hardly sound like materials that are deeply woven into the local history of a place like rural Gambia. But these technologies are becoming as integral to the commonsense tool kit for managing reproduction as relying on abstinence, Islamic medicine, or breastfeeding-induced amenorrhea. This does not mean that all of these methods are considered equally effective. Nor does it mean that they are considered equally appropriate for all women in every instance among those who use them. Indeed, differences among these methods, including differences between pills and Depo Provera, are central to the argument. It simply means that a wide variety of tools is available to women who, according to their different circumstances, may use one or more of them to try to create spaces in ways that some force that we usually call "nature" may not reliably accomplish.

Besides these domains of common sense, others on the Gambian side of things include age and bodily decline particularly for women. In matters such as these, I conduct a close inspection of the meaning structures of experience, but I leave a space open for the harder objective edge of the kind of experience entailed in physical aging and the trauma that may accompany birthing: pain, muscle loss and damage, hemorrhage, anemia, energy depletion, and the loss of life.[18] There is no necessary correspondence between the real world and perception. Yet if a person senses the world through the body, then the fact that this sensing instrument changes radically over the course of life—and even more if it changes in ways very different from how our writings have described the process—cannot be a trivial matter.

The second phenomenologically inspired thread that the book pursues is that of Western perceptions and the analytical frameworks to which they give rise. Just as rural Gambian women seem to act in certain ways because

18. A highly engaging effort to describe women's experiences of their bodies in eighteenth-century Germany is Barbara Duden's *The Woman Beneath the Skin* (1991).

of certain views of the world, the disciplinary practices that guide our writings may be precipitates in some ways of our own experience. This means that what we as analysts are predisposed to consider "natural" with respect to fertility and aging very likely becomes embodied in the techniques we use and the concepts we develop. We frame people's experience of the world, and we develop methods for collecting and analyzing data with these frames in mind. Whether we call ourselves demographers, anthropologists, art historians, physicians, or gerontologists, the problem that we perpetually confront is to discern between deceptively commensurate logics.

Two Visions of Time and the Body

Commensurabilities in the common sense by which we think about reproduction emerge starkly in the following accounts of time and the physical life course. One version, that of linear chronicity, sees the essence of fertility as a time-based ability to conceive. The other version, which I call a contingency logic, is used to describe high and risky fertility. These two frames are not spelled out anywhere in quite the way that I describe them. Nor do I presume that other members of my culture would describe them exactly as I do. I trust, however, that they are sufficiently familiar that the contemporary Western reader will be able to follow both accounts.

Time in the Body

The first frame, what we might call "time in the body" or "time as nature," arises most prominently in Western descriptions of fertility and aging. It equates the process of aging with age, the duration since birth. This duration is expressed as a linear grid of equivalent chronological segments, consisting of days, months, or years.[19] Age language saturates our speech, our analytical concepts, our most fundamental assumptions about life. Whether we are working in a scientific, a humanistic, or a popular genre, we describe the forces that control this degeneration as genetically programmed and that degeneration itself as largely linear with time. We gauge our lives in the terms set by the logic of time, and we pit ourselves against the clock. We complain about our age-related ailments and treatments and note that the years are creeping up on us. We do, of course, draw attention to variation among ourselves in the pace at which our life course stages

---

19. For an analysis of this propensity in American culture, see Chudakoff 1989.

transpire, and we recognize that some of us may die before the standard sequence is finished, whether by accident, disease, or suicide. We joke that we "look younger than our years" or that we are "getting old before our time." We also recognize that what we call being "fit" can increase longevity and that we can become fit, and hence live longer, through diet and exercise. For this reason, many of us buy products and engage in practices that are promoted in health magazines on the basis of their alleged ability to prolong life or to make us look young: alternative medicines, natural foods, herbs, vitamins, and so on. From our position in the frame of time in the body, though, most of us regard measures such as these with ambivalence if not derision.

We apply the frame of time as nature (or the bodily clock) as much to reproductive capacity as to aging. Much as Emily Martin (1987) observed that medical texts often construe the female body as a machine, it is also the case that we think of female reproductive capacity in the metaphor of a clock. We plot reproductive capacity, which we equate with the ability to conceive, along a pathway that converges closely with aging. Our belief in a time-based end of reproductivity is so pervasive that, as is true for common sense in general, it almost goes without saying. Our emphasis on a time-based ability to reproduce takes us in two diametrically opposed analytical directions. One is that usually taken by our international family planning specialists, who see high fertility as a problem in the developing world. Programs developed in this frame promote contraceptive use for spacing births on the conviction that doing so will reduce fertility by blocking out irreplaceable pieces of time from a woman's total span. Critics may censure these measures on the grounds that they exert pressure for fertility reduction in countries that do not have problems of overpopulation. The key point, however, is that both sides, despite their political differences, are based on precisely the same assumption of time in the body. Certainly these attempted assaults on time by family planners do in fact represent efforts to suppress child numbers, and so in this, both sides are right. But whether blocking off fecund time will actually limit fertility is something neither side has asked.

The other direction that our conviction that time as nature takes us is one we more commonly perceive in our own lives: anxiety that our reproductive time is running out. Most of us want children, yet women see this goal as something that is most easily achieved within a defined window of time. For those of us who delay reproduction, innumerable writings in our society portray the capacity to bear children as a clock ticking inexorably down to menopause as it lowers our chances of conception and pregnancy and increases our risk of miscarriage. The dust jacket of *The Biological Clock: Balancing Marriage, Motherhood, and Career* (McKaughan 1989), for example, states, "Careers, financial independence, and birth control have given today's women new choices about raising a family. Yet, one fact remains: the years of fertility are finite." The Downers Grove (Illinois) *Reporter* (20 September 1989) introduced a story thus: "Tick, tick, tick, tick. . . . That noise you hear is the biological clock of the women who are putting off having babies while they establish their careers. It is also the sound of a time bomb. . . . Women wait until they are in their 30s to begin starting a family. If they have trouble getting pregnant, they have to look for the problem and, hopefully, a solution to it. All of this takes time, time they no longer have." And the *New York Times* science section on October 3, 1999, carried as its lead article "Timeless: Buying years for women on the biological clock." Among its statements was a quotation from infertility specialist Dr. Maria Bustillo, "We should be using this technology to help the truly infertile . . . , not just people who are infertile because they are 45."

We know that there has been a profusion of new technologies for enhancing reproductivity that can stretch out a deteriorating ability to reproduce or even bypass many of the usual reproductive mechanisms altogether. These new technologies allow us to prolong our reproductivity in a spiral of financial, bodily, and psychic costs (see, for example, Franklin 1997). As is the case with aging, we recognize variation from one individual to the next. Yet our conviction that time is the "natural" basis of reproductivity induces us to track the passage of time closely so as to gauge our reproductive and financial strategies within its boundaries. One could even argue that it is precisely because we hold so tightly to the idea of time as nature in the body that such technologies can provoke enormous ambivalence or even animosity, on the grounds that they are "unnatural" (see also M. Strathern 1992a on this point).

The conviction that time is the essence of fertility means that the ability to conceive is what draws our attention in the reproductive process. It is the unknown, problematic element. As a result, we tend to take for granted the assumption that a pregnancy, once securely implanted, will be brought to a successful conclusion. Accordingly, we focus our technological energies and our popular imagination on the creation and viability of a conceptus, especially (and increasingly) its genetic constitution, and its first precarious days of existence. In doing so, we relegate to peripheral vision all the other troubles that can intervene in producing a child (see, however, the contributions in Cecil 1996 and Layne 1996, 1999 for some notable exceptions). We also minimize the possibility of problems for the next birth that the last one may have created and the cumulative dynamic that may build from one birth to the next.

Western society attaches one final culturally perceived quality to time that is relevant here: an assumption about its intrinsic causal force. Particularly in living organisms, we speak of time as if it had the ability to bring about life changes and to do so at a pace that is similar among all like entities. Note, for example, the sense of causation that is implied in these *Oxford English Dictionary* examples from literary sources: age-weary, age-cracked, age-despoiled, age-dimmed, age-enfeebled, age-gnarled, age-stricken, age-worn. Implications of age as causal even appear in this entry on the nonliving world: the increment in strength of an alloy over time is a process known in the field of metallurgy as age-hardening. Examples from the field of demography are readily found. *Population Index* abstracts describe examples such as the age effects of mortality from lung cancer, cerebrovascular disease, and stroke. And in the case of fertility, Frank et al. (1994) describe "[T]he influence of age on fecundity" (350) and "the time limits of fecundity" (361). Of course, if pressed on the point, our conviction that the passage of time itself causes aging or the demise of fecundity (or anything else, for that matter) evaporates. What takes its place is usually an acknowledgment that it is not time that causes these outcomes but certain metabolic processes that lead to an organism's growth or decline, processes that can be measured over time. Still, the assumption that time acts as nature on a biological template so thoroughly enshrouds the formal models in all of our fields that it passes unchallenged and therefore is submerged below the surface of everyday consciousness. Even in anthropology, which has been endlessly intrigued with cultural perceptions of time and has recognized the chronological definition of time as but one of many culturally marked durations, this feature of intrinsic causality appears to have escaped our probes.

The idea of an irreversible force of linear time in nature is the ground on which a tremendous amount of cultural activity is focused. In the case of reproduction, much scientific as well as popular effort is engaged in attempting to transcend the limitations of time and, where possible, to reverse its course. Postmenopausal pregnancy, the new reproductive technologies, and so on, are the most recent examples. We believe as well that we can take action to add time to the natural allotment we have to live—that is, to improve our longevity. The fact that we can speak of concepts such as "agelessness" or "timelessness" or, conversely, "getting old before our time" suggests that age is not necessarily joined to biological decline. Indeed, virtually all the titles on the subject of aging on the Evanston Barnes and Noble bookshelf now imply that time can be defeated, aging reversed, memory regained, sexual potency regained, and so on: for example, *Stopping the Clock: Dramatic Breakthroughs in Anti-Aging and Age Reversal Techniques* (Ronald Klatz, 1996) and *Strong Women Stay Young* (Miriam E. Nelson, 1998). However, these strategies for defeating time are found in a semantic context in which the reader is being exhorted to some course of action that would reverse what would otherwise be the body's natural course. So although this suggests that a more contingent view of aging may be gaining credence in the United States, the fact that these are considered self-improvement books is material evidence of our underlying belief that time works in a linear if not a causal fashion.

I leave for later a consideration of the directions the cultural logic of chronological time in the body has taken us and turn elsewhere for an alternative.

Contingent Lives

Although the great bulk of our academic writings describe reproduction and aging as part of a framework of linear time, we also recognize a strikingly different frame: one I am calling "contingency." This frame posits that a person ages (that is, becomes senescent, or "worn out," as the Mandinka notion of aging is best translated) as a result of the traumas encountered over the course of personal history. The organizing idea of contingency is that of proximity or contiguity, usually both physical and social. The fact that one person is proximate to another implies that the acts of one will likely have repercussions for the other. These repercussions may be beneficial. A Gambian woman whose daughter marries a productive young man, for example, may find her material life improving. From her new son-in-law she may receive grain supplements, cash to start a small business, and medicine from a pharmacy. He may even send her on the *hajj*, the pilgrimage to Mecca. But the repercussions of proximity also can be deleterious. A man who falls into debt threatens the well-being of his entire family, since they are expected to help him out of his predicament. Similarly, a man who cannot keep a wife threatens his family members in that the bridewealth that they helped him pay may not be returned.

Being contiguous or proximate to something or someone also implies a sense of vulnerability: being at the mercy of what can be a random act of fate lying outside one's control. Writing about death, which may not wait until old age but may strike at any moment, Whyte (1997) stresses how often anthropologists overlook this highly tenuous quality of life: "[W]e often fail to appreciate the reality of misfortune. . . . We skip quickly over morbidity and mortality figures, if we have them at all. We describe healing rituals, and the effectiveness of symbols, without going back three weeks later to learn how the patient is doing. We are entranced by the logic of ritual, the form, the assertions, but we tend to ignore the logic of affliction when it resists efforts to shape it" (21).

Attempts to deal with uncertainty have no warrant of success. The Nyole of Uganda, relates Whyte, "know they may spend large sums of money, sacrifice animals, and inconvenience themselves in vain. The fact that affliction is likely to have its own unrelenting logic is not something that Nyole hide from themselves. They acknowledge that misfortune may overtake them anyway" (22). A sense of vulnerability applies even to intimate social relations, despite the security these relations appear to offer. In a vivid quotation, Whyte captures the menace that can lie beneath the surface of apparent congeniality of everyday social proximity: "With a human agent, you must try to guess the details of sincerity, capability, and feelings, as these are revealed through a myriad of subtle indications. You go on living with human agents in the coincidences of daily life, and new clues are continually revealed. . . . [I]t is difficult to really know the heart of another person. . . . Nyole imagine the human agent as a self, ruminating on experience, resentful, angry, or grieved" (31–32).

The potentials for harm that underlie close social relations are an enduring African theme. My 1981–82 fieldwork in Sierra Leone turned up a key example in the idea of the "next-to" person. A next-to person is someone in whom you confide and who knows you well enough to advise you on how to proceed in difficult situations. For a woman, this person may be her younger sister or her co-wife—someone who pounds millet for her, brings her water and firewood, looks after her young children, and tends her when she is sick. A man's next-to person is often a younger brother or an older son; when his sons or their mothers are at odds with one another, it may be a young man who came into his household as a fostered child. The next-to person knows much about you: what foods you should and should not eat, what your habits are, who you do not like (and, conversely, who does not like you), what secret wrongs you may have committed, and so on. All the knowledge you convey to your next-to person—intentionally or not—can render you vulnerable to someone who has such potential to capitalize on it.

The sense of vulnerability to the risk of harm that stems from proximity resonates strongly in The Gambia. Here, childbearing and early pregnancy are perceived as times of intense danger, and a pregnant woman is considered highly vulnerable to those who may bear grudges against her or who may be jealous of her. Sisters-in-law and co-wives are frequently suspected of malign intentions, but even a mother-in-law trying to play favorites among her daughters-in-law or feeling that a daughter-in-law is trying to steal the attention of her son is not considered above evil tactics. To protect herself and the child she is carrying, a pregnant woman must have a close confidant who may be able to sense where harm lurks and advise her on how to side-step it. Yet this need itself makes her vulnerable to her confidant, who, if she herself feels some slight, can turn her intimate knowledge to malice.

Finally, the idea of proximity implies a dynamic of accumulation, in which the effects of events build upon each other. Applied to reproductive life, cumulative effects can be either additive or decremental, and both addition and decrement can result from the same event, as when a woman experiences a drain on her physical or economic resources as she accrues children. A cumulative dynamic underlies subjects as diverse as the Freudian theory of repression, maternal depletion in reproductive biology (Miller and Huss-Ashmore 1989), physical "weathering" among poor African American women in the United States (Geronimus 1992), lifetime mortality risks among working-class British men (Davey Smith et al. 1997), and the effects of stress or sleep loss. In addition, gerontologists long ago believed that cumulative "wear and tear" explained aging, although today we tend to treat such ideas as the stuff of novels (for two examples, see Moberg 1951 and de Maupassant 1969). The idea of cumulation is not new. Yet its implications for the life course have been thinly explored. The key feature of a cumulative dynamic is that the effects of contingent events may be not simply additive (or decremental) but spiraling. Once an injury occurs, an individual becomes increasingly vulnerable to the consequences of the next. Implied as well is the idea of a threshold or tipping point after which the repercussions of a new event may be catastrophic. In this way, a spate of physical assaults can intensify the effects of previous ones and destroy a fragile balance of health.

As this description suggests, the logic of contingency—with its attendant implications of cumulative susceptibility to proximate forces—applies as much to the process of aging as it does to reproduction. The whims of fortune to which our lives are subjected produce immense unevenness in the pace and character of bodily transformation, both within the span of our own lives and from one person to another. We all face certain inevitabilities of growth, decay, and death. But for rural Gambians, random acts of fate — a sudden illness, the loss of income from a son who is laid off from an urban job, a poor farming season, and particularly (for women) a difficult childbirth — can make these experiences vastly different. Linearity is not out of the picture; indeed, as I will argue, it is a critical type within the contingency framework of bodily decline. But on the whole, there is no systematic way to predict what adversities may befall an individual and therefore how decline will occur. All that can be said is that senescence will likely be saltatory: abrupt, random, and punctuated.

In rural Gambia, women are more vulnerable than men to the precarious unpredictability that this sort of dynamic can produce. For them, it is not time but rather the cumulative effects of reproductive events, especially those of obstetric trauma, that age their bodies and limit their reproductivity by injury and wear. Suffering the effects of mounting reproductive afflictions is especially perilous to a woman living on the edge of security. The greater the number and intensity of assaults she suffers, and the greater the pace at which their effects accelerate, the more difficult she finds it to offset them, and the more damage she sustains. Such forces can alter entire life paths in which social and physical facts are mutually defined.

Besides its associations with precarious paths of cumulative bodily trauma as well as the social proximity that may help or harm, the concept of contingency implies one final element that will be pivotal to the analysis: the possibility of taking action to prevent or mitigate misfortune. Drawing on John Dewey's work, Whyte (1997) argues that Nyole take highly pragmatic approaches to uncertainty and misfortune. By contrast with a "spectator theory" of experience, which tends to overlook the plights of those under study, Dewey's "practice" or "doing" emphasis stresses that actors try to grapple with life's predicaments in the face of uncertainty, pain, and perishability: "When Nyole speak of agents of misfortune, make sacrifices, carry out rituals, and manipulate medicines . . . , they are neither adjusting their social structure, constructing narratives, staging performances, expressing the nature of personhood, nor exercising their symbols. At least these are not their primary intentions. They are dealing with agents in order to alleviate misfortune" (21).

Similarly, Gambian women are not conducting their reproductive lives on the basis of fate alone. They may see themselves as having a certain reproductive potential assigned to them by fate or by God. But paradoxically (as I explain in chapter 6) it is their *action*, and that of people to whom they are close, that determines how many children they will end up with. Whether through strategies of economics, ritual, contraception, or medicine, women try to manage or contain the effects of deleterious events by laying what we would call "contingency plans," an etymological link that has particular significance in this context. This English phrase, found most prominently in the vocabulary of disaster planning or military operations, implies taking action to forestall deleterious outcomes. One does not simply sit back and wait for the unknown to occur. Rather, one tries to calibrate a trajectory by assessing the present and reflecting on past experience, then laying plans by anticipating the most likely outcomes. Instances of contingency strategies like these appear in chapter 4, in the descriptions of women's contraceptive decisions. More complicated instances appear in chapter 6 in the discussion of men's and women's diverging responses to birth interval dynamics.

The role of agency with respect to aging is perhaps the most challenging, if not counterintuitive, element in the contingency framework.[20] On the surface, it is unclear why action would be relevant to a discussion of the physical course of life. Few of the people I know in the West would concede that the pace of aging might be altered by intentional practice, at least in the ways that Gambian women describe. Certainly most of our scientific writings do not reflect this possibility. Yet in The Gambia, the following logic has emerged. Because action is a strong determinant of the outcomes of reproduction, and because reproduction is closely linked to aging, then by extension, action is also linked to aging. Thus, the possibility that reproduction is in some empirical sense a lever for aging means that a woman is said to be able to guide the pace and character of her aging in culturally specific ways by managing her birth events. Her primary motive in doing so, however, is not a cosmetic effort to preserve youth. Nor does she seek to alter the overall process. She seeks instead to smooth the roughest edges of risk. Taking all this a step further yields an even more provocative implication: a woman can seek moral gain from the way she ages. Because she can exert some control over the way her body declines, the character of her decline is read as socially meaningful and, by logical extension, as subject to evaluation. By shaping her aging process on behalf of a certain man and his family, a woman can build a moral reputation and establish her conjugal security. Indeed, since the efforts that age her are seen as helping to build her

20. See, e.g., Giddens 1977; Comaroff and Roberts 1981; Carter 1995.

husband's family, the number of children she has produced may well matter less than how she has conducted the process of aging itself.

My use of the word *contingency* covers a good deal of ground. It implies randomness, uncertainty, and risk. It also implies a sense of vulnerability and a sense that the wearing effects of harsh ordeals can have cumulative effects. This suggests that a woman's body may deteriorate rapidly with the stresses of reproduction. Yet *contingency* in the sense of containment also implies a capacity to take action to check harmful repercussions of events, especially through cultivating social ties with those who can help in a crisis. This means that the success with which a woman can prevent or contain future bodily harm depends on her investing broadly and deeply in social relations. Indeed, the word *contingency* connotes a sense of social ties that underlie all aspects of life, including the physical growth, development, and decline of the body. Relations with kin, marriage partner, and in-laws, whether these relations are good or bad, all have significant impacts on a reproductive career. The sense that the social and physical facets of life are inextricably intertwined thus applies not only in the individual's life but in ways that link the physical lives of different individuals. Classic works in sociology have described with immense insight how one person's life intersected in social terms with those of another (for example, Simmel 1971; Mead 1934, 1980). But in the Gambian view, the course of physical life itself is a product of social relations.[21]

What does all this mean for high fertility in Africa? Whereas we have come to believe that aging puts an end to reproduction, Gambian women see the relation as the reverse: reproduction causes the body to age, a process that, in turn, precludes further reproduction. Becoming pregnant, bringing the pregnancy to term, and giving birth to a healthy baby (not to mention doing so multiple times)—and undergoing a process of contingent aging—all these are not simply biological processes that occur within a given window of time. They are products of action in a precarious social and physical world.

Such assertions, especially those relating senescence to agency, might appear at first to be little more than an attempt to romanticize a set of exotic African cultural constructions. There is powerful support for the contin-

---

21. For two exceptionally important treatments of analogous subjects, see Hrdy (1999) on views of motherhood from the perspective of a biological anthropology and Lock (1993b) on the idea of "local biologies," the ways in which biological differences shape subjective experience.

gency framework, however, from within Western science's own standards. Clues to this extraordinarily different way of seeing have been strewn everywhere. It is consistent with findings from elsewhere in rural sub-Saharan Africa on subjects as diverse as marriage, birth intervals, contraception, and men's reproductive conundrums. It even appears to have figured significantly in more distant times and places, including our own past. It draws support from every discipline that has touched on reproduction—demography, reproductive biology, medicine, anthropology, art, literature. In much the way that Schutz described, each would probably see the framework as common sense: it seems so obvious that it scarcely bears stating. Yet if this view seems so commonsensical once we think about it, then how have we managed to construct, from our vast historical, cultural, and scientific repertoires, a dominant set of analytical practices that is so at odds with it? This question I cannot fully answer. What is clear is that despite our divergent orientations, we have all shared a most unreflective consensus. Tracking through numbers, quotations, and cultural ideologies, both African and Western, I identify some of the breakdowns in the logic and explore the new alternative.

Analytical Strategies

The key to the puzzle of anomalous reproductive behaviors in The Gambia turns not on the question of how fertility begins but on how it ends. The central question for a woman is this: Given her particular economic, health, and marital situation, how does she envision the challenge of bearing and raising all the children God gives her in a reproductive life trajectory that is determined not by time but by the cumulative effects of contingent events? The biggest problem I face in addressing this question is that the 1992–95 birth intervals project was not set up with anything like it in view. Circumstantial evidence and reinterpreted data are sometimes the best I have. Shortcomings such as this are compounded by the fact that the analytical conventions for describing life under high-fertility conditions have been partial if not distorted. My attempts to grapple with these problems lie in three related directions, all stemming from attempts to juxtapose logics.

The primary effort focuses on the logic underlying the Gambian materials. Here I scrutinize as closely as possible variations in social categories of fertility and the life course: men versus women, fertile versus infertile women, and so on. Second, I engage in comparative exercises, looking for evidence in different times and places and placing it alongside the Gambian materials. Examples of these efforts appear throughout the book in foot-notes but especially in chapter 9 and appendix A. Finally, I juxtapose different disciplinary perspectives. Some of these, such as obstetrics, demography, and gerontology, border on the technical and quantitative. Others come largely from history but also from art history and literature. I also draw on a wide range of materials: interview transcripts, print materials from the popular press, and numerically coded survey responses. Only a corpus of this breadth can stand up to all the sifting and resifting that must be done. In all this, I attempt to lay out phenomena side by side and reposition overlapping and redundant pieces of information, much as the example of the two visions of time and the body sought to do earlier in this chapter, to search for the understandings that produced them. If there is a fundamental difference, the edges should be "off" just about everywhere, and systematically so, if we stare hard enough.

The effort to detect relativities by exploiting phenomena with a linear character (and vice versa) appears throughout. I seek examples of "straight-edges," whether they consist of geometrized time, subfertile women, men, or Western women.[22] I allude persistently, for example, to a group I call "Westerners," who usually describe reproduction and aging from the frame called "time." This group might be narrowed further to refer to people raised in the West who are middle-class-plus, educated, professional, and even academic. This is not to say that all people living in the West who occupy these statuses voice these views all the time. Westerners of the past appeared to describe the life course more as Gambian women do than contemporary Westerners do. Nor does it imply that rural Africans always speak in ways that seem to reflect a contingency perspective. Among the most salient points of variation within The Gambia are men and women. But there is immense variation as well among Gambian women on the basis of their fertility, wealth, access to food and money, work demands, and rural or urban residence. A Gambian woman who is still becoming "old" from bearing children is in a very different situation from a chronological peer who is now becoming "young" *after* childbearing once her children began caring for her. Among the most mind-bending paradoxes are the plays of time among African immigrant women as they consider their reproductive lives in Africa and in the United States (chapter 7). Equally absorbing

---

22. In her repeated trips to Niger over a number of years, the anthropologist Susan Rasmussen implies that she seemed to become an aberrant linear measure against which Tuareg women measured their own normal contingent decline (1997, 88).

is the life course logic of Gambian men (chapters 6, 7, and 8) which, because men do not bear children, is said to manifest a far more linear pattern of decline than does that of women. Furthermore, because men may have more than one wife simultaneously, some of the most illuminating facets of the contingency framework emerge when a man comments for us not simply on one wife but on a shifting group of women, each with her own complex social and physical temporalities, who, for long or short periods of time, share him as their husband. Keeping a vigilant eye on the dynamics of gendered temporalities such as these, we may discern very different visions of time and the body.

I do not pretend to dignify this sort of exercise by calling it "controlled comparison," as cross-cultural exercises in anthropology (for example, Murdock 1975) or international surveys in demography might have attempted to do. Still, if we are dealing with a general principle of contingent physical decline, albeit manifested and described in locally specific ways, we can in theory launch a search for insight from almost any potential node, as long as we specify the conditions that each entails. We are in effect allowing Gambian perspectives to challenge those of the West, scholarly disciplines to challenge one another, and the understandings of the past to challenge those of the present. Whether clues come from demographic tables, from textbooks in medical archives, or from awkward uses of English — or across great gulfs of location, translation, transcription, and interpretation — the choice of places and genres is entirely secondary to the insights they may yield. Forcing improbable combinations of discourses into uneasy correspondence, we can watch for cracks in the logic. From the fissures and cracks that criss-cross this terrain, the book searches for fresh cultural and scientific understandings of fertility, time, and aging.

Anthropology is the discipline that frames the questions about conventional understandings of fertility and the life course. I draw as well on material from the medical specialties of obstetrics and gerontology and, to a lesser degree, reproductive biology. However, demography is the principal thematic focus because it is the discipline in which contemporary Western assumptions about time have shaped some of the most sophisticated analytical tools for examining fertility in the life course. The fact that the book deals so centrally with numbers is a point of special note. The use of numbers can take many forms. My interest here lies less in the classic demographic concerns with overall population levels and trends than in understanding the vital events they represent: the lives behind the numbers. Indeed, although numbers hold clues to the cultural world from which they were elicited, they also hold clues to the cultural world that generated them through acts of enumeration. The challenge is not only to use numbers to understand reproduction in The Gambia but to use those same numbers to learn something about ourselves.

Although anthropology's trademark methodological eclecticism and its efforts to seek out a wide and varied corpus of materials offer guideposts, two further methodological points are worth highlighting. First, the book alters the grounds of inquiry into matters of reproduction by broadening the notion of the "costs" of reproduction to include the medical toll from childbearing. Second, it broadens the notion of time in reproduction to include more general "temporalities," of which chronological time is but one type. To this end, I create two general clusters of terms. Ideas such as "time," "chronology," and "age" fall under the heading of an absolutist or universal linearity model. For notions such as "emergence," "relativity," "cumulation," and "plasticity," I settle on "contingency"; hence, the contingent life course. The distinction between linear time, on one hand, and contingency, on the other, is vital to every bit of the Gambian material we will encounter. With so many pitfalls posed by mutually reinforcing loops of flawed logic, the need for semantic vigilance may appear small at first, but its significance becomes intense as the evidence mounts.

To avoid the perils posed by the vanishing chronological baseline and retain some bearing against the power of the contingency frame, I never fully jettison time. Rather, I keep a grip on it as an external orientation scheme (see also Gell 1992, 218). In this, I try to exploit time's ballast at the exact points where its tension with alternative principles becomes strongest. I take as points of orientation age, birth intervals, and the end of reproduction—domains in which temporal anchors are often employed in fertility studies. I dwell particularly on chronological ages in a society that seldom cares about them. By holding onto these abstract absolutes, however illusory their purchase, I search for places where many small commensurabilities have led us astray. It is at the edges of conventionally defined temporal events that the most fascinating breakdowns in logic appear and the convergence with conventional understandings most glaringly crumbles. Here, time stands its greatest test. George Herbert Mead (1980, 58) captured the possibility that such a situation presents in a striking metaphor. In calculating motion, he said, the danger lies in continuing to explain an aberrance in our own time frame, as in the case of a clock's malfunction. Instead, the point at which the correlation breaks down can be the basis of an experiment. In the thick descriptions of temporalities that ensue, the most telling evidence of slippage between the two visions—time versus contingency—can be detected.

An analytical strategy that relies so heavily on juxtapositional exercises is fraught with problems of method and interpretation. Among the most obvious are dualistic terminologies that appear throughout the text. "Western versus rural Gambian" is the most obvious example, followed closely by "linearity versus contingency," "women versus men," "youth versus elders," and so on. And although I focus on rural Gambia, similar troubles lie in the codification of "Western." There are many different kinds of people who live in the West: those who were born and raised there, those born in the West there but raised elsewhere, and those born and raised in the West but having very different cultural orientations and different levels of resources. There are also enormous differences among kinds of countries and socioeconomic stations within them. (Analogous observations can be made even for "rural Gambia.") Dualisms such as these have come under strong challenge in recent anthropological writings. In his book *Orientalism* (1978), for example, Edward Said argues that anthropology has invented difference in what it sees as exotic locales and overemphasized coherence in what are inherently fluid categories. Creating the illusion of otherness, anthropology has used such efforts to dominate (for variants of the overall theme, see Abu-Lughod 1991; Appadurai 1990; Hannerz 1996).

Dualisms, objectifications, biological reductionisms—all pose hazards to the enterprise at hand. As for the first two, every study is in some sense vulnerable to a heuristic vocabulary—one that becomes objectified as soon as it is invoked, consciously or not. Whether there are two categories or twenty does not matter. The challenge is how to think about the two frameworks identified here, linearity and contingency, as different ways of seeing the world and yet also as inextricably linked.[23] Linearity is the background against which the contingency frame is brought to the fore, and vice versa. Thus, the fact that a woman is subfertile may be the way her abnormally linear pace of decline is understood. On the other hand, rapid aging for a man in rural Gambia, because it is not ordinary, may flag his low status. And a woman's rapid decline may confirm everyone's conviction that she has a disagreeable character, as evidenced by the fact that her husband

---

23. Speaking of his work in Samoa, Shore (1996) describes a related sensation. He found himself trying to grapple with things that were both very different from what he knew back home and yet also obvious and familiar to him. This latter sensation was one that anthropologists of the past called "psychic unity": having the capacity to entertain similar versions of reality despite fundamental cultural differences. Shore explains his resolution to the paradox thus: "Sometimes I was certain that Samoans had a mind of their own. At other times I was equally convinced that we were all of a common mind. I eventually came to realize that I was not really flip-flopping. I was just experiencing different aspects of the mind. The longer I lived in Samoa, the more I was able to use the Samoans' cultural resources to reconstruct my own mental models" (6).

must have withdrawn support from her. In truth, therefore, these two facets of experience, linearity and contingency, are not mutually exclusive but rather elements of the same framework. One cannot be understood without presuming the existence of the other. I emphasize the concept of contingency both because it arises so strongly from the Gambian materials and also because it brings to the fore a framework that has been almost invisible in both scientific and popular writings on reproduction and aging. And yet the concept of linear time is always on the sidelines, whether it represents a hypothetical biological phenomenon that no one case will ever match or (in the Gambian cultural ethos) a device against which moral worth can be measured.

Finally, there are the risks of reductionism, such that one could make the case that biology "causes" certain social outcomes. But it is also the case that social factors produce patterns of biology, in ways that our science has only thinly acknowledged. To the extent that one takes "contingent" or "containment" actions, the line that is presumed to divide cause from effect in sequences becomes blurred.

In writing this book, I have two larger goals. One is to document things about the empirical world that have been understood very differently. Toward this end, I hope to convey to the reader some of my own unabating confusion in trying to apprehend the social and physical world from the perspective of a person whose bodily characteristics, experienced sensations, and likely risks I still can scarcely comprehend. The other is to create a sharper edge of doubt about the conventions that lead us to define and handle facts in certain ways. In both of these goals, I am searching for ways to gain perspective on our contemporary academic habitus.

Organization of the Book

The interrelations among the phenomenal, the scientific, and the commonsensical form the critical nexus within which the book attempts to rethink temporality and reproduction. In its mission, the analysis moves between two conventionally opposed orientations to an overlapping set of facts about reproduction and the body.[24] On one hand are the disciplines of biomedicine and demography, in the empiricist-statistical tradition, sometimes labeled "nomothetic," objective, positivist, and so on. On the other are the more interpretive, subjective traditions of sociocultural anthropol-

24. See Keller 1985 for an analogous strategy.

ogy. Within this space, the book sets up a tension between a logic of linear time in the body versus one of contingency. Exploiting this tension on multiple fronts, it argues that we often err in substituting time for contingency and cumulativity in part because our own life experiences have led us in different directions. Besides these disciplinary bases, there are several thematic bases. The most fundamental is reproduction in the time-honored understandings of sociocultural anthropology: kinship, politics, marriage, the life course, domestic cycles, subsistence, and so on. Next are the conventions surrounding the collection and analysis of quantitative demographic data on reproductive events. There are also medical understandings of reproduction, whether these are found in biomedical textbooks about pregnancy and childbearing, in the statements of individuals informed by this tradition, or in experiential accounts of reproductive careers.

Within the various disciplinary frames, demography and biomedicine are usually said to resemble each other in their emphasis on objectivity more than they do sociocultural anthropology, which concentrates on more subjective modes. Yet among all of these frames are perpetual tensions between the science of medicine and the discourse about this science, whether we are describing domestic compounds or international policy circles. There are also tensions between the universal and local and between baseline and variation. In all this, the book draws inspiration from the interpretive tradition in anthropology. Yet it also takes an empirical leap: it attempts to be accountable to good science. This does not imply a restriction to logico-deductive hypothesis testing or to what we have become accustomed to calling "objective" data. It simply connotes an effort to discern regularities about the world by paying close attention to evidence.

Since the book is as much about how we in the West look at the empirical world as it is about Africa, I begin (in chapter 2) and end (in chapter 9) with Western perspectives, albeit very different ones. As this chapter has done, chapter 2 begins with an apparent anomaly, this time an example from contemporary Western reproductive medicine: a case of an egregious inconsistency in our collective perceptions about the body. From there I move on to examine Western beliefs about time and reproduction as reflected in reviews of the literature on reproduction in anthropology and demography. Although the subject matter and the approaches in the two disciplines appear to be vastly different from one another, some surprising similarities emerge.

After a description in chapter 3 of the ethnographic and demographic background of the study and some of the research methods, we turn to the five analysis chapters focused on Africa, chapters 4 through 8. The arc of the argument around which they are organized moves from chronological time to contingency. It also follows, roughly, the track of my explorations during the project. Beginning with a critique of the natural fertility paradigm's minimalist views of reproductive intentionalities in high-fertility societies, I move in for a close inspection of the dynamics of child spacing (chapter 4). In the thick descriptions of this apparently straightforward subject, close attention to the details soon begins to fray the edges of the logic of time by which child spacing has been understood. In chapter 5, evidence of the slippage that at first emerged imperceptibly is now stark and unavoidable. Among the examples: people pay almost no attention to age in reckoning female fecundity, the proportion of women who use contraceptives in the wake of a child death or loss of a pregnancy is much higher than that for women who had a live birth, and men often seem to be on an utterly different temporal wavelength than women. As we further probe the relation between time and fertility, in chapter 6 I describe the alternative framework: what I am calling contingency, detailing some of the principles by which women gauge reproductivity and relating these principles to the conduct of social life. The dynamics of conjugal politics are kept in constant view, both as a key example and a test, through complex mirrors, of this alternative way of seeing the world.

By the time we reach chapters 7 and 8, which take on the subjects of aging and the end of reproduction, I hope that we will have left behind a taken-for-granted faith in time. In chapter 7, in which I scrutinize the process of becoming "spent," the two frameworks are pitted against each other. Using findings on contraception, body states, age, and number of further pregnancies that individual women say they want, I venture some empirical tests to see which framework appears to offer the more satisfactory explanation. In chapter 8, I turn to the social and moral nature of bodily decline over reproductive life and to what Gambians call "retirement" from reproduction. Using this culturally specified lens, I then reformulate fertility. Comparing a contemporary Western version of a fertility questionnaire with how rural Gambian women might reckon it, I show a woman's reproductive record as a set of physical expenditures that have value only relative to a specific man for whom her fertility actions are carried out. Her fertility record thus becomes an accounting device: a history of conjugal virtue earned through sacrifice and through the conversion of physical expenditure to moral gain.

The Gambian findings raise the question of why the people described in this study seem to have views of the physical demands and temporalities of reproduction that are so different from how we have come to imagine the process. In this spirit, in chapter 9 I return to the history of the West, drawing on two descriptions of childbearing: one each from turn-of-the-century America and Europe. These examples reinforce the point that by contrast to Gambian views that bodies differ as a result of their individual histories, contemporary Western analyses of fertility assume a universal body that is not only healthy and intact but undifferentiated from one woman to the next. In smoothing out the contingent nature of life into one of linearity, this tendency undermines our ability to describe life conditions in societies where fertility remains high and resources few.

I make one final methodological note, and this is on the numbers and charts in the book. Gambian calculus undermines practically every fertility object that Western society counts and how it is counted. For this reason, the book's narrative covers considerable thematic ground, yet its perpetual anchors are several simple sets of numerical data on contraception, usually in combination with some reproductive outcome and some measure of time or temporality. Acting on the conviction that what people count and how they count them can point to critical cultural patterns, I sort and slice repeatedly through these numbers on contraceptives. As this takes place, it will be critical to watch how the axes begin to split away from time to accommodate alternative temporalities.

CHAPTER 2

Reproductive Tolls and Temporalities in Studies of Reproduction

I have come to believe what might seem to be a set of highly counterintuitive propositions about aging and reproduction for two reasons. One is the empirical weight of the Gambian findings, which depart sharply and consistently from current Western academic writings about fertility. The other is a disciplinary conviction that cultural frames, whether our own or those found elsewhere, are so powerful that they can "naturalize," or assimilate to common sense, beliefs gained through scientific procedures as easily as they can the religious efficacy of amulets containing texts from the holy Qur'an.

Yet common sense is also fragmented, distorted, contradictory, and selectively utilized. Because I consider the notion of common sense so important, I preface the Gambian story with an example of the conflicting versions of common sense within which contemporary Western society seems to perceive reproduction. It starts with a case of high-technology-assisted reproduction in the United States that was reported in a major scientific journal and in the popular press. I use this case to move us into a state of high alert about the traps that common sense poses.

On April 24, 1997, the leading medical story in the United States was that of a sixty-three-year old woman, the oldest recipient of oocyte donation and the oldest woman ever known to give birth, who had just borne a healthy baby girl: Apgar scores of 9 and 9, and, at thirty-eight weeks' gestation (delivery by cesarean section), having a weight of 2,844 grams. Television stations and newspapers across the country picked up the story of the nulliparous woman in very good health who had understated her chronological age by ten years—that is, she had said that she was fifty-three—in order to qualify for an assisted reproductive technology program at the University of Southern California. The patient had revealed her true age only later, when she was referred for obstetric care at thirteen weeks of gestational age. Before then, all tests, including one on a treadmill, had attested to her health and supported the chronological age she had reported initially. Summarizing the scientific significance of the event, the *Chicago Tribune* reported: "USC doctors say that the case shows that women may have two biological clocks—one for ovaries and eggs and a later one for the uterus" (April 24, 1997).

Of course, biogerontologists have long posited that the body has more than one biological clock: that is, a genetic mechanism that controls the pace of maturation and decay of biological entities. In fact, people have multiple biological clocks (Hayflick 1994, 13), so on this point, the *Tribune* was at least partly right. Yet what interests me here is the implication about the sequencing of the two clocks in question. In the abstract of the journal *Fertility and Sterility* from which the national news story was drawn, the investigators, Paulson et al. (1997), reported, "This case demonstrates that the uterus is capable of supporting nidation [the implantation of a fertilized egg through mucus membrane in the uterus] and subsequent gestation for many years beyond natural menopause" (abstract, *Medline*).

The implication here, and throughout the article itself, is that the biological clock that controls the uterus's muscular tone outlasts the clock that controls the ability to conceive. But the conclusions drawn from the case, in both the popular press and the scientific journal, are almost a complete reversal of what another version of our common sense would say. It may well be that the uterus retains its muscular tone for a long time under the conditions of low fertility that our society maintains. But we might expect women living in a society such as The Gambia, with expectations of high fertility, to say that repeated acts of giving birth wear out the uterus long before the body's ability to conceive deteriorates.

When variant versions of common sense such as these confront one another, we find ourselves struggling to reconcile them. In the present case, we might splice the two stories, the U.S. experiments in reproductive technologies and the ordeals Gambian women report from high fertility, to restate the journal's conclusions. Body parts may well deteriorate at different rates. But which deteriorate first is contingent upon many things, including (particularly in the case of the uterus) the wear and trauma they undergo. The irony in this case is that this woman used to her advantage the fact that chronological time can be so literally disembodied *physically* from a scheming agent to surmount the criterion of age, which otherwise divided populations into those who can quality for treatment and those who cannot. The publication of such a blatant oversight in one of the world's most respected scientific sources on the subject of fertility, and in a case that drew such massive international attention, suggests that it is easy to take statements such as this at face value and to pass over the contradictions they can pose.

Let us turn from this example to another crack in our collective vision: our popular discourse about the relation between contraceptive use and fertility.

We would all agree that for some time, contraceptive use in the United States has been high and fertility has been low. We would all agree as well that there is very likely a causal connection between these two facts: that high levels of effective contraceptive use have led to low fertility. But although the relation between contraceptive use and fertility seems so obvious that it scarcely bears stating, a close study of the content of our popular discourse might suggest the opposite conclusion: American natives have *culturally* dissociated contraceptive use from the idea of low fertility. To be sure, if contraceptive-using women in America are asked point-blank, as I have done, whether they are using contraceptives to try to prevent excess or unwanted births, the overwhelming majority answer in the affirmative, the respondent usually looking shocked at the question.[1] The popular media, however, give no such indication of this. My textual examination of a decade's worth of popular print media (1984–94) revealed that American women do talk about "having" children or "planning" them (Bledsoe 1996). But much as in rural Gambia, where few women describe their use of contraceptives as action taken to limit unwanted children, women in the United States seldom describe their actions in this way, either. Instead, U.S. discourse about contraception is focused on the potentials of contraceptives for enhancing relations with sexual partners, the side effects of contraceptives on health (either beneficial or detrimental), or a whole other range of

---

1. Just as strongly, rural Gambian women who are using contraceptives deny that they are trying to limit births.

uses.[2] Somehow contraceptives keep our fertility low, yet in our everyday consciousness we do not link them to low fertility. The phrase "unwanted births" now appears in writings only about people whom mainstream America holds at arm's length: welfare mothers, adolescents, and women in developing countries.

The realization that the country that provides most of the contraceptives for the developing world for purposes of reducing fertility has also decoupled its own fertility levels from contraceptive use, at least in its popular print media, came as an eye-opener to a researcher who has been steeped in the population literature for developing countries, in which contraception is linked *exclusively* to fertility levels, even if local people themselves do not necessarily see it that way.

In presenting these two cases, I have attempted to disorient the reader with accounts that might represent multiple realities in our science or "self-evidencies" that change from situation to situation (Schutz and Luckmann 1973, 10). Alternatively, they might represent small pieces that make sense when seen in a larger picture. Whatever we conclude, we should be braced to take nothing for granted as we wend our way through themes of time and reproduction. Let us first consider how reproduction has been handled in the two disciplines I have targeted for special scrutiny: demography and anthropology. I make no particular attempt to look for mirror-image topics in the two disciplines, but start with an open-ended scan of the topics that each has chosen to illuminate.

High Fertility in Demographic Theory

For demography, the central concern of which is increment or decrement to a population, numbers of births have posed a paramount issue. The question for my purposes is how these numbers are handled, how they are counted and analyzed. For calculating or predicting fertility at the individual level, demographic studies have relied on an implicit formulation. This consists of the number of children a woman will have over a given period of time. This formulation I describe as "children over time." The following discussion focuses on the two components of this implicit expression.

---

2. See Bledsoe 1996. A recent study conducted by the American College of Obstetricians and Gynecologists also reported birth control pills being used for purposes other than fertility limitation. As many as 48 percent of women responded that they were aware that birth control pills had benefits other than preventing pregnancy, for example, clearing the complexion, regulating menstrual periods, protecting against certain cancers, and reducing menstrual cramping (*Chicago Tribune*, 7 July 2000).

Children . . .

Ever since Malthus first raised the specter of population growth in the context of limited resources in 1798 (Malthus 1923), the question of how to balance numbers of people against available resources has been a major point of debate. The key questions for societies with high fertility have been, "Why are couples having so many children?" and "When and why will these numbers fall?" To address these questions, demographic studies have divided societies into two types: those that have begun a transition to lower fertility, so that their fertility is "controlled," and those that have not.

In societies in which fertility is not yet controlled, reproduction is said to be governed by "natural fertility," as the French demographer Henry employed the phrase, the term "nature" implying no effort to control numbers of children. In such societies, "the very idea of limiting births is more or less foreign" (Henry 1961, 81), and fertility levels are said to reflect the conjoined effects of local customs and biological rhythms that function by default in the absence of conscious human control. The hallmark of such populations is regular birth intervals, a pattern assumed to result from consistency in behaviors across all intervals. Only when traditionalism is said to lose its grip over reproductive behavior can the transition from high to low fertility occur.

The opposite of natural fertility is controlled fertility. By contrast to natural fertility societies, those with controlled fertility are said to manifest parity-specific measures: patterns that are aimed at limitation and hence become visible after a particular number of births. That is, people try to stop bearing children after they have borne a certain number.[3] In such situations, the number of children a woman wants is said almost invariably to be a precise number—a target one does not wish to exceed. This means that child numbers are hardly something to leave up to God—not in the United States, nor in the Catholic south of Europe, where Italy and Spain continue to vie, as they have for a number of years, for the world's lowest fertility rate. Since almost all sexual acts, except the very few that are meant to lead to a wanted pregnancy, are "protected" by some form of contraception, women use contraception for long, continuous spans of time. In Europe, for example, a high age at marriage is said to have kept fertility

---

3. Some, such as Leridon (1975), argued that the use of modern contraceptives would disqualify a society from the natural fertility classification. Others (e.g., Knodel 1983, 63) saw intent to limit births and parity-dependence control as the most important criteria.

lower than it could have been (Wrigley 1969, 117–18); yet fertility declined rapidly when women began to take active measures to limit births through contraception and coitus interruptus. Today, whether and to what extent a population has begun to limit births, as indexed in large part by levels of modern contraceptive use, have become key indicators of societal development. In developing countries the small set of users is seen as a group apart: urban, young, educated, economically secure.

Read very tightly, the natural-controlled fertility dichotomy takes an agnostic view of the intentionalities with which fertility-relevant patterns might be enacted. It implies merely a lack of parity-linked changes in fertility behaviors that would signal an intent to limit child numbers. Henry, to his credit, recognized the issue of intentionality as a point of potential confusion in the paradigm. He also recognized that levels of natural fertility could be variable, depending on local social and cultural practice. Still, the uncertainties surrounding the term "control" have created enough ambiguity for the natural fertility framework to continue, despite significant critiques (for example, Knodel 1983; Campbell and Wood 1988; Caldwell and Caldwell 1981; Santow 1995).

If it is no easy matter to determine whether people are limiting births, the question of why they might begin to do so is even thornier. Classic demographic fertility transition theory (Notestein 1953) posited that fertility would remain high until child mortality dropped, in effect allowing parents to limit their fertility without fear of being left childless as a result of child deaths. Such a transition was likely to occur in the wake of shifts to urbanization, industrialization, literacy, and so on. When the Princeton project found little support for Notestein's thesis (Coale and Watkins 1986), explanations of fertility decline turned to the possibility of cultural influences, such as those that could be traced through the diffusion of low fertility values. Others have turned to the effects of factors such as women's education and autonomy.[4] Another prominent strain of work, a refinement of the earlier broad-brush emphasis on economic development, has been that of the costs and benefits of children (Easterlin 1978; Easterlin and Crimmins 1985). Based in part on work by the economist Gary Becker (1976), this theory weighed the economic and social benefits of children for parents against their costs. Numbers of children produced are assumed to be a function of

---

4. See, e.g., Caldwell 1980, Mason and Taj 1987, Adamchack and Ntseane 1992, Ainsworth et al. 1996, United Nations 1995, Jejeebhoy 1995, Diamond et al. 1999

how quickly they can be biologically "supplied" and the "demand" for them, as determined by assessments of their costs and benefits. Caldwell (1982), for example, in his "wealth flows" thesis, posited that fertility would decline in the developing world when the benefits of having children began to be superseded by the costs of their upbringing. Thus, in populations like those of sub-Saharan Africa, where the costs of children are seen as small compared to the expected benefits of labor and future support, children's labor and earnings constitute a net gain.[5] As such, it is not surprising that most people continue to report on surveys that they want "all the children God gives them," a response often taken as reflecting superstition or resignation to fate. Nor is it surprising that typical reactions to suggestions to reduce fertility range from polite interest to outrage. Since the demand for children is high, a woman's fertility is assumed to be limited only by how quickly she can produce them, given the biological rhythms resulting from local customary regimes. When the costs for children begin to rise, however, and children incur more expenses for food, medical treatment, and school fees, desires for high fertility decline and women take marked efforts to reduce their numbers.

It is important to note, however, that significant works on political economy have disputed the entire premise that child numbers themselves can be discussed independent of regional and global inequalities (see, for example, Feierman and Janzen 1992). Thus, whereas many demographic works hold that Africa's current population growth crisis stems from a combination of high rates of fertility that have continued unchecked from the precolonial past and declining death rates under the impact of colonial rule, Cordell and Gregory and contributors (1994) argued that the crisis of high fertility, a departure from precolonial systems of careful control of numbers, could be traced to colonial policies, which stripped women of their autonomy in fertility control, built factories to produce canned milk to shorten birth intervals, sanctioned slave raiding, and demanded labor for cash cropping and taxes.[6]

5. Clear signs of fertility transition were noted in a few countries in the early 1990s (B. Cohen 1993). See B. Cohen 1998, among others, for evidence that a number of African countries are beginning to follow suit, albeit along highly divergent pathways.

6. Whether fertility rates have actually increased in contemporary times is unclear, although the idea that Africans, like other people, actually kept their numbers under control by prolonged abstention from intercourse, abortion, and infanticide has a long history in demography (e.g., Carr-Saunders 1922, 214).

Having examined questions about numbers of children as well as ways of counting and controlling these numbers, let us turn to time, the basis on which demographic convention has calculated reproductive capacity.

. . . over Time

Fertility studies in demography have produced some of the most sharply articulated elaborations of the notion of chronological time in all of social science. (For two of the best examples, see Ryder 1965, 1992.) At the population level, virtually all standard measures of fertility are built from quantifiable units with precise chronological boundaries. The most common measure of time is a rate, the frequency by which certain events occur over a specified period. Age-specific fertility rates, for example, are calculated by number of births to women within a certain age range (usually five-year groups) over a number of woman-years. Building on this, the total fertility rate is the sum of all age-specific fertility rates multiplied by the length of the age interval. Other standard measures include cumulative fertility (the mean number of children ever born to women of a certain age at the time of interview) and age-specific parity distribution (the proportion of women of a certain age who have produced a certain number of offspring by that age). (See, for example, Wood 1994 and Livi-Bacci 1989.) All of these measures assume a continuous time line along which births will likely occur. Perhaps the most notable exception is the parity progression ratio, which describes the probability that the women in a certain population will go on to have another birth, independent of their age (Brass 1985).

The linear, geometrized logic of time that is used to describe and estimate population-level fertility is also applied to the individual level. Women are seen as having a maximum reproductive span of roughly thirty-five years that begins at menarche (around age fifteen), when they are first able to conceive, and ends at menopause or shortly before, when they can no longer conceive (at around age forty-nine). The capacity to conceive—fecundability—is depicted as an inverted U that rises sharply from the early point in this span, peaks in the late twenties, and tapers off slowly. Since demographic convention tends to equate the ability to conceive with the ability to reproduce,[7] knowing a woman's age allows the analyst to estimate how many more children she can bear.

---

7. Bongaarts and Potter (1983, 3) point out that this tendency conflates the concepts, implying that there is a potential for confusion. Indeed, Wood (1994, 3) draws attention to the problem as a primary point of departure for his book.

The logic of time is applied particularly to what has been called the "proximate determinants" of fertility: factors close to the biological heart of the subject because of their direct effects on reproduction (Davis and Blake 1956; Bongaarts 1978). Examples include contraception, lactational amenorrhea (the absence of ovulation and menstruation during lactation), postpartum abstinence, pathological sterility, and abortion—all inhibitors of fertility. This framework offers precise points of temporal reference for fertility calculations. Applied to natural-fertility populations, where people are thought to want all the children God gives them, it helps to estimate on the basis of time the number of children a woman will likely bear. This framework also gives ample recognition to cultural practices surrounding marriage, which usually initiates regular childbearing among a highly fecund group of women: the young. Changes in age at first marriage have thus been taken as a key sign of potential fertility declines, as have lengthy marriage negotiations that influence the timing of first birth. Other examples include terminal abstinence (the cessation of sexuality before menopause) for women who become grandmothers and norms of lengthy breastfeeding that might cut into a woman's temporal allotment of fecundity. Using all these chronological measures, one can estimate the total number of children a woman is likely to bear. The schematic drawing of a female reproductive life course in Bongaarts and Potter (4), showing the occurrence of menarche, first birth, subsequent births, and menopause, excluding the duration added for intrauterine death, accounts for the distribution of every potential segment of time in a reproductive span. This diagram displays graphically the conviction that time is the basis of fertility calculus.

Some of the most subtle reproductive temporalities in demographic formulations of fertility are the timing, pacing, and circumstances of birth intervals, or the spaces between births. The total length of a birth interval—the duration between two consecutive live births—is said to be determined by several subsidiary durations: (a) a full term-pregnancy, (b) the postpartum infecundable interval just after birth, during amenorrhea, (c) the duration of abstinence, (d) the duration and effectiveness of contraception, (e) the waiting time to conception after ovulation begins, (f) and (in some cases) the time added by a spontaneous or induced intrauterine death, consisting of a shortened pregnancy, a brief infecundable period, and a wait until conception (Bongaarts and Potter 1983, 5). In the event of an intrauterine death, analytic convention has folded what might be more than one "pregnancy interval" into one live birth interval. Demographic analyses have placed particular emphasis on the birth interval as a determinant of levels of marital fertility in natural-fertility regimes, where desires for children are said to be unlimited. Livi-Bacci (1989, 15 n) sums up the relation between the reproductive span and the total number of children in such populations: "the number of children (TFR [total fertility rate]) is obtained by dividing the length of the reproductive period (age at the birth of the last child minus the average age at marriage) by the birth interval." Similarly, Bongaarts and Potter (1983, 4) observe: "While married and fecund, women reproduce at a rate inversely related to the average duration of the birth interval. Short birth intervals are associated with high fertility and vice versa."

As much as demographic works hold to the logic of time in calculating fertility at both the population and the individual level, a source that presses even harder on the logic is found in biological anthropology. In his benchmark book, Wood (1994) states the position thus:

> Fundamentally [fertility] is a time-dependent process: women produce
> a certain number of children by the end of their reproductive lifetimes
> because of the way in which they time (deliberately or fortuitously) various reproductive events over the course of their lives. . . . The entire
> female reproductive life course can be envisioned as a series of time intervals. . . . *The proximate determinants exert a direct effect on fertility precisely
> because they determine the distribution of these time intervals.* (80, emphasis in
> original)

Using these temporal bases, Wood argues, one can estimate the number of children a woman will have. The importance of birth intervals for fertility is obvious: "Each proximate determinant has its impact through the effect exerted on the time intervals between births" (67). Reproductive capacity can be linked closely to the time spent in various reproductive states during the life course: "[W]e can build up entire birth intervals from their separate, sequential parts. Thus, once we have the sum of lactational infecundability and waiting time to conception, we can tack on the time added by fetal loss; and once we have *that* sum, we can add the length of the next gestation" (513), and so on.

The end of the reproductive life has drawn far less attention in population studies than have age of first marriage and birth intervals. This is so because women nearing menopause typically make minimal contributions to overall fertility levels. Nonetheless, the end of reproductive life, like the rest of the reproductive span, has been analyzed through the inevitable filters of time. According to Wood (1994), the age at last birth in most populations is around age forty, and it precedes menopause by about five to ten years.[8] The factors typically used to account for this tapering off are lengthening menstrual cycles, increasing numbers of anovulatory cycles, declining coital frequency, and increasing likelihood of tubal damage and fetal loss. In populations said to have natural fertility, both the onset of permanent sterility and social expectations of grandmotherhood roles are said to be the most important factors in ending reproduction. Having regular birth intervals up until the onset of permanent sterility or grandmotherhood (with some expectable tapering off of fertility due to decreasing fecundity or sexuality) is taken as a sign that fertility is a function of biology and tradition, whereas an early age at stopping reproduction is interpreted as an attempt to control fertility.

Although there has been serious critique within demography of the concept of natural fertility, the conventions surrounding measures of reproduction continue to be mapped onto time in every domain of population studies and the reproductive life course. Formulas employed in the analysis of family planning programs are an excellent case in point. Two prominent examples include couple years of protection (CYPs) and births averted, both of these being measures used to assess the success of a family planning program. A "couple year of protection" is defined as the protection from pregnancy gained by a man and a woman for one susceptible year of the woman's reproductive span. "Births averted" refers to how many births would likely have occurred had the family planning program not been in operation (for example, Ridley 1979, 124). As a rule of thumb, four CYPs are required to avert one birth (Chan 1982, 55). Couple years of protection can also be assessed for various contraceptive methods. One CYP, for example, typically requires thirteen cycles of oral contraceptives, 100 condoms, or 100 foaming tablets (Ross and Frankenburg 1993, 27). Thus, in Hong Kong, where 386,548 pill cycles were provided by the national family planning program in 1976, the total CYPs for the country would have been 29,734 (386,548/13) (Chan 1982, 54). According to these estimates, the use of birth control pills averted 7,434 (29,734/4) births in the country during that year.

8. There is far more reported age variation in fecundability at the end of the spectrum than the beginning. In well-nourished populations of industrialized societies, menopause occurs at around 49 to 51.5 years, compared to an average age at menopause of 43–47 among women in New Guinea, India, Pakistan, and the Philippines (Leidy 1994, 240). In addition, early menopause seems to be associated with leanness, being unmarried, having lower socioeconomic status, and smoking (Pavelka and Fedigan 1991, 28).

Whatever point in the reproductive span is described, whether the focus is the population or the individual, and whether one looks at biology or the technology that is used to regulate it, assumptions about the relation between chronological time and fertility structure pervade virtually every convention governing the analysis of fertility (see also my own work, e.g., National Research Council 1993b; Bledsoe et al. 1994).

Economic models and the leverage provided by time have yielded powerful tools for understanding the population dynamics of reproduction. Yet there are some looming problems. One of the biggest is the costs-benefits framework, which, in its most basic form, is extremely confining. To whom are children costly or beneficial? The model assumes that parents alone must pay their children's costs and, conversely, gain their children's benefits. Abundant empirical work, however, shows that families exert prodigious efforts to manage the costs of children through time and over extended family membership. In fact, the major question is not *whether* people try to contain costs by controlling births or shaping families; it is *how* they try to do so.[9] In West Africa, for example, my work (1989, 1990c, 1994) has shown that young children are commonly fostered to "grannies" living in low-cost rural areas. When they are older, they may be sent to urban households that offer specialized apprenticeships or a place to stay while attending a respected school. Because parents can spread out children's costs so broadly, adults in much of West Africa prefer to have a number of children, investing heavily in the most promising ones and cultivating different opportunities for the others. Adults also treat childbirth not as a secure hold on a child's future support but as the beginning of a long, continuously negotiated relationship in which they try to structure household composition and oblige children to support them. Although the use of the term *nature* in studies of high-fertility societies has tended to imply lack of conscious decision making about numbers of children, fertility-relevant actions are driven by highly intentional decisions, and total numbers of children alone seldom motivate them. Most outsiders assume that reducing fertility is the best way to address economic troubles; most local people find it a drastic solution.

Even more serious problems are found in the cost-benefit model's basic concepts. The notion of "cost," in its narrow confinement to the domain of

9. For Africa, see Oppong and Bleek 1982; Townsend 1997. For elsewhere, see Mussallam 1983; Mason 1997; Skinner 1997. More generally, see Hrdy 1999.

economic production, has obscured hints of other costs that may loom large in people's fertility calculations: specifically, the *physical* costs or tolls of child-bearing.[10] Gambians' depiction of reproductive life as a medical struggle over the course of a high-fertility life suggests that there is much to gain by opening up the concept of cost. Equally restrictive has been the treatment of time as the baseline on which reproductive capacity is reckoned. A number of works imply that maternal exhaustion can be a limiting factor. Here are two examples: "older women are much more likely to stress the problems of recovering full health after a birth . . . and hence for their own sake and that of the baby are more likely to abstain longer" (Caldwell and Caldwell 1977, 211); and "the health of women, who constitute both the productive and reproductive capital of kinship groups, requires protection against exhaustion by rapid procreation" (Lesthaeghe 1989, 16). Observations such as these, though often presented, tend to be relegated to the margins and are not treated as potentially central principles that may guide action. The emphasis on the proximate determinates of fertility—or, more accurately, the proximate determinates of conception—leaves little space for other possibilities.

Just as problematic as restricting the costs of children to economics and using chronological time as the base against which births must be counted has been the exclusion of anything other than live births in the fertility calculus. The convictions that live births are the essence of fertility and that fertility is in turn a function of time are deeply embedded in our demography's indices and formulas. Yet even the critiques of demography in disciplines such as anthropology and history take the terms of the debate at face value: that child numbers are the critical point of discussion. Indeed, if child numbers have increased under Western influence, then in some sense capitalism has helped individual women achieve what they have probably wanted for a very long time (see Iliffe 1989 for a parallel observation).

Having scrutinized the most critical demographic conventions for analyzing reproduction, let us turn to anthropology's traditions of considering time and nature in studies of reproduction. As we will see, the natures of the enterprises are clearly different. But the parallels are surprisingly close to those we have seen in demography.

---

10. It is well known in the field of reproductive biology (e.g., Wood 1994, 204–5) that the mother's childbearing exacts physiological costs from a growing fetus and nursing infant, though this field has not seen intentional action as critical points of analysis. Further, concern is almost exclusively with maternal physiology and does not include anatomy.

The Study of Reproduction in Sociocultural Anthropology

Historical demography has long drawn on history for materials relevant to fertility change, especially with respect to Europe. But only within the last two or three decades, as demographic interest in fertility spread to developing countries, have practitioners actively begun to seek insight from anthropology, the discipline that has so routinely sent observers to these societies. To say the least, these are unusual steps for a field that ranks well above anthropology in the usual hard-to-soft pecking order of the disciplines. The magnitude of the response from the anthropological side of the fence has been small, however, relative to the size of the discipline. Concepts such as natural fertility and the conviction that people may not be exercising conscious or intentional choice over fertility pose obvious barriers to a discipline whose first principles are those of cultural relativism. Yet the lack of response to such appeals arguably manifests a more general move over the last three decades in the anthropological mainstream to abandon the subject of reproduction, at least in the way that demographers and biologists understand typically address it.

Reproduction, as anthropology understood it until the late 1960s, referred to the replication of the group through the production and socialization of children. British social anthropology took on the subject of reproduction as a matter of course, as long as kinship was the scholarly idiom, with its meticulous attention to jurally framed analyses of families and households. Inspired by early works such as *Studies in Ancient History* (McLennan 1886) and *Systems of Consanguinity and Affinity of the Human Family* (Morgan 1970), studies produced from the 1940s through the 1960s explored kinship as a mechanism for recruitment into kin groups, labor pools, succession to high office, inheritance, and domestic cycles. These remain among the field's great achievements (e.g., Fortes 1970; Goody 1958). Kinship was also central to studies of marriage insofar as it was seen as creating alliances between groups or laying the basis for the reproduction of new family members (Fortes 1962; Lévi-Strauss 1969a; Needham 1974; R. Fox 1967). It was also the backbone of analyses of political action, law, and witchcraft.

While European-inspired social anthropologists studied reproduction through social structure and economy, scholars on the western side of the Atlantic began to grapple intensively with cultural meaning. Authors such as Goodenough (1955) and Scheffler (1978) mined ethnographical work on kinship and reproduction to probe cognition, while others saw in the complexities of kinship the potential to remake the field of anthropology around interpretive issues (for example, Schneider 1968 and Geertz and Geertz 1975). Very different routes into familial relations were taken by anthropologists who took on topics such as socialization and personality development. Whiting et al. (1958), for example, argued from Human Relations Area Files data that life in harsh environmental conditions required parents to protect a child by a long period of breastfeeding and a ban on sexual relations. Such practices, because they led to strong psychological attachment of the child to the mother, were said to necessitate dramatic manhood initiation rituals for boys, to separate them from their mothers and to foster the development of their masculinity.[11]

The 1970s were marked by two major changes in the discipline. The first involved growing defections from static jural analyses of social relations to "processual" or "constructionist" approaches (for example, Barth 1959, 1965). Rejecting the determinacy of rule-centered categories and explanations, many anthropologists began to incorporate views that social identities such as that of "wife" or "mother" were fluid, or continually re-created (Comaroff and Roberts 1981). Di Leonardo (1987), for example, shows that rather than a family creating expectations such as holiday gatherings, visiting, and letter writing, such activities are more realistically understood as creating a family.

The second watershed event of the 1970s was the commencement of many anthropologists' personal and professional campaigns to bring women to the forefront of social life. Inspired by the new constructionist ideas, interest in the symbolic constitution of culture fueled growing views of gender relations as arenas of contestation. Early debates on gender often centered on the tendency to associate women with things considered to be close to nature, a usage with an obvious parallel to demography's emphasis on natural fertility. Extrapolating from binaries in Lévi-Strauss's structuralism (1969b), Ortner's early work (1974) attributed universal female subordination to women's confinement to domesticity or to nature and to their association with the raw, unstructured messiness and fluids associated with bearing and caring for children. Men, on the other hand, in their dry, structured distance from reproduction, were linked to culture.

Views of biology as a set of behavioral hard wires had long troubled sociocultural anthropologists, as I noted in chapter 1. But in particular the tendency to relegate women to nature and to the domestic domain drew fire

---

11. For extensions of this theme, see also Saucier's (1972) analysis, which, using Murdock's Ethnographic Atlas, sought associations between birth intervals and factors as diverse as practices of farming, marriage, and inheritance, and a belief in a malicious high god.

(MacCormack et al. 1994; Collier and Yanagisako 1987; Bourgignon 1980). Countering Ortner's depiction, MacCormack et al. (1994) argued that "nature" was itself a set of ideas created by and infused with culture,[12] a theme that Yanagisako and Delaney (1994) developed in their descriptions of the process of "naturalizing" power. As Jean Comaroff (1985, 4–7) explains, by contrast to earlier tendencies to see cultural beliefs as structures that rationally mediate rational action, anthropologists came to treat ideas as distorted, if not coercive, representations of the real world. These ideas became encoded in symbols that people learn, through socialization, to take as natural: taken-for-granted qualities of the world that were thought to exist independent of social attempts to manage or describe them. Linking the idea of naturalism to the subjective experience of the female life cycle, for example, Lock (1993b, 1993c) showed that the dominant Western ideology assumed a certain "natural" chemistry of menopause that brought on health failures, decrepitude, and emotional impairment and rendered the body the target of medicalization in ways that were quite different from medical approaches in Japan. Of increasing interest were aspects of women's identities that had been underplayed before, particularly those in the domains of work, politics, and ritual. Even among women who simply became mothers, holding this status could entail considerable power (Collier 1974; Bledsoe 1980). As Marilyn Strathern (1994) noted, anthropologists were often forced by their own critiques into the paradoxical position of having to grasp for words other than "nature" to capture what they perceive as a freedom from external control. Nonetheless, the consensus was that the entire nature-culture dichotomy was wrongly conceived (for example, Collier and Yanagisako 1987; Hansen 1992), as was the practice of locating gender studies within any particular domain, whether that of kinship and marriage or politics and economics (for example, Whitehead 1981).

By the 1980s, many discussions of reproduction had been drawn into wider political economy discourse in ways that further distanced women from children and other entities construed as being of nature. The term "reproduction" was used increasingly in the Marxian sense of a society's effort to perpetuate itself, often through oppression and coercion (Etienne and Leacock 1980; see also Robertson's [1991] critique and Moore's response [1994, 90]). Modes of societal reproduction were shown to be historically and socially constructed within wider systems of power and gender inequalities—whether in pre- or postcolonial contexts (for example, Bour-

---

12. See also the subsequent debates in Ortner and Whitehead 1981.

gignon et al. 1980; Meillassoux 1981; Leacock and Etienne 1980; Stichter and Parpart 1988). Authors working in this vein saw the fallaciousness of speaking only of biological reproduction to the exclusion of politics and inequality. To them, the production of children was meaningless without knowing how labor and its surplus were appropriated. Building from Engels's evolutionary vision of family structures, costs associated with domesticity were shown to be borne inequitably by women (Edholm et al. 1977).

Broader concepts of reproduction, then, were worked out carefully by a new generation of scholars who sought to suspend assumptions of naturalism and genetic determination in categories that were increasingly seen as products of culture and history. Paradoxically, however, efforts to extricate women from a necessary association with the cultural entailments of nature in reproduction also reified the low status of this domain. As it came to connote a sense of female inferiority, reproduction became a subject that almost no one wanted to own. The result was an almost wholesale abandonment of the domain.

In the late 1980s and early 1990s, the topic of reproduction returned with an infusion of fresh emphases. Particularly important was the publication of a review article by Ginsburg and Rapp (1991) that placed reproduction at the center of reconceived anthropological theory. In what the authors termed the politics of reproduction, reproduction was recognized as a locus of power struggles in the domestic domain as well as in the global order. Among the many strengths of the article was its unveiling of paradoxes. While adoptive babies went from the poor to the rich countries, for example, technologies of reproductive control went in the other direction.[13]

Running on parallel tracks has been attention to the body as a locus of political struggle. By using notion such as that of "embodiment" (the symbolic inscription of cultural principles onto the body), it became possible to "read" the body—its health, illness, beauty, gestures, sexuality (for example, N. Fox 1994, 20). Foucault, for example, described modes of disciplining a populace through the proliferation of state surveillance of the most intimate aspects of its citizens' lives and through adjusting bodily and habitual temporalities (1972, 1979, 1980). New work in this vein began to ask

13. There is a growing anthropological literature as well on the new reproductive technologies, biogenetics, and the human genome project that challenge ideas of biological naturalisms (e.g., Martin, 1987, 1991; Franklin, 1997, 1998; Franklin and Ragoné, 1998; Rapp, 1999, Ginsburg and Rapp, 1995, eds.; Strathern, 1992b; and so on). In non-Western countries authors such as Inhorn (1994) and Feldman-Savelsburg (1999) have explored other cultural understandings of biological processes such as reproduction and feeding.

how political agendas were inscribed on the bodies and consciousness of women through enforced idealizations of thinness, genital mutilation, and restrictive clothing codes. Among the most important examples of this work for reproduction were the fragmentation of women's identities and the erosion of their reproductive rights with the rise of medicalized birth practices (for important treatments, see Gordon 1974; Jordan 1983; Gordon 1990; Lindenbaum and Lock 1993; Sobo 1993, 1994). Other researchers have challenged what is seen as cosmopolitan medicine's attempts to subject women to surveillance and to monitor and manipulate the most intimate aspects of their lives (for example, Poovey 1986; Boddy 1995, 134–35). Among the themes this work generated were critiques of new reproductive technologies that effectively disembodied reproduction, eroding the organic unity between mother and child and exploiting Western society's obsession with biological reproduction as the only acceptable form of parenting (for example, Baruch et al. 1988; McNeil et al. 1990; Hartmann 1987; Holmes et al. 1992; Edwards et al. 1993; Franklin 1998).

The principal counter to the charge that the female body has become a target of control and surveillance has drawn on the notion of resistance (in Scott's [1985] terms) to imposed authority. Thus, Comaroff (1985) lent caution to monolithic approaches to hegemony; there is also a growing awareness of people's scope for maneuvering as they attempt to influence fertility practices.[14] Turner (1994, 44) went further. Criticizing Foucauldian treatments of bodies "as products or projections of cultural discourses or symbols rather than as pragmatic individual and social activities of production and appropriation," he showed that emphasis on the individual body as the subject of sensations of pleasure or pain has obscured the physical aspects of reproduction and the biological interdependence of conjugal and filial bodies. (For two notable exceptions, see Jackson 1997 and Devisch 1993.) Applying ideas of resistance to childbirth, Martin's landmark monograph *The Woman in the Body* (1987) traces the history of obstetrics in the United States from a personalized, midwife-based profession to one dominated by male doctors. Synthesizing a rich body of material from multiple fields, the book argues that as the hospital increasingly became the normal place for childbirth, pregnancy came to be regarded as an illness: a condition fraught with risks. Women came to feel that birth happened to them rather than because of them and, as a result, they felt greater detachment from the child

---

14. Besides the work of Ginsburg and Rapp (1991, 1995), other excellent reviews can be found in Lock 1993a, Csordas 1990, MacCormack and Strathern 1994, and Davis-Floyd and Sargent 1997.

after birth. One of the most innovative features of the book is its search for the overall "grammar" that has guided scientific medicine in its attempt to describe women's bodies (14). A number of examples show that medical textbooks have often depicted the woman's body as a machine that the usually male physician alone is qualified to manage at the time of delivery. Interventions such as the use of drugs, forceps, and cesarean sections can thus be adopted as a matter of course. In Martin's view, however, these intense efforts to medicalize birth have often backfired, sparking resistance among women seeking to reclaim an active role in childbirth. In many instances women seek out midwives and opportunities for home birthing and birthing centers. In other forms of resistance, women have refused to go to the hospital at the time of birth, snatched a scalpel from a surgeon's hand, and so on. Authors such as Martin (1991), Rapp (1999) and Lock (1993b) have even challenged the findings of science itself through the leverage offered by cultural perspectives.

The study of reproduction in sociocultural anthropology and its close disciplinary kin has undergone extraordinary changes in less than half a century. The field that was immersed in kinship algebra is almost unrecognizable as the one that is concerned with symbolic control over women's bodies and with birthing as an experience of women's self-fulfillment. Particularly productive have been steps to broaden the concept of reproduction to include the reproduction of societal values and systems of stratification and to work toward a vision of gender as socially made, if not an object of continual construction, rather than a fixed product of nature. Together with sociocultural anthropology's classic concerns with taken-for-granted biological naturalisms and its attention to context and motivation, these strands of study create new ways of understanding how reproduction is made social.

The importance and scope of such contributions, however, should not be allowed to obscure some less obvious facts. First, as the focus has shifted from the child as the product of the fertility event to the identity experience of the woman, there is less attention to the production of a new family member and its implications for the reproduction of a family. Topics such as infertility treatments, the subjective experience of childbirth, and forms of parenting such as adoption, surrogacy, and fostering have become our discipline's subject matter. Yet it is hard to avoid the speculation that these topics have risen to such prominence precisely because they hold the greatest potential to challenge conventional views of the principal form of

reproduction: by married heterosexual partners.[15] Second, although mainstream sociocultural anthropology has focused enormous attention on the
ideational, economic, and kinship dimensions of fertility, it has almost consistently left reproduction a numberless event, as if the number of births did
not matter. And although increasing proportions of the world's women are
using contraceptives from the West, little anthropological attention has
been paid to how people may be configuring them to their lives (for some
recent exceptions, see Nichter 1989; Greenhalgh 1994; Morsy 1995; Asdar
Ali 2000; Russell et al. 2000).

Finally, whether they have stemmed from interest in the alliance or descent debate or in realizing an identity in the childbirth experience, interests in the temporalities of fertility have been underdeveloped. The literature from which anthropology has built itself as a discipline is rich in
discussions of culturally marked durations and sequences (Durkheim 1915;
Gell 1992; Munn 1992). Temporal regularities have comprised some of the
most elegant works in anthropology, from studies of periodicities in marketing (Skinner 1964) and seasonal and agricultural cycles (Bell 1979) to
Evans-Pritchard's masterful descriptions (1940) of the fusions of social, historical, and ecological time. With respect to the temporalities of a woman's
reproduction of children, however, anthropological attention has been re-
stricted to broad sequencings: ritual efforts to bestow fertility at the beginning of reproductive life (for example, Richards 1956; Douglas 1970),[16]
social censure for premarital births (Friedl 1962), or social changes that
may occur at the end of fecund life (for example, Stenning 1958, 11; Lock
1993b). Although techniques for studying the addition of new members of
the population and analyzing the temporalities of reproduction have comprised some of demography's great achievements, birth spacing temporalities seldom take up more than a paragraph in most ethnographic writings,
even those describing reproduction in high-fertility situations. Virtually the
only topic in regard to which the interval from one birth to the next drew
any noticeable anthropological interest was the postpartum sex taboo. (See,
however, Sargent and Cordell 1998.)

In sum, the task of challenging conventional cultural understandings of
the meaning of matters such as reproduction has continued in anthropol-

15. My own project on child fosterage in Sierra Leone (e.g., 1990c) emerged from precisely such a
motivation.

16. Such interests have been sustained in later work as well (MacCormack 1979; Bledsoe 1984;
Abu-Lughod 1986; Boddy 1989; Jacobson-Widding 1991; Devisch 1993; Inhorn 1994; Kratz 1994).

ogy. But questions of the numbers of children and the temporalities of their arrival, the very center of demographic interests in the matter of fertility, have drawn far less anthropological attention.

Disciplinary Common Ground

Having drawn some broad contrasts between sociocultural anthropology and demography, I pause to gather some common points.

Despite vast differences in their vocabularies and agendas, both fields share to a remarkable extent a baseline common sense about two critical domains. One is the relationships among nature, time, and reproductive potential. Assuming no "assisted" reproduction, both fields see the female capacity to reproduce as a chronologically based bodily potential that will unfold naturally unless blocked by societal or political forces (the emphasis in most anthropological writings) or by mortality or morbidity (in most demographic writings). Both fields also focus on fecundity as the essence of fertility. In demography, this emphasis is most obvious in the proximate determinants framework, which is based almost entirely on events surrounding conception. In anthropology, nowhere is the Western cultural emphasis on conception more obvious than in studies of new reproductive technologies or assisted reproduction, where the politics of conception and surrogacy pose such fascinating challenges to our chronological common sense.

Anthropology, in treating both nature and time as products of cultural construction, would seem well placed to avoid demography's universalizing sins in handling reproductive events. But although we have had little interest in subjects such as birth intervals or fertility rates, and the few practitioners who know anything about the concept of natural fertility have viewed it with ambivalence at best, we seem to share demography's naturalized common sense about time in the body: that reproductive capacity is limited by time and that physical senescence occurs at a linear pace. To be sure, this cannot be directly demonstrated in the literature I have examined. The sections above on demography and anthropology have been quite asymmetrical in this way. The first was a focused analysis of the organizing themes of time and of cost and benefits that deeply structure demographic views on reproduction. The second turned up an assortment of themes that arose as anthropology marked out ever-wider definitions of the term "reproduction." Yet even though specifically anthropological visions of reproduction and how it might intersect with time in the body were seldom found, it is clear that neither classic nor more contemporary anthropology has questioned the veracity of linear time in the life course.[17] While demography encodes the assumption of chronological linearity overtly into its practices through its tables and formulas, this evidence by default in sociocultural anthropology suggests that both disciplines have taken with little question the cultural assumption that the adult life course is one of time as nature. The possibility of the wearing effects of reproduction on the process of aging has drawn virtually no attention. We have thoroughly studied adolescent fertility, child numbers, and birth intervals. But whether this omission has stemmed from our own unreflective habitus or from our flight from biology, we have paid almost no attention to how women cope with the cumulative physical costs, the "long haul," of high fertility.

The notion of common sense is central to all this. Whereas having common sense implies that one makes judgments that stem subconsciously from a cultural milieu, being technically proficient implies a mastery, through specialized training in a craft or a subject matter (such as engineering or law), that lies well beyond that which untrained people would have. However, it is my conviction that demography, despite its highly technical orientation to mathematics and statistics, stems from the same pockets of common sense that produce the rest of our culture's vast stock of knowledge.

Patterns surprisingly analogous to these in demography and anthropology can be discerned for the field of gerontology. When queried individually, gerontologists seem to agree that the pace and character of bodily decline can be affected by life events, and hence that the process of aging is not linear but episodic and cumulative. Yet until recently the field has pressed a temporal grid upon a physical template in ways that reify convictions about linear time. It is no accident that the cutting edge of research is on the genetics and cellular bases of senescence, an enterprise in which the inherited elements of life are assumed to bring on senescence at a predetermined pace and minimize the importance of contingent events. Parallel distortions fostered by our belief in linear time in the body are reflected in gerontology's apparent lack of interest in whether pregnancy and childbearing can be levers for the process of aging among women.[18] We readily

17. New anthropological work on the subject of aging is beginning to question conventional suppositions of time in the body, from different yet promising angles. See, e.g., Lock 1993b and L. Cohen 1998. And Rapp (1999) shows how warnings about the risks of fetal maladies as a function of maternal age are sometimes used in misleading ways in amniocentesis.

18. In 1997, these were some representative titles of medical textbooks in the OB/Gyn section of the University of Chicago bookstore's shelf: *Reproductive Endocrinology, Surgery and Technology, Human Spermatazoa in Assisted Reproduction, Management of Perioperative Complications in Gynecology, Fetal Sonographic Biome-*

acknowledge the fact that people can reach a certain physical stage before or after others. But we rarely ask why some people reach one physical stage of senescence more quickly than another. There is no direct contemporary literature on a possibility that must be a pivotal concern in areas where fertility is high and conditions of life are difficult.

The common sense that gives rise to our disparate disciplines has led us into a series of mutually reinforcing traps. Our taken-for-granted access to some of the world's best preventive medicine and backups for obstetrical emergencies, together with our excellent nutrition and low fertility, means that if we are demographers, we can strike from the record reproductive events that do not result in a live birth;[19] if we are anthropologists, we treat them in symbolic terms. (See, however, Rapp 1999, 102.) We are spared from sickness, insecurity, and poverty on the scale that our own forebears knew or that people in much of the world still experience. All the developments that have made childbirth safe have smoothed out our bodily trajectories, allowing us to believe that bodily decline occurs at a pace independent of exogenous influence. Our sense of the physical experience of fertility is flat. Because our writings conceptualize thinly the idea of cumulative costs across an individual's entire life span, we treat all births as discrete events of uniform or ephemeral medical impact and pay scant attention to potential problems of subsequent births. We may note the timing or social significance of the first birth. On the whole, however, our disciplinary assumptions and practices—as diverse as they are—treat all births as the same, and we write as if pregnancy and delivery will follow unproblematically once the conceptus is securely implanted.

Setting the perils of childbearing into peripheral vision, we can imagine that the costs of fertility can be limited to economics, that the reproductive process reflects desire, whether for children, sex, or identity fulfillment, and that a time-based ability to conceive is the crux of fertility. Because we assume a healthy reproductive body, we can focus our technological energies and our popular imagination on the genetics, creation, and viability of a conceptus and on its first precarious days of existence. On the basis of time, we can estimate when our fertility window will close and hence how sharply the costs of "assisted" reproduction will escalate. It is not surprising that we

---

try, Practical Gynecological Oncology, Home Births, Assisted Human Reproduction, Hormone Replacement Therapy, Invasive Ultrasound, Comprehensive Management of Menopause, Genetic Disorders and Pregnancy Outcomes, Sports Gynecology, and *The Augmented Breast.*

19. In maternal morbidity and mortality studies, nonlive births are sometimes often noted as evidence or causes of health problems, though the lasting and spiraling tolls that these pregnancy outcomes may take receive far less attention.

identify the reproductive problems of older women as those of the ability to conceive and the risk of genetic defects among their children.

Whether the analytical frame has been that of natural fertility or of the expression of female identity in the birth experience, the state of our theory on the relation of social action to the pacing or character of transformations in adult physical life is virtually empty space. The fact that such a void exists is evidence by default of our collective cultural belief in the naturalism of time in the body: that reproductive capacity is limited by time and that physical aging occurs at a genetically programmed pace, with individual variation stemming largely from chance. Observations of such striking parallels among such otherwise improbable disciplinary bedfellows suggest that we are glimpsing some deeply held and unexamined irreducibles of contemporary Western culture.

Neutralizing Concepts of Reproduction and Time

To open up alternative understandings of reproduction and aging, several terms that have been used in demography and reproductive biology will be starting points.[20] In demographic convention, the term *fertility* has been used to refer to the number of children born to women in a particular population. It refers to the production of a living child and hence to the addition of one person, however briefly, to the population. To express the more physiological side of fertility, *fecundity* has been used to refer to the ability of a woman to reproduce a living child. Thus, a woman may be infertile, having had no live births, but not infecundable or sterile, being unable to reproduce at all. But the problem is that the term *fecundity* in this sense of the ability to produce a living child has been conflated with the ability to conceive (or, to become pregnant). A woman may be able to conceive, but she may not necessarily be able to bear the child that results from this conception. This failure to distinguish between the ability to conceive and the ability to give birth to a living child will (as we shall see) become increasingly misleading. The fact that a woman can conceive and even that she may have had a nonlive birth can also be important not only in cultural conceptions but in behavior and social life.

20. For helpful analytical discussions, see United Nations 1959; Bongaarts 1983, 3; Wood 1994; and Weeks 1999. See Wood (1994, 3) on the importance of delving more deeply into the notion of fecundity, which has been a much more ambiguous notion for demographic counting purposes than has fertility.

I try to avoid neologisms or direct translations that are awkward and therefore distracting, though some of this will be necessary. A case in point will be what I sometimes call a "child potential." In addition, I will confine the term *fecund* to a nonpregnant, non-amenorrheic state during which a woman can conceive. Such a state is a critical condition on which conjugal politics may turn. But at times I will stretch the term *fertility* to refer to the production of a fetus that was dead at delivery. I will also leave myself enough ambiguity to refer to the production of a child who survives long enough to achieve some degree of sociality, say, weaning or walking.[21] The term *reproductivity* will refer to a capacity to reproduce, a category that includes not only fecundity but other capacities such as the anatomical and physiological capacity to carry the child and give birth to it. *Reproduction* will refer largely to the physical events surrounding childbearing. But stretched further, it can imply the production of a child who eventually brings prosperity to the family. As all this suggests, although demographic works tend to use *children, births,* and *pregnancies* interchangeably to refer to outcomes with a living child, I try to use these terms as carefully as possible.

Finally, I need a more neutral starting point for thinking about time. A candidate emerges in Plato's conception, from *The Timaeus* (1949), of space: *khóra*.[22] Stripping away any necessary connotation of time or even of geographic expanse, Plato describes this as a room or a receptacle (or "nurse") in the sense of being an aggregate of all of the potentialities that can be realized (McKeon 1994, 20). Khóra is not empty space in the sense of being a void. In Sallis's interpretation, it is amorphous and even invisible, but it moves, and, as it does so, it nurtures and shelters new images. "One could call it . . . a ghost scene that . . . endows the fleeting specters with whatever trace of being they might enjoy" (1999, 122).[23] It suggests a giving way or withdrawing to make room for things that are new, if not unexpected. The

---

21. The fact that concepts for fertility and children might convey different meanings from those we assume is aptly described in an anecdote from Sierra Leone. Ferme (2001) describes an instance in which a mother of a three-year-old boy who had died was reprimanded by a male relative for crying loudly in the manner that was allowed for deceased adults. Upon being rebuked that it was "only a child," the woman explained her grief by saying the boy was "already a little big"—that is, he had already been weaned and was walking.

22. I thank Douglas Mitchell for bringing this concept to my attention and for his guidance in this discussion.

23. Castoriadis's (1984) description of Plato's use of the term *techne* evokes the sense of a formless template of space that can endlessly reshape the same materials by reshaping itself. In the *Timaeus,* "we find Plato's god constructing the world out of pre-existing elements of every kind which he assembles, mixes, transforms and adjusts to one another in the light of his knowledge, playing the part of a true *technites-demiurge* in the classical sense of the term, what we nowadays call an 'artisan'" (232).

values placed on these new forms can be beneficial or detrimental, depending on the perceptions of those who may be affected by them.

The idea of space that gives way to create new forms imbued with a constantly shifting set of values provides a bridge to the numerous departures from chronological time we will encounter. By *time* I mean, in a literal sense, *chronology:* a linear set of ordered durational units of identical length that are anchored to absolutes point in history. Examples include calendrical dates or years of birth. By contrast, temporalities, which the idea of khóra suggests, are not necessarily reducible to fixed points in history. The points that mark them are not necessarily equidistant from one another, though they generally connote an ordering of events relative to each other. Taken in the phenomenological mode, temporalities are a rich source for describing experience. Cyclical time, a motionless present, "telescoped" time, time in reverse—all would be examples (see, for example, Lightman 1993). The replenishment of some bodily elements would be an example. In the case of birth intervals, using a more neutral idea of temporalities allows us to discern the meanings that might be entailed in the duration of breastfeeding relative to the return of sexuality, the conduct of disputes over when to wean a child, the long, ambiguous silence that might signal a wife's betrayal, and the extent of maternal sacrifice required to earn eventual reward. These phenomena may be indexed to chronological time, but they are best described simply in vocabularies of sequencing, pacing, and potentiality.

I begin, then, by using words that describe time in a more absolute sense. But as we move toward a vision of fertility and aging with no necessary chronological time entailments, the vocabulary increasingly edges away from these usages, and I try to render temporal terms as free as possible of the entailments of time, stripping even adjectives such as *young* and *old* of their necessary chronological attributes. A woman's physical stage will become far more important than her chronological age. Hence, I will restrict the noun *age* to the amount of chronological time a person has been alive: the number of years, months, or weeks that have elapsed since birth. Used in its other forms *(to age, aging, aged)*, the allusion will be to the process of physical deterioration or "senescence," a term that does not rest on time. Temporalities such as these I will take as time-neutral or non-time-dependent. That is, events may occur in time and they can be described in chronological terms, but their temporal characteristics may not coincide with chronological time. (Gell 1992, 315, takes a stance that appears similar, though as I explain in chapter 6, I will depart from it in one significant way.) Temporalities such as these will eventually overtake time to comprise the core of the book.

Using a more neutral starting point for temporalities also opens up the question of how they may be created. Where bodily states and temporalities are minutely monitored in order to anticipate and mitigate risks, high rates of fertility and child survival are best seen as complex social as well as biological achievements. The actions one takes and the resources one can muster bear strongly on how these hardships will be inscribed and therefore on how quickly one both ages and comes to the end of reproduction.[24]

24. For a different play on the theme, see Munn's (1986) analysis of "spacetime," in which space and time are brought together in the cultivation of social relations.

CHAPTER 3

Setting, Data, and Methods

Throughout sub-Saharan Africa, reproduction is a matter of intense concern. In this chapter I describe some of the social, cultural, economic, and historical background that shapes fertility in contemporary rural Gambia. I then turn to some of the methodological background: how the data for the study were collected and some of the many complexities that began to surface during the course of the project.

   The Gambia is the smallest country in continental Africa, a tiny sliver of land that lines the Gambia River. It seldom exceeds twenty kilometers on either side of the river. Only about 15 percent of its total land area of 3,860 square miles is arable. In 1996, the Population Reference Bureau's World Population Data Sheet estimated the country's population at 1.2 million, with a total fertility rate of 5.9. (For a more detailed demographic analysis, see Sonko 1995.) As is the case in other African countries, many Gambian citizens are young and few are old: 45 percent are under age fifteen and 2 percent are over sixty-five. One-quarter of boys of secondary school age and half as many girls are currently enrolled in secondary school. English is the official national language. Ninety percent of the populace is Muslim. Christians, living largely on the coast, comprise 9 percent of the population, and people professing indigenous beliefs 1 percent. Islamic religious leaders called imams are schooled in Arabic and in the holy texts of Islam, particularly the Qur'an and the Hadith, which chronicles the life and deeds of the Prophet Mohammed. Many Arabic trainees, largely boys, live with private masters, exchanging hardship and hunger for the blessings of a religious education. Learners who gain basic skills in Arabic are permitted to lead prayers for their villages. A few continue their studies to become imams.

With an active Ministry of Health and assistance from donor organizations, childhood mortality has fallen rapidly in recent years. Despite these gains, infant mortality was ninety per thousand live births, and children had a 20 percent chance of dying before age five. Figures from WHO/UNICEF for 1990 estimate that for the country as a whole, the maternal mortality rate (death during the period from the onset of pregnancy until forty-two days following a live birth) was 1,100 per 100,000. That figure for the United States, by comparison, was 12 per 100,000 (WHO/UNICEF 1996). Most of the mortality risks, particularly for children, lie in a combination of ecological and economic conditions. Although the long dry season, September to May, is a time of relative plenty, the rainy season, June to August, is difficult since the crops are not yet harvested. It is also difficult for health. The Gambia is one of the world's most hazardous areas for malaria. Mosquitoes are plentiful, and small weaned children, no longer receiving antibodies from their mothers' breast milk and having as yet few of their own, are at great risk. The younger they are when weaned and the more closely that weaning coincides with rainy season, the greater the risk.

The Wider Context: History, Politics, Economics

Before examining the immediate parameters of the project and the methods, we need to widen the lens to the broader historical and social context within which reproduction in contemporary rural Gambia occurs. As early as the fourteenth century, Portuguese explorers, lured by the possibilities of finding gold, began to draw detailed maps of coastal West Africa. Some of the most notable features of these maps were the navigable Rivers Gambia, Casamance, and Senegal, where European slave traders began to make their way inward. With the growth of production of sugar, rum, and tobacco in the Americas, West African coastal trade in slaves increased. In 1617 the Dutch built the first permanent European settlement in West Africa as a slaving port on the island of Goree, off the coast of Senegal. Similar European settlements followed, all designed to ship out gold and persons. Islam reached the Senegambia region by the eleventh century, and by the time of formal establishment of colonial rule, Islamic leaders were engaging in active political resistance, which in turn provoked the establishment of yet more French and British forts. The British eventually took over the region and in 1768 created their first crown colony in Africa, Senegambia. In a highly awkward geographical resolution of conflict, two territories were eventually split in 1884 from this original colony into French-controlled Senegal and, inside it, the British-controlled Gambia: the strip of land surrounding the River Gambia. Since then, tensions between Senegal and The Gambia have arisen continuously. A point of perpetual aggravation for Senegal has been the difficulty of travel between its northern and southern regions and constant secessionist threats in the south, meaning that The Gambia is often caught literally in the middle of the conflict. In the wake of continent-wide independence movements in the early 1960s, The Gambia acquired independence from Britain in 1965. In 1970, the country came under the leadership of President Alhaji Sir Dawda Kairaba Jawara and his People's Progressive Party.[1] After a coup in July 1994, a military government headed by Yahyah Jammeh took over. In 1996 a contentious election returned the country to ostensible civilian rule, converting Jammeh from a military to a civilian president. As has been the case in many other African countries, The Gambia has continued to suffer from widespread allegations of graft and from a brain drain to the private sector and to countries abroad as a result of low pay in the public sector (*Africa Confidential Headlines*, September 1997).

The national economy reflects a combination of the country's history, ecology, geography, and status in the world economy. In this semi-arid region of the Sahel, deforestation and the encroachment of the desert are perpetual worries given growing demands for farmland and firewood. Having no important marketable natural resources and a limited agricultural base, The Gambia is one of the world's poorest countries. Most of the population, with a per capita cash income of far less than $1,000, is engaged in agriculture or in tending livestock. Although the country was created as a colonial artifact because of its potential for river traffic, this traffic has all but died because of both increasing siltation of the river and the construction of improved roads along the river. Given this potential for expediting land-based

1. The following sources are some of many on the general histories of the region: Oliver 1967; Ajayi and Crowder 1971; Hopkins 1971; Davidson 1977; Fage and Oliver 1982. On Islamic history, see Quinn 1972; Barry 1988; Linares 1992. On colonial history, see Oliver and Atmore 1967; Crowder 1968; Linares 1992. And for independence movements, see Davidson 1987.

shipping of goods, groundnuts and other goods are highly profitable. More-over, because of its low import duties and its odd geography, the country has also seen the enormous growth of what has been called the "re-export industry" of goods from Europe and North America. Gambian dealers can rapidly re-export goods such as clothing and electronics north to Senegal and Mauritania, west to Mali, and south to Guinea and Guinea Bissau, buying them cheaply and shipping them for sale at high profits to its close neighbors, where import duties are high. Besides groundnuts, the country's major export crop, other agricultural products include millet, sorghum, rice, corn, cassava, fish, vegetables, cotton lint, palm kernels, and livestock (cattle, sheep, goats). There is also some small-scale industry. Tourism is a major industry; nearly 100,000 tourists from Europe and America arrive each year. Tourism was given a powerful boost by the 1976 publication of Alex Haley's *Roots* (see Ebron 1993, 1999) and the subsequent television miniseries based on the novel. In 1996 the First International Roots Home-coming Festival was held in The Gambia to celebrate a common heritage among African descendants, a festival that is planned for continuation each year. A host of development organizations have long been active in the country, advocating change on such issues as diverse as forestry preserva-tion and female genital surgery.[2]

Like other African countries, The Gambia faces the perpetual challenge of meager resources to meet the needs of its growing population. It also endures problems of inequality. In Banjul and on the beaches to the south lie elegant houses and tourist hotels, with their swimming pools, air con-ditioners, and watchmen. Such scenes offer a sharp contrast to the corru-gated metal lean-tos in other parts of the city, where small children play near garbage heaps and open-ditch sewers. And yet, the problems and in-equalities somehow seem less extreme here than in some of the other coun-tries in the subcontinent. The health care system may not provide the promised services all the time, but basic medical supplies can usually be found, whether in the clinic or in the physician's nearby pharmacy, and rates of child mortality, as noted above, have fallen significantly. There is no national university and usually only the wealthy can send their children abroad for a college education; still, most elementary and secondary schools graduate their students at the end of term. The economy is a perpetual

---

2. For insightful social and historical analyses of development work in the country, see Shipton 1992; Carney and Watts 1991; Watts 1993; Schroeder 1994, 1999.

source of worry, and government salaries are often late, but most people find ways of at least getting by.

Economics and Social Life in Farafenni and the Surrounding Villages

Farafenni, a town of approximately 25,000 at the time the study was conducted, is located beside a major ferry crossing in the Gambia River, about a ten-minute walk from the Senegalese border. It contains a wide national mixture of residents and sees a constant flow of travelers (Gambians, Senegalese, Mauritanians, Malians) who come to take advantage of the weekly market and the ferry crossing that links the lively international trade and currency network. In fact, Farafenni, as the first point east of Banjul where the river can be crossed to the north, is a major locus of the re-export trade. Several times a day the ferry crosses back and forth, heavily weighed down with transport trucks, personal vehicles, sacks of goods, and foot passengers who come to do business in the town. The town has a large government regional hospital and health center, which offers, among other services, a daily prenatal and contraception clinic for women and an "under-fives" clinic. Market day is particularly busy for the clinic. Many women who come into town to buy and sell at the market come to attend the clinic.

Research for the 1992–95 field study was collected in forty villages surrounding the town of Farafenni in the North Bank Division of the country,[3] under the joint auspices of the Maternal and Child Health unit of the Ministry of Health and the British government–sponsored Medical Research Council (MRC),[4] which has several small offices and laboratories in the country. The modest field station at Farafenni, seventy-five miles inland from the capital city of Banjul, contains a small set of labs, a computer

---

3. In this chapter, some of the demographic calculations describing the villages surrounding Farafenni are drawn from the work of Allan Hill (1997; Hill et al. 1992). See also a report based on the work of Mary Hill (A. Hill et al. 1996) and an M.A. thesis by Catherine Hill (1994). A dissertation by Margaret Luck (1997) contains an extensive treatment of patterns of health and contraception for the area and a general description of the socioeconomic context. For other details of the study see Hill 1993; Bledsoe et al. 1994, 1998; Bledsoe with Banja 1997; Bledsoe and Hill 1998.

4. Besides multiple offices and laboratories throughout the United Kingdom, the MRC has three international units that concentrate on research in, among other things, sickle cell disease (Jamaica), AIDS (Uganda), and global tropical diseases (The Gambia). In conjunction with the Gambian Ministry of Health, the Gambian MRC research laboratory in Banjul supports research on diseases such as malaria, HIV/AIDS, and tuberculosis and on disease control and clinical research (MRC Annual Report 1995). For a more critical analysis of the MRC, see especially Beinart (1989), who argues that the history of the MRC was one of seeing "an inner world of bugs and dietary deficiencies," rather than an "outer world of critically altered social relations, unfavourable terms of trade, and land hunger" (135).

room, a meeting room and two attached offices, staff houses, and guest houses for visiting researchers. Numerous medical projects have been run out of this station. In 1981 the MRC began a demographic census of the surrounding forty-village area, largely for malaria work.

In villages, people live in large households or compounds consisting of one or more dwellings. Compounds are encompassed in turn by *kabilos*, villages, and divisions. Of the latter there are five in the country. Villages have a headman or chief (an *alkalo*); women have a leader (a *kafo*). The chief is drawn from a leading family, often called the "landowners," most of whom, in this particular area, are Mandinka. Most houses, built close together, have thatch roofs. Some have walls constructed of wattle and daub; others are made of cement blocks. Cows, goats, and chickens are kept, and many of the villages are surrounded by thatch fences to keep certain animals in and others out. Almost every village has a well and a few have clinics, run usually by a resident of the town on a part-time basis or when medical supplies are available. Almost all villages have a mosque, even it is simply a room in someone's house. None has a secondary school, though a few have primary schools. The few children who go on to secondary school go to live with friends or relatives in Farafenni or places farther away. Some commute the distance each day. The villages have ready access by vehicle to the main arterial road that bisects the country. People needing to get crops to market or sick relatives to the health center can usually do so in less than a day by hiring a driver with a flat wooden horse cart or by riding on a passenger lorry.

In 1995, the forty study villages contained a total of 16,642 people, with individual village populations ranging from 60 to more than 1,300. Three ethnic groups were represented: Mandinka, 44 percent, Wolof, 36 percent, and Fula, 20 percent. All have patrilineal ideologies, with strong preferences, particularly in a man's first marriage, for a match with his mother's brother's daughter. The Mandinka, the "landowners" or first settlers in most of this particular region, are largely farmers, cultivating groundnuts, rice, millet, and sorghum. They lend usufruct farming and grazing rights to some of the land to members of the other groups or to lower-status Mandinka. At harvest time, people who borrowed the land bring part of the harvest to the landowners, and at the beginning of the rains, they ask permission to use the land again. Thus, many Fula and Wolof farm as well. The Fula in particular raise cattle for milk and for sale, grazing their cattle on Mandinka land. The landowners benefit from the fertilizing and remove the cattle when the rains come, around June, to make way for the farmers. The Fula, when they cultivate, grow primarily maize and millet. A few

Mandinka have cattle as well, but most buy them for ceremonial occasions, especially for bridewealth, to gain rights in a woman and her future children.

Single ethnic groups tend to dominate each village, although villages of different ethnicities are often close neighbors. Mandinka compounds tend to be the largest (with about nineteen people), followed by Wolof and Fula compounds (with about seventeen and twelve people, respectively). In Mandinka villages, several women may live together in a large house, the old supervising the young. Each woman sleeps with her small children in a curtained-off bed, and co-wives alternate nights to sleep with the husband in his house. The Wolof and the Fula tend to have a small house for each woman, whom the man visits in rotation (Wittrup 1990, 129–30). In all ethnic groups, children come and go readily from households and villages, whether to perform domestic help, to learn a trade, to attend school, or simply to be raised by a relative. Such fluidity among children yields an entirely different sense of reproduction from the one with which most of us are familiar. Rather than a fixed group, children comprise a moving wave of young family members.

In the rural areas, the various ethnic groups recognize a hierarchy based on their occupation but also on the alleged order and circumstances of their arrival. In the past, the differences among groups were marked sharply by hereditary castes. As was the case for much of West Africa, there were freeborn people: those of noble descent who had a direct (and preferably recent) connection through the father's line to a chief. Below them were people of lower standing such as weavers, blacksmiths, leather workers, and praise singers. At the lowest level were slaves, of whom there were two types: those born into the household and those bought or recently captured, the former enjoying higher status than the latter. Today these hierarchies endure to some extent, although slavery per se is illegal, but the boundaries among groups have become quite porous. Especially in urban areas, the possibilities for rising to wealth and prominence through schooling and through government and business employment usually render the notion of caste meaningless in everyday life.

Farming families grow both staple and cash crops in ways that attempt to stagger labor inputs at peak seasons. Men cultivate groundnuts and millet in the uplands, while women cultivate rice in the lower wetlands. During the dry season women grow vegetables, which they use for consumption in the household or bring to local market towns to sell. Among the Mandinka, who are seen as the landlords to those who arrived later, land has classically been of two types. One is "household land," available through members of the patrilineage to sons and their wives and children to support the household. The other is the individual plot, which a woman, with the help of her older children, can use to farm crops to sell, although access to this land is contingent on her continued good graces in the household. In general, women put in far more work on the farms than men. Especially during planting season, around mid-June, as the ground is prepared for the rains, the only women to be found in the villages during the daytime are the very young, the very old, the very sick, and those who have just given birth. Use of migrant labor is a long-standing practice, and many young men, both married and unmarried, leave for several months of the year to work for cash (see Enel et al. 1994). Over the course of the rounds, 19 percent of women stated that their husbands were absent, whether for work or other purposes.

Although the notion of "population" implies a group in a fixed location, it is more useful to think of the idea as one of "being" in a specific time and place. The patterns of labor and migration that one sees today have changed significantly over time. Indeed, the history of agrarian change and gender relations in The Gambia is one of the richest and best-documented cases in the African record. Carney and Watts (1991) have shown that the sexual division of labor by crop that is visible today is not the outcome of a "traditional" division of labor but of an increasing commoditization of production in the mid-nineteenth century. Whereas men and women had previously worked alongside each other, producing both upland and swamp rice, the introduction of groundnuts as a cash crop in the 1830s produced greater segregation of male and female tasks. Aided by migrant laborers ("strange farmers"), men increasingly worked on the upland cultivation of groundnuts and cereals such as millet and sorghum, and women moved into intensified lowland cultivation of rice. To meet the food needs for their families and the migrant laborers, women had to intensify their work, expanding the growing season for rice, traveling longer distances each day to more distant plots, and drawing ever-younger women (sometimes under the age of ten) into the labor force (Haswell 1975). In the 1940s, upland rice had all but disappeared (Gamble 1955). Starting in the mid-1970s, a critical development in agriculture for women was the advent of efforts to promote vegetables and, later, tree crops such as citrus and mangoes for home consumption, for sale in local markets and in the country's thriving tourist hotels, and for shipment in the winter to Europe (for example, Carney 1992). The result was a number of instances of what Carney and Watts (1991) termed "renegotiations of the conjugal contract" as men and women jostled for access to land for cash or subsistence production. Schroeder's (1999)

complex account hints of an instance of men and women pitting international advocates of "women in development" and advocates of "biodiver-
sity" against one another in the continuing struggles over access to land.

Marriage, Childbearing, and the Political Economy of Reproduction

For women in rural Gambia, marriage is of major consequence. About
88 percent of women aged fifteen to forty-nine in the study area were currently married. More than one-fifth had been married to more than one
husband because of divorce or widowhood. So important is marriage that
a woman's entry into childbearing is usually preceded by a marriage that
is both early and arranged. The average age at marriage was 16.1, and
among women who had given birth, the average age at first birth was approximately 18.4. Although Islamic norms governing conjugal union, with
their emphasis on female purity, are sometimes said to weigh heavily in producing early marriage and fertility, Islam itself may have less effect on these
patterns than local recruitment of young women into marriage pools.[5] Marriage is entered into at a very young age, but full sexuality may be delayed
for another year or so until the state of bridewealth negotiations permits the
young wife to be "transferred" formally to her husband's compound. A formal transfer may even be delayed for two or three years, until she has borne
and weaned her first child. Once in her husband's home, she may remain
under the watchful eye of a senior wife who ensures that sexuality is initi-
ated sparingly until she appears ready to undergo the rigors of childbearing. Because of households' need for young female labor, there is often an
undercurrent of struggle between the mother of the young woman and the
mother of the prospective husband. A mother who can delay her daughter's
transfer until her son is able to marry and bring in his own wife is able to
maintain a steady source of young female labor as well as money and gifts
from an anxious prospective son-in-law.

First marriages are almost invariably arranged. English translations of
the men's marriage survey in the forty-village area frequently quoted both
women and men as saying they were "forced" to marry their first partner. This phrasing, however, appears to mean simply that the marriage was
obligatory. A young woman may even come to learn that her family be-

---

5. Certainly marriage is no longer early or universal in much of the Muslim world (Obermeyer
1992).

trothed her to a particular man when she was small. In the rural areas, a young man may ask his father to arrange a marriage to a girl he already admires. But in some cases, conjugal partners may not know each other ahead of time. There are some quite touching stories of men who reported that they were initially forced to marry a woman they did not want, yet whom they eventually came to love and respect. A young man's first marriage is almost always to a woman he calls his "cousin-sister," an actual or classificatory mother's brother's daughter. In marrying a woman from his mother's family, he reinforces what is often a chain of historically established "uncle-nephew" relationships involving claims to land, leadership, and wealth (see Murphy and Bledsoe 1987 for Liberia). Marrying a cousin-sister is advantageous to his family as well in that it usually requires less bridewealth. According to some people, it also reduces the risks of adultery because of the moral consequences of bringing discord into a family. In any case, the overriding concern for a young man's family is to obtain a woman from a family known to train its children properly: to accept responsibility, to respect elders, and to bear hardship without complaint.

If anything is more important in life than marriage, it is the production of children.[6] Most mothers spend considerable time with their babies, picking them up, feeding them on demand, taking them to healers if necessary, and so on.[7] Although babies are indulged, older children are expected to bend to their responsibilities of schooling, training, or work, and their future marriages and careers are of intense concern to families. So important are children that the primary purpose of marriage is said to be having them. Throughout West Africa in general, wealth and security lie in people and relationships far more than in money or property (on Mandinka patronage politics, see Weil 1971 and Beckerleg 1992–93). The uncertainties of both urban employment and of rural agriculture draw the two spheres closely together. For rural cultivators, ties to urban relatives and to patrons can provide critical access in times of crisis to food, money, and petrol and to the international world of mobility, jobs, and hard currency. Thus, whereas much of the classic African kinship literature casts families as conservative forces seeking to uphold tradition, the reality is quite different. The diverse skills and social ties that a family cultivates through children are the keys to its ability to cope with economic insecurities and political perils

6. It would be wrong to argue that women's lives are organized entirely around reproduction or that all the other aspects of their lives—whether productive labor or agency in general—are subsidiary to reproductive activity. Reproduction, however, is of major consequence to women in The Gambia.

7. See Whittemore 1989 for an insightful study of Mandinka socialization in southern Senegal.

(see Rasmussen 1997). Vital to families' political goals is the task of identifying and cultivating children who have the potential to strike out into the world beyond the home and farm: to enable them to become something *other* than what the family is now. Much as I found in Sierra Leone (1990a, 1994), bearing many healthy children and training them for success under such conditions lies at the heart of security for rural Gambian families. A son may move to Banjul and acquire a job with ready access to hard currency; a married daughter living in Europe may send money to her mother during difficult times back home. Since children are the family members who are most poised for training as new economic enterprises become available, adults watch children, trying to cultivate their potentials to take advantage of these opportunities. In pursuit of such ties, parents may foster their children to a household that offers new skills and contacts or a nearby school with an excellent reputation. Here, the children may have to work and study hard, receive meager food, endure low status, and suffer sickness to mold their characters and earn knowledge and blessings from those who teach them. The greater the status differential between the sending and the receiving families, the greater the hardships the children must endure. Such ordeals as seen as building character. The success that children achieve, of course, may aggravate competition among their mothers. Observing the benefits her co-wife was reaping from well-positioned children, a forty-year-old woman made explicit the advantages of outside ties that children can bring: "My co-wife . . . has five children, all of whom are living in the outside world. . . . She receives very good support, financially, from all her children regularly. This is why she is better off than me."

Children who become successful find themselves deluged with requests from former supporters, all of whom now claim to have been instrumental to their success. Whereas Western scholarship tends to relegate the topic of children to socialization or to what has sometimes been depicted as an uncomplicated "domestic" sphere, the West African domestic domain, if indeed this is where the subject of children should properly be placed, is anything but uncomplicated. Children, like other objects of value, have highly contested histories of claims upon them (for related discussions, see Appadurai 1986; Kopytoff 1986).

Although the primary reason for marriage is the production of children, not all marriages produce children. Some women never manage to bear children or to raise any who survive. Another type of marriage that is not expected to yield children is a "charity" marriage. Local Islamic practice requires that a woman be married in order to have a husband who will pray for her when she dies so that she can enter Paradise. A widow or divorcee who is past childbearing may therefore ask a man to marry her "by name." She may live outside the compound, visiting occasionally with a cooked meal for him. In such a marriage, the tables have turned from youth to senescence: now it is the woman who goes looking for the man and not vice versa. A related deviation from the expectation of reproduction in marriage is that of a woman whose husband dies. A widow may be given a choice: she may marry a relative of her dead husband, go back to her own family, or marry someone outside the compound. The less likely she is to produce more children, the more choice she is given in this matter.

For everyone in rural Gambia, polygyny is in one way or another a fact of life. Men from families eligible for local chieftaincies see it and the additional children it can bring them as key for maintaining their political strength. Polygyny is also explained as a way to allow a man to maintain sexual life while a breastfeeding wife abstains from or minimizes sex. For this reason, not only a woman's breastfeeding status but even her monthly menstrual patterns may be well known to all conjugal members, even if nothing is ever spoken directly. West Africa has the highest rates of polygyny in the world (Ezeh et al. 1996). In the project's 1992 survey, about 58 percent of married women in the study area had one or more co-wives. So common is polygyny that even women who are not currently in such a union for the first part of their married life are likely to be in one at some point because of divorce or widowhood. Most polygynous women had only one co-wife but sometimes there were two. Among married women, 38.7 percent had one co-wife and 15 percent had two. By Islamic decree, a man can have as many as four wives, although taking on an additional one as a "charity wife" is regarded locally not as a sin but a beneficent act, and a man need not count such a wife as part of his religious limit. Men who were especially likely to be polygynous were middle-aged or older. Whereas a young man's father usually pays for his first wife, the second wife, married perhaps a decade and a half later—sometimes over the protests of the first, sometimes at her insistence—is usually acquired by the husband himself.

If, as Simmel suggests, persons are composite collections of identities stemming from multiple sources, such is true in the extreme for a man whose reproductive life usually derives meaning with respect to more than one wife, whether simultaneously or in sequence.[8] As is the case elsewhere in Africa, the central question for a man is not whether but how intensely

---

8. For more on the social and demographic implications of polygyny for a man, see Bledsoe et al. 2000b and some of the contributions to Bledsoe et al. 2000a. For just two of a number of excellent demographic works on polygyny, see van de Walle and Kekovole 1984; Goldman and Pebley 1989.

he is married or partnered (see Blanc and Gage 2000). That is, how many partners does he have, at what points in time, and how strong are his links to them? Individual men tend to have peaks and troughs in their sexual lives, in situations we might find quite paradoxical. As Orobaton (2000) reports for Nigeria, a young man actually sees the early years of his marriage, his period of maximal biological reproductivity, as a "rest" from the increasing sexual expectations he was facing before marriage from peers and potential sexual partners. By his mid-forties or so, his rest is over, and pressures to strike up new partnerships begin anew. Wealthy men tend to have more wives than poor ones, and, hence, more children as well. But as Riesman (1992, 57) suggests, as much as a man wants many children, he is more concerned with maintaining a continuous supply of them in order to maintain the labor he needs. This, he hopes, will delay as long as possible his relegation to an inconsequential role in the compound. Hence, a man would find the demographic notion of "final family size" meaningless because he can in theory continue marrying young women up until his death, and his last child may grow up never knowing him. Because men usually stagger their marriages throughout their lives, it is risky to assume, as family planning programs tend to do, that a man and his wife are a unified "couple" and that hence men can be won over once and for all to family planning.

As for the woman's view of polygyny, having a co-wife is said to allow women to share housekeeping duties and to fill in for each other during sicknesses or absences or to maintain spousal distance when they need to avoid pregnancy. Sometimes common household expenses such as food are the responsibility of the man. When they are not, they are shared, in rotation, by each wife, according to who is to "take her leg," a metaphor that refers alternating the weight of the body while walking. That is, each woman takes her turn cooking for the man and sleeping in his house. There are longer-term cycles, as well, as older women yield these roles to younger women.

Co-wife relations are pervaded by inequalities. Most inequities are expected and tolerated; others are deeply contentious. Status relations are determined by temporal precedence, numbers of surviving or successful sons, and so on. Information about junior wives should be known by senior ones but not vice versa; younger co-wives should do heavy labor and let the senior ones handle the household's administrative and fiscal tasks; senior wives may help junior wives give birth but not vice versa; and so on. If relations are cordial, co-wives call each other "mother" and "daughter" or (for wives closer in age) "older (younger) sister," and cooperation may take place amicably. In the worst cases, however, rivalries over food, labor, money, and children reduce co-wife relations to bitter enmity. As was true in Sierra Leone, small acts of favoritism, whether real or perceived, infuse polygynous life. One wife may be perceived by the rest as enjoying better clothes, more money, or more benefits for her children. To avoid fueling these rivalries, husbands should avoid overt signs of favoritism, although some women feel that this norm simply gives men the license to shirk responsibility, leaving a mother to furnish practically everything for herself and her own children. Not surprisingly, the separation between men's and women's incomes, for which Africa is noted, is strongest in polygynous households. As the number of wives increases, the stipulation that a man should refrain from favoritism intensifies. If he must have a favorite, he is expected to choose the first one he married, out of respect for her seniority. But youth and beauty influence his sentiments, and everyone resents a pretty, young wife who attempts to "turns the husband's head" through mystically powerful "juju" (Islamic ritual medicine) to escape drudgery or to seize what the others see as an unfair share of household resources.

As is the case with his wives, a man should treat all his offspring equally, but given limited resources, he may try hardest to educate older children with the expectation that they in turn will help younger siblings go to school. He may also favor the children of a wife from a high-status family, regardless of their mother's temporal precedence. Differences in treatment may carry far beyond the immediate household, a fact that worries women who are concerned that such signs foretell future imbalances in educational and family leadership opportunities for their children.

In rural compounds, then, men and women have overlapping concerns about reproduction. Everyone would like as many children as God gives them, and preferably soon, to establish their security and gain a competitive edge over present and future competitors, whether these be (in the case of men) male agnates or (in the case of women) co-wives and sisters-in-law. For men, with their formal authority in matters of marriage, inheritance, and land, especially desired are sons, who will retain rights of residence, inheritance, and succession to leadership roles. Yet men welcome daughters as well. A daughter's bridewealth will allow a man to acquire a wife for his son or to take another himself.[9] As for women, they enter their husbands' compounds with a highly tenuous status, having rights to farmland and to the compound's titles and possessions only through their husbands and children. Like their husbands, women very much want daughters—they, more

---

9. For a discussion of sex preferences among offspring in The Gambia, see Nyabally and Sonko 1997.

directly than men, are the beneficiaries of girls' farm and domestic work. Even when they leave home for marriage, daughters (if they are dutiful) will try to send remittances and lend help whenever possible to ease their mothers' material worries in elderhood. Yet as much as women want daughters, they describe boys as holding more long-term value for them because of men's rights to family property and leadership. The importance of securing optimal positions for her sons is a strong incentive to a woman to establish her own position in the marriage home.

How are descriptions such as these borne out in the Farafenni study area's fertility numbers by ethnicity and gender? In the first part of the 1990s, the birth intervals project showed no statistically significant difference in the fertility among women of different ethnic groups (the total fertility rate, as reported earlier, was 7.5). Although comparable data were not collected for men at the time, a 1998 study by Ratcliffe and Hill in the same area showed an average of 6.5 for women aged forty-five to forty-nine but no statistical difference among the ethnic groups. Men aged sixty to sixty-four, however, showed significant differences by ethnic group. The mean number of children they had borne by all wives was 9.7 for Mandinka, 8.5 for Fula, 8.9 for Wolof, and 9.3 for all, with differences probably attributable to rates of polygyny.[10] And although the intervals between women's birth's lengthened with age, those between the births of men's children became shorter as they acquired additional wives. Fertility experiences for men and women are likely envisioned through the life course in quite different ways by men and women, even those who are married to each other.

Now there are signs of changing attitudes about the value of high fertility. The costs of educating a child for any length of time severely strain a family's income. They also pose an increasing gamble. Because of the shrinking market for wage employment, the chances diminish that any one child will become highly successful or will remit benefits to elders who invested in him or her (see Berry 1985). Still, children remain immensely valued, and a woman who tries to achieve long birth intervals may be accused of withholding children from her husband or of thwarting his political ambitions.

For a woman, the transition from adolescence into marriage and childbearing is best described, as it is through much of the subcontinent, as a process. During this process, gifts and bridewealth are exchanged, visits are made, a change of residence occurs, a child is conceived, and so on. For a young woman, the inception of sex, pregnancy, and childbearing are com-

10. Ratcliffe 2000, tables 17 and 18, pp. 125–26.

mingled. Whereas a woman with older children to care for usually remains in her conjugal home to give birth, assisted by a midwife and by older women, a young woman having her first child typically goes home to her mother to give birth and to stay for several months. In doing so, she receives help in delivering and in tending to the baby, and she is better able to maintain sexual distance from her husband until it is safe for her to get pregnant again. The following account from the monthly rounds is typical:

> I spent one year whilst [newly] married to [my husband] with my parents, during which I used to come over to his home [in the same village] to sleep with him. . . . By the end of the first year, I moved to his home [permanently] with a seven month pregnancy. After delivery of that [first] child, I went back to my mother where I stayed and abstained from my husband for six months. I breastfed [this child] at my mother's for two years. I got pregnant and delivered my second child while I was still at my [mother's] house. (R. 1)[11]

Breastfeeding usually commences after the colostrum ends and breast milk proper appears. Most women breastfeed fully, supplementing only with water and (occasionally) animal milk for several weeks or months, until a thin, watery pap of millet or couscous is introduced and then thickened gradually. About a week after the birth, the child is carried outdoors, named, and blessed, to establish its place in the paternal family.[12] Once marriage begins, whether it is delayed by bridewealth negotiations or (in a very few cases) by schooling, a woman's birth intervals take on a fairly regular rhythm. After reproduction is finished, sexuality tapers off or ends altogether, an event that may or may not coincide with becoming a grandmother, though the practice is usually explained in these terms.

Infertility is possibly the worst fate an individual can suffer. After you are gone, explained a woman, your children will remind people about you. If you have no children, everything about you disappears: you leave "as a whole" (see also Fortes 1978). Childless men may turn a blind eye to their wives' efforts to seek fertility help from other men. As for women, a few become so beloved that they take on the role of nurturing "mother" to all the compound's children, but most are simply given a child to raise by relatives or co-wives. Anguishing delays in pregnancy may be attributed to witches,

---

11. Throughout, I will refer to responses to open-ended questions from (say) Round 2 of the monthly multi-round survey as "R. 2."

12. On analogous "outdooring" practices in Ghana, see Anarfi and Fayorsey 2000.

spirits, or jealous co-wives. Suspicions may also arise that an infertile woman has been consorting with other men, polluting her blood and making it impossible to conceive. Other theories about infertility include body pain, unclean womb, weak sperm, or impotence. Since conception is believed to require a mixture of male and female fluids that are compatible, individuals who are childless in one marriage may marry again to try with someone else whom they hope will make a more compatible blood match. Islam explicitly allows partners in a marriage that has been unfruitful for seven years to divorce, although such relationships usually end well before then. For an infertile man or woman, each subsequent union is increasingly likely to be ephemeral or marginal (for a woman, it is likely to be one with an already married man), and divorce, remarriage, and abandonment are common themes in the life histories of subfertile individuals. A referral hospital in Banjul can perform a medical inquiry for infertility, although the costs of these services and the travel expenses required to reach them make them prohibitive for most individuals. For those with abundant resources, however, it is possible to go abroad for treatment. Other curative efforts consist of dilation and curettage, medicines, and even birth control pills, which may be used to try to induce menstrual regularity. Most infertile or subfertile women also consult marabouts, Islamic ritual specialists, or they join the Kanyaleng Society, which provides advice on ritual as well as medical measures and gives social support (Sundby 1997; Skramstad 1997; Sundby et al. 1998).

As for how the child grows in the womb, the mother is said to be like an empty container; whatever is put in is what she will produce. Thus, although her blood is said to contribute modestly to the child's growth, the husband is the primary contributor, and he must keep the fetus growing with regular infusions of his seminal fluid and with food that he provides for the mother. Both of these substances denote, symbolically and physically, his significance in the reproductive process. One of the worst things a mother can do is commit adultery while pregnant. In doing so, she is mingling in her husband's child his substance and that of another man. For a woman whose child misbehaves, defies authority, or refuses to learn properly, the product of her suspected transgression may be painfully exposed into the next generation.

The most important fact about a pregnancy is its precariousness. Throughout, a woman should exercise care about what she eats, lest the child be deformed or be unable to function properly. Some of these taboos are general. Thus, all pregnant women should avoid eating eggs, lest the child be unable to speak. (The reasoning: because there is no opening in an egg, the child, like the egg, will not have a mouth.)[13] Other taboos are more specific. Certain families may say that they cannot eat a particular animal or a particular leaf, lest the child be born with a defect that the taboo food can cause. In some cases this is a rash or an inability to walk. A woman who is pregnant must be careful not only about her own family's taboos but those of her husband's family, since the child is of this line.

There are more significant risks to pregnancies than food taboos, however. An early pregnancy is highly susceptible to miscarriage, and the mother must be extremely cautious until it is stable, or until it "stands."[14] A pregnancy is said to stand when fetal movements can be felt; thus, it is at greatest risk in the early period. Among the greatest risks to an early pregnancy are witches and spirits called *jinns*. A witch is a human who changes form to eat other people, particularly children, either before or after they are born. Whether it acts out of jealousy or spite, a witch always acts for evil and always to destroy. Jinns are different. Some can do good and may adopt a human for this purpose, although they expect some reciprocities; they can even bring fortune. Others are mischievous. But most jinns are evil. Unlike witches, jinns try to populate their own world, and they do this by trying to seize fetuses and change them into their own kind. Hence, people might explain a miscarriage or a child death by saying that a certain baby "went back" to the jinns.[15] Because jinns rove about in the air and winds, a pregnant woman is admonished to stay inside her compound as much as possible and to wrap her clothes tightly about her to avoid exposure to these elements. She should particularly avoid going out in the early afternoon and in the late evening, when jinns are most apt to be out.

A pregnancy can draw jealousy from just about anyone outside of a very tight circle, even relatives. The more people who know about it before it stands, the greater the potential harm, and a woman must take extraordinary care to hide her condition from the people she most fears would have reason to be jealous. Such people are often co-wives or sisters-in-law, but a woman may even suspect her mother-in-law, who may have opposed her marriage or who may favor another daughter-in-law. Fearing the spread of news of her pregnancy, a woman may not even tell her husband she is pregnant. She must, however, confide in one or two people she trusts: usually

13. There is inevitably transgression of these taboos, and many people put little faith in them. Only if something goes wrong later might a taboo food be suspected as the source of the problem.

14. *Kono loo: kono,* literally, "stomach"; *loo,* "stands," the double *o* denoting emphasis; hence, the pregnancy is *definitely* there.

15. See Gottlieb's (1998) excellent work on babyhood as a period of highly tenuous connection to living personhood. For a novel based on such beliefs, see Okri 1992.

her mother or a sister. Whoever she confides in will be an "extra eye" to watch over her. By listening to gossip and watching for subtle cues in the social environment, this person will bring her back in line should she transgress any social or ritual boundaries. This person can also go to a marabout on her behalf to obtain ritual amulets to protect the pregnancy, without revealing who the pregnant woman actually is. Since a pregnancy is not said to stand for a few months, most women delay at least this long before going to government-run clinics for prenatal care. Here little confidentiality is possible. Seated on the long wooden benches in the waiting area, everyone can see everyone else. What is more, the nurses themselves are very likely to be their patients' neighbors or kin. Especially if a woman lacks the cover of a small child who can be presented for "under-fives" checkups, going in for prenatal care would make her instantly vulnerable. Maternal and child health programs that try to persuade women to come in for medical checks in early pregnancy are notoriously unsuccessful. Even the nurses who staff these clinics and advocate the need for prenatal care may themselves avoid declaring their own pregnancies until their pregnancies stand or their condition is obvious (see Chapman 2001 for Mozambique).

Methods of Fertility Regulation

In chapter 2 I described very broadly practices such as fosterage as instances of exerting control over reproduction. Here I describe methods of regulating births more specifically, including internationally distributed products of high-technology research. In later chapters I move on to specific strategies of contraceptive use. I omit a discussion of abstinence since chapter 4 takes up this topic in detail.

In a context where births and the spaces that separate them are matters of intense concern, women resort to a variety of means of maintaining control over them. In making fertility control decisions, they take into account several criteria, including their own marital and fertility histories as well as characteristics of the contraceptives themselves. Some of these criteria include ease of acquisition and use, perceived efficacy and health effects, and degree of confidentiality.

A number of techniques that local women use would be classified in the medical and demographic literature as "menstrual regulation" (see van de Walle and Renne 2001; Levin 2001). Abortion is one possible solution to an unwanted pregnancy. A woman may try to abort a fetus by inserting a long, sharp object into her womb (or having someone do it for her) or by drinking a liquid mixture of local herbs made from the bark of a particular tree *(jalafato)*. Everyone, however, recognizes the dangers of hemorrhage in the use of perforating instruments, and herbs have uneven efficacy or may be taken in doses that are toxic. Thus, a woman may try to flush out a fetus by taking strong doses of birth control pills to produce heavy bleeding. Even a woman who does not think she is pregnant might drink a certain kind of honey twice a day as a preventive measure. Thick and reddish in color, like menstrual blood, this honey is said to "wash the stomach." Even local birth attendants dispense such potions.

Widely prevalent in The Gambia, and in West Africa more generally, is the use of "juju," sometimes called a "charm." Written in Arabic by an Islamic holy man whose powers rest on controlling the mysteries of the Qur'an, juju typically consists of secret texts from the Qur'an sewn tightly into a small leather amulet and tied around the client's waist or neck. Among the virtues of juju as a contraceptive is that it only needs to be obtained once. It can be used throughout reproductive life at the times when pregnancy is not wanted. In addition, it is easy to use. Once it is put on, it is always worn, so there is no need to remember to put it on anew each day. Birth control pills, by contrast, require daily vigilance. Furthermore, juju is highly amenable to user control. Its effects on fecundity can be switched on and off as easily as turning the amulet over and wearing it front to back. At one moment a woman is said to be fecund; at the next moment she is not. For a woman who seeks close control over the timing of her fecundity, this "on/off" feature of makes juju ideal. Juju also has the benefit of having no effects on future fertility, making it suitable for young married women who are deemed too immature to bear a second child soon after the first or to fend off the husband. In addition, juju is written for specific purposes, and so a woman whose husband is anxious for her to become pregnant may construe it, because of its ambiguous physical appearance, as a measure for preventing sickness or bringing luck, instead of avoiding pregnancy. Only the wearer knows the real purpose. Juju is also used by women who worry about gossipy clinic nurses who dispense pills and injections but trust the professional demeanor of secrecy among Islamic ritual specialists. Juju is used even by educated women who worry about the possible harmful effects of Western contraceptives. Said a twenty-five-year-old schoolteacher with two children: "I am not taking [Western] contraception . . . because of the medicines [chemicals] which can cause complications in my body, as I learn from a lot of my friends. I think I am too young in marriage to start introducing such strong medicines into my body that can cause some serious problems for me to have children in the future."

Such readiness by the educated to use juju is by no means uncommon.

My ad hoc survey, one day, of the five young female fieldworkers who were working on the project, all of whom had at least some secondary school education, revealed that all four of those who had begun childbearing were either using juju at the time or had done so in the recent past. One woman, who was breastfeeding, was using two jujus.

Despite its virtues, however, juju has decided drawbacks for a woman. One is that in most cases, it must be commissioned by the husband or an elder relative to lower the chances that it will be used to cover up an affair, and many ritual specialists refuse to prepare it without such approval. This means that a nonbreastfeeding woman can in theory become pregnant again even if she continues to wear her juju. The husband may even stipulate, in commissioning it, that its ritual efficacy dissipate as soon as the child is weaned. The following quotation from a woman implies how tight this control can be: "I have four children alive. [One died.] Each time I am breastfeeding my husband gives me a juju to tie to my waist which prevents me from getting pregnant until I wean my child. After weaning, he collects the juju from me" (R. 3). (The implication is that he is making her fecund again.)

Perhaps the most serious drawback of juju, however, is its questionable efficacy. A number of women complained about getting pregnant while using it. When other methods have failed or produced complications, juju and herbs are clearly preferred to nothing at all. But outsiders would not be surprised at responses such as the following to the open-ended questions or by the comment that the interviewer appended:

> I was given a juju by my husband's elder brother. He said it was going to protect me from getting pregnant, for I intended to breastfeed my child for two years. [However,] I came to realize that I am pregnant recently. If I deliver with no problems I will go in for a different method than the in-law's juju. [Interviewer's comment: The child she is breastfeeding is, frankly speaking, too young for weaning. She never wanted to get pregnant. This woman is very shy [ashamed] about this pregnancy and was at the verge of crying while doing the interview.] (R. 1)

As for Western contraceptives, several types are available locally. Foaming spermicide tablets can be found in town pharmacies, although no one in the rural villages that were surveyed reported using them. Intrauterine devices can be inserted by practitioners at the government health center, although only one woman in the 1992 survey reported using one. Condoms, widely available in the larger towns, have two principal advantages: they are cheap, and discontinuing them permits an immediate return to fertility. The retail market had at times been so saturated with condoms from international AIDS programs that town pharmacies gave them away. On the negative side, they are troublesome to use and they connote promiscuity because they are associated with extramarital relations (see, for example, Pickering et al. 1992; Bledsoe 1994). In addition, their use obviously requires the man's consent. The 1992 survey of the study villages turned up only four admitted users, though some cases may have been missed of women who found the question confusing since it was arguably not they but their husbands who were using the condoms.

The most common types of Western contraceptives reported were oral contraceptive pills and Depo Provera injections. Although taking a pill every day is difficult to remember and a packet of pills might be discovered by an irate husband, pills permit a fast and controllable return to fecundity. Insofar as the contraceptive effects of pills can disappear quickly, women perceive far more commonalities between pills and juju charms than they do between what outsiders collectively term "modern" contraceptives: pills and injections. (For more on this point, see chapter 4.) Pills and juju are similar also in being susceptible to male control, because a husband's approval is often required to gain access to them. Such facts lend very obvious qualification to the conviction that Western contraception offers women unmitigated liberation from pregnancy or from male control over their reproductive lives.

Contraceptives are also used in The Gambia, as they are in the United States, for many purposes other than preventing pregnancy. Pills are the best case in point. Premenopausal women are sometimes said to use them to postpone their periods so that they may go to Mecca in an unpolluted state. Others may use them to abort unwanted pregnancies by "washing out" an incipient fetus along with menstrual blood or to prevent sexually transmitted diseases by reducing the chances that their husbands will seek sexual satisfaction outside the compound. Not only are contraceptives used for reasons that depart from those we might expect. They can be used for the opposite purpose: to try to *facilitate* fertility. Pills, for example, can be used to purge the reproductive tract of "bad blood" that may be inhibiting fertility, and many health workers actually issue them for this purpose. A village health worker reported that he sometimes gave out pills to women who sought to hasten a new pregnancy as soon as they finished breastfeeding, much as we saw with the phenomenon of menstrual regulation.

The most commonly reported Western contraceptive in the 1992 survey was Depo Provera. Depo Provera is ideal for women who dislike the daily annoyance of remembering to take pills and for women wishing to prevent conception in secrecy. Very occasionally, a young woman in a forced marriage may use it in hopes that her husband, discouraged by her failure to conceive, will conclude that she is sterile and free her to marry a man of her own choosing. Depo Provera, however, is seen as a powerful contraceptive, and its use is not taken lightly. The fact that it is injected is a potent act in itself. And the user has little control over the duration of its effectiveness. Although it is administered in doses whose effects are supposed to last for three months, local conditions that require exhausting, dehydrating work and precipitate frequent illness seem to make Depo Provera spill over longer than it would in more benign conditions. A chemically enforced inability to conceive can be doubly distressing since, once a pregnancy is wanted, each sterile month can be a cumulative indictment of a wife's conjugal loyalty. Depo sometimes inhibits fecundity for more than a year, and many women worry about the possibility that it might impair their fertility permanently. As I document in later chapters, however, the "spillover" features that younger women fear are precisely the ones that older ones may value. Only older women in The Gambia, for the most part, use it, and clinic personnel dislike giving it to younger women. These patterns are vastly different from those in the United States, where some of Depo's most common users are young women finishing an education or carving out a career.

At the end of reproductive life is the possibility of "closing the stomach": bringing a permanent halt to reproduction. In indigenous practice, this consists of a midwife symbolically tying the placenta when it comes out and then turning it over as she buries it in the ground. Nowadays, the most common referent for the notion of closing the stomach is hospital surgery, a procedure that can be conducted, only with the husband's permission, at regional and district health centers. Twenty-one women in the 1992 sample reported that they had been sterilized, which I have taken to mean hospital surgery, though the possibility that they were referring to a ritual procedure cannot be ruled out. Sterilization, whether ritual or surgical, is an extreme measure, usually undertaken only in situations wherein further pregnancies would be life-threatening.

Contraception: Channels of Distribution

The Gambia's health and family planning programs have had input and resources from numerous sources, both national and international. During the past few decades, agencies such as the United Nations Fund for Population Activities and the International Planned Parenthood Federation have stepped up support throughout the developing world, and in 1989, the Gambian Ministry of Health began to add family planning services to its list of measures to improve child health. The government provides inexpensive contraceptive supplies, when they are available, through a national network of clinics and health workers. Indeed, by comparison with some of its West African neighbors, the country is highly medicalized. Outside of Banjul, the Ministry of Health runs several health centers, including the one in Farafenni. Besides dispensing contraceptives, these centers perform prenatal examinations and deliveries and can perform cesarean sections. Women at parity 7 or higher and those in high-risk pregnancies are advised strongly to deliver here. In smaller villages, supplies of contraceptives, though irregular, are distributed by community health nurses (overwhelmingly male) and sometimes by traditional birth attendants (always female). A few larger towns support family planning services, although supplies of contraceptives can be unpredictable here as well as in villages. Even clinics may have no contraceptive supplies when a woman visits, or they may have no supplies of the type that she has been using.

Alongside these direct government sources of contraceptives is the Gambia Family Planning Association, an affiliate of the International Planned Parenthood Federation. The GFPA established an office in Banjul in 1968 with a network of regional offices throughout the country, including one it established in 1975 in the North Bank area. Here, clients can come for services and "community-based distributors" are dispatched to villages, selling contraceptives for small fees. Save the Children, a private voluntary organization, has been also active in family planning in the country, stationing representatives in a few of the larger villages. The organization launched several projects, including a national project concentrating on Islamic leaders. Co-sponsored with the Population Council and the Ministry of Health (Askew et al. 1992), the project subsidized textual searches of the Qur'an and the Hadith, seeking material that could be used to counter claims of clerics who declared that Islam opposed the use of Western contraceptives. To this end, it attempted to bring together large groups of religious leaders to persuade them that spacing births through contraception was acceptable to Islam because it promoted women's and children's health, and that limiting families allowed a man to support the children he brought into the world. It then asked the leaders, with equivocal success, to spread the message.

Despite these efforts, local response has not fulfilled all the hopes of outside family planning agencies for use of contraceptives. Besides the problem of uneven availability, people worry about side effects of weight gain, blood loss, and infertility.[16] In addition are worries, often fueled by those who claim that Islam forbids family planning, that women may take advantage of their contraceptive-induced infecundity to engage in sexual impropriety. In many cases the collusion of birth attendants is feared, as are private pharmacies in the larger towns and individuals who obtain contraceptives through professional connections to health facilities, a phenomenon commonly described throughout West Africa as "private practice." The fact that Western contraceptives can be obtained outside of the control of the husband or in-laws makes everyone nervous about them.

Data

The analyses in this book draw on multiple sources designed in collaboration with Allan Hill. Besides the continuously updated census that began in 1981, a 1992 baseline fertility survey was taken of the forty villages east and west of Farafenni. Those interviewed included 2,980 "women of reproductive age," following demographic convention. They ranged in age from fifteen to fifty-four,[17] and the survey included only women who reported that they had had at least one pregnancy. This survey linked existing documentation from the years of the census with new data in cross-section on marriage, education, and fosterage. Fertility questions included those on breastfeeding, postpartum abstinence, current sexual status, and contraception. Information was also elicited on each pregnancy the woman had undergone: the outcome and (if surviving) sex, date of birth, date of death (if relevant), present location, and so on.

Besides the 1992 baseline survey there were a number of other surveys. The most important was a fifteen-month multi-round survey during 1993 and 1994 of about 270 women each month in eight of the forty villages. The aim was to see how their fertility-relevant behaviors changed as new pregnancies occurred and were terminated, and as their children progressed.[18] A total of 4,054 responses were collected throughout the fifteen months. For

16. Sometimes users of pills and Depo Provera complain of an increase in weight. But since most women of childbearing age worry not about being fat but about being thin, they often find these contraceptives appealing for this very reason.

17. The group included eight women aged fifty-five to fifty-eight. Since the ages of the women at the upper end of the age range could have been underreported (and there were only a few), I leave them in for the analysis.

18. The analysis uses only thirteen of the fifteen rounds. At the time I was conducting the analysis, Rounds 5 and 14 were not in a format compatible with the others.

the rounds, eight villages were chosen to obtain a wide range of size, degree of access to health care, and predominance of one ethnic group or another. The women participating in the rounds were queried every month. Because of the emphasis on child spacing, the initial group of women included those who reported that they had had a live birth in the past three years. From then on, more women from these eight villages were recruited into the study as new births occurred.

The monthly rounds included a core fertility questionnaire with a number of yes-or-no or multiple choice possibilities. Several of these questions were followed by "please explain" follow-up questions. Rounds 1–3 concluded the interview with an open-ended cluster of questions and probes, the answers to which were entered separately in word-processing files. The theme of these first three rounds was getting pregnant and avoiding pregnancy. The questions, edited slightly, read thus:

Rounds 1–3: General Fertility
Tell me more about your efforts to get pregnant, or avoid pregnancy. (If using a particular method, such as pills or juju): Where, or from whom, did you get the advice/the supplies to do this? For what reasons are you using this particular measure now (e.g., pressure from husband, in-laws, own family, co-wives; worries about health of children; difficulty of last pregnancy; illness)? Have you used any other methods or strategies to get pregnant (or avoid pregnancy) in the past? If so, why did you stop using them?

Repeated every month, however, these questions became tedious to many of the women, and so starting in Round 4 (October 1993), a new component was substituted: a "question of the month." [19] Here are two examples.

Round 4: The Beginning of Marriage and Childbearing
I would like to ask you about the beginning of your married life—when you were first married and started to have your children.
1. How was your marriage arranged? Who picked your husband—you or your parents? What age were you when the marriage negotiations began? Were you a girl or a woman when you married this man?

---

19. This substitution was Allan Hill's suggestion. The wording in Rounds 4 and 11, shown here, was largely his work.

Were you promised to him as a girl? Were you consulted during the negotiations?

2. Were you pregnant or did you have a child before the final marriage payments/transfer took place? After the public ceremony, how long was it before you transferred to your husband's compound? Did you see your husband regularly during this period? How long was it between the ceremony and your first birth? Did you try to delay the first pregnancy? If so, why? Was your first child born before you finally transferred?

3. Where did you have your first child (husband's or mothers compound)? Who helped you? Did you return to your mother for the first birth? Why? How long did you stay? Who decided you could go? At what stage of physical development was the child when you went back to your husband?

Round 11: Islam and Fertility

What do you think is the most important rule in Islam pertaining to women? What difficulties do you encounter in trying to follow this rule? How do you try to manage these difficulties?

Once these substitutions were made, interest picked up again and many of the women, as they responded every month to the first part of the questionnaire with its invariant questions, looked forward to the new question of the month. For Round 12, which was conducted in June 1994, a special questionnaire was incorporated that I describe in chapter 8.

In this book, the numerical analyses that use the rounds do not, for the most part, represent individuals. Although I describe the units, for facility, as if they were individual women, they represent instead single "observations" or "events." This means that some women are represented in as many as thirteen of the monthly rounds, whereas those who were absent for part of the time may appear only once or twice. There will be occasional breaks from this event-based practice, which I will note. The major exceptions will occur when we examine Round 12's special questions. There, the units will be individuals.

It is critical to note that because of the project's emphasis on birth intervals, the decision was made in both the 1992 baseline fertility survey and the later monthly round surveys to omit women who had had no pregnancies. This excluded very young women who had not yet begun childbearing and women who were barren. It also undoubtedly excluded a number of women who were subfertile. At the time, however, the need to concentrate on the question of the intervals between live births made the decision to focus on women who had borne a living child in the previous three years an uncomplicated one, and women in the more anomalous categories easily slid into peripheral vision.

Besides the 1992 background survey and the monthly rounds, some of the other activities in the project were large and relatively systematic, and some were small. Of the large variety, the two most important examples included a fertility questionnaire for some of the husbands of the women involved in the rounds and the male marital history alluded to above. Other projects were small and impromptu, devised as new issues arose. These included some observations of and open-ended interviews in venues such as family planning clinics at the Farafenni Health Centre. Smaller projects included monitoring the sale of contraceptives in pharmacies in the town of Farafenni and recording the content of public media campaigns on family planning in the *Gambian Daily Observer* (the principal national newspaper) and on Radio Gambia.

As for staff, the project was fortunate to acquire part of the time of several MRC fieldworkers and data entry clerks and of the manager of the computer lab. Several individuals living in the nearby community were also hired to be fieldworkers specifically for the project. All fieldworkers were recruited on the basis of spoken and written English skills and geniality and diplomacy in dealing with people. Whenever possible, women were interviewed in their first language and by a person whose first language was the same, so recruitment was also based on the need for particular languages. Still, in some cases, respondent and interviewer had to speak to one another in languages that were second languages for both. The other crucial matter was the gender. Because the study focused on women's reproductive lives, the preferred fieldworkers were women. However, the men who presented themselves as candidates for employment were sometimes much better qualified than the available women, and in the end some of the best interviews with women were conducted by men. On the other hand, the best interviews overall in the study (in my view), those on men's marital histories, were conducted by three young women, two of them unmarried. Given such a societal emphasis on both patriarchy and gerontocracy, the fact that young women could so successfully interview men who were on average so much older and more highly placed than themselves, and on a topic that was clearly distressing to some of the respondents, was not something I would have predicted at all.

With some of the background of the study and the region laid out, along with an initial look at marriage, childbearing, and contraceptives, we move on to birth intervals, the subject of intense concern, both local and international. The international overlay that I have sketched here and will touch on in chapter 4 is critical for understanding the local context of contraceptive use. Yet as we will see, contraceptives take on very different meanings from those that motivated their manufacture and export.

Managing the Birth Interval: Child Spacing

In this chapter, written largely through the lenses of my initial understandings of fertility, I examine the birth interval: the small, apparently nondescript duration that separates one birth from the next. The chapter's central theme is a critique of the natural fertility paradigm's minimalist views of intentionalities with respect to birth intervals specifically and to reproductive behaviors generally. The natural fertility framework has presumed that in societies where people do not want to limit children, fertility levels will reflect the rhythms produced by biology in combination with local custom. Contraceptives, which are used to limit fertility, will play no role or a minimal one. The findings for rural Gambia suggest some initial commensurability with this interpretation, and the level of contraceptive use is indeed low. But contraceptives seem to be used in very different ways than they are in the West. This raises an obvious question: "What *are* they used for?"[1] Overall, the findings make sense within my mission of a critique of natural fertility, which will fare poorly as a way of explaining patterns of child spacing. But closer attention to the details of time and the

---

1. This question was particularly intriguing to me because of earlier work on cultural transformations of Western technologies (1985, 1990) and of Western education (1992) in Sierra Leone.

sequences it is alleged to describe will soon begin to fray the logic of child spacing itself, as it is conventionally understood.

International Depictions of Birth Intervals and Child Spacing

Efforts to space children's births at safe temporal distances from one another have drawn some of the most detailed attention in the demography of developing countries. With its continuing high fertility rates, Africa has been the prime case study in recent decades of birth interval analysis. Given the strong desire for children in this area of the world and the low usage of Western methods of fertility control, postpartum abstinence practices in Africa have long been regarded as critical in keeping fertility lower than it might otherwise be by maintaining lengthy spaces between births (for example, Cantrelle and Leridon 1971; Caldwell and Caldwell 1981; Hobcraft 1992; Hobcraft et al. 1983). Now, however, a number of societal changes are said to be putting pressure on lengthy birth intervals. Forces such as urbanization and education appear to have discouraged long periods of breastfeeding. Also hypothesized to play roles are declines in polygyny, women's growing need to maintain a sexual link to a supportive man, and (in some countries) a rise of strong Islamic doctrine, which many see as promoting postpartum sexual norms that run counter to more indigenous norms favoring long periods of abstinence.

With specters of mounting population problems in view, international organizations have been pressing for fertility reduction. Western contraceptives are promoted as the most efficient way of achieving this goal. But reducing fertility remains a sensitive issue in many areas, and so the idiom in which contraceptives have been promoted has centered largely on a need to lengthen birth intervals—that is, "spacing" births[2]—in order to improve mothers' and children's health (for example, Ross et al. 1993). Within the past two decades, and especially following the publication of the ground-breaking *Child-Spacing in Tropical Africa* (Page and Lesthaeghe 1981), which dealt insightfully with indigenous people's concerns about child spacing—and on anthropological evidence for them—public appeals to space

---

2. Although the idea of child spacing remains a strong and highly elaborated cultural ideal in Africa, it has a long history in the West as well. According to the 1998 Margaret Sanger Papers Project Website, for example, the Birth Control Federation of America, the largest organization of its kind in the country, changed its name in 1942 to the Planned Parenthood Federation of America to reflect a redefinition of the organization's goals from family limitation to child spacing. In doing so, it sought (says the Website) a more "mainstream" approach to a broad range of programs related to reproductive health.

births have sounded more openly throughout the subcontinent, from national radio broadcasts and local health clinics to illiterate elderly midwives. Besides improving health, using contraceptives to space births is said to allow parents to educate all (rather than a few) of their children, to free up the family's financial resources, to encourage male responsibility toward the family, and so on.

But although the limitation potentials of contraceptives are frequently muted—and the ideals of the Cairo 1994 International Conference on Population and Development (United Nations 1994) have given priority to women's reproductive health rather than to limiting numbers of children—most observers would likely concede that the overriding concern of outside supporters of family planning remains one of fertility limitation. As a result, the politics of fertility control programs is one of the most contested areas of population and reproductive health studies. In Morsy's (1995) view, for example, contraceptive and maternal-child health programs obscure population control efforts and pose as humanitarian concerns. In Egypt, she argues, programs such as the government's Safe Motherhood Initiative have exaggerated the harmful qualities of indigenous birth attendants' practices, portrayed mothers as incompetent caretakers of children, and obscured the sources of reproductive risks that the spread of capitalism spawned. At the same time, government policies have promoted practices that increase people's risks from exposure to pesticides, industrial contaminants, and biomedicine. They have also minimized attention to infection and malnutrition that can be traced to Egypt's increasing importation of food and to new patterns of consumption that are themselves the sources of many reproductive ills.[3] Whatever the origins of contraceptives in the fertility-reduction motives and financial backing of the West, their use has increased significantly throughout the subcontinent from almost nothing in most countries in the late 1970s to double or almost quadruple those rates in the late 1980s and early 1990s (National Research Council 1993a, 32; for an update, see B. Cohen 1998). And yet the connection between contraceptives and local birth interval dynamics remains a complicated one.

A cursory look at the numbers from the national level and from the 1992–95 study population in The Gambia would appear to bear out suppositions that people are ignorant and recalcitrant to change. The 1990 national contraceptive prevalence study found that in the country as a whole, many women know about Western contraceptives (74 percent of

---

3. For just a few of the other important challenges to population control efforts, see Hodgson 1991; Hartmann 1992; Szreter 1993; Pearce 1995; Greenhalgh 1996; Watkins 2000.

married women aged fifteen to forty-five), yet only 7 percent were current users (Republic of The Gambia 1993). In the rural Farafenni study area, the 1992 birth interval's baseline survey showed only 5 percent of women of reproductive age (fifteen to forty-nine) using a Western contraceptive, while another 5 percent were using what demographic practice calls "traditional" methods: abstinence, juju, withdrawal, and herbs. Further, the few women who were using modern contraceptives were doing so in ways that seemed uninformed. They might use a contraceptive briefly and then stop after only a few months, perhaps claiming objections from religious leaders or husbands. Others reported what family planning analysts call "redundant" use: using pills while still amenorrheic or even (in a tiny number of cases) using pills and injections simultaneously.

These patterns of low and apparently erratic contraceptive use seem consonant with conventional suppositions about users in developing countries and their motives. Two frameworks have been used to explain such patterns for rural Africa. The first depicts the few users who appear in fertility surveys as a tiny island of users (alternative terms include "acceptors" or "limiters") in a sea of the unpersuaded. Efforts to discover what are sometimes labeled "barriers to contraceptive use" seek to ask what makes the users different from the nonusers. Members of the nonuser group may (for example) resist modernization, lack education, fear religious transgression, belong to ethnic groups with fatalistic or conservative outlooks, or find themselves isolated in rural communities with poor access to family planning media messages. Alternatively, they may be too set in their ways to adopt Western contraceptives. Whereas young women are said to be open to change and willing to experiment with innovations, older women are sometimes depicted as fearful traditionalists who resist them. Whatever the defining criteria, the strategy in this two-type model is to identify characteristics of users (for example, age, ethnic group, religion, educational level, possession of a radio) that might separate them from nonusers. To this model, the second mode of analysis sometimes adds an interstitial group: women who use contraceptives not to limit but to space births. That is, they are currently using contraceptives although they want more children later (for example, National Research Council 1993a). As a result, the temporal spaces between their births are similar, given biological limits on fecundity as menopause approaches. Whether the two-type or the three-type model is used, all groups are portrayed as distinct from one another. Limiters and spacers are different from one another and from people who do not use contraceptives at all.

These depictions, though highly schematic, begin from several critical assumptions. First, despite their differences, both the two-type model (users and nonusers of contraceptives) and three-type model (users, nonusers, and spacers) begin from an assumption that these are fixed groups. There are types of individuals who use contraceptives and others who do not. Even the terminology itself—"acceptors" versus "nonacceptors"—implies this assumption: certain people approve of contraceptives and others do not. Related to this is a sense of failure. The fact that African women use contraceptives in short spurts, rather than for long, sustained periods as in the West, has often been phrased to imply that the users themselves were not responding as they were being urged to do. Instances such as this are phrased as "discontinuation of protection" or "noncompliance." Failure can also lie in family planning programs. Scanty numbers of users are taken as evidence of failure to convey sufficient information about contraceptives or sufficiently motivate women to reduce their fertility. Finally, there is an assumption that the meanings attached to these contraceptives where they were manufactured, in the West, is the same in the new setting: a contraceptive was manufactured to limit fertility. Thus, levels of contraception are taken first and foremost as indices of desires to reduce fertility, and people who do not wish to limit births are seen as unlikely users of devices that would do so.

Initial Findings: Contraceptives and Child Spacing through Time

In the 1992–95 birth intervals project in rural Gambia, problems with the ignorance and deficiency views emerged almost immediately. Interviews with local family planning and health officials and with women themselves quickly revealed that most family planning programs were highly active and that virtually everyone knew about one or more forms of Western contraceptives. Those who claimed ignorance of them were simply being evasive. The point, however, is that they seemed to be used for spacing births. Viewed diachronically, across the postpartum months since a woman's previous birth, the most common users proved to be breastfeeding women who wanted to avoid overlapping children—one in the womb and the other nursing—but who had resumed their menses before the child could be weaned.[4] In virtually all cases it was explained that contraceptive use was

---

4. For a more extended discussion of the nutritional problems of overlap, see Merchant et al. 1990.

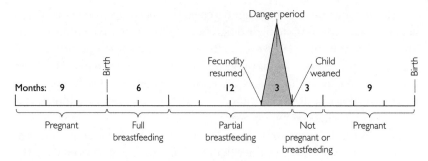

Fig. 4.1 Timing of major birth interval events

intended to protect the health of the children and the mother and not to limit births. Verbal responses as well drew attention to meticulous planning around the period in which a new pregnancy could be dangerous to a young breastfeeding child. Voicing a common aphorism, a local male elder declared that women should give birth not like mango trees, which drop hundreds of ripe fruits in rapid succession, but like elephants—*sama wuluwo:* "elephant reproduction"—with long, generous spaces in between.[5] All the descriptions conveyed a sense of dynamism: many people took contraceptive actions that varied according to the point in the birth interval. Figure 4.1, a schematic diagram, displays several key components of a hypothetical thirty-month birth interval to show how contraceptive use is framed within a more diachronic perspective of spacing. It is plotted with rough chronological correlates of the postpartum events and danger points.

This figure shows nine months of reproductive time taken up by a pregnancy, followed by a birth and then fifteen months of amenorrhea: a lengthy period characteristic of many Sahelian populations. In this case, a new birth occurs two and a half years after the previous birth, though the time tends to be short for young women and long for older ones. Peaking at around fifteen to eighteen months after birth, Western contraception among breastfeeding mothers, when it occurs, usually lasts no more than a few months, when the mother is susceptible to a new pregnancy but the baby is too young to be weaned safely. After weaning, contraceptive use dwindles rapidly. For many women, so important is it to become pregnant quickly after weaning that this interim yet hopeful state is culturally inscribed with the term *kanchango:* a woman waiting to be pregnant. By now,

---

5. I am grateful to Margaret Luck (pers. comm.) for recording this statement.

what family planners refer to as "protection from the risk of pregnancy" has become a misnomer in most cases.

These results, revealing that women use Western contraceptives for short, highly targeted slices of time, make a strong case for departing from views that users act in ignorance. Many instances of "discontinuation" or "noncompliance" represented highly intentional attempts to become pregnant again after a successful spacing effort. Most contraceptive users are members of a fleeting group who are simply trying to delay a new pregnancy as they juggle the conflicting demands of husbands and mothers-in-law and the health of their children. Most acceptors rapidly become nonacceptors during the sequence of pregnancy, lactation, and weaning.[6] Thus, it may be true statistically that users of contraceptives at any given moment are more urban or wealthy than the nonusers. But far more interesting is the fact that rural users are not a discrete group whose background characteristics set them apart from nonusers. They are instead the crest of a moving wave of numerous *temporary* users who are simply using contraceptives for small slices of time during the birth interval if they find that their fecundity resumes too soon.

This finding is critical. It suggests that a woman's immediate fertility situation weighs more heavily in her contraceptive actions than do background characteristics such as ethnicity or education, the categories with which contemporary readerships are usually concerned. Neither of these characteristics made any statistical difference at all in the birth interval patterns among the 2,980 women in the survey area. Take first ethnicity. The Mandinka, Wolof, and Fula peoples, who together made up the study population, have quite distinct histories as well as economic and political status on the land. And yet a lack of difference among the ethnicities was found not only in the 1992–95 study but also in a 1998 survey of the same area. According to Ratcliffe (2000, 163), the median birth interval for women of all ethnicities in the study area was around thirty-one months with no statistically significant differences among the groups.

Even more provocative are the results involving education. Modernization theory would suggest that education imbues individuals with the ability, if not the will, to break with high-fertility traditions and become limiters of births. The 1992 baseline survey, however, showed no evidence for this conclusion. Educated women only seemed to be better "spacers," in the

---

6. See Bledsoe et al. 1994; for additional observations on contraceptive use for child spacing, see Lorimer 1958; Caldwell and Caldwell 1981; Greene et al. 1997.

sense that they, more than uneducated women, more often used Western contraceptives to finish breastfeeding a child and not to "limit" births. If anything, the results would appear to suggest that educated women are *more* traditional with respect to fertility behaviors than their uneducated counterparts, once the dynamics of the birth interval are taken into account. In the 1992 survey, only ninety-eight women had any education, and the average number of years was small: 4.1. Of these "educated" women, only 14 percent of those using Western contraceptives had infants who were weaned, compared to 57 percent of the women with no education. Among the four women who had ten years of schooling (the most reported), only one was currently using a Western contraceptive, and her child was not yet weaned. To be sure, most educated women in the country do not live in very rural areas, and so educated women in these villages are unusual. They likely have better access to Western contraceptives and higher levels of contraceptive use than their uneducated counterparts, whether through language skills or through being able to command respect from local health officials. Yet in this rural situation, these educated women appear to have no more desire than the uneducated women to limit numbers of children. The fact that individuals with such different ethnic and educational backgrounds can assimilate to a common set of situational practices in their fertility behaviors underscores forcibly the importance of avoiding cultural stereotyping.

The findings on child spacing, then, undermined static depictions of women as being of one type or another: users, nonusers, or spacers. The problem in conventional analyses of contraceptive use has been that users and nonusers are treated as distinct groups of people, when contraceptive use is instead a temporary role. At one point in time, people may find this role compelling; at other times, it may be the last thing they want. To make predictions about social action on the basis of current roles is quite legitimate, as long as it is recognized that how individuals move through them is distinct from the roles themselves. These observations bring to light a striking oversight for a discipline that places such emphasis on precision in measuring time. Even in the model that incorporates spacers as one of the categories, spacing is treated as a fixed characteristic, a snapshot in time.

To be sure, a number of women did not use contraceptives at all because they were abstaining or because they did not return to full fecundity until the child was weaned. Others had what people (having heard so much media publicity on "family planning" as a euphemism for Western contraceptives) called in jest "God's family planning." They knew, on the basis of experience, that their periods would not resume until their previous child was safely weaned and out of danger. Using the polite local idiom that expressed sexual intercourse as "contact," one mother of three illustrated the reasoning with impeccable case-control logic:

> You take family planning [Western contraceptives] for spacing and if it happens naturally that your child spacing is all right, there is no need to try other methods. It would duplicate things and you may not come to know which has affected it the most. I am contented with my birth intervals. . . . I do not "menses" when breastfeeding until the child is able to walk. I normally resume contact forty days after delivery [in accord with the Islamic norm]. My children are healthy. (R. 2)

Here we have looked at contraceptive practices and the birth interval chiefly through the eyes of women, through both their survey responses and the verbal explanations offered for these practices. Some of the best testimony on women's contraceptive intent, however, comes from men, who comment on the reproductive experiences of their various wives. To what extent are men aware of birth interval matters? And, most particularly, what about men as the potential husbands of multiple wives, with the welter of reproductive temporalities that these relationships entail?

A man is usually as scrupulous as his wife about birth spaces and their possible effects on children's health. This concern is strongly reflected in this remark by a thirty-three-year-old monogamist whose wife had a sickly child: "The child is not well even since birth, so I [allow the mother to abstain] even though she is my only wife." For a wife who cannot sustain amenorrhea through the period of breastfeeding, a man is usually an enthusiastic backer of contraception. He may even describe *himself* as spacing births by agreeing to abstinence or to condom use or by taking a young wife to the local imam to obtain juju. He may even go to the village health worker or to the town pharmacy to obtain oral contraceptives for her. Once the child is weaned, a man may see little further to be gained in terms of the child's health by delaying pregnancy, and male approval of women's use of contraceptives usually falls off rapidly.

So concerned are most men about their children's health in relation to birth interval difficulties that they become astute observers of the details of female reproductive physiology. Said one man about his wife: "She never sees her period until two months after weaning, which has helped her to be breastfeeding for two years." Another, explaining why he was not using contraceptives with a particular wife, said: "She doesn't see periods while breastfeeding. [Regular contact] is not risky for such types. She has a good spacing of three years." Men even become meticulous observers of the relationship between sexuality and the child's health. Most men take an attitude of cautious experimentation about sexuality during the danger period of potential overlap. They also voice a willingness to alter their practices if a particular situation deteriorates. If the child gets sick or loses weight, sex stops. Said one man: "When [my wife] had a child, I started to use a condom for a period of four months then I stopped it for the child got sick. I thought it was the condom I was using. I waited for a period until the child got well, then I continued to use the condom."

Men's scrupulousness with respect to women's physiology and children's health becomes most obvious in the context of polygyny. Among the most vivid descriptions were those of a man, who, in comparing his two wives, articulated the idiosyncrasies of their reproductive temporalities: "Mariama is unlike my first wife for if I allow her to come to my house within two months she will get pregnant and I have said that I would like her to take a rest for three years. . . . Though Mariama is not seeing her periods . . . , the moment the child walks she can get pregnant now. It is a problem that worries us."

However we look at women, natural fertility fares poorly as a way of explaining patterns of child spacing largely because of its overall dismissal of intentionality. What makes the case most compelling is the determination with which people are taking active measures to shape fertility events, *irrespective* of their total numbers of children, through the use of modern contraceptives.[7] These findings suggested two immense ironies: First, people were using high-technology Western contraceptives for very "African" purposes: to ensure the survival of *many* children by spacing their births carefully; second, people were *socially constructing* what looked like "natural" fertility patterns through careful strategies of spacing children's births.

Strategies for maintaining safe birth intervals are by no means limited to contraceptive use. National newspapers occasionally carry disturbing stories of newborn babies found in pit latrines, cases involving not just schoolgirls trying to avoid expulsion from school but married women whose pregnancies overlapped too closely. Polygyny is often explained as a way of managing the problems of child spacing, and the cultural repertoire of strategies for managing reproduction becomes even more revealing when women are envisioned not as individuals but as co-wives or even as potential co-wives (for example, Madhavan and Bledsoe 2001). Thus, a woman

---

7. See Bruce 1987 for a feminist analysis of conjugal power relations underlying the use of contraceptives in developing countries.

herself may press for a co-wife in order to maintain safe birth intervals. A thirty-year-old mother of three children outlined her own crisp, no-nonsense approach to ensuring proper child spacing by presenting a united front with her co-wife:

> I never contact my husband during breastfeeding. I never use family planning [Western contraception] nor juju nor any other. [Using] family planning is a strategy, but the best and most reliable is not to have contact with a man. That is what I do. . . . I am open to my co-wife on discussions on issues concerning our childbearing. We advise each other and share a residence together. Our husband is not concerned with these issues but we make him abstain forcibly as we like it. (R. 1)

Similarly, a thirty-four-year-old woman implied that having a co-wife was an aid to avoiding pregnancy, although in her case, the risk of sexual pressure from the husband seemed less intense: "I have never used any family planning method at all. I only avoid my husband when breastfeeding until my child is able to walk and I don't see my periods when breastfeeding. My husband . . . is an old man with two wives so I can avoid him for some time" (R. 3).

What, in Fact, Are "Spaces"?

So far we have examined some of the central dynamics surrounding efforts to shape birth intervals through the use of contraceptives. The implicit model of a birth interval has been one of a chronological duration. If post-partum events occurred in a fashion as orderly as these descriptions suggest, there would be little else to say. But as we force the cultural observations about child spacing into tighter confrontations with time, doubts begin to surface about the meaning of birth intervals and child spacing. Chronological time is without question a practical way to depict birth intervals, and the events that affect a birth interval provide cardinal reference points that can be mapped onto units of time such as days, weeks, months and years past a child's birth. Let us look, though, at some of the cracks in the logic of time as we pursue it more closely.

Take first the question of birth intervals and a child's age. Gambian women themselves often describe a child's age in chronological terms. Yet time-based marking points seldom seem to be what they have in mind. When independent evidence such as a "Road to Health" card (now issued soon after birth for virtually every child born in The Gambia and many other African countries) or careful census entries are available to check the calendar date on which a birth actually occurred, women's reports of their children's chronological ages frequently prove wrong if not erratic. The monthly round surveys showed a number of cases in which a woman would report her child's age (for example) as four months old, the next round eight months, the next one month, and so on. A determined interviewer can use various methods of cross-checking to pin down a more reliable age. But the most important point is that the mother herself rarely keeps track of a child's age as a meaningful piece of knowledge. In her birth interval narratives, a woman may speak of the ideals of weaning in two years or of spacing births two years apart. But when pressed to specify what she means, her explanations almost invariably move away from time. Indeed, I sometimes had the distinct impression that the survey interviewers, who shared the women's sense of temporalities yet also understood the Western emphasis on chronological time, were translating responses of "walking" or "weaning" as "age two."

Numerous demographic works have tried to be sensitive to cultural temporalities of sexuality according to the most recent child's development and feeding progress in societies that pay scant attention to age. Some of the most imaginative work in the demography of Africa has grown out of these observations.[8] Among the most systematic was an analysis of child spacing by Schoenmakers et al. (1981, 27–29), who tried to follow the scheme of anthropologist George Murdock, who, in the Human Relations Area Files, used local cultural markers to classify periods of abstinence (for example, child's head is shaved, child is weaned, child can walk; see also Adeokun 1983). Faced with overwhelming complexity among all the schemes, the authors gave up and reduced them all to time markers: forty days or less, forty days to a year, one year or more.

If the child's age is a misleading marker of birth interval events, what *do* most people seem to have in mind when they describe the spaces between births? In fact, there are three major kinds of spaces. The first, and the one most often described as ideal, is one in which the woman becomes pregnant as soon as the previous child is weaned. Such a space is said both to ensure an acceptable pace of childbearing for the woman and to bolster a child's chances of survival through a long period of breastfeeding without nutritional competition from an unborn sibling. The second type of space is a

8. See, e.g., van de Walle and van de Walle 1991, 1993; Caldwell and Caldwell 1977; Page and Lesthaeghe 1981; and Lesthaeghe et al. 1989.

"rest," *fonyondingo*, a word that implies an effort to replenish resources between taxing events. In such contexts a productive capacity requires rest lest its potential be exhausted. With respect to reproduction, it implies a nonpregnant period after the previous child finishes breastfeeding. More will be said about this in chapter 6. For now, I note simply that rest is not always a good thing. Women sometimes rest involuntarily. Whereas having a physiology that maintains a lengthy space can be desired, failing to become pregnant for some time may begin to provoke comment.

The third type of birth spacing I call "overlap": a situation in which a woman becomes pregnant while her young child is still breastfeeding. The African ethnographic and historical record contains innumerable mentions of overlapped births, or births that occurred in rapid succession. Such births are *juruma*—"many," "very close," "unchecked," "one on top of another"—"rampant," as the word is often translated. A grievous insult is to tell someone, "You are a goat seed [offspring]," an irresponsible woman who bears child after child, uncontrollably and indiscriminately. Overlap, which draws by far the most concern for the child's safety, is the dominant theme in the rest of this chapter. In subsequent chapters, as we shift attention from the child to the woman, the kind of spacing called resting will move into broader view.

There are two distinct types of concerns with respect to overlap: those surrounding the resumption of sex while breastfeeding and those surrounding the possibility of becoming pregnant while breastfeeding. With respect to the former, a significant worry is that male fluids may dilute the breast milk, exposing a breastfeeding baby to nutritional risk. As a result, the baby may become "dry" (thin) and weak from fever and diarrhea. As it gets older and begins food supplementation, the dangers posed by dilution recede and increasing the frequency of sexual contact is considered to be safer.

Overlapping a new pregnancy with a breastfeeding child is quite a different matter. Because a woman can only produce so much nourishment at a time, all three entities—the mother, the breastfeeding child, and the fetus—are competing for the same sustenance. At the core of the dilemma is the breastfeeding child, who is consuming the blood of the mother, making her anemic, and of the unborn sibling, making it small and fragile. Further complications arise in that the breastfeeding child is effectively committing an act of cannibalism. Reacting to the polluted milk, it may lose weight and suffer increasingly violent, debilitating episodes of nausea and diarrhea. As for the mother, she is caught in a catch-22. She must decide to wean or continue breastfeeding (see McDade and Worthman 1998). Whatever she does, the child will be susceptible to malnutrition and life-threatening diseases, requiring costly trips to the local healer or to the clinic.[9] Moreover, a pregnant woman may lack energy to care for a small child, especially one who gets so sick, and it will suffer all the more. The risks of early weaning may be exacerbated by a lack of support (whether of money or labor), the privations of the rainy season, heavy labor demands, the decimation of a crop, and the times when the threat of malaria is great-est. Given this "limited good" calculus, a woman's attempt to nourish one child in the womb and another who is breastfeeding is seen as perilous to all (see Cantrelle and Leridon 1971). The tighter the interval, the more pre-carious the situation. By the third or fourth month of pregnancy, with the woman's body being consumed simultaneously by two growing babies, breastfeeding becomes downright dangerous. One woman who found her-self especially vulnerable to such overlaps related, "I always get pregnant while still breastfeeding. In some cases, the child starts losing weight and the result is always deadly. . . . I lost five children [in this way]" (R.1). A woman who has no protection from the risk of pregnancy when her child is very young, whether from amenorrhea, from contraception, or from a co-wife who can draw the husband's sexual attentions, can only wait in fear of the inevitable.

Small overlaps usually pose few problems if the fetus is quite small and the breastfeeding child is well established on solid foods. Many young women actually see a small period of overlap between breastfeeding and a new pregnancy as quite acceptable, if not ideal, since they have much to gain in establishing themselves in the compound by rapid childbearing. One man implied that if all is going well, getting pregnant and *then* wean-ing may even be part of a normal cycle of reproduction: "[My wife] has not yet weaned, but as soon as she gets pregnant she will wean the child for the child is old enough." But in cases of severe overlap, a woman will probably

9. The diversity in tactics that women can use in juggling the demands posed by postpartum events is reflected in a key contrast between my Gambian and Sierra Leonean research projects. In Sierra Leone in the 1980s, many rural women fed their babies canned milk to solve the dilemma posed by the need to both maintain sexual relations with a supportive man and to nourish a small baby. Bot-tles and canned milk were highly visible in the local markets and stores. Responding to international concerns, The Gambia's activist government of the early 1990s had discouraged infant bottle feeding and was trying to promote sustained breastfeeding through long birth intervals and the use of Western contraceptives. On the face of it, this is excellent health policy. However, one might wonder whether raising it to greater heights of public sensitivity, encouraging long breastfeeding periods and discourag-ing the sale of bottles, may have the unintended consequence of whetting public condemnation of too-early weaning. (See Lockwood 1995 for a broader political economic interpretation of the different postpartum situations in these two countries.)

try to abort, using local herbs or Western medicines, including strong doses of birth control pills. Her husband may try to help her, even to the point of sending her to Banjul, if he can afford it, for a hospital procedure. So intense can sanction be, especially if the child becomes sick or malnourished, that fears of social condemnation may induce the mother to wean it even more quickly: "When I had that unplanned pregnancy," related one woman, "the child was breastfed only one year, so I had to wean him and hand him over to my mother. Still, the child looks very weak" (R. 1).[10] If abortion is impossible, the breastfeeding child must undergo a process called *buruu:* it is weaned too young because of a new pregnancy. Such early weaning is one of the worst things a mother can do. A short birth interval may signal a failure on her part to control her husband. It may also signal avarice: trying to "turn her husband's head" (to monopolize his attention vis-à-vis her co-wives) through sinister dealings with ritual medicine. Whatever the charge, the greater the overlap and the more the child deteriorates, the greater the censure the mother faces. One woman, still breastfeeding a nineteen-month-old child, described her combined social and medical plight: "I was not using any method to avoid pregnancy. . . . I am pregnant three months now [unwanted] for my child is still young. According to my observations, my friends do discuss my pregnancy, for the child I am breast-feeding is still young and unable to walk. He has begun to lose weight. I am very much ashamed of the pregnancy. Since I found out about the pregnancy, I have avoided my husband" (R. 1). In such situations, weaning does not necessarily lead to conception, as a straightforward biological interpretation of fecundability might lead us to expect. Rather, as a woman pointed out with singular clarity, social pressure to avoid dangerous overlaps makes conception lead to weaning:[11] "We wean when we have breastfed for 24 months. This can be interrupted by conception, of course; for example, the conception of this child I am breastfeeding overlapped with the breastfeeding of the last child by one month. In fact, in our community, generally if one stops breastfeeding her child earlier than 24 months, it means she has conceived."

Overlapped pregnancies can be intentional, however, especially (it would seem) in cases where enmity dominates co-wife relations. Women in

10. Such facts suggest a line of questioning that my previous study in Sierra Leone on child foster-age overlooked: although I noted that small children being raised by grannies are sometimes malnour-ished, the possibility that a child might have been weaned and sent away because of the mother's new pregnancy did not occur to me.

11. See also van de Walle and van de Walle 1991.

such relationships refer to polygyny not as a strategy for lengthening birth intervals but a reason for tightening them. Said a twenty-eight-year-old woman who had borne four children, of whom two had died: "When I weaned my child I was contacting my husband as frequently as possible because he married a very young girl recently and I want to have more children than her" (R. 2). Polygyny-related pressures to shorten birth intervals arise even from the wives of husbands' brothers. Agnates are notoriously competitive for status and rights to property. Because male status depends heavily on the productivity of women, fertility is a domain in which agnatic competition visibly surfaces. One twenty-three-year-old woman underscored such pressures in her comment: "I am not avoiding pregnancy though I am breastfeeding because I am the only wife of my husband and we have only two children. . . . My husband is pressuring me to have as many children as possible because his brothers are in the compound and their wives have many children" (R. 2). In situations of extreme threat from competing relatives, a woman may try to space her births by an interval that almost everyone agrees is far too short. The following case illustrates such a situation, even though a co-wife was not yet on the horizon. In this case, a woman in a small rural village had arranged a marriage between her daughter and an educated man with a regular salaried job who had been posted upcountry as a fieldworker. Since such men are among the most desired husbands, the mother urged her daughter to secure her tenuous position by bearing as many children as possible before a co-wife arrived. When the first child, a boy, was four months old, the young woman began to demand that sex resume on the grounds, provided by her mother, that it was not "natural" to abstain any longer. The husband, worried about his child's health, refused initially but finally agreed on the condition that the wife take action to prevent an early pregnancy. To ensure her compliance, he took her to the family planning clinic to obtain birth control pills and kept them himself. He then handed her a pill every night and dispatched her for a glass of water to drink it with. To his outraged surprise, however, his wife soon became pregnant and confessed that she had been throwing away the pills when she left the room.

In exploring birth intervals we have encountered some complex histories of negotiation, in which the most important tactics involve child feeding, the pace of resuming sexual relations, abortion, and (as we will see) contraception. Behind a vast number of birth intervals, moreover, lie some counterintuitive histories of causation. Rather than biology producing a social response, a social action may produce a biological response. What should be apparent in all this is that whereas people do try to distance births from each other, it is not time that determines the distance but rather "safety" or "strength," with reference to the health of both the child and the mother. None of the relevant fertility events has any necessary relation to time. All can be located in time, but none derive their significance or force from it.[12] What should also be clear is that the phrase "child spacing," though it seemed an acceptable starting gloss for reproductive practices in rural Gambia, ultimately painted too broad a stroke. There are very different kinds of spaces between children and different conditions under which one type or another might be desired.

Controlling Spaces, Crafting Intervals

Given that sexuality may resume for a breastfeeding woman, what can she do to avoid the risks to her child that this may entail, yet also sustain a viable marital situation? The transformation of Western contraceptives into an "African" technique will figure strongly here. I begin, however, with the most common form of contraception in sub-Saharan Africa: abstinence.

Postpartum Abstinence and the Resumption of Sexuality

Bans on sexuality for significant portions of marital life are one of the hallmarks of African reproductive regimes (see, for example, Caldwell and Caldwell 1977 and the contributions to Page and Lesthaeghe 1981).[13] At the early part of reproductive life, a very young woman may be allowed to delay full sexual relations for several months or even years after she marries so that she can mature physically. On the other end of the scale is the possibility of terminal abstinence, when grandmotherly obligations are said to override those of sexual or reproductive partner. In addition, most African groups consider a menstruating woman to be unclean and therefore unavailable sexually. However, the marital sexual ban that has drawn by far the most attention in demographic analyses of Africa is that governing

12. Gell (1992, 36) describes a variant of this observation in his distinction between the "topology of the time-dimension" versus "representations of what characteristically goes on in the temporal world."

13. Abstinence, or "avoiding the husband," the closest translation in The Gambia, is frequently reported as a contraceptive measure, although this is often a gloss for simply reducing the number of sexual contacts to minimize the risks of a mistimed conception. Such categorical ambiguities undoubtedly apply elsewhere.

the proscription on sex after a birth: the "postpartum sex taboo," as it was called by anthropologists of an earlier era. European interest in postpartum abstinence practices appeared in print in the writings of Thomas Winterbottom, a physician working in Sierra Leone at the end of the eighteenth century: "[U]ntil the child is able to bring to its mother a calabash full of water, they [women] are entirely separated from their husband . . . [because] the mother, upon whom devolves the whole care of her children, is afraid of being burthened with a second offspring before the first can in some degree dispense with her continued care" (1803, 1:149).

Postpartum abstinence in many parts of Africa is said to have been as long as three years in Yoruba-speaking areas (Olusanya 1969), although in most areas it seemed to last simply until the child was weaned or could walk. Today, such practices receive singular demographic attention because they are regarded as a key factor in keeping fertility much lower than it might otherwise be.

Stages of the Child's Physical Development and Feeding

Discussion about when postpartum abstinence should cease and sex should resume hinges on whether the child is set on a secure path to development and health. The most salient points in the cultural repertoire are pegged to two related trajectories. One is the stage of the child's physical development (in Mandinka, these stages consist of "wet infancy," "neck straight," sitting, crawling, standing, walking, and "grown up"). The other is the child's feeding progress (breastfeeding only, breastfeeding plus thin pap, breastfeeding plus thick pap, breastfeeding plus solids, and weaned).[14] The markers in the birth interval to which people most often refer, however, are the Islam-mandated "forty days" after a child's birth, closely related in time to a point called "neck straight," and walking or weaning. These points form the bases for quite distinct strategies for achieving intervals of various lengths. They also lay the groundwork for potential discord. I start with the very first phases of a child's life and the temporalities that surround it.

---

14. The developmental stage of "wet infancy" and the feeding stage of breastfeeding only are not precise analogues of one another. In the rounds data, almost half of the events in which children are breastfeeding only occur at a later stage of the child's physical development, such as "neck straight" or "crawling." Some of these appeared to be cases of sick children who were recorded as "breastfeeding only" because they had temporarily stopped eating solid foods.

"Wet Infancy"

One of the most engaging themes in anthropology has been the symbolism of the bodily fluids of reproduction. Past studies described the power inherent in the fluids of reproduction as "polluting" (for example, Douglas 1966) and as harmful to those without ritual protection. Female fluids were often seen as particularly polluting, especially to men. Such notions were used to explain why women in New Guinea, for example, were confined to menstrual huts during their periods. More contemporary symbolic studies of power and aesthetics (for example, Arens and Karp 1989; Hardin 1993; Buckley and Gottlieb 1988; Boddy 1989) suggest a broader view. Substances such as menstrual blood, like the notion of power itself, are better seen as having "transformative" capacity. With respect to reproduction, the potent fluids of reproduction can be seen as mingling and congealing: transforming the raw elements of life into a human being.

In the Gambian case, such observations are highly apt. A newborn baby is called a "wet infant," a metaphor with dual referents to the baby's pliability and lack of muscle tone and to its proximity to the powerful, life-giving fluids that nourished and protected it for so long. These fluids are seen as accompanying the baby into the world and continuing to cling symbolically to it for weeks after birth. A newborn infant is considered to have boundaries that are permeable and fluid, still commingled with the fluids of the mother. This means that the mother is also, in some sense, "wet" for some time after giving birth, if not symbolically then literally, with the general messiness of a small baby. Wet infants are fed almost exclusively on breast milk. License to traffic with the ritually powerful fluids of reproduction thus belongs for the most part to women. Wet infants, like the postpartum fluids their mothers are expelling, are considered perilous for men to touch. Men display acute discomfort in the close proximity of a baby less than a week old who has not yet been brought outdoors ritually and introduced to the world. They are also uncomfortable around a wife who is in this liminal state, and sexual relations at this point are out of the question.

"Forty days"/"Neck straight"

Male discomfort with a small infant, and with its mother, decreases markedly as the baby progresses to the next stage of development: "neck straight," a period from about forty days to two or three months after a child's birth. At this point the neck muscles have become stronger, and a baby that can hold its head upright can be carried in a lappa cloth on the mother's back. The baby may move also to light supplementation with a thin pap made from rice or couscous. For present purposes, however, the most important implication of the neck-straight stage of child development is that parental contact can now, in theory, resume. The phrase "neck straight" inspires endless plays on words and images. In its simplest form, neck straight connotes the rough temporal equivalent for the Islamic forty days. By logical extension, it also refers, as does the forty days, to the resumption of sexual contact between the parents. "Neck straight" can also be used to allude to the action of the man's vital organ, which, about this time, is said to replicate the action of the baby's neck. And the sight of a new baby on its mother's back for the first time, a sudden public statement of her renewed availability, is said to rekindle the husband's amorous interests. The child's feeding stage itself is both a sign that the man monitors to ascertain the risks of sexuality and a flag to outsiders about the level of sexuality that is likely occurring. A woman who begins to feed thick pap to a very young baby must resign herself to a period of teasing allusions from other women who claim to know that sex has begun or is imminent simply by observing what her baby is being fed.

From descriptions such as these, an unmistakable symbolic configuration emerges. Immediately following birth, the baby and mother are wet, pliable, fluid; the man is straight, dry, hard. As the birth interval progresses, however, the qualities of the mother and child change from wet and fluid to dry and hard. The overall movement in these physical and symbolic temporalities forms what we might call symbolic "intermappings" among qualities, entities, and persons: softness, hardness, food, necks, organs, men, women, babies, and so on. Observations such as these underscore the relevance of Bourdieu's insights on the notion of habitus, wherein not only social structure but its temporalities are lived in the body: "[S]ocialization instills a sense of the equivalences between physical space and social space and thereby roots the most fundamental structures of the group in the primary experiences of the body. . . . To control the moment, and especially the tempo, of practices is to inscribe durably in the body, in the form of the rhythm of actions or words, a whole relationship to time, which is experienced as part of the person" (1990, 71, 76). As these movements transpire, the possibility of starting a new pregnancy becomes progressively safer, and more sexual activity is permitted.

The association between the resumption of sex and a firmer, neck-straight child who has moved beyond pure breastfeeding to light pap supplementation is not only symbolically striking; it is quantitatively unambiguous. With virtually no exceptions, women maintain abstinence at least until the fortieth day after birth, the point when Islamic practice decrees her ritually cleansed of the blood and fluids surrounding the birth event. During the course of the monthly round surveys, a total of 118 mothers (and now I am using individuals and not events) reported that they had a wet infant at some point. Of those who had a wet infant, only six reported any sexual contact in the previous month, far less than was the case with women at other points in the birth interval. Even the six apparent exceptions were illusive. Five of the six mothers of wet infants who reported contact had given birth in the previous few days, a point that every one of them hastened to explain in their commentary, unprompted by the formal structure of the questionnaire. The episodes of contact they reported as having occurred within the previous month, as the survey's format specified, had thus occurred *before* the baby's birth.[15] In other words, it was the structure of the survey itself that made the cases appear aberrant.

The fortieth day, the point at which many spouses recommence sexual relations, however, is a potential point of marked disagreement. For a young wife who has gone back to her mother's home to bear and nurse her first child, her husband might make a special visit to enact what he may see as this religious mandate. A man, especially a young one, sees the forty-day decree as a requirement to resume sex immediately. This does not mean that he wants her to get pregnant immediately. To him, his wife should make herself available so that his religious rectitude will not be tarnished by "going outside" the house.

Most women, however, emphasize the meaning of the fortieth day differently. To a woman, it is not that sex *should* resume after forty days; rather, sex *might* resume after forty days. This way of expressing the precept implies a hope that the husband will allow her to abstain longer, to take every precaution to avoid an accidental pregnancy. Women thus tend to refer to indigenous norms—the child's health, their own health—that might justify later points in the postpartum cycle as the time to resume sex. To bolster her case, a woman may fuel her husband's fears that she is not yet ritually clean and that he, therefore, will become polluted if he insists on sex. One woman admitted as much in the case of her own struggles to avoid pregnancy, which began on the fortieth day after birth:

> I have abstained completely from my husband since delivery of this child, though he had attempted to go to bed with me several times during this

---

15. In the one remaining case the woman had given birth in the previous month, very likely more than forty days earlier.

period. I have been refusing his attempts with excuses that I was realizing unusual menses. His first attempt was on the fortieth day after delivery. He had made other attempts and finally, as my last resort, and also exhausted of excuses, I decided to consult a nearby Community Health Nurse to seek advice on contraception. He [the nurse] asked me several questions and recommended the injection to me.

In general, then, women prefer weaning as the time to resume contact, whereas men eye the forty-day target. Because women usually prefer the longer goal, they are often caught between norms of conscientious motherhood, which pressure them to avoid an early pregnancy while nursing a young baby, and those of conjugal duty, particularly when there is no sexually available co-wife.

From these observations, it might appear that men seek to conduct their sexual lives out of a much more deeply held set of religious convictions than do their wives, who, by comparison, appear to have more pre-Islamic "animist" leanings. It is true that men in this area of the world have more formal Islamic training, on average, than do women. Their greater literacy and devotional opportunities might allow them to learn rules governing marital life and punishment for transgressions. Since girls are needed in the home for domestic work and marry soon after menarche, few of them have the luxury to attain the levels of Arabic training that their husbands have, and most women have only a vague knowledge of Islam's precepts. It would be wrong, however, to conclude that men are religious zealots with uniform views and women are ignorant traditionalists. Women frequently express religious devotion that is as eloquent as that of men, even if they disagree on the points of doctrine. Conversely, men themselves often express quite different interpretations of Islamic decrees on sexuality and childbearing. Compare, for example, these statements from two men. One said, "According to my tradition and religion, normally when a woman delivers a baby boy, you should contact her after forty days; if female, the contact should resume after one month. So that is what I am practicing"; the other said, "I do according to the Qur'an, and that is that a man should leave his wife to breastfeed up to two years, then after they can start to have sex."

Although the fortieth day can be a tense moment in the postpartum cycle for men and women alike and there is some worry about diluted milk, everyone knows that fecundity usually resumes only when the menstrual periods return, a point often coinciding with weaning time. Far more worrisome, especially to women, than the forty-day point itself is the pace of sexual activity in the subsequent phases of the birth interval: after fecundity resumes but before the child is weaned. These worries are not unfounded even in Western terms. As most reproductive biologists would acknowledge, the transition to supplementary foods makes breastfeeding less frequent and more erratic, and it often precipitates the return of the menses.

Walking / Weaning

Rural Gambians describe several advantages of abstaining from sex until the child can walk or be weaned. Doing so, they say, reduces the possibility of an overlapped pregnancy, thus allowing the older child to become more independent physically. It also gives a mother time to recover from the physical strains of child-bearing and caring for a small baby. And in a subcontinent where co-wife jealousies are a perpetually sensitive issue, a long wait gives the other wives a chance to engage the husband's interest. The principal disadvantage to waiting this long, especially for a monogamous wife, is the risk that the husband will seek satisfaction elsewhere. In Sierra Leone, I found, so closely linked were the idioms of weaning a child and the resumption of sex that "weaning" was often used as a euphemism for "resuming sex," regardless of the child's age or breastfeeding status. Much as a Gambian man might describe himself as spacing births, in Sierra Leone, the man's role in weaning seemed to be articulated even to the point at which the man, not the woman, was seen as the decision maker in weaning. He was even said to be the person who actually weaned the child. (Said one man to me, "I weaned my child, I think, at eight months old.") "Weaning" could also refer to the act of cuckolding by a man who took advantage of a husband who had been maintaining a responsible sexual distance from his breastfeeding wife. Allegations of this crime surfaced repeatedly in civil cases in which a man was sued for weaning another man's child. Reporting on the petty complaints with which the president of the country was continuously besieged, a 1984 Freetown newspaper editorial noted: "Today, everybody wants to see the President for everything. From marriage quarrels, to failure to settle debts, to weaning a child to everything" (*The New Citizen*, 16 July 1984). Read with a Western eye, this makes little sense; the cessation of breastfeeding is hardly a reason to complain outside the household, much less to the president of the country. In this context, however, it can mean only adultery or, even worse, adultery followed by a pregnancy, both being charges so serious that they were normally handled in court.

Numerical Analyses of Abstinence and the Birth Interval

Let us now examine some numerical associations linking abstinence and the resumption of sexual contact to child feeding events in the birth interval. We will use the 1993–94 monthly rounds and the stages of a child's development defined therein: (1) breastfeeding only, (2) breastfeeding with thin cereal pap, (3) breastfeeding with thick pap, (4) breastfeeding plus solid foods, and (5) weaned. This continuum connotes a certain set of risks for the baby and, thus, a set of cues to the mother for adjusting her fertility behavior. Figure 4.2, from the rounds, displays the number of sexual contacts reported in the previous month by women in three age groups (under twenty-five, twenty-five to thirty-four, and thirty-five to forty-five), according to how their most recent child was currently feeding. The figure includes only women whose most recent pregnancies resulted in still-alive children and women whose husbands were currently in residence, although this latter choice obviously selects against women who go to live temporarily with their mothers as part of a broader abstinence strategy.

Overall, this figure shows a clear increase, as the birth interval progresses, in the likelihood that a woman will report having had sex in the previous month. At the outset, among mothers whose children are breastfeeding only, the number of actual contacts reported is very small: on average

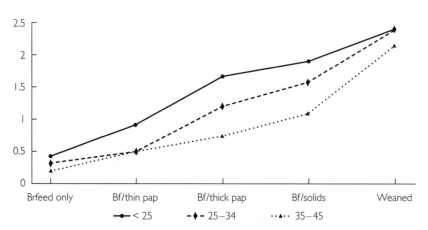

Fig. 4.2 Mean number of sexual contacts in previous month by mother's age and child's feeding stage

Note: Thirteen rounds done in 1993–94. Women with child from last pregnancy alive and husband present.

.3 times per month. By the time the child is weaned, this number has reached a mean of 2.3 times per month. Yet within this overall pattern there is considerable variation. The most immediate is between the age groups. Although we might assume that younger women are under more pressure to comply with an early resumption of sex, age seems to make little difference in the timing of initial contact. At the outset, women reporting contact during the breastfeeding-only phase were 26.1 years old, whereas those reporting no contact were 27.3. However, patterns of contact in the *middle* of the interval show clear age differences. Women younger than 25 engage in sex nearly twice as often as their counterparts aged 35 to 45, a variation that may stem from the youthful appeal of a young woman to her husband. Other sources of variation are not shown. Some women report steady numbers of contacts throughout the months. Others report fluctuating numbers, with marked decreases if their fecundity resumes too early to wean a child, or increases if a co-wife leaves temporarily or a child dies. And although the resumption of sex after forty days appears to be a symbolic necessity for many women, for some, sex may not occur again until they are ready to get pregnant again. For everyone, however, sexuality ceases abruptly as soon as the next birth occurs, and it begins no sooner than the forty-day point, as noted above.

These results might seem to describe an unproblematic picture of biological events. With some variation among age groups, women recommence sexual life as the child progresses along a developmental feeding continuum. And yet whereas the discussion so far has highlighted the deceptive traps for the unwary that are posed by commensurability among cultural categories, there loom new dangers in taking for granted "natural" causal sequences that putatively link key events in the numerical associations that we have just seen in figure 4.2. I describe three examples. The first involves the visible increase in sexuality as the baby moves to thick pap. Since the introduction of solid foods and the move from a thin to a thick mixture may precipitate fecundity, the scenario depicted in figure 4.2 might suggest that mothers of small babies who are beginning to eat solid foods would encounter the biological risk of an early pregnancy. But causation may have run in quite the opposite direction. A young woman anticipating sexual pressure from her husband—or herself desiring to begin a new pregnancy soon—may have intentionally accelerated her baby's feeding to thick pap. Her goal in doing so may have been to build up the baby's weight to offset the threat posed by the possibility of deficient milk and the consequent need for an abrupt weaning. In a similar instance, a woman who discovers through bitter experience that she has "hot luck" (that is, she conceives easily and early) may start her child quickly on solid foods before sex recommences. In such cases, it would be erroneous to assume, as might those of us with some presumptions of Western biological knowledge, that the initiation of solid food supplementation precipitated fecundity. This may have been true in part. It is more accurate to say, however, that the woman introduced solid food in order to make sex or fecundity possible.

A second potential trap in inferring causality concerns the question of whether a young woman should move back to her mother's house before giving birth. Whereas a young woman's residence with her mother in the postpartum period might be attributed to custom, it may have come about instead from learning that she is susceptible to resuming fecundity early. Thus, she may go back to her mother only when fecundity is imminent, and not prior to the child's birth at all. Such a train of events is apparent in the assertion of a twenty-five-year-old woman with four surviving children: "I will go back to my mother immediately when the child is a bit older. If not, I may have another child on top of this one and that will give me much trouble" (R. 1).

Finally, whereas we might assume that women would try to abstain from sex in order to prolong breastfeeding for the child's sake, the following case suggests a very different conclusion. In this case, a thirty-two-year-old woman with five pregnancies (the last a living child, almost three years old at the time of the survey) confided that she was prolonging breastfeeding in order to maintain the appearance of needing to abstain. Her husband, she reported, was anxious to begin a new pregnancy, and he would surely insist on intensive sex as soon as the child was weaned. As for herself, she reported: "I am tired of having children all of the time without [sufficient] intervals. . . . Even before the child is weaned I start to see my monthly periods and during which I see myself pregnant. . . . My child is due to be weaned but I am delaying his weaning so that my husband will not [suspect] a thing" (R. 2).

Descriptions such as these yield strong evidence of anticipatory action and of an elaborate repertoire of excuses that would make a certain outcome a fait accompli. A woman's declaration that she must prolong breastfeeding, that she has a sick mother in a distant village, that she is unclean or sick, or that her daughter needs help with her own children—all may be excuses to minimize the risk of pregnancy. Conversely, declarations of devotion to Islam or of a spouse's reproductive duties may reflect a desire to hasten a new pregnancy or to keep a husband's interests from straying. In short, although it may be true that abstinence ends and sex begins after breastfeeding is finished, action, anticipation, and subterfuge can produce a logic of action that defies cause-effect relationships that might otherwise be ascribed to the workings of biology and custom. Bourdieu's description captures perfectly the spirit with which a woman may manipulate the biological ambiguities of her child's development, her own fecundity, and her relations with her husband: "Only a virtuoso with a perfect mastery of his 'art of living' can play on all the resources inherent in the ambiguities and indeterminacies of behaviours and situations so as to produce the actions appropriate in each case, to do at the right moment that of which people will say, 'There was nothing else to be done,' and to do it the right way" (1990, 107).

Western Contraceptives and Child Spacing through the Birth Interval

To achieve adequate—if not finely honed—birth spaces, some women abstain through the course of breastfeeding. Others commence sex but rely on amenorrhea, taking pregnancy-avoidance measures if their periods resume before the child can be weaned safely. To this cultural repertoire for managing the temporalities of sexuality, birth, child care, and conjugal life through the birth interval,[16] the advent of Western contraception has added new possibilities.

Figure 4.3, from the monthly rounds, shows the proportion of women using Western contraceptives (here, they are exclusively pills and Depo Provera) according to the most recent child's feeding stage. Much as we saw a steady rise in sexuality as the child's feeding capabilities progressed (fig. 4.2), we see a steady rise in use of Western contraception: from 2 percent among mothers of children who are breastfeeding only to 11 percent among women with children who are breastfeeding and eating solid foods. By weaning time, when most women want to get pregnant again, contraceptive use falls sharply to 6 percent.

The strong message from this figure is that in rural Gambia, Western contraceptives are devices used to delay pregnancy while breastfeeding a child. This kind of contraceptive use occurs not for long blocks of years before and during childbearing, as one sees in the West[17] but for short slivers

16. See Ware 1976 and Bracher and Santow 1982, among others, for innovative analyses of the relationship between breastfeeding, pregnancy, and contraception.

17. My use of the term "Western" breaks down in many places in this book, and this is a key instance. In Sweden, for example, state parental leave policies have induced couples to create very short birth intervals between their two children (e.g., Hoëm 1990).

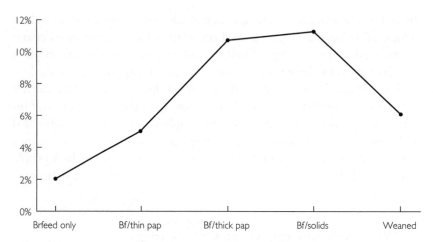

Fig. 4.3 Women using Western contraception by previous child's feeding
stage

Note: Nonpregnant women with child from last pregnancy alive (rounds data).

of time following the resumption of fecundity (or in anticipation of it) before
the child is ready to be weaned. Women who use contraceptives in these situations tend to be those with a previous history of close spaces or a tendency
to resume fecundity before it is safe to wean a breastfeeding child. These
understandings of child spacing are far more precise than current international understandings of contraceptive use in high-fertility societies imply:
actions taken now although more children are wanted later. They are also
quite different from the chronological portrayal of contraceptive use in the
informational pamphlets prepared for the Gambia Family Planning Association by international organizations. One drawing depicts a woman who
is grasping the hand of a walking child and who has apparently taken two
years' worth of pills—twenty-four month-long cycles of thirty tablets—after the child's birth. After this, we are to infer, the child is healthy and the
mother can get pregnant again. Time is directly embodied in the figures of
the mother and the child. The finely differentiated child feeding and development phases that people use as cues to change their sexual behavior are
thinly acknowledged.

Given this general rise in Western contraceptive use during the birth interval, let us examine the conditions under which women use what are seen
as highly effective Western contraceptives as opposed to any other strategy,
whether abstinence, juju, or nothing at all, as the child's feeding progresses
(fig. 4.4). If Western contraceptives are being used to help space births when

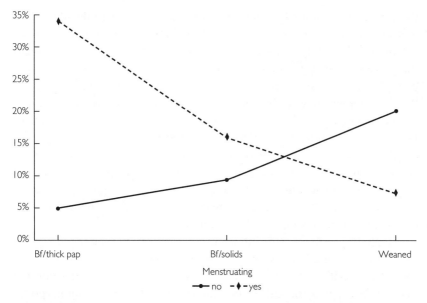

Fig. 4.4 Women using Western contraception by previous child's feeding stage and whether menstruating

Note: Nonpregnant women with child from last pregnancy alive (1993–95 rounds).

there are fears of an early pregnancy, this usage might appear most frequently among women who have resumed fecundity early in the postpartum period. Since there were almost no cases of women using contraception in the earliest phases of the birth interval, the figure starts with the phase of breastfeeding plus thick pap.

Women know that amenorrhea is generally a time of infecundity, yet their use of Western contraceptives bears strong evidence of fears of an early pregnancy. In figure 4.4, we see these fears manifested throughout the birth interval in sharply differentiated contraceptive patterns, depending on whether the mother saw her period in the previous month.[18] Among women whose periods have not resumed, there is a modest rise in contraceptive use through the feeding stages of the birth interval.[19] Since fecun-

18. For similar observations in Thailand and Zimbabwe, respectively, see Knodel et al. 1985 and Sambisa and Curtis 1997. These countries, of course, have undergone substantial fertility declines, whereas The Gambia as of this writing has not.

. 19. The fact that Depo Provera often suppresses periods undoubtedly helps explain why contraceptive use was higher among mothers of weaned children who reported no period in the last month than among women who had. All fifteen of those using Western contraceptives who had not seen their periods and whose children were weaned were using Depo Provera.

dity has not yet resumed in such cases, contraception might be interpreted as a precautionary measure, perhaps taken in anticipation of an early resumption of fecundity. But for women who did report a menstrual period in the previous month, the pattern is the opposite. Contraceptive use is very high among women whose children are eating thick pap, tapering off to 8 percent by weaning. If the magnitude of contraceptive use reflects anxiety about a new pregnancy, then the sharply elevated use of contraceptives in the early part of the birth interval among fecund women reflects powerful fears for a young child. Particularly for women with very young babies, contraceptive use is extremely high. As many as 33 percent of fecund women whose child was breastfeeding and eating thick pap (thirteen out of thirty-nine cases) were using Western contraceptives, compared to only 8 percent of fecund women with a weaned child.

Finally, figure 4.5 includes all women irrespective of their fecundity status to analyze differences among kinds of Western contraceptive use with respect to specific points in the birth interval. Pills and injections are the major contraceptives of interest, but juju is also included as a counterpoint. This figure shows two patterns of note. Both center on the latter phases of the birth interval and both underscore the danger of drawing hasty conclusions about apparently clear-cut cultural categories. The first pattern is a substantial difference between uses of pills and injections. In the early feeding phases of the birth interval, the percentage of women using pills and injections is almost exactly the same. Both begin at minimal levels among mothers who are only breastfeeding (around 1 percent) and rise to 5.1 percent each among mothers of children eating thick pap. With the switch to solid foods for the child and (likely) the resumption of fecundity for the woman, however, the use of pills and injections diverges sharply. Pill use falls to 3.8 percent with solid foods and disappears completely by weaning time (.5 percent), while the use of injections rises to 7 percent with solid foods and remains at around 6 percent at weaning. Whereas conventional analysis treats all Western contraceptives as cut from the same mold, these results suggest that people use pills and injections for quite distinct temporal ends.

The second notable point that figure 4.5 highlights is a much stronger resemblance between the use of pills and the traditional juju in the crucial latter phases of the birth interval than between the two Western contraceptives. At the thick pap phase, the level of all three contraceptives converges at around 5 percent. But there the similarity ends. Injection use rises steadily to a high peak, 6.8 percent at the stage of solid foods, and it remains

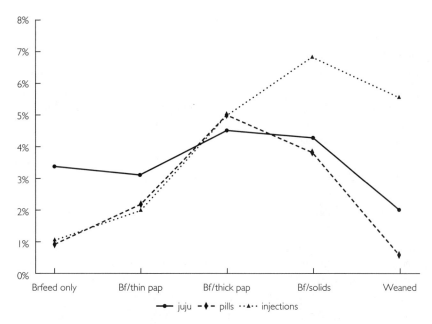

Fig. 4.5 Women using juju, pills, or injections by previous child's feeding stage

Note: Nonpregnant women with child from last pregnancy alive (1993–94 rounds).

high at weaning: 5.6 percent. Pills and juju, however, descend together, pills declining eventually to .5 percent at weaning and juju to 2 percent. These findings suggest that pills and juju are best for creating tight, closely controlled spaces between births.[20] Depo Provera, by contrast, seems to be used to create longer, more vaguely defined durations that may continue for some time after the child is weaned. The significance of this distinction is taken up later.

To flesh out some of the numerical patterns that have come to light, let us take one case from the rounds, that of a young monogamous woman who had resumed fecundity early. Twenty-year-old Binta Mbye had two

---

20. There are two kinds of pills, low-dose and high-dose estrogen, whose differentiated actions are well known locally and are undoubtedly reflected in patterns of use and among different kinds of users. The project's surveys, however, were not set up to catch these differences in types of pills. The only possible category of response in the surveys was "pills."

children, the younger still breastfeeding. As early as Round 1, when her daughter was nine months old, Binta explicitly linked her use of pills to breastfeeding and not to any attempt to limit child numbers: "I am . . . breastfeeding; it's only the breastfeeding, but [when] I wean I would like to get pregnant again. . . . My child is too small for me to be pregnant" (R. 1). Later, as we might expect by now, pill use stopped as soon as the child was weaned at twenty-one months. On several counts, however, Binta was an exception. Twenty-year-old women are infrequent users of Western contraceptives of any kind. Even for spacing births, most rely on abstinence or juju. In Binta's case, she had gone to stay with her family during her first breastfeeding experience. There she had discovered that she was susceptible to early resumption of fecundity—well before the baby could be weaned. As her husband's only wife, however, she felt compelled to return early to her husband, and the next child was conceived quickly, forcing her to fully confront the conundrum posed by her physiology and her monogamous status. In addition, her breastfeeding daughter was sickly, having dangerous bouts of diarrhea and a poor appetite. Both of these symptoms would likely have been attributed to the effects of sexual contact on the milk. All this made the prospects of an early pregnancy doubly risky and led Binta to use birth control pills:

> I am avoiding pregnancy because I am breastfeeding and my child is unhealthy which leads to her [being] unable to crawl and walk [even though] she is nine months old; she is suffering from diarrhea and chest pains since a month ago. I [decided] to join the family planning because I have two children and the second child is not well and I am the only wife of my husband whereby if I don't [take care] I will keep on having children rapidly. . . . I am avoiding pregnancy very well now because of my unhealthy child and I am still using the pills. (R. 2)

Women are highly attuned to their physiological proclivities and to the risks that they entail and in this case, as in many others, the contraceptive strategy follows the stage of the child's physical development. Yet women like Binta are not only acting with intention with respect to apparently natural phenomena by laying contingency plans. Such women, who fear hazardous outcomes, based on previous experience, take anticipatory action. From such cases, it is quite possible that had Bourdieu known, when developing his notion of habitus, about birth interval dynamics such as those we have seen, he might well have seized upon them as a riveting example of social necessity embodied in some of life's most transformative moments. Yet the temporalities of birth intervals are almost too starkly consequential for the level at which Bourdieu writes and is read. Their social and physical contingencies carry consequences that go far beyond their symbolic significance.

These contraceptives have become the implements of a rural West African techne: a set of practices that, along with abstinence and juju, become commonsense techniques for achieving not low but high fertility. It is paradoxical, to say the least, that uneducated women in rural Gambia use state-of-the-art Western contraceptive technologies that were exported for long-term use to limit births as short-term strategies to sustain high rates of fertility and child survival.[21] In observations such as these, the question of commensurability comes strongly to the fore in the form of meanings that are overlapping and mutually intelligible but somehow not identical. Yet it is at the edges of the received categories where the contradictions most arise.

There is high commensurability among Gambian women and Western population scientists concerning the value of spacing births for avoiding maternal depletion and child morbidity. However, this commensurability quickly unravels once we look much beyond this fact. Western ideas of a birth interval do not encompass an elaborated cluster of worries about sexuality in the interval after birth, worries that include a religious mandate, the problems of semen and blood commingling, or the level of the child's development or feeding progress as an index for resuming sexual life or beginning a new pregnancy. On the other hand, the commonsense concerns that Western women of today express about the intervals between children are highly remote from ideas to which Gambian women are attuned. In American popular literature, I found numerous worries about child spacing with respect to sibling rivalry, parental attention, mother's employment, and children's I.Q. But spacing never seemed to arise in conjunction with health concerns (Bledsoe 1996). Compared to Gambian women, American women have quite a casual attitude about closely spaced births. In fact, it appears to be quite acceptable for an American woman who becomes preg-

21. It is equally paradoxical that, as Santow (1995) points out, methods such as withdrawal, which are usually regarded as "natural" (or as "ineffective" or "traditional," in WFS and DHS terminologies, respectively) appear to have played a key role in the fertility decline in the West.

nant to continue breastfeeding almost until the new baby is due.[22] The cultural commensurability, then, on these matters is thin. There are also, of course, subcultural versions of common sense about birth intervals. For example, the degree of Western technical knowledge in chemistry and endocrinology that is applied to the physiology of breastfeeding and maternal depletion has no immediate parallel in either The Gambia or in Western popular literature. And in The Gambia, the level of knowledge and experience that elderly midwives have about childbearing far exceeds that which young women have. The problem in all these cases lies in assuming that the terms by which the phenomena are described are mutually translatable from one domain to the other.

Implications of the Findings for Natural Fertility

This close inspection of birth interval dynamics in rural Gambia has uncovered a number of conundrums for the notion of natural fertility, the lens through which African birth intervals have conventionally been inspected.[23] This concept, as we saw in chapter 2, implies two things of note: (1) an absence of parity-dependent changes in reproductive behavior, indicating no desire to limit births, and, related to this, (2) a secondary or negligible role of intentions in fertility behaviors. As for the first, the findings reveal that a woman's fertility-relevant behaviors do change markedly throughout reproductive life, although it is not the number of children born that makes her behaviors change. Women's birth intervals may be regular, but they are hardly natural, at least in the sense of being unintentional. Women are socially constructing birth intervals that appear, because of their regularity, to be the outcome of natural biological phenomena.[24] Indeed, one might well conclude that birth intervals themselves, not numbers of children, are the focus of the calculus of conscious choice in fertility behavior (compare Coale 1973, 65), a vision quite different from that which the natural fertility framework would lead us to assume.[25] It is not, then, that a space appears because of the passage of time. Rather, some agent act-

22. A *New York Times Magazine* article—"The Breast Offense" (6 May 2001)—described in approving tones an American mother of four (a nine-year-old, a six-year-old, and four-year-old twins) who had nursed for such lengthy periods that at one point all of them were nursing. The twins were still nursing.

23. William Hanks helped immensely with this summary discussion.

24. These attributions of naturalism probably have multiple origins. Among the most likely are the tendency to throw out "unclean" data or to tuck them away into categories of "other," to infer motives and causal directions from statistical associations in conventional ways, and so on.

25. See Lockwood 1996 for an application of this idea to situations of fertility decline.

ing with intent skillfully creates a biological space that can be described by time. Moreover, these measures are taken not to limit children but to increase their numbers.[26] This is space in the Platonic sense of an empty yet nurturant space that can give rise to new, even unexpected events.

Henry (1961), the originator of the term *natural fertility*, recognized that culturally prescribed practices that may have a biological influence (whether intended or unintended) on fertility might be included under the rubric of natural fertility as long as these practices were unrelated to parity. Natural fertility could thus, in theory, apply to situations of delayed marriage, prolonged breastfeeding, lengthy postpartum abstinence, premenopausal terminal abstinence, the use of contraceptives (or polygyny) to space births, or (as I document in chapter 6) to heal the damage caused by traumatic pregnancies. Nor did Henry's theory specifically exclude the possibility that people in a natural fertility regime might use modern contraceptives to space their births. Yet if the principal test of a theory is its ability to shed explanatory light on a wide variety of practices and motives, then attempting to incorporate all these definitional challenges into the concept of natural fertility holds no obvious advantage over a simple assertion that people do not want to limit fertility. If anything, they take measures to enhance it. Natural fertility would therefore appear to be an ideal type in which the empirical reality never fulfills all the required criteria. The analytical task remains one of exploring the variations in fertility practices that have existed across time and space.

Although these results render natural fertility irrelevant to understanding African fertility, it is possible to make one final observation about the framework as a formal proposition. In its stripped-down logic, the theory presumes that any intents to interfere with fertility are enacted in order to limit children. Yet, as I have stressed, spacing patterns in The Gambia result *precisely* from intentional intervention and for the purpose of *not limiting*. In regimes where people want few children, mistakes or problems will increase fertility; where they want high fertility, mistakes will limit it. In The Gambia it is at the point when local intentionality breaks down—when the spacing strategy fails and the woman has not played her bodily or conjugal cards right—that this will appear to us as "controlled" fertility. Natural fertility, in sum, is exactly backwards.

---

26. This observation may help to explain why Howell (1979, 132), in her sample of !Kung people in the Kalahari, found that "the more successful women [i.e., those who produce the most live births] go on bearing children over a longer period of time, rather than simply crowding more children into a similar length of time."

Blurring and Slippage

In the course of this assault on natural fertility, some highly systematic relationships among biology, action, and temporalities have emerged. These relationships make intuitive—even "common"—sense in a regime that so
emphatically promotes the importance of careful child spacing. Certainly it
is engrossing to watch husband-wife, mother-child, and co-wife relations in
social, temporal and bodily play at once, with respect to one another and to
shifts in the available resources and technologies. Yet if we take a step back,
it becomes clear that the individual pieces of the child spacing framework
no longer fit together tidily. The apparently simple question of how people
space births has dissolved into more complicated ones. What are people
spacing, and how are they doing this? And what, moreover, are "spaces"?
We may have dispensed with the notion of natural fertility, but the notion
of child spacing that once seemed so safe also begins to crack, and we find
ourselves scrambling to invent ever more qualifications to salvage it. At first
these problems surfaced in a trickle, then a stream of conditionalities and
exceptions opened up. It is this growing chasm that I now want to bring forward and place on center stage.

The primary fault lines in the child spacing thesis lay in the fact that
highly intentional actions are taken to shape the spaces between children,
actions that vary according to circumstance. This hardly sounds like natural fertility. Yet neither does it sound like child spacing, as it has been described, either in chronological time or in terms of a child's developmental
phase. A long list of contingencies clouded the descriptions of spacing
strategies.[27] Subsidiary fault lines lay in puzzles such as age-related delays
or graduated entry into sexuality over the birth interval, life-cycle declines
in postpartum sexuality, and differential use of pills and Depo Provera. In
addition, people try to sequence not just births but many events relative to
one another: sexuality, pregnancy, menstruation, breastfeeding, the introduction of solid foods, and so on. Not only were events calculated relative
to each other, but the application of norms was as well. Normative conditionalities rested on the arrival of a co-wife, a lack of money, seasonal
hardships, strenuous labor demands, the decimation of a crop, a lawsuit, a
child's infirmity, an early resumption of fecundity, or an insistent husband.
A woman might adopt different pregnancy avoidance norms at different

---

27. A number of these observations have been made elsewhere. See particularly Caldwell and
Caldwell (1977, 212), who describe a sliding scale of duration of abstinence based on many things, including the mother's history of child mortality.

points in her life, and a man might apply different norms to different wives. Complications emerged in the debates over who should be enacting which pregnancy avoidance strategy, with respect to whom, under what conditions, and for how long. If a breastfeeding child is strong, a brisk pace of childbearing is desired, and the woman is young, it is acceptable to bend the rules on avoiding overlapped pregnancies. In other instances, it is advisable to slow down. Different puzzles arose in hints of male ambivalence about family planning and about causation in a birth interval sequence. On top of all this, rather than the workings of biology necessitating social accommodation, we saw intentional efforts to engineer biology to accommodate social needs. Among the most notable examples were attempts to abort a fetal competitor of a young breastfeeding child or to nudge along a child's development to keep pace with the mother's sexual activities.[28] Everywhere we looked, things were just slightly "off." The more intensely we stared, the more the edges of common sense began to blur and slip.

As all this has transpired, the temporal bases of action have shifted both absolutely and relatively. In this chapter I have edged noticeably away from the notion that there can be any stable chronological reference points within a space and begun a retreat to the cover of a more neutral Platonic sense of a space within which transformation may occur. Terms such as *soon, early, far,* and *later* seemed to refer less to the time when sex (or a pregnancy) should begin than to the temporalities of the baby's feeding and developmental progress. Besides these points of confusion, we saw that when sexuality is the explicit focus, the forty-day point after a child's birth is a perpetual point of contention. Men see it as the time when sex *should* begin; women see it as the time when sex *might* begin. Even the concept of forty days itself, the clearest chronological anchor in the birth interval, turns out to be a religious metaphor for a host of other things.

The language of child spacing thus manifests high commensurability between the two cultural frameworks, African and Western, that speak in its terms. New public norms promoting the health and welfare of women and children through contraception or child spacing readily become publicly acceptable rationales that lend an air of legitimacy to actions of many sorts.[29] But commensurability does not necessarily mean equivalence. At the outset, child spacing appeared to be the common sense laid down by

28. Rasmussen (1997, viii) describes parallel attempts in the past by Tuareg mothers to hasten their daughters' puberty by ritual force-feeding.

29. See Bledsoe and Hill 1998; for related discussions, see Feldman-Savelsberg 1999 for Cameroon, and Clark 1989 for Ghana.

time. By now, it has become apparent that none of it works that way. The farther the chapter progressed, the more that time began to collapse. In chapter 5, the notion of child spacing unravels altogether as we begin to lose our grip not only on time but on children as the most significant anchoring units in the reproductive trajectory.

CHAPTER 5

Disjunctures and Anomalies:
Deconstructing Child Spacing

As I explained in chapter 4, findings on child spacing seemed piv-otal to understanding contraceptive use in relation to the Gambian project's results. That is, rural women seem to have added Western contraceptives to a large repertoire of strategies for managing birth intervals in order to increase, rather than decrease, numbers of surviving children. To be sure, anthropologists might not be sur-prised at all to see reproductive behaviors that subverted the in-tentions of family planners. Criticizing both modernization theory and apparent naturalisms is standard fare for sociocultural anthro-pology. But a number of pieces of the new picture itself were not hanging together. Indeed, they were falling apart rapidly. Before I unglue even them further, I need to explain how the problems be-gan to surface. For this purpose, I take two methodological digres-sions. The first describes a data entry and analysis program called Epi Info that I began to learn. The second defends the value of awkward English translations in questionnaire responses. A proce-dural note: This chapter works backwards, sifting through findings that had begun to materialize and picking out of the mass a few "hindsight" findings. Yet it also looks forward, putting in place some critical pieces of evidence that will open up a new logic.

Making Numbers Talk: Anthropological Logic and Numerical Semantics

Anthropology's greatest strength is its enduring conviction that the cultural frames from which our questions about human action and motivation spring are likely partial, if not altogether wrong and therefore misleading.[1] All our work, both theoretical and empirical, is directed toward exploiting this fact for immense gain. The ethnographic method thus privileges attention to people's "voices" over formulaic concepts. But if numbers are the primary data at hand, how can we possibly hear this voice? Statistical methods are seen as applying standardized techniques to identify relationships among key variables in quantifiable ways to make powerful deductive arguments on the basis of quantifiable statistical significance. To find this significance, social science research often uses questionnaires to derive the data by means of which to test hypotheses. The key variables of interest are framed into questions, and response choices are created that will provide variation to test the hypotheses. These questions are then organized into thematic cluster areas (for example, "background information," "marital history," "fertility preferences"), in the order the questionnaire writers deem logical according to their understandings of the subject matter. The problem is that by the time the data have been filtered through all the processes from standardizing questions and coding to translating, transcribing, and tabulating—converted from talk to numbers and subjected to increasingly standardized recodes, filters, and cross-checks that delete ambiguous responses—people's voices seem dimly perceptible indeed. A different assessment also seems possible, however, one that exploits surveys and the numbers they produce for close cultural use.[2] For working with numbers, I happened upon a computer program called Epi Info.[3] Now it is unlikely to be obvious to most readers why a computer program and the numbers it records and analyzes should be of any utility to a discipline

---

1. This section draws on a document written in collaboration with Jane Guyer, Barthélémy Kuate Defo, and Shobha Shagle (Bledsoe et al. 1999). Each, from their quite different disciplinary perspectives, helped capture perceptively the rationales underlying these methods. See especially Guyer 1998 for a theoretical treatment of the anthropological thrust to research methodologies such as these.

2. I use the term *culture* here to include the way in which agents engage with the world, whether these engagements consist of thinking, speaking, or (in this case) performing analyses of numbers.

3. The discussions of Epi Info in this book apply to the versions I used, DOS-based Epi 5.01b and Epi 6.0, which have now been superseded by a Windows version. However, the general points concerning the interplays among the technologies, the genre of numbers, and the style of thinking remain relevant.

that so values cultural voice. Yet if culture is as powerful as my discipline maintains it is, we should be able to seize for interpretive ends even instruments and genres that have been handled by the most universalizing conventions. Indeed, numbers can "talk" through a kind of "numerical semantics." We can thus put them to use for open-ended, ethnographically inspired thinking.

Following the initial findings on contraception and child spacing, the next phase of the project was intended to be a time to fan out in a more open-ended fashion, to enrich the child spacing results and to acquire a more precise view of their dynamics. The field workers were collecting some brief case studies, but the principal instrument for this phase was to be the fifteen-month multi-round survey, in which women who had borne a living child within the past three years were to be interviewed once a month. The data in the monthly rounds were largely "quantitative" or (more neutrally stated) coded in numbers, a medium generally considered to be mutually exclusive from "qualitative" data and antithetical to concerns for cultural meaning. The data from the 1992 survey had been entered in DBase at the MRC field station and then exported for analysis into SPSS, a powerful statistical and programming package. However, the new monthly rounds were being entered in Epi Info, a program created largely for data entry by the Centers for Disease Control in Atlanta and disseminated freely throughout the world for work in epidemiology and related fields.

In the preface I confessed that I spent a significant amount of time during my short visits to Farafenni in the field station's computer room. There was much to do to review materials that the fieldworkers had collected, create mini-surveys or interviews for them to try out, and write new protocols before leaving. But as I worked with the fieldworkers, I began to notice the activities of the Gambian data entry clerks who came in occasionally to enter the monthly rounds data in Epi Info. What particularly drew my attention was not Epi Info's data entry capacities but its fluid "analysis" mode. Seeing my interest, they began to teach me the program as well as some tips they had discovered for maneuvering within it. Because the program's movements were uncomplicated and my technical skills were minimal, I began to experiment with it to see what the rounds were beginning to produce.

To a field whose practitioners start with a mindset of being wrong, several methodological elements are critical. Of these, open-ended approaches are the most important. Whether we are inspecting interview texts or statistical data, we walk around phenomena, mentally sorting and re-sorting ideas about how they are linked. We look intensely, continually adjusting the "zoom lens" to different levels of resolution in search of meaningful patterns. We mentally reconfigure the data into visions of personal careers, social relationships, and cultural meanings, and we use these visions to generate further questions. The exercise, even if we seldom call our thinking hypothesis testing, seeks to make powerful configurational arguments about phenomena that may deviate significantly from all conventional understandings.

Another methodological element involves the handling of the extremes of variation that we call exceptions or anomalies. These cases, occurring in tiny numbers at the extreme edges of the logic, are easy to dismiss as statistical noise or recoded in the all-purpose category of "other." Yet if the whole explanation is sitting awkwardly with respect to what we have gleaned from other sources about how people conduct their lives, a continuing search for the anomalies and the conditions that produce them may provide, by the very power of their illogic, the handles needed to force reconsideration of the entire framework.

The third methodological premise essential to a mindset that is professionally expectant of being wrong is the need to create redundant data. Students of writing are taught to shun repetitious, superfluous prose as an impediment to clear thinking. But redundancy, in the sense of collecting copious overlapping information, is one of the most fundamental tools of sociocultural research. In conversations, we ask different questions of the same respondent, the same questions of different respondents, and the same questions endlessly rephrased of the same respondents—all in search of tiny divergences that might yield clues about lines of variations and deceptive commensurabilities. (Ethnosemantics is possibly the most systematically developed methodology in this vein, but most anthropological methods share the emphasis.) The more important the question, the more we build up redundancy around it.

The final methodological premise is that of listening for "voice": people's statements about themselves, from the distinctive positions they occupy. Regardless of the filters through which they must speak and we must listen, we try to stay as close to the data as possible. In survey research, it is the questionnaire, with its copious, overlapping—but critically redundant—information that holds the semantic keys to this voice. A completed survey can be seen as the record of a conversation between two people: one who posed questions that may have been both incommensurate with local concerns and phrased in an unfamiliar idiom, and another other who tried to answer them. An apparently anomalous response may thus reflect an attempt by the respondent or the interviewer, or both, to fashion an answer from a misguided question. Translated back across the cultural divide into the closest approximation of what the interviewer and the respondent believe those who wrote the survey can comprehend, these awkward responses to wrong-headed questions may remain embedded in the data set. To the astute eye and ear, such apparent inconsistencies, felt as almost imperceptible traces at first, may appear with increasing clarity as we tack back and forth across the data with a particular issue in mind. By watching for patterns among the tails of the normal curve and the unusual single cases, we may begin to discern a facet of reality that was not envisaged when the survey was written but to which the responses now bear witness. Detecting such possibilities in a data set demands play and experimentation in the freest possible way. One needs vision, for keeping many alternative interpretations in view; accessibility, for drawing them into view easily; and speed, for sorting through different configurations as new ideas arise.

All of today's computer statistical packages can perform tests on quantitative data in terms of their numerical significance. They can sort variables, select cases, define new variables, set conditions, recode, create graphs, and so on. Epi Info, however, seems to have two features that set it apart from the others. One is its navigational potential, which allows close control over vision and rapid movement. The other is its capacity to record and display commentary features.

Epi Info permits fluid maneuvering by allowing the analyst to wade directly into the data set itself, much as a data entry clerk would do, selecting certain cases and setting up, side by side, a few relevant variables at a time for visual checks. After running preliminary frequencies, tables, and statistics on key variables to get a feel for the data, we can descend for a more in-depth look. Selecting, for example, women under the age of twenty with more than one child and currently using oral contraceptive pills, we can bring up onto the screen a few columns of key variables for close scrutiny in an order that is independent of their original ordering in the survey. We can then re-sort the variables quickly to look at new configurations. Being able to disengage the questions from their original ordering in the questionnaire is crucial for efforts to avoid reifying, or erroneously fixing, their meaning. Although we might assume that contraceptives, for example, are devices for suppressing numbers of children, being able to reorder the "contraceptive use" variable on the screen and set it beside variables encoding a woman's age, number of surviving children, and medical condition may suggest an entirely different meaning. As we glean new ideas, we can look even closer, turning up the zoom lens to inspect individual cases. When a pattern appears that might offer a promising new lead, each step can be unraveled for closer scrutiny and the entire data set can be re-sorted and recalculated to try new interpretations. Oddities can thus be seen not necessarily as errors or as noise but as potential points of leverage toward solving the next step in the puzzle. Trawling rapidly and repeatedly through the data, we can engage with a moving set of unfolding ideas. The technology can approach the speed of the mind as we identify new questions to ask, test logical inferences, and make comparisons with other groups.

Besides its remarkable capacity to yield clues about cultural meaning through greater maneuverability and visibility, Epi Info can also encode and display open-ended textual commentary in "string" variables alongside the quantifiable responses, allowing people to explain in their own words their answers to key questions. Thus, the question "Last month did you want to get pregnant?" can be followed by "Please explain." Or, "What means [if any] to avoid pregnancy did you try last month?" can be followed by "Why did you use this method [or nothing]?" This allows us not only to make particular numbers talk, but to do so in prose. In fact, as the data are repeatedly sifted and sorted, a kind of "synesthesia" develops. The information begins to fuse, so that one begins to forget where it came from, whether from numerically coded responses to a survey, from lengthy interviews, or from the national newspaper or radio broadcasts. Clearly, attempting to attach a "quantitative" or "qualitative" designation to data that result from methods such as these does no justice to the possibilities they offer.

Building a bridge between the "raw conversation" and the fixity of a conventional statistical package, Epi Info's simple features make the program highly suited to reproduce an anthropological style of close juxtapositional questioning. As partial and misguided as our survey questions inevitably are, the ability to reconfigure the responses in any combination with such analytical impunity, at any level of resolution (from the whole sample down to the individual respondent), and to envision the patterns against data from field notes and interviews—all may unveil an utterly new experiential landscape. Probing commensurabilities by assembling richly redundant information, scrutinizing anomalies, and scanning contexts, one enters a "discovery," as opposed to a "confirmatory," mode (Chomsky 1965; Guyer 1998).

This exercise is not one of "mining" data, a term sometimes used to criticize efforts to fiddle with data to get the results to "come out right." It is instead exploring the data, assuming that the most relevant patterns are unknown at the outset and must be unveiled through careful sifting and inspection from infinite angles the logic of ethnographic knowledge of the area and the people. Nor are efforts like these meant to "operationalize" talk and turn it into countable variables. Rather, numbers are asked to "talk" as if they were being interviewed, whether by totaling them, sorting them, or juxtaposing them with one another and with commentary. We are trying to listen for the original voices speaking from a cultural repertoire, a set of sociopolitical positions, and a historical moment. At every point, the ethnographic eye is open, searching for the meaning that the numbered responses may encode, imagining individuals who are acting in ways that the survey is somehow capturing, though not necessarily in ways that were anticipated when it was written. Nor, finally, is this exercise a substitute for ethnography. A sense of the ethnography is the crucial background against which plausible links between the numerical codes must be made. Indeed, the analysis itself ideally takes place in situ, where, as the survey explorations bring new puzzles to light, local people can be asked for interpretations that may open up new directions. Even when being in the field is not feasible for much of the time, as was the case for me, such explorations can be conducted through a rapidly expanding corpus of global communications media such as overseas phone calls, fax machines, and email.

The combined effects of having commentary variables plus quick access to full view of all the questions is extraordinary. They bring a survey to life. They provide wide-angled views of the individuals whose complex lives and worries have been sorted and packaged into the survey's a priori variables and cluster areas. Transforming an apparently universally standardized and quantified set of numerical responses into a rich field of persons embedded in a moral economy of complex social relations, such methods can turn common sense on its head. Inspired by this sudden ability to see the data up close and to explore the meanings they might somehow encode, I spent increasing amounts of time playing with Epi Info. During my visits to The Gambia and when I was in Evanston, these odd methods and the data to which they were giving such unprecedented access became powerful discovery heuristics for cultural ends. I eventually asked the Gambian manager of the Farafenni computer station to convert all the project's numerical survey files, including the prior 1992 survey, into Epi Info for me.

Hearing Voices through Linguistic Filters

Besides the Epi Info exercise, the other methodological source of both confusion and inspiration was awkward English. With little time to spend in the field, I experienced unending frustration at trying to listen through filters of social status, language translation, and geographical and cultural distance, all stacked thickly on top of one another. Given the logistic difficulties the study entailed, I occasionally found myself on the other side of the Atlantic, pondering a response from an illiterate Fula woman to the misguided question I had written that had been duly posed to her by a male Mandinka interviewer, himself having only passable skills in either Fula or English, as he attempted to translate the question for her and then translate and transcribe her response into something he guessed would be understandable to an absent foreigner.[4] Such an instance, although an extreme one, is a shocking violation of the canons of the anthropological method, which so values linguistic competence and face-to-face interactions. Yet such gaps had odd advantages. The very awkwardness of translation, the frequent mistranslations, and the alternative interpretations they suggested sometimes highlighted facets of meaning that otherwise might have been overlooked. In fact, my absence itself undoubtedly allowed numerous anomalies to be recorded that I might (had I been present) have pressed the interviewer to reconcile in a frame that made more sense to me at the time.

Let us take the example of chronological time, which already has begun to unravel in our scrutiny of child spacing, women's health, and contraceptive use. What appeared to be oddities in women's survey commentaries became increasingly difficult to attribute to translation problems alone. Here is just one example: "I do not want the space [between births] to be short. I will grow elder in strength gradually." Uses of the English terms by which the interviewers were translating descriptions of the spaces between children (for example, "distant," "close") were puzzling as well. There was little mention of time per se (for example, "It is not good to have births too close to each other"). Women did refer to time and sometimes to age, especially for young children. But on the whole, time, when it was mentioned, served simply to locate events in a narrated sequence ("I had a stomach pain the time I was seeing my period") or in a duration in which something else, such as the growth of a child or the achievement of health, might occur ("I have natural spacing and I can regain my health and strength out of this lengthy period"). The fact that similar vocabularies can overlay entirely different referents is a trap of deceptive commensurability for the unwary. But when a speaker applies a word to a domain in a way that seems awkward to a listener, this also provides a research opportunity.

---

4. Ellen Ross (pers. comm.) reports that my efforts to carry out the project at a distance, and via translations and mentalities of researchers whose questions were different from the ones I was posing, all had surprising parallels to her experience as a social historian, whose informants are almost always dead and whose data arise from purposes that were rarely her own.

Growing Empirical Anomalies

The fanning-out activities that introduced the second phase of the project, then, began according to plan. These activities consisted of (among other things) intensive interviews, Epi Info explorations of the survey data, and discussions with local staff and health and family planning officials about the accumulating results. But the more the high-intensity beam was turned up on specific domains, the more anomalies seemed to come to light and the less sense the child spacing framework alone began to make as an explanation of reproductive behaviors. There were several major breakdowns, some of which began to emerge in the previous chapter. For example, the almost routine Western analytical tendency to peg the dynamics of birth spacing and reproductive capacity to the passage of time now seemed to be incongruous with local women's perception of contraception as a technique to ensure the production of *more* living children than they would have achieved in its absence. Whether they actually brought more children to survival than they could have otherwise is a question so counterintuitive to the thrust of Western assumptions that its logic has never been pressed in demographic analysis at all. This is so even though the goal of insuring child survival is precisely the rationale on which contraceptives are promoted in many developing countries.

The Ambivalence of Men

Some of the biggest challenges to both natural fertility and to the child spacing framework were the reactions by men—and often mothers-in-law—to women's contraceptive use.[5] A man's efforts to monitor his wife's reproductivity often stemmed, as I described in chapter 4, from genuine worry for her and the child. Some men were not only enthusiastic backers of their wives' contraception; they saw themselves as spacing births by agreeing to abstinence, by using condoms, or even by taking their wives to the local imam to obtain juju or to the village health worker for pills. This we might expect from the perspective of a child spacing framework. Yet men were hardly uniform on this question. Some men were supportive of women's use of contraceptives, while others expressed moral outrage. "I don't like my wife to use family planning," asserted one man, "because it is against Islam and we are all Muslims." Said another, "Family planning is used to destroy

---

5. For his insights and collaboration on this section, and especially on those in the section in chapter 6 on men, I am enormously indebted to William Hanks (see Bledsoe and Hanks 1998).

life because I hear from people that the pills cause abortion." Stormy arguments can arise when a husband discovers his wife's secret cache of tablets or hears from an indignant elder female relative that she was seen in the family planning clinic. Women whose husbands object to contraceptive use thus find themselves in a catch-22. A man may see his wife's contraceptive use as quite legitimate for her efforts to attend to both maternal and conjugal duty. But after the baby is weaned and the mother's fecundity has resumed, her use of contraceptives might be interpreted as a sign of an adulterous affair. One man stated his objection flatly: "I don't like the idea of contraception, especially when my wife is not breastfeeding, and any one of them who practices it and I am aware, I will divorce you."

Throughout the subcontinent men have a long-standing reputation as obstructionists to family planning, and promoting male involvement in reproductive control was a major goal of the 1994 Cairo Population Conference. Conversely, a significant proportion of women actually appear to be using contraceptives secretly in order to avoid detection by their husbands (see Watkins et al. 1997). One woman described her own use of Depo to the interviewer with a fear that spoke unambiguously through the filters of language and transcription:

> I am using the injectable contraceptive for this first time. I started it two months ago. My husband is not aware of it. I wish he will never be aware of it. It may result in a divorce. It was in deep secret that I decided taking contraceptives because my husband is a stern man. I trust you and hope he will not know from you people! It was a strong decision to take the injection after I have nearly failed my strategy [abstention].

Clearly, contraceptive use and the nonpregnant time it creates can evoke strong moral tension in a marriage.

Suspicion of overly long birth intervals or of sexual straying on the part of wives means that men who allow their wives to use a contraceptive measure during breastfeeding may try to maintain tight control over it. In the following instance a man describes a traditional contraceptive measure: "I give my wives a string from my trouser to tie on their waist whilst breast feeding. When I feel they should get pregnant I just take this string from them." In another instance, a twenty-five-year-old woman, describing her attempts to avoid another overlapped pregnancy, referred in a quite matter-of-fact way to her husband's control over her contraceptive options through the rules and documents of the government health bureaucracy.

I once had an unwanted pregnancy, so I was advised by my husband to join the family planning. I had one injection of Depo one month after delivery. I am due to have my second injection but I was away for one year with my mother, leaving my family planning card with my husband. That deprived me from taking my second dose. Now, I have come back to join my husband. So, I will see the CHN [community health nurse] for my second injection or advice. (R. 1)

Here once again is evidence that a husband is highly attuned to both his wife's pattern of fecundity and the child's stage of development. Most important, however, this woman's statement implies that her husband was trying to keep her away from extramarital temptation by withholding her family planning card. If she became pregnant in his absence, this would be clear evidence of her transgression. Younger men, who need to establish themselves in the compound vis-à-vis their brothers by the production of children, seem to be particularly scrupulous about their wives' spacing activities. A young husband may keep Foucauldian track of the timing and duration of his wife's monthly cycles in order to know when she is fecund.[6]

The fact that men can be so suspicious of contraceptive use is mirrored in the fact that women can be deeply invested in the confidentiality that various contraceptives afford. Clearly, neither abstinence nor condoms can be hidden from a husband. And most imams and marabouts will provide ritual protection against pregnancy only with the husband's permission. As for pills, they are easy to hide from a husband, who spends little time in the wife's room, though they can be discovered by children or suspicious cowives. Injections are best of all since there is no visible trace of their use. Still, whether he uses a trouser rope or a government-issued family planning card, the man is seen as the ultimate legitimator of the woman's contraceptive efforts.

By no means do women simply acquiesce in male control. There is considerable use of contraceptives to space births without the husband's knowledge or approval. Yet the logical problem that remains is this: If a woman is simply using contraceptives to ensure her children's health by safe birth

---

6. This phenomenon can be transferred seamlessly across the Atlantic. A young woman from a francophone African country, a recent immigrant to the United States who knew little English, asked a friend to come with her to a family planning clinic to help translate as she went to get a supply of pills. The young woman's husband, a U.S. resident, insisted on going as well. When the clinic attendant asked the woman, in English, how long her periods lasted, it was the husband who answered, even before the translation exchange could commence, "Five days" (Fatoumatta Banja, pers. comm.).

spacing, why would her husband be opposed? These are, after all, his own children. Why should she have to resort to secrecy? To press the case even further: If women really wanted all the children God gave them—which in the overwhelming number of cases they do—why should they try to delay pregnancy at all?

Old-Young Distinctions

Although some puzzles arose in observations of male resistance to contraceptives, the domains containing the most striking inconsistencies were those that have remained farthest from the gaze of population concerns. One of these domains was that of older women. The emphasis thus far has been on the significance of birth intervals for stages of the child's development. Now we turn to the meaning of birth intervals for the woman herself: her age, her fertility history, and her conjugal situation.

Let us consider first age patterns in women's fertility desires. It is well known that older women in high-fertility populations have lower fertility and longer birth intervals than do younger ones. The most common explanation offered is that women are less fecund at older ages. Because of the fertility implications of early marriage among a highly fecund age group, the start of the reproductive years has attracted by far the most demographic attention (my own work is an archetypal case: National Research Council 1993b). As a result, older women's low fertility rates, whether produced by declining fecundity or by terminal abstinence, have almost completely marginalized this group as a focus of demographic interest. It is certainly the case that older married women had lower fertility in this population than did younger ones. But contrary to natural fertility theory, the rounds data showed age patterns as well in women's expressed preferences about a new pregnancy. Among the nonpregnant women in the rounds with weaned children, those who said they did not want to be pregnant at the time were significantly older than those who did (31.8 versus 30.0 years; $N = 647$). Suggestions of a desired slowdown appeared as well in women's expressed wishes for more pregnancies. In an add-on questionnaire to Round 12, women were asked how many more pregnancies they wanted for their husband. I group the possible answers into three categories: no more pregnancies wanted for him, a numerical answer more than zero, or either a nonnumerical answer like "up to God" or no answer. Figure 5.1 shows the responses by five-year age groups, with the number of respondents in each age category at the top. On the whole, it shows a decreasing number of women willing to leave their number of future pregnancies up to

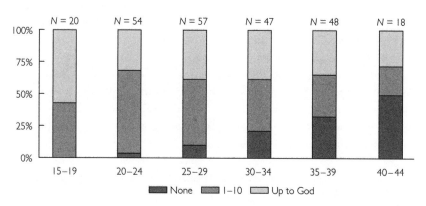

Fig. 5.1 Women wanting more pregnancies for husband, by age group

God as age increases, although there is some indecision among women in their twenties on this matter. But the proportion of women saying they wanted no more pregnancies rises smoothly by age group from no one at all less than age twenty to half of those forty and older.[7]

To be sure, many of the women who said they wanted no more pregnancies might later change their minds—especially the younger ones. And many did. Still, because this is a "nonlimiting" population, it is mysterious that any woman in a population with such normative emphasis on high fertility would express a reluctance to be pregnant after weaning her child. The fact that older women say this more often than younger ones would make their situations especially important to understand.

Some of the most telling clues to the old-young distinction in birth interval desires appeared in the Epi Info expanded commentary responses. When asked, "Are you trying to take a 'rest' between your births?" (that is, to create longer spaces between weaning one child and conceiving the next), younger women generally proved anxious to get on with childbearing. Some sample explanations:

"I love having children."
"My husband wants more children."
"I want more children so I want as soon as my child is weaned, [I want] to get pregnant 1 month after weaning."

7. The number of women who wanted no more pregnancies was very likely an underestimate, especially in the older groups. Because this questionnaire was designed as a postpartum survey, it omitted women who had had no children in the prior three years. Many of these women probably would have responded "none."

"I did not reach the age of delaying my pregnancy because I only have
3 children."

Whereas young women often seemed willing to overlap children and to
use contraception "for spacing," what stood out in many older women's responses was a determination to "rest." By this they referred to an effort to
slow down the pace of childbearing by delaying a new pregnancy past the
point when the previous child is weaned.

"I want to delay the next pregnancy because I am weak and want to wait
until I have a little strength again."
"I don't want to get a child any more. I want to rest now and take care of
my present children."
"My womb is now slight [weak, thin] and I delivered my present child in
Banjul [that is, an emergency]."
"I am not well."

Convergent with these verbal testimonies were differences in the reported use of particular contraceptives. Women in the 1992 survey who
were using Western contraceptives such as pills and Depo Provera were
significantly older than the women using traditional methods: 33.8 and 30.3
years, respectively ($p < .01$). Juju users, the youngest of all users of contraception, had an average age of 27.8. Thus, the young, normally considered
to be the progressive wave of the reproductive future, were using predomi-
nantly what standard surveys classify as "traditional" methods: herbs, juju,
or abstinence. Especially conspicuous among older women was their use of
strong injections. Whereas the mean age of the fifty-six pill users was 30.7
years, the seventy Depo users averaged 35.5 years ($p < .01$).[8] Depo Provera
is the overwhelming contraceptive of choice for older women. Table 5.1,
from the 1992 survey, shows that among women who reported they were
using some method to avoid pregnancy (whether pills, abstinence, juju, or
Depo Provera), the use of Depo increases smoothly, starting from only 7.3
percent among those who had had one or two pregnancies to 66.7 percent
among women with ten to thirteen pregnancies. Interviews revealed that
Depo Provera alarms young women because its effects can spill over for

---

8. These ages are in keeping with the Gambian Ministry of Health guidelines, which recommend
Depo Provera in particular to "women of proven fertility." However, the use of Depo by older, higher
parity women seemed to be in keeping with the stated desires of these women quite irrespective of ministry guidelines, of which most were unaware.

Table 5.1 Women using Depo Provera as a percentage of women using any kind of contraception, by parity

Parity	Percent using Depo	N
1–2	7.3	41
3–4	13.6	44
5–6	38.6	57
7–9	44.4	45
10–13	66.7	27

Source: 1992 survey.

months and delay the next conception. By contrast, although "traditional" measures like juju and herbs are known to carry high risks of failure, they are considered to act in mild ways that do not endanger future reproductivity and are thus preferred by young women.

Further, although older women are more likely than younger ones to be using Western contraceptives at all phases of the birth interval, this age difference increases as the developmental phases of the birth interval progress. Among mothers of children who are feeding on breast milk and thick pap, users of Western contraceptives are two years older than nonusers (29.7 versus 27.5 years). By the time children are weaned, users are four years older than nonusers (33.0 versus 29.2).

Desires for a co-wife reveal age patterns that mirror those of contraceptive use and birth interval desires. Older women spoke with considerably more favor about the prospects of polygynous marriage than did younger ones, and many older women took matters into their own hands to launch the search for a new wife for a diffident husband. Once a woman had undergone several pregnancies, the virtues of having a co-wife seemed to override the drawbacks. In fact, the purpose of acquiring a co-wife was often stated explicitly as one of lengthening birth intervals or, in some cases, of stopping child bearing altogether.

In sum, many older women, although their fecundity might be ebbing, sought far wider birth intervals than child health alone seemed to demand.[9]

9. My 1997 analyses of data from eight of the eleven African DHS countries that, at the time of their last DHS surveys, did not seem to be undergoing a fertility transition (Burkina Faso, Cameroon, Central African Republic, Malawi, Rwanda, Senegal, Zambia, and Nigeria) showed significantly higher ages for modern contraceptive use among women whom one would least expect to be using contraceptives. These women were not currently breastfeeding but had had at least one live birth and were also rural, uneducated, and married. This age difference did not, however, occur in Ghana, Niger, or Tanzania.

This means that if they wanted all the children God gave them, they would appear to be obstructing divine will by blocking off irretrievable segments of the reproductive clock. Child numbers were often mentioned, but more as after-the-fact reckoning than as a prior goal that, once reached, would justify limiting childbearing. Said one thirty-six-year-old woman, "I am avoiding pregnancy now because I have nine children and all are alive. So, I am praying to God so that it stops there, because when I get pregnant I am always sick like bleeding and I get anemic." A thirty-four-year-old woman related, "I have nine pregnancies and I am exhausted now. I have decided using the injection to enable myself avoid getting pregnant. . . . Not that I do not want another child. My situation is that I want to rest for a while."

This word—"rest"—will form a core concept of what I am calling the contingency thesis. The semantic distinction between this word and related ones, though translated, points to a key observation: neither "resting" nor "stopping" seemed to these women to imply "limiting" children. Together with the findings on ages of users of various kinds of contraceptives, they hinted at critical health differences separating young from old. Young women, with their youthful base of strength and health, seem to recover quickly from a birth. They start out wanting many children quickly, but with the accumulating demands of childbearing and the care of surviving children, they find that they must slow down as their strength flags. Most women over thirty-five, finding their strength increasingly hard to regain after each successive birth, expressed fears of the rising health risks of high-parity childbearing: prolonged labor, hemorrhage, and death. Some of the health concerns of this older group and their contraceptive efforts to extend the birth interval beyond the time of weaning had been described in an earlier article (Bledsoe et al. 1994) to critique the natural fertility model. Yet the article did not fully confront the analytical significance of the fact that these findings were inconsistent with the view of child spacing that the article itself employed. Its framework remained bound to a certain set of cultural assumptions about the role of time in reproductive life.

Besides the numerical puzzles posed by views of age and aging in a society with such high fertility goals there were semantic puzzles, most notably people's perceptions of the terms *old* and *young* themselves. One of the questions the 1992 survey asked was the following: "Why do you think you cannot have another child?" It was included as a follow-up to the question, "Do you think you could have another child if you wanted one?" on the assumption that a response of "too old" would indicate a woman who had reached menopause or was nearing it. However, in working with Epi Info, I began to see something quite odd in peripheral vision. A number of women who were only in their mid-to-late thirties reported that they were "too old" to have another child. Selecting this group for special attention, I could see that several of these women were having regular menstrual periods and a number were using long-term contraceptives. Among the 220 women under age fifty who said they were too old to have another child, sixty-three had had a period in the previous month, nineteen had had a live birth less than three years earlier (thirteen of them less than two years earlier), and five were taking pills or injections. Nine were even breastfeeding at the time of the survey. Some age reports were likely wrong; the women surveyed almost never care about their own ages.[10] But similar findings appeared later in the rounds surveys, in which age by this time had become a subject of great interest, and extensive efforts were made to obtain accurate ages. Still, the question remained: Why should women with high fertility aspirations care so little about their ages when according to the Western view this should be a subject of intense interest for them?

A response of "too old" may well have captured some cases of premature terminal sterility. Yet the fact that the current fertility activities of these women were quite at odds with what one would expect to find in a perimenopausal population lay unnoticed for some time simply because the subject of older women was of no interest at the outset of the study. It was equally odd that despite the societal passion for high fertility, menopause was a subject of negligible interest. Although everyone in The Gambia knows that reproduction cannot occur after menopause, such profound cultural lack of interest in a subject that now draws such immense attention in the United States was striking.

Reproductive Mishaps

Emerging as anomalies, then, were the following puzzles: men sometimes manifested inexplicable outrage at women's apparent efforts to ensure the health of their children, there were many kinds and causes of "child spaces," and neither age nor menopause seemed to draw much interest among women in a society with high fertility expectations. Results such as

---

10. A telling case in point is that of Isichei (1978), who asserted that the Ibo in Nigeria are intensely concerned with "age." Closer inspection, however, suggests that he was struggling with the limitations of the English word. What he clearly referred to was not chronological years but people's age relative to others, a point on which much social status rests. A similar lack of interest in age seems to have applied to other high-fertility times and places. Working-class Englishwomen wrote about their childbearing experiences to their guild organization in the early part of the twentieth century (Women's Cooperative Guild 1916). When they noted their age at all, they did so largely to mark the severity of childbirth ordeals they had experienced in a short time, not as an index of proximity to menopause.

these were beginning to cast severe doubt on child spacing as a useful explanation of the observed patterns of contraceptive use. Taken together, these incongruities of time, age, and men's attitudes suggested that Western precepts about aging and reproduction bore little resemblance to the cultural understandings that had generated the responses these women were giving.

The domain of inconsistencies that posed by far the most troublesome stumbling block, however, was the fact that in a number of cases of Western contraceptive use, there *was* no last child to space. Selecting only the users and examining their characteristics and comments in detail through Epi Info's visual capabilities drew stark attention to the fact that some women were using contraception in the wake of what I am calling a reproductive mishap: a child or fetus that had no signs of life at birth (a miscarriage or a stillbirth) or the postnatal death of a neonate or a young child. In a high-fertility regime, using contraception in such situations would appear to make little sense. It is precisely those women who were trying to have a child and failed who should be most anxious to start again. Such cases had been swept aside by both the logic of the child spacing analysis and adherence to the conventions that count only live births as significant data. Western demography has now amassed vast amounts of data on the deaths of living children, especially those of neonates and infants. But the recognition that there are also nonlive births, many of them quite traumatic and injurious to the woman, has remained outside the vision of fertility research. The full significance of the fact that a woman may have more pregnancies than live births did not occur to me for a long time.

If information on reproductive mishaps is scarce, information on maternal behaviors following mishaps is even more so. Maternal behaviors preceding the deaths of small children have drawn vast amounts of demographic attention, as have behaviors preceding and following live births. But what a mother does after a child's death or a nonlive birth has gone unnoticed.

Investigating reproductive mishaps is no easy task. Because these events connote infertility and cast doubt on a woman's conjugal worth, they tend to be underreported. There are definitional and technical problems as well. Although the death of an infant that survived the birth process is a standard source of demographic data, far less so are nonlive births, sometimes referred to as fetal losses, intrauterine mortality, or wasted pregnancies. A miscarriage is typically defined as a fetus that is expelled before about twenty-eight weeks' gestation, whereas a stillbirth is a fetus of longer gestation that show no signs of life at birth. Miscarriage and stillbirth thus refer, respectively, to intrauterine deaths that occur before and after the conceptus might have been viable in the outside world, a point usually near the end of the second trimester.[11] Older women may be more susceptible to these losses (Casterline 1989b; Wood 1994, 250−52).[12] According to Wood (1994, 246), as many as one-third of all pregnancies end in fetal loss, although a sizeable proportion of these losses occur so early that they are detectable only by hormonal analysis.[13] If the proportion is in fact this high, then nonlive births were highly underreported in the Gambian project's 1992 survey, which showed 8 percent of all pregnancies resulting in nonlive births. Still, this proportion is quite similar to the levels reported in other surveys that collect fertility histories. (A nontrivial proportion of pregnancies may be absorbed in the placenta rather than expelled in miscarriage.) Although the project was not equipped for hormonal analysis, nor did it begin with any sense that nonlive births were worth collecting, more of these instances undoubtedly could have been elicited with careful probing had the importance of these data been anticipated.

Another reason why investigating mishaps poses problems lies in Western cultural understandings about these events. The Western convention of distinguishing a miscarriage from a stillbirth reveals three cultural emphases: it is seen as a temporal division, it focuses attention on the fetus, and it indexes (roughly) the viability of the fetus outside the womb. Gambian understandings, however, emphasize the mother's experience of the event and its health implications for her. In local understandings, a miscarriage (commonly translated into local English as an "abortion") refers to the loss of a pregnancy before the fetus becomes a discrete entity that is clearly separate from the mother. This point occurs some time early on, before it has a recognizable human shape; a pregnancy lost after this point is translated as "stillbirth." In some instances, a baby who lived for a short time might be reported later as a stillbirth (see also Ross's descriptions of births to poor women in London around the turn of the century, 1993, 94). Yet restricting the analysis to miscarriages and stillbirths omits another group that local people see as having important similarities: young children who died,

11. See Wood (1994, 240) on the complexities that developments in neonatology have posed for this distinction.

12. These apparent effects, however, may be complicated in low-fertility populations by the fact that women who are continuing to try to have children at older ages tend to be those with a history of losses (Santow and Bracher 1989).

13. According to Townsend and McElroy (1992, 23), fertility may be affected by infections and parasitic diseases such as tuberculosis, Chagas' disease, and malaria, which are not sexually transmitted. Malaria, for example, affects reproductive health at each stage, from increased likelihood of miscarriage and stillbirth to increased risk of malarial symptoms in the postpartum period.

particularly, like Kaddy Seesay's last child, before weaning. These are imperfect terms. "Reproductive mishap" is unconventional, and "nonlive birth" does not always involve a birth as we typically understand it. But for my purposes, they draw attention to two key cultural concerns: the failure of a pregnancy to add a child to the compound and the possibility of adverse medical consequences for the mother.[14]

Issues of quantity pose even greater difficulties. The demographic notion of "parity" generally includes only live births, and it counts twins as two. The closest approximations in the medical field of obstetrics would be the terms *para* and *gravida,* in which nonlive births are included in pregnancy counts but twins (whether live or nonlive at birth) count as one. Rural Gambian women have a system of counting that is commensurate with these but not quite the same. They distinguish between fetuses that were live or nonlive at pregnancy termination, but foremost in their minds is the total number of fetuses born, whether as single or multiple births. There is no English equivalent at all, either in demography or medicine, for this emphasis. Since most of the study's surveys were set up before this distinction was recognized, the assumption in the surveys was that the response would refer to the number of times a woman had been pregnant, whereas the woman herself may have been referring to the number of fetuses she believed she had borne. The problems that these confusions entail for calculating numbers of children, births, or fetuses, not to mention intervals between these events, I do not need to elaborate. The best I can do is take the data at face value. Let us look, then, at some of the relations between mishap events and women's subsequent use of contraceptives.

Taking the 1,756 women under age forty-five in the 1992 survey whose most recent pregnancy had ended after 1987 (within the previous four or more years), figure 5.2 displays patterns of contraception according to the status of the woman's most recent pregnancy: a child currently breastfeeding, weaned, or dead, or a nonlive birth. The results are displayed in histogram format to convey a sense of how tiny the numbers are of women who reported a mishap, compared to women who reported other outcomes.

Among the large group of breastfeeding women, slightly less than 6 percent were using Western contraception; the same is true for those using traditional methods (that is, juju or herbs). This pattern was the only one that might be admissible under the original understanding of child spacing: using contraceptives during breastfeeding to avoid a pregnancy that is too

14. For noteworthy anthropological treatments of pregnancy loss, see the contributions to Cecil 1996.

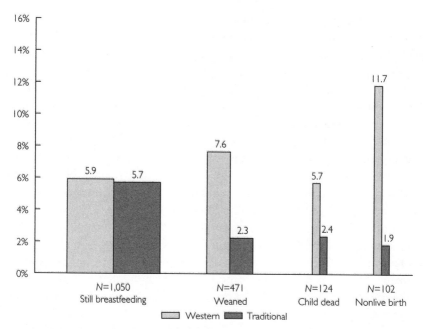

Fig. 5.2 Women under forty-five using contraception after 1988–92 pregnancy outcomes

Source: 1992 survey.

early for the health of the breastfeeding child. And yet, Western contraceptive use among the other groups was actually higher. Among women with weaned children, 7.6 percent were using contraceptives even though their previous child was weaned: probably those who, as shown in the quotations from the monthly rounds, were "tired" and wanted to "rest" past the point when the child was weaned. The set of bars of central interest, however, is the small set on the right. This set reveals that the proportion of women using some form of contraception in the wake of a nonlive birth (nearly 14 percent altogether) was greater than that for any other group.[15]

The methods these women are using is even more telling. Although half of the users who were breastfeeding were using traditional contraceptives and half Western, the bars on the right show that very few of those using contraception after a mishap were relying on half-way measures such as

15. Given the emphasis on the tight time frames in which contraceptive activity usually occurs, the time span that figure 5.2 shows is somewhat longer than the "normal" childbearing sequence of breastfeeding and weaning. Yet even with sequences that start as late as 1990, nonlive birth remains consistently the best postpartum predictor of contraceptive use, never descending below 11 percent.

juju. Like Kaddy Seesay, whose case introduced the book, they were using strong, "effective" contraceptives: pills or Depo Provera.[16] The proportion of Western contraceptive users among women whose most recent pregnancy ended in nonlive birth, almost 12 percent, exceeds that of any other outcome and is twice that of women breastfeeding. Even young women, who otherwise avoid Western contraceptives, use them after mishaps. There is a telling difference as well in contraceptive use between women in the two types of mishap situations: women whose child died versus those who suffered a nonlive birth. The proportion of women using Western contraception after a nonlive birth is considerably larger, although the mean ages of women in the two groups are almost the same (32.0 years for a child death and 32.4 years for a nonlive birth). Although the use of strong contraceptives toward the end of reproductive life in order to stretch out the spaces between children is a pattern that fertility transition watchers might seize upon—older women seem to be stopping because they have had as many children as they desire—there is a critical distinction to make here. Limiting pregnancies or even births, as noted above, is not necessarily the same thing as limiting children.

Figure 5.3, focusing on nonlive births, examines the phenomenon of post-mishap contraceptive use from another angle. Removing all constraints of age and time since prior pregnancy termination, it shows that at each parity, the percentage of women with at least one completed pregnancy ($N = 2,466$) who are using Western contraceptives is consistently higher among those who have had one or more nonlive births than for those who had only live births. Although separated at the early parities by less than one percentage point, the disparity rises to 6 percent among those with more than ten pregnancies.

Figure 5.4, also freed of age and time constraints, is equally striking. It includes only women who have had two or more pregnancies but whose youngest is still alive. It suggests that whether these outcomes occurred recently or in the distant past, the effects of a nonlive birth reverberate throughout reproductive life. Among low-parity women, those whose youngest child is still alive are more likely to be using a Western contraceptive if they had only live births than if they had one or more nonlive births.

16. In this group were three cases of women who reported they were sterilized. There is no way to tell from these data when or why the three cases of sterilization occurred, although two instances occurred after a nonlive birth and the third after a live birth. Some women may become sterilized voluntarily after the birth; others may become so as a result of a life-saving measure during an obstetric emergency. If these cases are removed, the number of women using Western contraceptives after a nonlive birth (10 percent) is still higher than any other outcome.

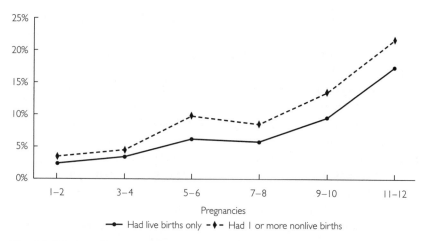

Fig. 5.3 Women of various parities using Western contraceptives by live/nonlive birth experience

Source: North Bank, 1992.

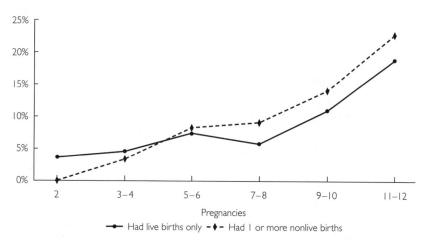

Fig. 5.4 Western contraceptive users with previous child still alive, by prior nonlive birth experience

Source: North Bank, 1992.

Around parities four and five, however, the pattern shifts decisively, and women react more visibly by using contraception. Even though women with one or more nonlive births are likely to have fewer surviving children than those whose fetuses were all born alive, women with any nonlive births are more likely to be using Western contraceptives than those with only live births.[17] Like the previous figure, this one suggests that the effects of nonlive births on contraceptive use operate with increasing intensity as parity rises. The idea of contraceptives simply as implements of child spacing is now eroding markedly.

Although the internal patterns in these data are both clear and consistent, the actual number of women who reported that their most recent pregnancy ended in mishap is very small. Of the 2,980 women in the 1992 survey, only twenty-five women, or 0.8 percent, of the 1,823 whose most recent pregnancies had ended within the prior four years (the basis of fig. 5.2) were using some form of contraception, usually Western. Further, although the results lie in the expected direction, logistic regression analysis reveals no significant differences in the type of contraceptive use between women who had mishaps or live births once we control for the effects of other factors such as age and number of pregnancies. Still, the logical anomaly remains. If contraceptives are being used simply for child spacing, to ensure an adequate period of breastfeeding before weaning, then there is no reason why they should be used after a reproductive mishap.[18] Because of the importance of these most unlikely cases, table 5.2 lists some of the details for women younger than forty-five.

Conventional fertility analysis, assuming contraceptives to be methods for limiting child numbers, might suggest that women such as these who are using Western contraceptives had reached the number of children they wanted and were trying to stop childbearing. As table 5.2 shows, though, very few of these mishap sufferers had particularly successful fertility records. Of their 149 collective pregnancies, only 53 percent had resulted in a living child, far fewer than the 92 percent reported for the population as a whole. Only six of these women had more than four surviving children—

---

17. Women with problematic fertility records also take greater contraceptive precautions while breastfeeding. Among the 902 women in the 1992 North Bank survey whose previous pregnancy resulted in a weaned child (excluding cases of less than six and more than forty-eight months at reported weaning), those with a low ratio (75 percent or less) of all pregnancies surviving reported breastfeeding the most recent child longer than did those with a high ratio (24.0 months versus 24.7 months, respectively; $p = .05$). As for the 1,077 women still breastfeeding, those with low ratios of surviving children were using Western contraceptives, as opposed to no contraception or traditional contraception, more often than those with high child survivorship: 7.5 versus 5.0 ($p < .1$). Similar findings occur in the 1990 Nigerian DHS, which included a country-specific variable on the question of health. When asked why they are using a method to avoid pregnancy, sixty-two women said they were using a method because of health. Of these, all seven of those who said their previous child was not alive were using a "modern" method, compared to 53 percent of the fifty-five women whose previous child was alive.

18. In theory, a contraceptive user who had had a nonlive birth could have been attempting to space a previous live birth, inducing an abortion in order to continue breastfeeding her previous child. However, no women in the 1992 survey whose previous pregnancy resulted in an unweaned living child were using contraception after a reported mishap.

Table 5.2 Women under forty-five using any form of contraception

		Previous Pregnancy				All Pregnancies			
Age	Parity	Outcome	YOB	Age at death	Present contraceptive	NLVBS	DTHS	SURV	PCFNA
18	1	liv	1990	14 mos.	pills	0	1	0	1
19	2	misc	1991		pills/IUD	2	0	0	2
20	3	misc	1992		abstinence	2	0	1	1
22	2	liv	1990	19 mos.	pills	0	1	1	1
23	4	liv	1989	2 yrs.	traditional	0	1	3	1
24	2	misc	1991		pills	1	0	1	1
25	5	misc	1992		pills	1	1	3	1
25	5	stbth	1990		DP	2	2	1	4
28	5	liv	1991	6 mos.	pills	1	2	2	1
28	3	liv	1990	14 mos.	traditional	0	1	2	1
29	5	stbth	1991		DP	1	1	3	1
30	4	liv	1991	1 yr.	abstinence	0	2	2	2
30	5	misc	1988		sterilization	1	0	4	1
34	6	misc	1990		pills	1	0	4	1
34	6	misc	1990		abstinence	3	1	2	1
34	7	liv	1990	<1 day	DP	0	4	3	2
36	5	misc	1990		DP	1	1	3	1
36	8	liv	1991	<1 day	DP	1	6	1	2
37	11	stbth	1991		sterilization	1	4	6	1
43	11	misc	1990		pills	1	4	6	1
43	10	liv	1991	<1 day	sterilization	2	1	7	3
43	8	stbth	1989		DP	1	4	3	1
43	10	liv	1990	1 mo.	DP	0	3	7	1
44	11	stbth	1991		DP	4	0	7	3

Source: 1992 survey.

Note: YOB: year of birth; NLVBS: number of nonlive births; DTHS: number of child deaths; SURV: number of surviving children; PCFNA: prior consecutive fetuses not alive.

"Age at death" applies to live births only.

five of these individuals being age forty or older.[19] And of the twenty-three
women with two or more pregnancies, seventeen had lost at least one other
pregnancy besides the most recent. Yet even among these most unlikely users
of contraception, a number stand out:

> the seven women with two or more immediately preceding pregnancies
> not resulting in a live birth, six of whom were using a Western, rather
> than a traditional, contraceptive;
> one of the twenty-five-year-olds, using Depo Provera, who had lost her
> four prior pregnancies (only her first child had survived);
> a thirty-six-year-old, also on Depo Provera, with eight pregnancies, seven
> of which had not resulted in living children, including the previous
> two;
> the two youngest women, ages eighteen and nineteen, both with no sur-
> viving children. The nineteen-year-old was only one of nine women
> in the whole survey using two Western contraceptives simultaneously.
> She was also the only woman in the survey using an IUD.

Although some of the older women with high numbers of pregnancy
losses command the most immediate attention, the most unexpected may
be the youngest two, who were among only three teenagers in the entire survey, which included 589 women below age twenty who were using Western
contraceptives;[20] the third was breastfeeding a baby.

Women who were trying to have a child and failed should be most anxious and the last ones to be using any contraceptives at all, especially very
effective ones. Such cases were among the best evidence that some other
domain of common sense besides that of time or child numbers was guiding decisions to delay a new pregnancy.

Similar oddities of contraception after reproductive mishaps appeared
in the other data sources besides the 1992 baseline survey: the monthly
rounds, a smaller version of the 1992 survey (including only women in the
rounds), and the case material on women who were not from the study area.
None of these sources had been collected with the possibility of such pat-

19. Of the ten sterilized women in the entire sample whose previous pregnancies had ended
within the past four years, two pregnancies had resulted in nonlive births and a third in a child who
later died. Two of these children died subsequently.

20. It is possible that the nonlive births these young women reported were actually induced abortions, in which case their subsequent contraceptive use might imply that they were simply trying, as
many urban teens do, to delay childbearing. Both teenagers, however, were married, a fact that dimin-
ishes the abortion possibility but does not eliminate it. They may, for example, have been trying to feign
sterility in order to extricate themselves from an older husband they had been forced to marry.

terns in view, nor did the patterns themselves come to light until most of the data collection was finished. Especially when the commentaries in the monthly rounds could be examined in Epi Info alongside the numerically coded responses, the anomalies of post-mishap contraception cases, male reactions to contraceptive use, incongruous declarations of reproductivity, and so on began to raise serious doubts about the child spacing framework itself.

Why Focus on Anomalies Such as These?

Both Western contraceptive use and reproductive mishaps represent statistical oddities, in both The Gambia and in Africa as a whole. Most women are not using Western contraceptives, and most pregnancies do not end in mishap. Why, then, give such intense attention to such anomalies as the even tinier intersection between these two sets? The reason is that they so profoundly contradict common sense. Not only natural fertility began to come under question but also Western notions of the proper units of fertility analysis: children, live births, and time.

The field of demography has taken the key fertility question, especially in developing countries, to be: How many children are women having, especially surviving children? What would seem to make no sense at all, then, are remarks like those of thirty-two-year-old Oumie Dibba. Oumie reported five pregnancies. One resulted in a nonlive birth, and one child died, leaving her with three living children: two boys and one girl. Reporting that she was nearing the end of reproduction, "because of many pregnancies and too much hard work," Oumie declared that she was nonetheless "tied" to the compound. That is, she felt secure and was committed to its future welfare: "The number of children I have borne in this compound makes me feel 'tied.' I have 5 children with this husband: 2 died and 3 are alive. . . . I'm more tied than my co-wife because she has only two children and I have 5" (R. 13).

This response would seem to imply that Oumie had five children, when in fact she had five pregnancies but was left with only three children. Had I been in the field when the response came in—and here is another instance of the odd advantage of being absent—I would likely have summoned the surveyor who wrote it down, lectured her on the need for accuracy, and dispatched her back to the field to resolve the numerical inconsistencies. It is far more difficult to take the quotation seriously. Doing so raises a critical question: are live births the sole units of reproductive currency? If not, then, what *are* people counting?

If fertility had never been questioned as the numerator in my fertility expression, anomalies in the Gambian material were beginning to cast doubt on something even more fundamental: the notion of age itself. Anthropology turns on the conviction that how people explain their lives is the starting point of any meaningful understanding. Still, most of us would find it hard to comprehend why breastfeeding women would assert they were too old to have another child. Nor is it clear why there should be such a paucity of interest in the ticking of the menopause clock in this high-fertility population. But when we confront such an egregious implausibility as the use of contraceptives among subfertile women who have suffered reproductive mishaps, the whole configuration sits uneasily indeed. Great leaps of the imagination seemed necessary to explain why women like Kaddy Seesay should be letting time, their most precious resource, slip away as they returned for dose after dose of Depo Provera. Evidence of slippage began to emerge: at first imperceptibly, and then starkly and unavoidably.

The key to handling these puzzles, and to perceiving the larger patterns at which they hint, lies in the power of the counterintuitive logic itself. Rather than seeing these results, as striking as they are, as statistical "proof" of anything—which many of them are not—we should see them instead as so aberrant from our own common sense that almost any case should give us pause. *No one* in this population should be using Western contraceptives when their previous pregnancy did not result in a living child. Time must be pressing hard on these women if they are to produce more children. The logic of their actions is so powerfully contrary to our common sense that contraception in *greater* proportions among women who suffered multiple mishaps and last-pregnancy mishaps than among women with other outcomes, and with such consistency across such diverse data sets, should stop us in our tracks.

The principal puzzles thus began to cluster not at the beginning of reproduction but the end. People who want all the children God might give them should be calculating closely the likely approach of this end, trying to squeeze into their final reproductive years as many children as they possibly could. Yet if the end of reproduction is bounded by time, then many of their reproductive actions made no sense at all. If women like Kaddy Seesay are like Bourdieu's ball player (1990, 82), who, in passing the ball to a teammate, takes aim at some imagined position and not the present one, what is the logic of the practice in which they are engaged?

The issue at stake is nothing less than how we have come to relate time to senescence. Time has become so embedded in our cultural ideas of physical development and decline that its passage is treated as if it had an intrinsic capacity to cause life changes, and at a uniform pace among all like entities. We not only assume that time acts on the body in a linear manner; we also seem to assume, in our statistical practices, which often cast "independent" variables as causal, that time causes senescence.

To be sure, one might well counter that it is not time that leads to the growth or demise of an organism but metabolic processes that occur at variant paces among individuals. And our science does offer some analytical models that circumvent the shortcomings of chronological descriptions of reproduction. Every relevant academic field seems to have them. A notable example is gerontology, which has drawn attention to the pliable and episodic, rather than linear, character of aging (see appendix B) and to the fact that the process of deterioration that we usually call "aging" can be affected by life events (for example, Rowe and Kahn 1997). Such realizations, however, have seldom been taken up outside the narrow field of aging, least of all in works on reproduction. And yet the possibility that childbearing, as a major life event, can accelerate the pace of aging, a possibility of obvious significance for high-fertility societies, has not been taken up at all in gerontology. Even in that field, as I noted in chapter 2, the greatest research interest by far lies in genetics, a field in which the weight of research posits a life course trajectory that is guided by endogenous forces.

Another notable exception to the view of chronologically based models of reproduction is closer to the field of fertility studies. This is the study of what has been termed "maternal depletion syndrome," in which the effects of past reproductive stresses result in an unrepleted loss of soft tissue and energetic reserves after closely spaced births (for example, Jelliffe and Maddocks 1964; Prentice et al. 1981; Tracer 1991). Usually implicated is some combination of lactational demand, sickness, and strenuous work. Such studies, however, are rarely concerned with fertility intentionalities that may guide behavior. Further, the notion of maternal depletion refers almost exclusively to the attrition of energy reserves during pregnancy and lactation, omitting consideration of other bodily elements that might be necessary to reproduction. Studies of maternal depletion also tend to omit non-live births as units of analysis, a bias that parallels the tendency to view reproduction through the lens of increase of a population. Finally, although the model focuses on the cumulative effects of a long-term trajectory of depleting events, it is not clear how variation in the pace and severity of depleting episodes may affect the character or the pacing or the end of reproduction. Nor is it clear what the end itself consists of, whether complete depletion of reserves, menopause, or death. All this remains secondary in the model. As I emphasized in chapter 4, processes such as these can be located in and traced through time, but none are caused by time.

The harder we pursue the logic of time into our common sense about the life course and the birth interval, the more time falls apart and the more we come to suspect that we have fallen prey to some highly deceptive commensurabilities in the logics.

A Fieldwork Story

Many contemporary anthropologists would argue that instead of finding structure and order in the field, observers encounter irresolvable situations of uncertainty, relativity, and indeterminacy. Yet despite the discrepancies in visions of reality that a field situation can present, anthropological research usually proceeds on the assumption that people have reasons for doing things that make some sort of existential sense, even if we do not go so far as to resurrect mechanical explanations to acknowledge this. Some identifiable patterns will emerge as the material is examined. In my case, however, the chaos seemed to increase as the project went on. People's actions seemed greatly at odds with what my culture would dictate as the way to behave if one wanted to maximize fertility. People's explanations of fertility-relevant actions seemed to make sense for a short time. Pressing further on the logic always seemed to bring up more incongruities than had been solved, and each could, in turn, be pursued for short, unsatisfying distances. In this situation of growing bafflement and frustration, I found myself narrowing the field down to a few key incongruities and looking for solutions to them that might shed new light on the whole picture. These incongruities were the puzzles surrounding contraceptive use with respect to men and mishaps and the odd reports of being old by women who had no apparent grounds for saying so.

We researchers like to tell ourselves that we pursue evidence in a systematic, logical sequence to derive a conclusion. In truth, however, we often resort to a puzzle-solving mode, and all pretense to systematicity evaporates. Taking its place is a no-holds-barred chase down myriad pathways to find the solution, through whatever shortcuts we can devise, through whatever solutions might work. We fling out odd questions, create ad hoc mini-surveys, draw diagrams with people, press logics to their absurd extremes. We take several pieces of the puzzle at once, strip them from their context, and sort and re-sort them, working both forward and backward. Such flagrant efforts to solve a puzzle by working backward from a hypothesized end point are highly risky, of course. It is quite possible to "discover" a false conclusion and work backwards to a false set of propositions that seem to support it. Trying to work backwards in puzzle solving is also awkward professionally. If we succeed, we must explain the results to our colleagues in terms that make the methods sound academically legitimate. When a significant proportion of these colleagues belong to the scientific community, as was the case in my situation, there is further pressure to explain the results in the discourse of logico-deductive hypothesis-testing: as if one really did arrive at the conclusion in a careful, step-by-step manner by rejecting a logical sequence of null hypotheses. The irony is that such pressures distort the ideal of discovery to which scientific epistemology aspires.

Solving a puzzle is all the more difficult if the ground on which one has been relying begins to sink. In this case, the ground (that is, its steadiest base) was time. Without time to rely on, our culture gives us little guidance for gauging how much reproductivity remains to a woman, unless we are high-technology infertility specialists. Even then, age is the first query we would put to a new patient. Solving a puzzle is doubly difficult if the original research question gradually evaporates and we no longer know what the question is to which such enigmatic answers are beginning to appear. Indeed, the question became increasingly opaque to me as the project went on. There were, in sum, a flood of disorienting relativities.

It would be gratifying to say that I independently found the solution to the puzzle. But credit is due as well to Fatoumatta Banja, who, under the pressure of relentless questioning from me, had begun to make a project out of studying me. Much as I was trying to read through her answers, she began to try to read through my questions. On my trip to The Gambia in March 1994, things came to a head. Fatou declared, after a long morning of interrogation, that she was going to bring me a fertility survey "as an African woman might write it." That evening we sat down in my flat with the single piece of paper she brought, a revised version of which I display in chapter 8. In trying to grasp the meaning of her chart, I finally realized that there was something very wrong with how I had been imagining reproduction to work.

It was a transformative evening. As I finally began to understand what people had been trying to tell me in conversations and in survey responses, whether coded verbally or numerically, all anchor ropes to comfortable absolutes were cut loose. I remember staring down repeatedly at the leg of the table. It sat glued firmly in place, at a precise right angle and in steady contact with the floor. My sense of orientation, however, was the opposite of these things. It was unglued, tilting, floating. I was reeling in the most intense culture shock I have ever experienced, and all of this after more than twenty years of submersion in field research, reading, and teaching on Africa. By the time Fatou finally managed to convey to me the thrust of her survey, a view not of children over time but of contingency and the cumulative effects of body resource expenditure in a moral universe of marriage, a two-dimensional black and white landscape had suddenly sprouted a full-color third dimension. During the rest of that trip, every conceivable anthropological and demographic exoticum in my head—polygyny, Depo Provera injections, maternal depletion, mother's brother's daughter's marriage, secret society masks from Sierra Leone, terminal abstinence, ancestors, bridewealth, widow inheritance—was battling with the others for a turn to race through this new filter. One by one, all understandings were ripped up and began to be hammered into a very different template.

The question that had finally come to the surface was the nature of the course of life itself. People around me, I finally realized, had an entirely different view not only of reproductivity but of the life course. The most striking fact about this experience, however, was that this question was not one that the original research had addressed. Not only that: it was a question I did not even know could be posed. Once I began to grasp the principles on which the new perspective rested, conversations in the field flowed far more easily. Back in Evanston in the months that followed, I found myself combing back through all the essays and numbers. I was drawn especially to the surveys' commentaries, which were suddenly coming into remarkable alignment with the numbers, unveiling patterns that had been invisible before. I studied every one of the thousands of responses that had been collected, reading them all with a new eye, with far fewer disruptions in flow than I had experienced before. When I did encounter a disruption, I tried (on return visits or in phone calls) to compose the questions about it as neutrally as possible, but with an idea in mind of what the answer should be if the new model were the one at play. Sometimes I was right; sometimes I was not, and I was corrected. The times I was not right were the most significant, for I was inevitably corrected in ways that were more consonant with the new perspective than the way I had guessed.

The pieces of the framework that Fatou managed to convey to me that evening, together with the pieces that other Gambians elaborated later, seemed at first to breach almost all demographic common sense. Yet both the clarity of the patterns and their consistency through a range and richness of data sources (not only from The Gambia but from elsewhere in Africa and, in fact, from other times and places) suggested that this explanatory framework had far more depth and reach than the one in which I had been socialized. It began with many of the same elements that were visible in my layman's collection of Western scientific fertility knowledge, though it added some new ones as well. But the total vision of reproduction and the life course that I thought I understood now appeared to have been a deceptive convergence with a wider reality. This explains why it had been possible to follow women's descriptions of reproduction and age for a few steps in every direction but why these facts as well as the rationales underlying them always seemed to fall apart when their logic was pressed.

Some of the empirical elements of the new framework I found difficult to accept. I still do. But many others are aligned, albeit through different concepts and emphases, with versions of my own culture's past science, most of which I only learned about later, over months of reading old medical texts.

CHAPTER 6

Realizing a Reproductive Endowment in a Contingent Body

Let me recount briefly how I believe most of us in the West, scientists and laypeople alike, think about reproduction and, if these things are so, then the challenges that the Gambian data pose to our logic.

The ability to conceive (fecundity) is to us the essence of fertility. We see reproduction as hinging on the production and fusion of an egg and a sperm and the chromosomes they contain, and on their journey down the fallopian tube to become implanted in the uterus. Highly salient as well in our descriptions are glands such as the pituitary and the chemicals they secrete—estrogen, progestin, progesterone, follicle stimulating hormone, luteinizing hormone, prolactin, androgen, and so on—which set these objects into motion or create the appropriate environment for them to develop.[1] Cross-cutting this story of tiny objects and chemicals is time. Whether we are trying to avoid conception or achieve it, we pay minute attention to time, which we regard as the index of the

---

1. The fact that we view reproduction as hinging on the conception of a microscopic entity is clear from this definition of human fertility in the *Encyclopaedia Britannica Online* (http://www.eb.com, accessed 22 August 2000): "the ability . . . of a human couple to conceive and reproduce. Fertility refers to the ability to become pregnant through normal sexual activity, and infertility is defined as the failure to conceive after one year of regular intercourse without contraception."

ability to reproduce. At a micro level is the timing of ovulation and of intercourse. At a higher level is a woman's age as the best index of both her ability to reproduce and the costs of "assisting" this ability to continue. When asked, therefore, how many children a particular woman might have in a society that valued high fertility (assuming single child outcomes and a full nine months for each pregnancy), we would likely do the following. We would divide the total amount of time we thought she could conceive (usually from menarche to menopause) by the average length of a birth interval from the start of one pregnancy to the start of the next. The use of contraception would play directly into this calculus. Since we see fertility as bounded by the temporal limits in which a woman can conceive, the proportion of fecund time in a woman's life course that contraception would block off would be a key determinant of how many children she would have.

These tenets (conveyed through a bit of anthropological distancing)[2] have a satisfying coherence, and they are based on countless acts of laboratory experimentation and personal observation. Yet if they are correct, why should rural Gambians, in their techniques of contraception, be behaving in ways that are so at odds with them? By now, the puzzles are inescapable. Among them are women's frequent efforts, despite their high fertility goals, to "rest" after weaning a child, to use contraception after reproductive mishaps, and to stop childbearing before menopause. In addition, women display almost no cultural interest in menopause or in their age, and they sometimes seem to count nonlive births as children. The enigmas surrounding men are equally perplexing. Men seem unaccountably opposed to contraceptive use, when common sense would suggest that their wives' efforts to avoid a new pregnancy while finishing the breastfeeding of a previous child would be in the men's best interests, since it would result in more surviving children.

It would be easy to dismiss these anomalies as "noise." But subsequent efforts that night with Fatou, as well as months of subsequent discussions with her and with other Gambians, to unravel the cultural logic embedded in both the commentaries and the numbers began to reveal the contours of a very different vision of fertility. This vision is commensurate—aligned at certain points—with what I just sketched. In overall shape and thrust, however, it is radically different. Taking up some of the puzzles that began to

---

2. The use of "Nacirema," in its backward spelling, was the famous device that Horace Miner used to exoticize American culture. For a similar telling of the story of reproduction in Western science from the perspective of a feminist critique, see Martin 1991.

emerge in chapter 4, on breastfeeding and the transition to weaning, and in chapter 5 on postpartum "rests," in this chapter I re-explain fertility. I show that the resolution to the anomalies that have been brought to light is found not in a time-bounded model of numbers of births or children. Nor is it to be found in forces that work their effects independent of human action. It is found instead in a vision of a divinely allocated reproductive endowment that is realized, or "spent," in a time-neutral "contingency" decrement of bodily reserves. Reproduction in this view is not limited by time but by the expenditure of a fixed sum. Under the conditions that women in rural Gambia experience, attempting to force the notion of a highly contingent reproductive capacity into a fixed temporal frame would make no sense. This alternate framework is not derived from the relative safety and predictability of the low-fertility West. It is derived instead from a premise of extraordinary life risks as the bodily costs of reproduction accumulate. As a phenomenological position would lead us to expect, visions of multiple temporalities and tolls emerge. In this chapter, on reproduction, and the next, on aging, I devote special attention to physical details because they set the stage for the cultural associations in chapter 8 that link a woman's fertility record and her bodily state to morality.

The more general question I address in this chapter is how such disparate forces of divine will, individual action, and a shaping social context function in combination. Particularly noteworthy are the depiction of reproduction and aging as highly related processes and the possibility that both of these processes can be managed.

Elements of Contingency

The vision of female reproductivity that rural Gambians describe identifies four key components: endowment, muscles, strength, and blood. They are set along several axes. Among the most important are fixity versus malleability, transparency versus impenetrability, permanence versus transience, and degree to which the elements can be replenished.

Reproductive Endowment

The local reproductive framework in rural Gambia departs in two significant ways from Western depictions. First, its most fundamental unit of fertility calculation is neither a live birth nor a surviving child but a fetus (*harijeo*) or a "child potential," of which every woman is considered to have a certain number: a *hapo*. *Hapo* literally refers to an "amount" or a "number" of anything, from mangoes to kilograms of rice. When applied to fertility, however, it refers specifically to what might be called a divine "endowment," a number of potential fetuses that God has bestowed upon a woman that she may bear throughout her life.[3] This endowment she is expected to expend on behalf of her husband and his family. Each fetus, whether it terminates in the form of a single child, as one of a pair of twins, or as a miscarriage, represents one entity of this fixed endowment. A twenty-four-year-old woman expressed the conviction as follows: "The number of children that everyone will have since when [God] created us and whatever the case may be, everyone will get that number." Once this endowment is finished, reproduction is finished, regardless of her age. Because reproduction is not limited by time, a woman with an endowment of nine fetuses who has had her pregnancies in close succession will finish childbearing before a woman with the same nine fetuses but longer birth spaces. As much as she tries, she will have no more. Some women, typically urbanites and foreigners, state flatly that they want no more pregnancies and may try to stop having them, irrespective of what they might imagine their hapo to be. But although everyone knows that people in such situations are under pressure, efforts to avoid bearing the child potentials with which one is endowed constitute a mild sacrilege of God's will.

There is no way to predict how many children a woman will have. Some people speculate that a large or strong body structure is a mark of more fertility potential. But physical structure is meaningless without a preordained number of fetuses, and it is impossible to know from visual inspection how large a woman's endowment is until it is finished. Some women have large endowments; some have very small ones. A few tragic women have none at all. Any link to physical attributes is incidental. The hapo is also unrelated to character. A congenial woman can have no fetus potentials; a spiteful

---

3. There are several related referents for this number of child potentials. Among them are a "seed" *(turo)* or a "placenta" *(nǎǎyoo)*, "something that comes with"; the implication is that when a child emerges, along with the placenta in which it grew, that particular potential is finished. The idea of a preordained endowment also appears in reports of multiple regions of the subcontinent. Writing about Benin, Sargent (1982, 38) notes that women say they have a certain limited number of eggs, each of which becomes a child when a man's substance enters it. (Sara Randall and Thomas LeGrand, pers. comm., report the same among the Wolof people of Senegal.) According to Adam Thiam (pers. comm.), the Bambara of Mali express reproductive potential in the metaphor of "placentas." And Johanne Sundby (pers. comm.) reports that in Zimbabwe women say that they are born with a certain number of "lumps" inside them that determine how many children they can have. That number can be reduced by birth control but cannot be increased. From Kenya, Susan Watkins (1994 field notes) reports similar ideas. On the idea of a predestined number of children, see Pearce 1995, 202. Observations of a fixed-sum reproductive capacity are seen as well in descriptions of herding animals. According to Evans-Pritchard (1940, 34), the Nuer observed that if a cow had no serious illnesses (and note the contingency element of this statement) it could bear about eight calves.

gossip can have many. Divine will is never transparent. What everyone does know is that although a woman cannot end up with any more surviving children than her God-given endowment, she can certainly end up with fewer. If she is lucky, all of her fetuses will be born as living children and survive to maturity. But this is not the end of the story. More likely, one or more of these child potentials will be lost in nonlive births or in child deaths. Still others may not be born at all. Thus, a woman's family elders or in-laws may pray for God's blessings, asking him to bestow many children on her, a practice recorded in innumerable ethnographies of the subcontinent. But they are not asking God to increase her total endowment. This would be presumptuous if not blasphemous. Instead, they are asking God to allow each of her fetuses to become a child who survives.

Taken together, these facts suggest an answer to the puzzle raised earlier: why so many women are reluctant to give a numerical response to the question of how many children they want. The question is probably being understood as a query about the hapo. To such a question there can be no meaningful response.

Bodily Resources and Reproductive Senescence

People in the West would likely see the ex post facto attribution of numbers of potential fetuses to divine will as an immense circularity. Certainly this is something that almost no Western scientist would accept. But it would be a mistake to dismiss the entire framework as superstition before asking how, precisely, God's will is said to be enacted. Involved are concrete anatomical and physiological changes that are immediately visible to the astute eye.

Whereas Western society gauges the limits of reproduction by the amount of time that likely remains in which conception can occur, people in rural Gambia focus on a woman's declining bodily capacity to carry a child to term and give birth. This capacity they gauge by the cumulative toll that wearing life events have taken on her bodily resources. Resilience is lost over a series of saltatory events that can have sharp transformative effects. The most prominent index of this decline is not how many children she has had. Nor is it live births or even surviving children. It is instead the number of fetuses she has borne.

Several key cultural phrases denote the stages of prenatal existence and growth. A *yɛlokunturo* (literally, "thick blood") is an entity that is on the way to being a fetus but is not yet recognized as such. It may advance further to become a fetus, or it may be discharged as an ambiguous mass. Sometimes, as I explained in chapter 3, a woman may try to effect such a discharge, especially if she has a young breastfeeding baby. At the next stage is a harijeo, an actual fetus that, if terminated too soon, would mark a clear miscarriage or abortion. Twins, in each case, count separately. Thus, a twin pregnancy would involve two harijeos. Up to this point a pregnancy would be unrecognizable to the outside world. But the next stage, *kono mɛrɛŋɔ* ("small stomach"), a pregnancy is plainly visible, and a too-soon termination would result in a stillbirth, which would be buried as a child. Only when the fetus gets to the stage of harijeo is it considered to comprise one part of the hapo.

In the scheme rural Gambians describe, pregnancy terminations are not discrete events of uniform or even minor health impact, as they tend to be depicted in Western writings, both demographic and popular. They are instead events that damage the body and contribute to the cumulative "aging" effect. Women are exceedingly attuned to these losses, or "costs," although their vocabularies and frameworks of understanding do not always coincide with those of Western science. The number of God-given fetuses a woman will bear as miscarriages, sickly infants, or children who can survive and prosper depends on her eroding bodily capacity to bear a child. (Appendix A, examining several domains of Western scientific scholarship, finds support for many of the precepts this chapter describes, although the configuration of elements described here is different.)[4] This means that the "normal" female life course trajectory is highly contingent on external events. It does not proceed autonomously or at a linear pace that is independent of other life events, as the process tends to be portrayed in the West.

Highly salient in women's descriptions of this process of bodily expenditure, or "finishing," of reproductive resources (as they more literally translate it) are the physical elements needed to conduct reproductive life: muscles, strength, and blood.

Muscles: Women express their capacity to reproduce in terms of "muscles" or "sinews," which they "cut" or "lose irreversibly" *(kuntu)* over successive pregnancy terminations.[5] The term *muscles*, a metaphor, is the most

---

4. The thesis that depleted bodily resources, rather than time, are the limit to fertility in high-fertility populations is highly consistent through a wide range of evidence. Parallels to the Gambian materials are found in ethnographies and in first-hand accounts from many other times and places, from historical Europe to contemporary North India, New Guinea, and Egypt. As for Africa, anthropological works suggest that a theory of contingency that governs fertility and the life course deeply permeates not only domains of social and ritual life but also literature (e.g., Emecheta 1979, 32, 213). Demographic evidence using DHS data on sub-Saharan Africa emerges in Lockwood 1996. Other evidence emerges from Blanc et al. (1996, 39) on Uganda, Watkins (field notes, 1994) on rural Kenya, and Eloundou-Enyegue (pers. comm.) on Cameroon.

5. See Rasmussen 1997, 109.

basic physical component of reproductivity. Muscles (*faso*—literally, "sinews," which give muscles their tautness) is a concept that appears to be most analogous to the concept of muscle tension or tone in the West. Having muscles connotes resilience: an ability to withstand ordeal and trauma. Like the divinely endowed number of potential fetuses, muscles are a divinely allocated, fixed resource that operates by decrement. No amount of feeding or cultivation can augment their number or replace them once they are lost. Unlike the abstract hapo, however, muscles are concrete entities. They can be seen in animal meat and, unless covered by heavy layers of fat, discerned beneath the skin of a person. However, the principles that govern the decrement of muscles are quite different from those governing the decrement of the hapo. In a figurative way, muscles are said to be "cut" over the course of any grueling physical stress. The analogy of an elastic band is often used to describe the process in which muscles, taut and strong in a young person, grow irreversibly slack with repeated stretching and straining. Because muscles are lost with wear and not simply with the passage of time, the pace of loss on the scale of time can range from slow to precipitous, depending on the prior state of the body and the availability of resources that can be drawn upon to help meet each succeeding assault.

Both men and women have muscles that they lose over the course of their lives during (for example) farm work or lifting and carrying heavy loads. But for women, the term *faso* refers specifically to reproductive potential, and muscles are the mechanical locus of this potential. The reason is that the most taxing events by far for women's muscles are pregnancy terminations. A woman who had undergone three deliveries explained in graphic detail: "Concerning muscles reduction, after each pregnancy [it] is true, because of the severe pain and the strong muscles' contraction. During this contraction all muscles open wide in order to give enough space for the baby to pass through. [The space] from womb to the birth canal is very tight and it needs to be widened for the baby to pass."

As muscles reach their end, they become weaker and the body becomes "old" or "worn out" (*kɔtɔ*; thus, *musu kɔtɔ*: "old, finished, or worn-out woman"). *Kɔtɔ* denotes flaccid muscles[6] and wrinkled, sagging flesh. The process of reproduction results eventually in total and irreversible muscle depletion. Muscles become thin and weak with repeated pregnancies and deliveries. Childbirth is so powerfully taxing that women who have suffered

---

6. Parfait Eloundou-Enyegue (pers. comm.) reports a very similar phenomenon in Cameroon; the verb *teg* in Ewondo is used to mean to "age," "wear out" or "soften."

difficult pregnancy and childbearing ordeals are said to become old more quickly than women who have not.

Just as the divinely endowed hapo is impossible to know in advance, the number of reproductive muscles a woman has is also unknown at the outset. With muscles, however, there is room for more speculation than is the case for the hapo. Some people contend that a strong body structure or an ample lower abdomen and thigh area, combined with a tight waist, is a good predictor of a large endowment of muscles in a young woman. As is the case with the hapo, however, everyone knows of cases that have confounded expectations.

As the reader has undoubtedly sensed, we are now sliding rapidly off the rails of contemporary Western writings on reproductivity. It is growing increasingly difficult to align these understandings, however schematic they might seem, with Western ones. Gambians do speak of conception and of the difficulties women sometimes have in conceiving when, for example, the blood of different men is mixed in adultery or remarriage. But much more important to them are the subsequent phases of a pregnancy. Most starkly different are the elements of time. People understand the general principle of chronological time, even if not everyone understands Western categories of minutes and hours and so on. With respect to the age of a person or even an object such as a table or a car or a piece of clothing, however, they think less of chronological age than of its physical condition, fresh or worn.

This wholly different understanding of reproductivity than the one we are used to thinking about, given our emphasis on the ability to conceive, is further developed in the idea that although one muscle is generally cut (or lost) for each fetus expelled, the number of pregnancy terminations is not necessarily the same as the number of muscles that are cut. When a woman terminates a pregnancy by regulating her menses ("washing the stomach"), this termination is hardly noticed, and it cuts no muscles. On the other extreme, a pregnancy termination may cut more than one muscle. Some people claim that giving birth to boys, who are often larger than girls and possibly more stubborn in the delivery process, cuts two muscles. And difficult or closely spaced births, in combination with a poor diet and strenuous work, can exact harsh costs, making further childbearing dangerous and making a woman feel, look, and behave much "older" than her empirically validated years would suggest. For a woman who is strong and healthy, a normal childbirth takes a minimal toll. The "older" (that is, more worn out) she becomes, the higher the toll, and the faster the pace of the decline, if it is not checked. As with the hapo, God's will with respect to numbers of muscles cannot be known until reproduction is finished. But unlike the hapo, it certainly becomes clearer as the end approaches.

The extent of muscle loss and the pace at which this loss occurs are also functions of how well a woman's body has recuperated, with diet and rest, from previous exertions. The accumulating effects of physical stress, compounded by unrelenting work demands, sickness, and short pregnancy intervals, makes each succeeding birth tax the body disproportionately. Each pregnancy exerts a mounting toll on a woman's body's reserves of strength and blood, and she may report additive, even spiraling, effects of the wear and tear of high fertility over the reproductive life course. The less she manages to rest and recover after one birth, the more muscles she must use for the next. Although there is a commonality in the general trajectory, each case of senescence is singular and the combined effects build up a unique corporeal record.

At some point, a woman realizes that she is "spent" (*sarifo*, a word apparently derived from the Arabic word "to spend"),[7] with an understanding that childbearing is the cause of this condition.[8] She might be able to conceive and to bear another child or two, and she may do so if she has few surviving children by her current husband, whether because of child deaths, infertility, or divorce. She is fully aware, however, that the risks have risen sharply. The most extreme manifestation of muscle loss is having a "deep womb" (literally, "birth nest," an allusion to a type of bird nest that sags down like a sock). One woman described the process that leads to this state: "Having many children makes the womb get deeper because each time you get pregnant [it] is the womb that takes care of the pregnancy" (R. 6).

---

7. I am grateful to Carla Makhlouf Obermeyer for noticing this word's likely Arabic origin *(sarf)* in the notion of monetary accounting and to John Hunwick for pointing out its likely subsequent West African transformation through vowel additions. The apparent application of the term *spent* to women may reflect the woman's perspective, insofar as she believes that she has exhausted her bodily resources in reproducing . It may also, however, stem from the perspective of her husband, who sees all his bridewealth investment as now fully expended, ideally with the result of many living children. Because the English translation "spent" is such an appropriate description of how people speak of the physical condition, I continue to use it.

8. Parallels are found in archaisms reported in Western popular culture. In an article titled "Sounding Off," in the "On Language" column, Charles Harrington Elster (*New York Times Magazine*, 31 August 1997, p. 22) notes, "*Effete* comes from the Latin *effetus*, worn out by bearing children, unable to produce offspring, from *ex-*, out, and *fetus*, productive." According to Elster, the word when it first appeared in the mid-1600s was applied to animals, plants, and soil to mean "barren" or "past bearing," a set of meanings the *Oxford English Dictionary* labels as obsolete. However, some of the present-day connotations of the term are "weak," "ineffectual," "superannuated," "barren of results," "fruitless," and "unproductive." (In chapter 9 I report some parallel terms in the self-descriptions of Women's Guild members in England in the early twentieth century.)

Thinly stretched by successive fertility events, especially if births have been "rampant," a deep womb has lost the power to expel a baby.[9] Using the metaphor of a well in the arid Sahel, a woman described this wearing process and its difficulties using a vivid metaphor of subtraction: "For every birth the stomach [womb] is scooped and it eventually deepens. The older the well, the deeper it becomes and the more difficulty in drawing water from it" (R. 6).

Muscle reduction and growing old can be the subject of bantering comparisons among women, but having a deep womb is no cause for humor. Once the body has lost its ability to expel a fetus, a woman risks prolonged labor, hemorrhage, and death. A woman who has reached the end of her muscle capacity—and this often occurs by the mid-thirties—should be spared from further childbearing. It is still possible to conceive with a deep womb, but labor and delivery are now life-threatening, and women fear situations in which things can go badly wrong. "Giving birth is between life and death," a common expression, captures the anxiety of the moment. A thirty-five-year-old woman implied as much when she explained why she wanted to try to have only one more pregnancy, even though only two of her eight fetuses had survived: "I have no more strength in me because all my muscles are gone due to many pregnancies. I may have difficulty in delivery again if I get pregnant and this time if that happens it will be more serious because I have no strength that will help me to deliver and strength and power are needed in delivery" (R. 12).

Acquiring a deep womb, regardless of calendar age, usually brings a sharp end to reproduction. So grave are the dangers that a deep womb poses *before* menopause that people almost invariably try to stop childbearing before then, an act that anthropology and demography have long termed "grandmother abstinence" or "terminal abstinence." One woman even declared that childbearing should stop before grandchildren begin to arrive, to conserve remaining strength in order to help raise them. In any case, getting pregnant beyond a certain stage of physical decline is simply inappropriate, as one forty-seven-year-old sarifo woman with eleven pregnancies made clear: "Even if I happened to get a new man, he would never want me to get pregnant again for he would also be an old man like how I am old. We would feel ashamed with any more pregnancies" (R. 12). To capture the importance of this more contingent sense of reproductivity,

9. According to Johanne Sundby (pers. comm.), Zimbabwean women say that reproduction ends when the uterus "turns its back to the sperm" because it is too tired to open up anymore.

Round 12 contained a special list of questions. Among the most important were the woman's stage of muscle loss, how many pregnancies she had had, how many husbands she had had, and how many more she wanted to bear for her present husband, all of which I discuss presently.[10]

What about the kind of linearity that a chronological model of aging suggests? Is it relevant at all? The answer is yes. In this scheme, where contingency rather than time is the normative scale, there are some critical potentials for linearity in the physical life experiences of men and infertile and subfertile women. Men and women enter their early years of pre-adult life about the same time: what they call their "twelve," that is, when twelve years old. The twelve is a lively, exuberant phase of boundless energy. Men, because they do not bear children, are said to remain in their twelve as late as age thirty or so. As for women, the few who have excellent health and ample domestic support may remain in their twelve for some time, reporting little discernible muscle loss. However, most women's twelve begins to dissipate rapidly with the onset of childbearing. Since it is the physical stresses of life that "age" a person, and since labor and delivery entail far more stress than any other life experience, senescence will likely occur faster for women than for men. Women who have had many closely spaced births thus say that they show the cumulative effects of aging well before their male age peers or before female age peers who have lower fertility or a better life. Here once again, the observation of a set of relativities undermines a process that Western science has tended to depict in absolute, linear terms. In fact, the plasticity implied in the notion of the twelve itself strongly conveys this sense. The word *twelve* used as such appears to switch to a chronological scale because the referent is literally twelve years. But although the phase is named by a linear duration of years, how long it actually lasts is entirely dependent on the hardships encountered and how they are withstood.

In sum, whereas we hold that aging puts an end to reproduction, Gambian women see the causal relationship as the reverse. Because how worn out something is depends on how much use it has received, reproduction causes the body to age, a process that, in turn, would make further reproduction dangerous if not impossible.

Strength: Strength (*sɛmbo,* "power" or "energy"), the second essential component of reproductivity, is what propels the body and allows it to move. A

---

10. Even Round 12, however, could have been constructed better. Besides the question on how many pregnancies a woman had had, there should have been one on how many fetuses she had produced, to capture the complexities of twin births, which are considered to take a double bodily toll.

traditional birth attendant (TBA) captured the relation between strength and muscles with a vivid metaphor. A motor vehicle, she explained, has an engine of a certain capacity: its "muscles." But without fuel, sembo, both the engine and the vehicle must sit idle. Strength is not a concrete entity like muscles, but its quantity can be estimated by body fat (see parallel discussions in Frische and Revelle 1970). This characteristic is reflected in carvings from West Africa of female figures, their corpulence representing life, energy, and strength.[11] Like muscles, strength is lost especially during times of physical stress such as hunger season, just before the harvest. It is also lost particularly during childbirth, and cumulatively with closely spaced or difficult births. But whereas muscles decrement is permanent (*kuntu*, "cut"), strength undergoes a process of temporary reduction *(baŋ)*, followed by repletion. Although it never again rises to the level of one's twelve, strength can be replenished with rest and nutritious foods such as meat and chicken. Dipping and surging during the life cycle, but in decline overall, strength is life itself. When all strength fades, whether slowly or abruptly, life ends.

As is the case with muscles, there is a close relation between strength and reproductive events. The amount of strength one has at the time of birth is a key determinant of how difficult a birth will be. To protect herself as she advances in parity, a woman tries to eat energy-rich foods that will keep some fat on her and to ease out of heavy work to conserve her body's resources. A woman with an ample diet and abundant help for child care and farm work (whether from co-wives, a mother-in-law, or a fostered niece) will probably have easy births because she can regain her strength readily. An undernourished woman who alone must tend to her husband as well as her elder in-laws and small children (including visits to distant medical facilities for routine well-baby checks and emergency treatments), all while trying to keep pace with heavy farm work and walking several miles to the weekly market to sell vegetables—such a woman will find it increasingly difficult to withstand the strain of pregnancy and childbirth.[12] A woman assesses the likely state of her overall reproductivity by noting both how her strength fluctuates through each delivery and the state of her body. Taking on this knowledge, in conjunction with the kind of social support she senses, she can try to go on to a new pregnancy, pause to replenish her bodily resources, or stop childbearing altogether.

11. The Fula people, who relate these notions to herd animals, point out that muscles can be seen on the top of the neck of a cow or a goat; fat can be seen on the bottom (Adam Thiam, pers. comm.).

12. On the parallel Western notion of maternal depletion, see National Research Council 1989, 32.

Blood: Blood *(yeloo),* the third physical component of a woman's reproductive potential, is the main substance required to build the body of a fetus.[13] Once a new pregnancy is desired, a clean womb is the ideal environment for a pregnancy to begin. "Bad" or "dirty" blood that accumulates
following a birth or in the wake of menstrual ailments must be washed out
to facilitate a new pregnancy and to prevent difficult labor, miscarriage, and
infertility. Women therefore worry about excessive or irregular menses that
can obstruct fertility or endanger their health. The womb, because it har-
bors a fetus, is a prime collection site for blood both good and bad, and the
time after a birth is one of potential contamination and illness if the womb
is not clean within a month or two. To wash it out, many women drink a
boiled herb called *jambakatapo* for several days after delivery, or they go to
the clinic for dilation and curettage. For womb cleaning, a few women take
birth control pills that local medical personnel may give them; the rationale
is that these pills, with their high estrogen content, can flush out contami-
nated blood. (Red pills, with their association with blood, are preferred.)
Here again, of course, is an instance of using devices that were provided by
international agencies to limit fertility with the opposite intent: to facilitate
fertility. This time, though, the temporalities are quite different. The usual
aim is not to rest for a long period of time following a birth but to conceive
as soon as possible.

Besides problems of quality are those of quantity. Like strength, blood
can be lost, but it is replaceable only with great difficulty, and the time frame
in which repletion can occur is much slower. The loss of blood through
menstruation is considered a normal process, although unusually heavy or
lengthy periods are feared to cause undue blood loss, and excessive or irregular menses can prevent fertility as well as endanger health. Breastfeeding is considered relatively neutral in its costs to blood, since a mother and
her breastfeeding child are not considered to be in direct nutritional competition with one another. Far less benign in its effects on blood is pregnancy. The fetus is considered to compete directly with the mother because
it eats directly from the food she eats and ingests her blood. The most serious drain on blood, however, is that which is lost at childbirth. Particularly
if there is hemorrhage or if the woman has already been under nutritional
stress from hard work and an inadequate diet, a series of "rampant" preg-

13. Problems and images of blood have drawn long-standing symbolic interest in cultural anthropology. Works such as those by Buckley and Gottlieb (1988), Sobo (1993), and Boddy (1989) have documented the multiple layers of symbolism concerning kinship, reproduction, nourishment, danger, and
so on that blood evokes.

nancies and deliveries will rapidly deplete her blood, bringing it to a dangerously low level. Being pale and listless, a state compounded by one of the world's highest malaria levels, is an ominous sign that a woman is unprepared for the next birth. At risk are her own safety and that of her baby, who, as a direct participant in her own bodily environment, may be born sickly. The best way to replace blood is transfusions in hospitals. Because blood is considered so difficult to replace, however, blood donated to one person is considered to be lost to someone else. Even close relatives donate to each other with great reluctance, a pattern widely noted throughout the subcontinent. The ferrosulfate and folic acid supplements now given to pregnant women in prenatal clinics are considered poor substitutes. Others substitutes (meat, chicken, palm oil, and so on) are at best partially effective. Blood seems to be regarded as replaceable mainly in the longer term, when a woman stops childbearing.

Interactions among Reproductive Elements

The three reproductive elements (muscles, strength, blood) operate in close synchrony during childbirth and its aftermath. A lack of one element must be offset by expenditure in the others during the next delivery. This synergy is reflected in women's descriptions of obstetrically salient events in blends of biology and social practice. Here is just one example from a woman living in a large town, a woman whose wealthy husband could afford the luxuries of blood- and strength-giving foods for his wives.

> It is true that women cut muscles when they deliver. As for me, I have
> four pregnancies but I am still strong. The reason why some women say
> that [they lack strength], is because they don't eat good food when they
> deliver. As for me, I started eating chickens immediately after my delivery
> until the naming ceremony took place then I stopped it and continued
> with the normal food. This is normally done for delivering women for
> them to recover the blood they lose when giving birth.

Revealed as well is an intricate mixture of propositions about God-given and socially controlled elements of reproduction, along with the principles governing the manner and pace of their decrement. Referring to the bodily constituents of reproductivity, one this thirty-three-year-old woman explains with poetic simplicity: "I am just a human being. I have no power to estimate the number of children I want to bear. God has the power to decide and give the luck of bearing up to a specific number of children. . . .

If he still makes the availability of enough muscles and strength to bear children, I will bear any number given to me to produce and look after them" (R. 12).

The "older" a woman is in terms of cumulative muscle loss, the more difficult she will find it not only to carry and expel a fetus but to regain her strength and blood after each successive birth. A woman with unrepleted strength will find that labor and delivery take a disproportionate toll on her muscles. In her tired, weakened state, closely spaced pregnancies or difficult deliveries that involve heavy blood loss will further drain her strength. Forced to use more of her physical capital during labor and delivery, she may lose two muscles rather than one during the next delivery. Giving birth with a serious deficit in any of these basic constituents of reproduction, and particularly with minimal support from her husband or his kin, is dangerous. Should an anemic woman become pregnant with a deep womb and little strength, childbirth poses severe risks. It is important to stress, in fact, that a similar event may carry very different risks, depending on the state of the woman who experiences it. A woman just starting childbearing may much better tolerate a trying delivery than a woman for whom the cumulative tolls of childbearing have left her few bodily resources. The two women will likely emerge from such an event in different conditions.

As we have seen, all of the physical elements in the process of reproduction and senescence are closely interdependent, yet separate principles underlie their expenditure. Each element differs from the others in the degree to which it is expended. It also differs in transparency, replenishability, and permanence. The termination of the hapo cannot be assessed visually, since it is an abstract entity, but the diminution of strength, blood, and muscles is felt and can often be seen. And both the muscles and the hapo, although they are fixed sums, differ in their transparency. There is no way to know in advance when the hapo will be finished, but the termination of muscles can be sensed and seen as the end approaches.

In this strikingly different frame for understanding reproduction and the life course, physical decline for a woman might occur over a linear duration, but it usually occurs in an episodic manner. The process also has a cumulative character. One event affects the next in an evolving set of interactions whose effects continually build upon each other. Eventually, of course, wear will take its toll and aging will occur. But the pace at which this process occurs is not set. It is dependent on the wearing and traumatic events encountered, the vagaries of personal history, actions taken, and the degree of support received from the husband and in-laws. Combined with the capriciousness of events, a cumulative dynamic can disrupt a fragile balance of subsistence or health, and with fearsome speed. As a result, reproductive events are highly variable among individuals and within the social worlds in which individuals operate. The result is not a demographic model of childbearing that calculates numbers of live births over a temporal span. It is, rather, a social, medical, and economic model, set against the background of hard physical labor, poor nutrition, and scanty medical infrastructure. It is also not simply a world of calculating individuals divorced from contextual influences but one of individuals whose acts arise from a set of social relationships and culturally mediated perceptions.

Findings such as these are echoed in the concept of emergence, found in abundance in the visions of Georg Simmel and George Herbert Mead, in which a unique character or life pathway is continually shaped. Emergence lay at the heart of Mead's (1980) inspired adaptation of time and movement in Einstein's relativity theory to social life. Conventional views had held that the reality of a physical mass lay in invariant qualities, no matter how it moved through space. Einstein, however, showed that the mass of a moving object is dependent on its history of contact with other forces. As an object moves, it changes the space and hence the other objects with which it comes in contact. In such a manner, said Mead, members of a social community carry over into a new order traces of their selves that were formed in an old order. Conversely, they change the social systems in which they possess temporary membership as they pass through. Strauss (1964, 340), summarizing Mead's vision, describes "a common plane of events" in which individuals are conjoined. Yet because of the experiences that brought them to this event and will carry them forward in different trajectories, each individual sees the world from the standpoint of a different time system. Individuation is paradoxically a social process, therefore, in that the self arises out of interaction with others (Mead 1934). Simmel (1971a, 1971b) makes analogous observations: not only does society select and limit individuals' choices, but, as they develop, they seize and incorporate elements of their surrounding social worlds.

The vision of the life course as described by rural Gambians reveals a similar sense of emergence: a function of particular interactions with, and incorporations of, a surrounding milieu. Outside or unanticipated influences may be experienced as sickness, a child's failure in school, a lawsuit, an attack of witchcraft, or an act of God. These experiences render each person a motley collection of historical events and social relations, all inscribed upon the body and affecting its potential. From histories like these, multiple life pathways emerge. Some lead to gain. Others can steer an individual further down a treacherous course, crystallizing a trajectory from which efforts to effect significant shifts become increasingly difficult. Since each contingency contains its own conditions and sets the terms for its own consequences, each emergent life is unique.[14] But whereas rural Gambians seem to attribute a large proportion of their adverse outcomes ex post facto to the workings of fate, they clearly try to take actions that would forestall these outcomes by anticipating possible results and by *containing* the adverse impacts of such events once they are in motion. Although women cannot control every event, they try to take efforts to curb or hold in check the adverse effects that such events might entail. The fact that outcomes are understood to reflect one's ability to manage the situation means that the lines that appear to divide cause from effect are blurred.[15]

Previously, I noted a prominent metaphor for the reproductive capacity in contemporary Western writings as one of a clock. In the Gambian context, however, economic metaphors of "costs," "tolls," and "expenditures" seem more apt descriptors of reproductive life and physical decline. Martin's (1987) observation that medical texts in the West have often portrayed the body as a machine has relevance. In her descriptions, the woman has been portrayed as a machine that produces a product (the child), under the guidance of the physician-operator. The Gambian imagery actually overlaps with this. Certainly the machinery image would apply to the metaphor in which the various reproductive components of a woman's body are

14. Such a composite conception of identity, deeply implied in much of the African ethnography, departs markedly from those often found in contemporary scholarship in the West, which posit a stripped-away, exclusive self. Some diverse examples include Karp's (1980) analysis of the dynamics of an inner and outer self; Riesman's (1986) observations of a small child's dual membership in the worlds of the spirits and of humans; Isichei's (1978) descriptions of the spirit familiar as a component of the self; and Ben Okri's (1992) novel depicting a man locked in a constant struggle with the capricious spirits that possess him. M. Strathern offers parallel observations (1992a, 71) from Melanesia: "a person is equal to all the relationships that compose it, and in that sense they in turn are integral to his or her composition as a living body." For theoretical statements along these lines, see Guyer 1996 and Shweder 1990, 2–3.

15. There are striking parallels between Gambians' efforts to contain the risks they face in livelihood, marriage, fertility, and health, and the emerging literature on uncertainty and complexity in other fields. The entire April 1999 issue (vol. 284) of *Science*, for example, was titled "Complex Systems: Beyond Reductionism." Contributing the piece on economics, Brian Arthur ("Complexity and the Economy," 107–9) notes (in a manner evocative of Mead's emphasis on emergence) that after two centuries of presuming to study static patterns that called for no further behavioral adjustments, "economists are beginning to study the general emergence of structures and the unfolding of patterns in the economy" (109). In this process, economic agents (whether banks, consumers, or firms) continually adjust their market moves to evolving situations. In Arthur's deft, almost symbolic interactionist prose, agents "react with strategy and foresight by considering outcomes that might result as a consequence of behavior they might undertake" (107). As for what produces these evolutions, Arthur notes that economic structures can crystallize and lock in around small events (108).

likened to a motor vehicle—not by a Western physician but by an elderly rural Gambian traditional birth attendant. In fact, the Gambian imagery of production in reproduction could extend very broadly to a highly complex economy. Terminologies could include relations of production, endowments, investment in (and expenditure of) social and moral capital, losses, gains, risks, conservation. Images of reproductivity might include as well the interests of various agents such as the husband and the mother-in-law, not to mention the woman herself. They could certainly include the values placed on children: investments in their food, bridewealth, medical costs, school fees, and blessings they require to succeed. So although economics is sometimes cast as a nomothetic, positivist endeavor, we should not retreat from the cultural readings it opens up, if such readings are faithful ones. We must ensure that the terms are specified as carefully as possible.

Some of the key pieces of evidence that support the contingency view were the anomalies that I identified in chapter 5: patterns of contraceptive use surrounding mishaps and older women and the recalcitrance of men regarding contraceptives. These patterns seemed at first highly counter to Western convictions about the dynamics of high fertility. Now they should seem less so. I now elaborate on some of these patterns, bringing the Gambian and the Western frameworks into closer alignment with one another.

The Medical Significance of Mishaps and Contraceptive Use in the Contingency Framework

The contingency view holds that all pregnancies are taxing if not dangerous for women. Yet of all the sources of risk and depletion, none are more intensely feared than nonlive births (stillbirths, miscarriages, and abortions).[16] In fact, the finding that most strikingly supports the Gambian view of reproduction is the pattern of using contraception after reproductive mishaps. This makes consummate sense, as we will see, if understood not as an attempt to limit children but to heal the anatomical damage and physiological tolls of pregnancy.

A woman expects—indeed, she hopes—to expend all her reproductive capital on behalf of her husband. Yet she much prefers to do so through normal childbirth. What she most fears is prolonged or injurious deliveries

---

16. For Gambian people, the distinction between a miscarriage and a stillbirth—whether the entity was anatomically distinct from the woman—has a ritual counterpart. A stillbirth can be buried as a person, whereas a miscarried fetus cannot.

that both fail to produce living children and destroy her remaining reproductive capital. Whereas contemporary fertility studies in demography have treated nonlive births as events worthy of note only insofar as they take up time in the interval between live births, local people understand them as events that can exacerbate medical trauma and wreak havoc on bodily resources. Mishaps and the events that produce them are not only costly to reproductive capital; they can endanger a woman's life. Nonlive births may be either cause or consequence of an infirm reproductivity. A non-live birth may be caused by a rapid pace of childbearing (rampant births),[17] a heavy workload, a shortage of blood, or simply being exhausted.[18] If the womb is not well, the pregnancy cannot survive. A reproductive calamity may thus reflect an underlying health problem. For a woman who has had little opportunity to recover from a previous birth, jeopardy confronts her on two sides of the horizon. The nonlive birth she suffers may so badly deplete her body that it precipitates another one the next time. Whereas poor health may have led to a nonlive birth, a nonlive birth may now set off a spiral of cumulative and interrelated health and pregnancy maladies that she must try to bring under control.

Unmistakable support for a contingent view of reproduction is found in women's verbal accounts of the experiences that distinguish miscarriages from stillbirths.[19] Giving birth to a stillborn child *(süriŋo)* is often described as extremely difficult. One reason is that a stillbirth may result from an obstructed labor, which was itself taxing. In addition, whereas a living baby is said to make small movements that render every push of the mother more effective in dislodging it, a stillbirth, which represents attempts to expel a large, inert mass, can exact an enormous toll on the muscles. In particular, women who undergo stillbirths at higher parities describe acute, prolonged suffering. A miscarriage *(wulu,* "delivery" + *kurɔŋ,* "extremely bad, taxing")

can be even worse. Whereas a stillbirth usually ends in expulsion of all the tissues and fluids, a miscarriage can leave residual tissues, producing infections, and the damage may heal slowly. More important, since the fetus is not yet a discrete entity, it is essentially a piece of the woman—her own flesh—that is being torn out, causing great pain, heavy blood loss, and pos-

---

17. The need for rest to prevent close spacing and reproductive mishaps emerges in descriptions from very distant places and times. For example, writing on North India, Jeffery and Jeffery (1996, 23) observe that a woman "should avoid strenuous work and take more rest than usual. Women also say that frequent pregnancies can weaken the uterus so that it cannot retain a baby."

18. Another cause, according to local and expatriate medical personnel, is venereal disease.

19. A miscarriage is generally considered to be the product of a pregnancy that has not yet stood; a stillbirth, by contrast, is the product of one that has stood.

sibly internal damage. A woman can even bleed to death. Using the analogy of the locally ubiquitous mangoes, a village traditional birth attendant vividly captured the miscarriage experience. When a ripe mango is picked, she explained, the fruit snaps off the dried stem easily. Its life moistures are sealed intact on both sides of the break: the tree and the mango. Trying to pick an unripe mango is quite a different experience. The fruit can be pulled off the green stem only with determined force, and both the mango and the tree undergo a dramatic, sustained loss of fluid.[20] (Later, I tried pulling an unripe mango off a tree, and saw exactly what she meant.) As a Gambian health center nurse confirmed, the sequelae of a miscarriage are often more severe than those of a stillbirth, especially if the womb becomes infected. All this is even more relevant in case of induced abortion, in which a woman may be reluctant to seek help. A woman who attempts to abort may destroy her entire future fertility potential, if not her life. The knowledge that schoolgirls sometimes attempt to abort in order to avoid being expelled may in some cases underlie families' decisions to withdraw from school a girl whose academic attention seems to be straying.

The cultural categorization of different kinds of miscarriages provide additional support for the contingency framework. Because many miscarriages are experienced simply as late periods, much like occasional efforts to regulate the menses by washing the stomach, they entail benign experiences. Given that anywhere from one-half to one-third of all pregnancies end in miscarriage, women do not even detect most of them, and a benign miscarriage that is recognized at the time may well fade from memory. However, miscarriages that occur later in the pregnancy, but before the fetus becomes clearly distinct from the mother, can be far worse. They may entail labor pains. The biggest fear, however, is the bloody loss of flesh that a late miscarriage and its aftermath can entail. Ordeals posed by miscarriages such as these, like stillbirths, may cut more than one muscle, especially if the woman is already in poor health from malnutrition, illness, or hard work. A costly reproductive event such as this can leave her exhausted and sick, if not more visibly "aged." Although God may have endowed her

---

20. One of the letters to the Women's Guild (1916) in England contains a virtually identical metaphor: "It is nature, and nature does or should do its own work. . . . Take, for instance, the apple. When it is fully ripe, it falls from the tree. So the child, when the time has arrived for its appearance. I say it should come as naturally, not to look upon the little creature distorted and bruised through having to be brought into the world" (125). Speaking from the framework of contemporary U.S. obstetrics, Patricia Woollcott's (pers. comm.) descriptions of the risks of miscarriage turned up further verbal parallels. Trouble with a premature birth often ensues, she affirmed, because the placenta is premature: it is not ready to detach from the wall of the uterus, and a woman who suffers such an event may need to have her womb evacuated.

with eight pregnancies, the experience of two miscarriages may leave her so drained that she is able to have only four more pregnancies safely.

The medical significance of mishaps, then, lies not only in their numbers but in their severity. What should now be very clear is that there is a wide array of units of reproductive currency. Recognizing the trauma or bodily expenditure that can accompany reproductive events explains why women whom standard definitions would label "infertile" can gain conjugal credit even if they never have anything but a nonlive birth. It also helps explain the response reported in chapter 5 from the woman who, though she was left with three children after five pregnancies, implied that her conjugal credit was comparable to that of a woman with five living children. Her rivals may well dispute this claim, but the physical basis on which such arguments will arise is clear.

Confirmation of the contingency thesis through the phenomenon of mishaps is also found in patterns of contraceptive use in the wake of a nonlive birth.[21] If both high levels of contraceptive use and the use of the most effective methods are indices of trauma, then the fact that many women were using the most efficient methods (especially Depo Provera) after a nonlive birth is especially significant. This finding suggests that women whose most recent pregnancy ended in a nonlive birth are more determined than women with surviving children to avoid a new pregnancy. Regardless of whether there was a live birth or a nonlive birth, the womb needs a rest. Given that the original sample for the rounds had been selected heavily for women whose previous pregnancy had resulted in a living child, the undoubtedly small proportion of nonlive births that the surveys captured may have been among the most damaging because of the dramatic contraceptive responses. If so, this would lend further support to the contingency perspective.[22]

If these observations begin to cast new light on the medical problems that nonlive births may reflect and the behaviors they precipitate, the death of a young nursing baby can be understood in similar terms, as a manifestation of the mother's health problems. A tired or infirm mother who is bur-

21. It was impossible to test the thesis by examining differential levels of contraceptive use following miscarriages as opposed to stillbirths. The numbers of nonlive births reported were small and the local categories that were translated into English were not refined in the surveys.

22. Although a number of women using Western contraceptives after a mishap or a difficult delivery seem to have been doing so because they sought the contraceptives themselves, others may well have done so because a local clinic practitioner recommended doing so. If the latter occurred, this would suggest that local medical personnel, like their clients, are highly attuned to the problems that follow difficult pregnancies.

dened with farming and domestic responsibilities and with her other children may be unable to ensure that a baby consistently gets nutritious food or unwilling to take it to the clinic unless its condition becomes serious. The younger the child (or the fetus) that must depend on a worn-out mother, the more likely its death will be attributed to her own infirmities because its life is so utterly dependent on her bodily substance and energy. An older child, by contrast, is better able to seek attention from the mother or other people in the household when it is hungry or in distress. Such a child learns how to appear at other people's houses just as food is being distributed, to pilfer small bits of food from the family cooking pot, or to make or embezzle small profits from the family market business.[23]

In sum, mishaps are not the only traumatic obstetric events, nor are they equally traumatic. All pregnancies are seen as taxing for women, some far more than others. Nor, obviously, are mishaps the only factors that influence fertility behavior. But the behaviors surrounding reproductive mishaps, especially the use of Western contraceptives, comprise some of the most compelling evidence that prevailing assumptions about the dynamics of fertility have been misconstrued.

By now the dynamics of the contingency perspective should be more evident. Let us pause to clarify it through an example of a hypothetical woman with a particular set of reproductive resources and experiences. My purpose is to illuminate the local calculus of the principles of reproduction. Figure 6.1 shows how various events are counted. It also attempts to convey a sense of the momentum and cumulativity that the woman experiences, as well as the impact of her actions as events progress.

The vertical axis represents the fixed number of "muscles" that the woman will deplete over the course of her reproductive life. I have bestowed on her nine muscles.[24] The horizontal axis represents time. In this, I depart from the Gambian cultural grid. I do so, however, to keep a foot planted on a familiar point of reference. For most of this woman's characteristics, I lean toward optimism. I give her an adequate diet and supportive in-laws, and I restrict her to one marriage. But I also give her a slight proclivity to resume fecundity before the child is strong enough to be weaned. This tendency, at first a blessing, later becomes an adversity. The

23. For a description of this phenomenon in Sierra Leone, see Bledsoe 1991.

24. The *hapo*, or number of child potentials (*harijeos*), could have been used as the vertical axis, but since this cannot be felt or acted upon as muscles can, the changes in this scale would be less meaningful for present purposes.

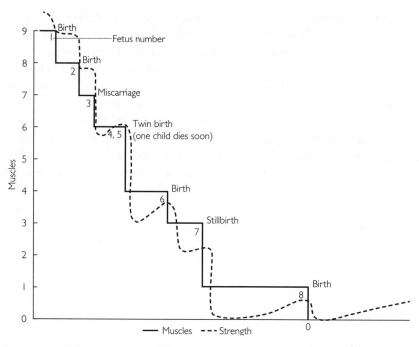

Fig. 6.1 Hypothetical case of expenditure of reproductive "muscles" and strength over a lifetime

units to be tracked include muscles, fetuses produced (among which there are live and nonlive births), child deaths, and total children surviving. Since reproductive capacity operates by decrement, individual events may be tracked from the top. The number of muscles, shown in the downward steps, are the primary focus, although the more ephemeral element of strength (the line with curves) will be kept in view as a critical determinant of the pace of the muscles' trajectory and of the woman's health.

The woman begins reproductive life with nine muscles, a sum that is unknown to her at the outset. She has as well a hapo of eight child potentials (and hence eight fetuses she can produce), although this also is unknown. She marries at age sixteen, and at eighteen, her first pregnancy termination (#1) is a normal live birth that depletes one muscle. Young, strong, and still in her "twelve," she scarcely feels the loss. Since she is anxious to establish herself in the compound, she is gratified when she discovers a new pregnancy (#2) as the child she is still breastfeeding begins to eat solid foods. Like the first pregnancy, this one ends in a normal delivery and a live birth.

Pregnancy #3, however, overlaps substantially with the preceding child, and the woman fears to wean her breastfeeding child (#2) so soon. This new pregnancy (#3) ends in an early-term miscarriage or an induced abortion; we are unsure which it was because the woman's account of the event is vague. The bodily cost of the nonlive birth was noticeable but not disastrous. The next pregnancy (#4), beginning as the second child is weaned and some time after the nonlive birth occurred, produces living twins. With little opportunity to rest and a difficult pregnancy and delivery, the toll is two muscles rather than one (although I could have made it three), and the woman's strength sinks low. By now, the mounting toll is making her considerably "older" in terms of bodily resources than she was at the outset. One of the twins, its health reflecting her own fatigue, is weak at birth. It succumbs within a few weeks.

So far, this woman, in her four pregnancy terminations (the twins counting as one), has expended five muscles and had five fetuses (the twins counting as two), and she has had four live births. Left with three surviving children (minus the abortion and the dead twin), she is more than halfway through her total muscle allotment of nine.

At this point, the woman, with her husband's full support, obtains birth control pills to delay the next pregnancy for several months, even past the time she weans the surviving twin. After she regains some strength, she becomes pregnant again, and termination #5 results in a live birth. Six muscles have been lost, six fetuses have been borne, and the woman is left with four surviving children. The next termination (#6) results in a stillbirth after a difficult, prolonged labor. The trauma of this experience is reflected in a precipitous loss of strength, and she nearly dies. She attributes this harrowing event and its toll of two muscles to the cumulative effects of her body's depletion, a product not simply of prior pregnancies but also of the unrelenting and accumulating work demands she faces to keep her remaining children fed and healthy. She is now "spent," a state she senses vividly.

After six pregnancy terminations, seven fetuses borne, and eight muscles lost, the woman still has only four living children. Fearful now for her life, she begins a search for a co-wife to take over the brunt of reproductive and farming duties. Inflated bridewealth prices and a poor groundnut harvest this year have stalled her husband's negotiations for the girl she wanted, so with her worried husband's encouragement, she begins to take the powerful, long-lasting Depo Provera. Three years later, her husband pressing for another child, she becomes pregnant again and delivers for the last time.

At the insistence of both her TBA and the clinic personnel, this time she delivers (termination #7) at the clinic. The result is a live birth. She and her husband finally manage to acquire a new wife, and she declares in no uncertain terms that she is "retiring" from childbearing. Her age at this point? I hope that the reader has become so engaged in the story and concerned about the woman's physical state and the experiences that led to it that the quantity of her years is of little interest. If pressed, however, I would put her at what to us would be a very "young" age to stop childbearing: thirty-six.

Let us now review the various counts and the relations among them. In the process of losing nine muscles and bearing eight fetuses, this woman has had seven pregnancy terminations. Six resulted in children who were alive at birth, although one (a twin) later died, and two were nonlive births. The other muscle was lost in the extra exertion required for termination #6. Happy with her five surviving children, whose rewards she has already begun to reap through the marriage of her oldest daughter (and satisfied as well with her young co-wife, whose training is coming along nicely), she begins to regain her strength and experiences menopause some time thereafter.

Stepping back, now, from the details of the chart, we see that two patterns of larger consequence become apparent. The first is the unmistakable character of contingency as opposed to linearity in this reproductive history. Pressed flat against the linear scale of time, the process of decline starts from a peak of muscles and strength, and it manifests a regular pace at the outset. But as the effects of reproductive assaults begin to accumulate (and especially when trauma strikes), the pace of the decline accelerates. We can sense the danger that a quickening pace implies in the precipitous drop in life strength, particularly when the woman reaches later stages of senescence. Even though later events occur with less frequency on the chronological scale than those that occur early, they tend to have a greater impact because of the spiraling effects. The second pattern of note is that action is the key component of the bodily dynamic. Once the decline is under way, its pace is affected *only* by action. Whether the woman uses contraceptives or finds a co-wife to step into the conjugal picture, or whether she does nothing at all, it is her own actions (or inactions) that make the difference in her own aging.

This exercise illustrates a very different calculus of fertility events and their relation to the life course than that usually encountered in Western science's models. No one thinks of this woman's reproductive life as a simple history of pregnancies and live births. The mix of elements such as children and time that appeared to have such clear empirical groundings is giving way to a much more textured and contingent vision.

What do findings such as these imply for the principal data sets that have been collected for international analysis? Contemporary Western ideas about how fertility works have decisively shaped the structure and content of the Demographic and Health Surveys (DHS), the largest and most comprehensive demographic project in history. The DHS does include numerous health variables, as the word "health" in the title conveys. But since the thrust of demographic concern for places such as sub-Saharan Africa has been to understand population growth, virtually all health emphasis in the variables—and indeed the most fundamental events that the DHS counts and measures in "low contraceptive prevalence countries"—has focused on the child. Hence, the births and deaths of live children have been taken as the proper units of fertility analysis.[25] We sense as much in the instructions to surveyors in the 1993 Kenya DHS for eliciting information about children who died after birth in the questionnaire's judicious yet persistent wording:

> Sometimes it happens that children die. It may be very painful to talk about and I am sorry to ask you about painful memories, but it is important to get the right information. Have you ever given birth to a boy or girl who was born alive but later died? IF NO, PROBE: Any baby who cried or showed any sign of life but only survived a few hours or days? (231)

This passage reflects a strong assumption that however emotionally painful, the birth and death of a no-longer-living child are critical events. Whereas this and other questions devote enormous attention to child sick-

---

25. Emphasis on population growth and decline can also be seen in the redundancy among the particular questions, response choices, and recodes on which the DHS rests. Besides the births and deaths of children, the Western cultural preoccupation that stands out above all is that of contraception. The reason is, of course, is that rates of "modern" contraceptive use are seen as indices of the likelihood of fertility reduction. Thus, the 1993 Ghana DHS contains forty-one questions on exposure to or practice of contraception, for example, the respondent's knowledge of, use of, and current use of various methods. In addition, there are questions about pattern of use of a current method and preferred future method. For each of these questions, there is a large number of response choices. For the question of contraceptive "method," Phase I, the early version of DHS, lists twelve response choices: none, pills, IUD, injection, diaphragm/foam/jelly, condoms, female sterilization, male sterilization, periodic abstinence, withdrawal, other, Norplant and abstinence. (DHS Phases II and III add three country-specific possibilities.) All twelve (or fifteen) of these responses are then recoded in another variable as contraceptive type, which includes "modern," "traditional," and "none." To these three types, Phases II and III add a fourth: "folkloric." Despite the richness offered by the "methods" variable, analyses using DHS data have almost always bypassed it and focused instead on the recoded types. Indeed, many analyses examine only "modern contraceptives," treating everything else—whether traditional contraceptives, folkloric, or no measure at all—globally, as one contrastive category.

ness and deaths, omitted almost entirely from the African DHS surveys are data on pregnancies that resulted in miscarriages and stillbirths. To be sure, nonlive births can be extremely difficult to elicit. Women do not want to draw attention to their fertility problems, so nonlive births can be as painful to recount as the deaths of small children.[26] As a result, women frequently omit them from their fertility histories. The World Fertility Surveys, the precursor to the DHS (conducted in a number of countries in the late 1970s and early 1980s), tried to capture nonlive births. With numbers of pregnancies so often discrepant with total sums of live and nonlive births, however, the result was often acute confusion (Casterline 1989a). Because nonlive births so confound attempts at measurement, and because of the difficulty of collecting data that would seem to have only marginal utility for illuminating population change, surveys have shifted massively to live births as the basis of fertility measurements. The "Model B" version of the DHS, used in countries with low prevalence of Western contraceptives and high fertility (*Interviewer's Manual For Use with Model "B" Questionnaire For Low Contraceptive Prevalence Countries*, 1997), scrupulously screens out all pregnancies except those that produced living children.[27] In effect, one breath of air, even if it is the only one, would qualify a nonviable infant as a subject of intense investigation, whereas all information would be omitted about a pregnancy termination in which two days of traumatic, obstructed labor caused the death of an otherwise viable infant. Most surveys have followed the DHS, eliminating the category of nonlive births altogether. Such data, when collected at all, have been treated largely as temporal placeholders for births that did not occur when expected, then discarded from further analysis. The only time Model B brings up nonlive births is as a check on the length of the interval between two live births. If the reason for a long live birth interval was a nonlive birth, this fact is to be noted in prose—a noncountable format—and then the interview is to proceed (64). Most surveys have followed the DHS, eliminating the category of nonlive births altogether. Such data, when collected at all, are treated largely as temporal placeholders for births that did not occur when expected, then discarded from further analysis.

26. Miscarriages are often indistinguishable from a late menstrual period, but if a much-wanted pregnancy is believed to have been lost through miscarriage, the same sensitivities in recounting them can arise as in reporting a child's death or a stillbirth.

27. Only recently has the core DHS included systematic questions on outcomes such as stillbirths and miscarriages or abortions. These questions, however, are found in the full-fertility "calendar" method that is used only in the "Model A" version, for countries with high contraceptive prevalence and low fertility (see *Interviewer's Manual For Use with Model "A" Questionnaire for High Contraceptive Prevalence Countries*, 2000).

Having data on nonlive births is not essential to grasping this very different understanding of fertility; many other clues can be seized upon.[28] In the absence of other relevant medical data on women, however, nonlive births comprise one of the most telling indicators of likely reproductive trauma. The DHS obviously was constructed with a very different set of assumptions about the concerns that are important to fertility decisions. But the fact that there was no definitive information on what pregnancy outcomes transpired recently, much less in the past, means that there was no way to discern the full fertility context in which contraceptive use may be occurring. In populations that are not trying to limit numbers of children, such omissions have impaired the survey's entire fertility framework. Even where people are trying to limit numbers of children, preoccupations such as these are no less evident in every cultural domain. In popular book stores in the United States, the emphasis in books on miscarriage and child loss is overwhelmingly on emotional loss, with almost no attention to the medical concomitants.

Those who draft international surveys are hardly alone in these ways of looking at the world, therefore. Most of us who were raised in the West share visions of the life world that would lead us, if we were demographers, to create such research instruments and analyze our data in very similar ways. I certainly did. The monthly rounds questionnaire used in the Gambian study was based on the presumption that the events surrounding the birth of a living child might have a major effect on women's subsequent birth interval behaviors in the multiple domains of sexuality, child feeding, and contraception. This proved quite correct. What I did not anticipate was that the fertility events that fell *outside* the scope of a live birth (miscarriages and stillbirths or even a child's death) might also have an impact on a woman's behavior. Looking back on it, this was a galling oversight. But when one is moving with a particular vision, customary research procedures are easy to adopt (indeed, compelling) because the assumptions that underlie them are so commonsensical that they go unnoticed.

In the case of the monthly rounds, these questionnaires did contain a question on "stage of the last child's development" that contained a response possibility for a child death. But subsequent questions such as "What is your last-born child feeding on?" contained no coded category for noting that the child or fetus was no longer alive. Following the question on the

---

28. In Phase III, which appeared in 1997, the surveys for low contraceptive prevalence countries added several other variables for the last and next-to-last births that I would now consider critical: "Around the time of the birth of (NAME), did you have any of the following problems: long labor . . . ?, excessive bleeding . . . ?, a high fever . . . ?, convulsions . . . ?"

last-born child's development there was an instruction for the interview to skip to the next page if the child was dead. But a number of interviewers had not followed this instruction in their questioning—that is, they had continued the questions on postpartum maternal behavior and child development. In what I now regard as a happy oversight, the checking program that was written to catch inconsistencies as the rounds data were entered had omitted this particular skip. In a number of instances, then, the circumscribed nature of the questions, together with the flow of the questions and the omission of the data entry check for the questionnaire's skip pattern, all seemed to have the following effect: Because the emphasis in the questions was on a living child and its feeding and development, the interviewer and the woman seemed to be indexing their conversation back to the last child born that was actually alive. A number of anomalies resulted. Among the most glaring was the fact that in the rounds entries nearly 8 percent of miscarriages, stillbirths, and dead children appeared to be continuing in their development: they were breastfeeding, breastfeeding with food supplementation, or weaned. As a result, the question on the last child's feeding and developmental status became not only irrelevant but highly misleading for every succeeding month until the mother had a new live birth. This anomaly came to light because of Epi Info's capacity to juxtapose re-sorted variables for visual inspection.

Revisiting Some English Definitions

Having examined some key distinctions in reproductive events and their timing, let us revisit some of the concepts with which we began in chapter 2. Has the analysis turned up possibilities for definitional clarification in ways that can illuminate new facets of reproductive life? Let us take first *limiting* and *stopping*, words used almost synonymously in population studies to refer to intentional efforts to suppress child numbers. What now becomes apparent is that a woman may in fact try to space her births and at some point she may even try to *stop* childbearing, in the sense of bringing an end to the risk that giving birth at high parities can entail. But trying to stop childbearing does not necessarily imply trying to *limit* children to a prechosen number. Since another delivery could jeopardize her surviving children if she becomes impaired, she may be trying to ensure that a larger, rather than a smaller, number of her children survive. If the ability to reproduce is limited not by time but by bodily resources, she can even delay a new pregnancy past weaning and by doing so produce children who are healthier if not more numerous than could have been the case otherwise.

Alternative shades of meaning and clarification emerge as well in terms such as *births, pregnancies,* and *fetuses.* Since a pregnancy can end in a stillbirth or a miscarriage rather than a living child, limiting births is not the same thing as limiting children. And whereas the Western method of calculating fertility collapses the notion of multiple fetuses that occupy one womb into the notion of one pregnancy or birth, the analysis presented here has underscored the fact that one pregnancy is not the same thing as one fetus. Because carrying and delivering twins is more taxing than having a single birth, each fetus is counted separately in the overall Gambian calculus.

Notions of reproduction that have emerged here also demand clarity in the difference between *fertility* and *fecundity.* In demographic convention, as explained earlier, the term *fertility* refers to the increment of one living person to the population, a use reflecting a Western preoccupation with population levels, whereas *fecundity* has been used to refer to the ability to conceive. Missing, however, is a technical term reflecting the fact that a miscarried fetus may take at least as large a toll on the mother as does a live birth. What is more, as Bongaarts (1983, 3) observed, pointing to related definitional quagmires, *fertility* and *fecundity* often have been used synonymously in the biological and medical literature. If vocabularies and definitions are indices of cultural preoccupations, then the conflation of fertility and fecundity, together with the lack of interest in a "countable" category for bodily toll, underscores the conviction that once implantation is secured, the rest of the pregnancy can be taken for granted. A woman who is able to conceive is able to reproduce, and bodily toll is not a concern. As the findings presented here have shown, this set of assumptions is far off the mark for rural Gambia.

Managing Bodily Resources

The ability to conceive is in some cases no small issue, especially when there is no conception throughout reproductive life. But in most cases, the question of physical endowment is more critical than a time-related ability to conceive. Apart from the need to retain a competitive position in the compound, most women pay no particular penalty for slowing the pace of reproduction to minimize the risk of dangerous pregnancies, especially given the precarious medical care they face in times of emergency and birth traumas they may endure. This suggests some strategies to cope with the rigors of high fertility. Gaining a set of cognitive skills, for example, can enable a woman to mitigate the expenditure of social and bodily reserves. She learns to read body signs, her own as well as those of her co-wives and other women.[29] By monitoring multiple sources of information, first with little concern and later with considerably more, she tries to brace for her remaining reproductive ordeals. The most important actions, however, involve maneuvering through social and bodily temporalities. I describe just a few examples.

Avoiding Difficult Births

The major risk to a woman's bodily resources is the strain of delivery itself. One concern is the size of a child relative to that of the birth passage. In Western medical terminology, cases in which the child's head is too large for safe passage in relation to the woman's pelvis are called cases of cephalopelvic disproportion. In areas of the world where women marry quite young,[30] cephalopelvic disproportion may create an obstetric fistula, a cavity between tissues. Gambian women's efforts to prevent such outcomes center around efforts either to keep the birth passage open while pregnant or to keep the baby small. As for trying to keep the birth passage open, it is generally regarded as beneficial to maintain sexual relations, even into the last month before delivery. The pattern of a young woman returning to her mother before giving birth to secure help in delivery and child care is sometimes said to exacerbate the problem of a narrow passageway, though a conscientious husband will visit occasionally to mitigate this problem. As for the difficulties posed by a large baby, a woman may try to forestall a difficult delivery by avoiding foods considered to make a fetus grow large: butter, bread, and eggs. Whereas one of the clearest messages in international maternal-child health literature for the past decades has been a concern with low birth weight (for example, Koblinsky et al. 1993), information from very disparate times and places suggests that low birth weight may in many circumstances be a desired outcome if not a result of efforts to "eat down." [31] (See chapter 9 for more discussion.)

29. See N. Fox 1994, 29, for a theoretical consideration of such possibilities in a postmodern vein.

30. One of the clearest examples is the Muslim north of Nigeria, where the average age at marriage in 1990 among women who had ever formed conjugal unions was 14.9, compared to 18.5 in the south (Nigeria Demographic and Health Survey 1990).

31. Nurse-midwife Patricia Woollcott (pers. comm.) relates that especially in northern Europe, where a high prevalence of rickets could result in badly deformed pelves, women often died in childbirth. Until the 1950s, American women were urged to try to keep the baby's weight low, sometimes by rice and water diets, to facilitate birth. See also Brems and Berg (1988) on the developing world.

Getting Rest

Besides attempting to minimize the physical stress of childbearing, a woman tries to mitigate future reproductive troubles. Her efforts to do so center on trying to recover from past pregnancy and birth events. Since the principal barrier to having as many children as God may give is not time but a deficit of bodily resources, it should not be surprising that a woman may try to create generous pregnancy intervals. In chapter 4 I described *fonyondiŋo* (rest) as an effort to avoid pregnancy after birth as a measure to protect the child from the risks of postpartum sex and pregnancy. There the point of orientation was the child. We now turn to the advantages and disadvantages of rest for the woman herself.

From a woman's perspective, there are two principal types of rest. The first refers to a major stage in the life course. It is the phase referred to as being "retired" from childbearing. A woman in such a state is usually "spent" as a result of childbearing. Being spent and retirement are phenomena that I take up in more detail in chapters 7 and 8. The other type of rest, described here, is the phase following a pregnancy termination when a woman is neither breastfeeding nor pregnant. She might stop childbearing, or she might, at some future point, become pregnant and give birth again. It is this ambiguous notion of rest, often marking a tense point in a marriage, that forms the most conspicuous sense of time-neutral yet potentially generative space, in the Platonic sense described in chapter 2. On these two paradoxically time-neutral notions hinges the remainder of the book.

Rest may have quite different connotations, depending on the context. Sometimes it represents a long, undesired hiatus without a pregnancy. On the other extreme is a rest that is highly desired. Such an idea emerges repeatedly in cultural analogies among animals, agriculture, and women's fertility. Analogies to land are among the most common. Many African societies have proverbs like this one in Mandinka: "Land is just like a woman; they both produce." Both can be not only "fertile" but "tired" or "old" (that is, "worn out"). A depleted rice field must be either fertilized and irrigated, or it must be "rested" for a number of seasons. Like a field, a woman should replenish herself in order to regain her reproductivity. She should eat rich foods, take curative measures when necessary, and go lightly on farmwork. The shorter she falls of the demands of work and nutritional privation, the more she should rest between births. Rest in this sense, then, is used simply to refer to a duration, usually created intentionally, in which she may recuperate from the rigors of childbearing by avoiding pregnancy. But it can also imply a carefree, sexually available state. A resting woman no longer encumbered by a breastfeeding child can move about town and farther afield. She is very likely to be the subject of her husband's renewed sexual interest.

If previous reproductive outcomes have taken a light toll and if ample food and domestic help are available, it is considered safe to begin a new conception just after weaning. If all has not gone well, though, a woman's best strategy is not to rush ahead at the risk of wasting a precious child potential out of her remaining endowment. Rather, it is to delay the next pregnancy.[32] The more strenuous the childbirth ordeals she has experienced and the weaker her body, the more she should rest. Because of the perceived intimate physiological link between a mother and a dependent child, a worn-out body is likely to miscarry or give birth to sickly children who will be malnourished because of the lack of adequate maternal resources. Mentions of rest as a critical element of a reproductive career appear repeatedly in women's comments. In the following case, a twenty-two-year-old woman, recalling the early period of her marriage with her in-laws in a remote village, attributed the death of her first child, a premature infant, to a life of arduous work, a meager diet, and no rest, either from work or from childbearing:

> I have had two pregnancies. In my first pregnancy, I delivered when I was 8 months pregnant. It was premature. The baby died a week after I delivered. My husband traveled when I was four months pregnant and he did not came back until after my delivery. I was staying with my in-laws in my husband's village. I was not having good foods there and I was doing all the domestic work and at the same time working on the rice fields during the rainy season. I think that hard work made me deliver early. A few months after my delivery my husband returned from his journey. He transferred me to the town, where I am still, living with him. My second child is two years old now, and still I want to delay my next pregnancy so that I can regain my strength. I was very sick and weak when I delivered my first child. He died and my husband came back [so] I did not stop to have a rest. I rushed to have a second one; that will not happen to me any more. I will have a good rest this time.

32. In the Gambian data, mean birth intervals following the death of a child or a nonlive birth are shorter, usually, than if the pregnancy/child had survived. This fact, however, poses no particular problem to the contingency thesis. In an expanding population, most pregnancies occur to young women, who are more able than older ones to recover quickly from an obstetric trauma and willing to go on quickly to the next pregnancy.

A case such as this, in which a young woman who has had only had one birth is anxious to rest after weaning before becoming pregnant again, is most unusual. This woman's desire to do so undoubtedly reflected the trauma of her experience.

Desire to rest is highly salient in the comments not only of women who had experienced close spaces between live births but of those who had a traumatic nonlive birth or a series of births that produced no surviving children. An example of the latter is a twenty-seven-year-old woman who had had six pregnancies, of which two resulted in children who died and two were nonlive births. Only two of her children survived. At Round 1, her previous child, still alive, had just been weaned, and she declared a desire to become pregnant again. Then, just before Round 7, she reported a stillbirth. No sexual contact was reported for the next three months, and for the remaining rounds she reported wanting to rest, an act which, in her situation, seemed to connote not only physical respite but an opportunity to pause and consider remedial actions.

> I want to rest for a while in order to regain my health and strength simply because I have just delivered a stillbirth baby and I want to do check up to know the cause of the death of the children I lost. I want to know whether all these stillbirths were caused by infection and if so, then I will treat the cause. That can help me to bear healthy children if I regain my health and strength in the future. I easily get pregnant and don't want to get pregnant without knowing the cause of the deaths of these three children. I believe that something is wrong which caused the death of these children. I want to treat the cause before resuming contact. (R. 10)

A woman in such circumstances may wait as many as three or four years before trying to get pregnant again, regardless of whether the outcome was a living child or a nonlive birth. In rest, the womb and the body can heal, and the blood and strength needed for further reproduction can be replenished. In this Platonic quality of time-neutrality, rest does not have a basis in time. It has temporalities but, as with child spacing, its duration is not thought of in months or years, and it is not necessarily seen as an action that limits numbers of children. Indeed, it is the "room" that creates a space for future reproductivity.

Connotations of timelessness also underlie van Gennep's famous insights into the liminality that often accompanies major life transition rituals, during which initiates drift "betwixt and between" various phases of ritual maturation. Victor Turner drew on these ideas in his analyses of

Ndembu ritual. On at least one point, however, he surely falls short. The phenomenon of timelessness, he wrote, is found especially in societies less complex than our own, "where change is bound up with biological and meteorological rhythms and recurrences rather than with technological innovations" (1969, 93). The implication of this passage, that people simply let time and biology drift, fails to capture the highly intentional efforts to create rest of a duration that is contingent on felt needs that lie at the heart of rural Gambian women's efforts to replenish reproductive resources. It also creates a highly arbitrary division between the natural world and a material product of human design. These observations come to the fore as we examine two further strategies: the acquisition of a co-wife and the use of Western contraceptives.

Polygyny

For a woman, abstinence from sex may be difficult, especially if she has a young husband or one who is under pressure from his family to keep up the pace of childbearing. Such sentiments are reflected in the fearful remark of one monogamous twenty-nine-year-old woman with six children:

> I would like to rest when I wean my child or to stop having children for I had a lot of difficulties with my last pregnancies. I know my husband will never allow me to practice family planning. He is totally against it. He never wants me to talk about family planning. I can only rest for a short period by avoiding him when breast feeding not for a long period because I am the only wife. (R. 3)

Polygyny does not appear to hold the solution to this woman's problems. But for others it may do so. Indeed, the desire for rest makes some women not only willing to accept a co-wife but (as my hypothetical case above showed) anxious to acquire one. As this quote implies, men are quite ambivalent on the question of their wives using contraceptives to rest from the ordeals of reproduction, a point I take up in more detail shortly. The possibility of acquiring another wife, however, they find less objectionable. In chapters 3 and 4 I described the contexts of co-wife competition and of child spacing, respectively. Here the context is men's attitudes about polygyny for solving the problem of their wives' need to rest after weaning a child or after having a reproductive mishap.

To illustrate this, I draw on a highly articulate rationalization of polygyny that appeared in the writings of Jacob K. Coker. Coker, the Nigerian leader of the African Church movement in the early twentieth century, took up the great "marriage debate" with advocates of monogamy.[33] Along with other Christian men and a growing number of clergy, Coker found it wrong for African men to be forced to accept monogamy (Dada 1986). In his view, neither the Old nor the New Testament bade men to be monogamous. All African men and women, irrespective of their conjugal status, should be brought to Christ. In fact, although he held that sex with an outside woman was wrong for a married man (as was "extravagant polygamy" because "multiplicity of wives brings multiplicity of troubles," Coker 1915, 9), Coker argued that taking a second wife was not a sin but a responsibility. His reasoning followed two lines: one a sense of obligation, the other a health measure. First, argued Coker, taking a new wife allowed an older one to be retained if a new one were acquired, rather than being abandoned in divorce as adherence to monogamy would demand.[34] Thus, the biblical prophet Malachi, he noted, had forbidden a man from turning out an old wife, the "wife of one's youth," for a new one (1915, 5). Second, and most important for our present purposes, monogamy could be risky if not fatal to both mothers and children. Coker detailed the cumulative health problems monogamy could entail: "the children born of such parents are seldom strong in constitution. This is because the mother being weak of frequent child-bearing, she must either stop or die of constant breeding" (quoted in Dada, 113). Arguing that a long nursing period for a mother and child was essential in a continent where people lacked the means to feed babies artificially, he emphasized the importance of rest: "Nursing of children, care of the house, assisting in the work of the husband and all home duties generally, become easier, being done together. Nursing for three or more years is not simply on account of the child, but to give the mother sufficient rest which is mostly needed in Africa. The absence of this has sent many a married woman [to an] untimely death" (quoted in Dada, 171). Men's practice of polygamy thus allowed women to pace the rigors of child-bearing: "Sometimes the unhealthy condition of the wife and the sickness of the child . . . call for longer rest. But nothing under 18 months is advisable, otherwise many wives will fail in health and die after a few years of child-bearing. Those who are not able to refrain for so long, take on a second wife" (172).

33. I am grateful to Kristin Mann for pointing me toward this case.

34. In a short story from Nigeria called "She Stooped to Conquer" (Kolon 1982), a man who takes a new wife already had two wives "but he had retired his two wives who were ageing" (52). Although "their mating days were over" (54), "[h]e didn't really discard them like unserviceable vehicles. He provided for them but left them in his home village to do whatever they found hands to do" (52).

Coker's report of an African bishop's trip to England in 1886 provided perspective on African practices from yet another vantage point. Upon inquiring about the ideal breastfeeding duration in his host country, the bishop was told by English physicians that the short birth intervals that apparently were then in vogue in England were unnatural and harmful and that the African practice of a three- or four-year period of nursing was best (171).

From this very surprising source emerge rich pieces of evidence that confirm the dynamics of the birth experience in West Africa today. Through the mirrors of history, religion, gender, and internationalism that Coker's texts bring to light, we see an intricate case of the phenomenological point that experience shapes perception. Coker wrote from the perspective of a man and a polygynist who could understand the experience of women who lived out a life of high fertility and suffered high rates of child mortality. The English physicians wrote from the perspective of those who dealt with problems of high fertility in pockets of their own society. To be sure, neither direct nor indirect experience necessarily determines which facet of perception will dominate in certain situations. And an experiential stance alone does not account for the language in which debates will likely be argued. Nonetheless, in listening to Coker argue his position to the multifaceted audience of his time—European missionaries and jurists, African Christian clerics, and lay monogamists (and very likely to many angry Christian women as well)—we gain perspective on the idiosyncrasies of our own vision.

Contraceptives

Drawing attention to rest as a means of replenishing strength and blood between childbirth events brings us back to one of the most provocative facets of the logic of time in this high-fertility regime: the use of high-tech contraceptives such as pills and Depo Provera to enhance rather than reduce fertility. The reason is that Western contraceptives are seen as one of the most effective ways of creating recuperative spaces for rest between taxing pregnancy and deliveries. The great majority of women who use them express a need to avoid the exhaustion and poor health that might result in nonlive births and jeopardize the children who are still alive. Previous chapters have already introduced evidence for these assertions. Here we look more closely at patterns of contraceptive use among women in different reproductive situations, particularly with respect to situations of great risk.

As the statements of many women attest (and figure 4.5 showed), the use of pills, with their short-term effects, tends to rise as far as the feeding stage of thick pap. At this point it drops sharply, as does the use of juju. Pills, like juju, tend to be used to craft tight intervals: to finish breastfeeding before beginning another pregnancy. Depo Provera, with its long durational effects, begins its rise much as pills do. But use continues to rise sharply as the child moves into solid food supplementation, and it remains high even after the child is weaned. High-parity women, finding their strength increasingly hard to regain after each successive birth, often welcome Depo's long-term effects, something that virtually all younger women just beginning their childbearing careers avoid. Depo Provera may even be used to cease childbearing completely, becoming in effect a "retirement" contraceptive.

Of particular note is the possibility that reproductive assaults are likely to result in a cumulative toll. We sense as much in the case of thirty-seven-year-old Fanta Juwara. Fanta had had seven pregnancies, the last of which had resulted in a child who was still alive at the time of the survey. Yet her third pregnancy had ended in a nonlive birth. Besides this, another child had died, leaving her with five surviving children. Because she had had at least one live birth after the nonlive birth, she might have appeared to be back on track and to have had no cause to delay a new pregnancy. But as we have seen, women who have had a nonlive birth, once they have more than four or five pregnancies, are *more* likely than those with no nonlive births to try to avoid pregnancy, and this is increasingly true with each successive parity. Such actions suggest that the nonlive birth event had an effect from which the sufferer still has not recovered. In Fanta's case, as in that of other such women, she did not want to stop childbearing altogether. But the impact of her nonlive birth remained vividly inscribed both in her memory and on her body. Here is how she described her fearful ordeal and its debilitating effects.

> The stillbirth I had was more painful than all my births because I did not deliver that one with life. He was dead inside me so I had to use all my power to push him out. If he had been alive he would be moving himself as I pushed but that was not the case. Because of that trouble over strength, my husband wanted me to rest for two years before I got pregnant again. . . . When I felt my stomach was well enough to have another child I got pregnant and my husband left again.

The possibility that reproductive events take a cumulative toll is also suggested in efforts to prolong the birth interval through contraceptive use for longer durations as parity advances. This means that the "crest-of-the-moving-wave" description of contraceptive use in chapter 4 was headed in the right direction: away from the idea of a discrete group of users and toward a vision of a temporary group whose membership changes rapidly. A more accurate rendition would retain the membership turnover idea but would show women of low parity with no peaks above the contraceptive use line, beginning to break into this line as their parity advances, and running over the line in broad swathes near the end of reproductive life.

But the strongest evidence from contraceptive use that rest is essential to reproduction in a high-fertility regime stems from the data on mishaps. We have seen that the pregnancy terminations that appear to be most physically traumatic produce the strongest contraceptive efforts to delay pregnancy. Without any doubt, the starkest case among all the women in such situations from whom I have commentary is that of Kaddy Seesay, the woman whose case began this book. With no surviving children after four pregnancies, Kaddy had begun Depo Provera injections as soon as her last remaining child died, apparently just after she was interviewed in Round 5. She next appears in Round 7 with comments such as the following: "My stomach is paining when blood is coming out. I would like to have a rest because I always have difficulties when breastfeeding. I want to have a rest. [I am using] injection to delay pregnancy because I always have problems while pregnant." And in Round 10 she said: "I used to suffer a lot before I delivered. I used to have 5 days in labor or more. I want to rest and also to regain my strength. I am afraid of labor [that is, she has difficulty during labor]. Since I started childbearing I always have difficulties before delivery. I want to rest now. . . . I am forgetful; therefore the pills which require everyday attention are not suitable for me. I take the injection once [every] three months, which is very convenient to me."

Kaddy's difficult fertility history is undoubtedly responsible for the conjugal troubles in her second marriage. So, although she wants more children (in Round 12 she expresses a desire for four more) and she sees Depo Provera as a means to this end, it is by no means clear that she wants to expend any more of her precious child potentials for this particular husband, with whom conjugal relations are fast deteriorating: "I am suffering in my marriage. I think I do not want a child here anymore. I do not talk to him [the husband] about it" (R. 14). Kaddy's most poignant response, however, was her answer to Round 11's question of the month, a query about which of Islam's tenets is most important for women and how the respondent tries to observe them:

A woman is ordained by Allah to follow the orders, advice and wishes of her husband. A good Muslim woman should not refuse to have contact with her husband when requested, and should also bear children for him. As said by the Holy Prophet, the best among his people is the one that increases the number of his people, because in the day of judgment, he doesn't want the people of other prophets to be more than his [own]. I encounter a great difficulty in following this rule. I was following it all along, but since I started bearing children, I have suffered a lot during my pregnancies and much more in labor, because in each delivery, my people thought that I would die, [yet] none of these children are alive. Now I am using family planning to prevent pregnancy in order to regain my strength, power and health. Though my husband does not like it, I am using it for prevention.

By now, it should no longer be mysterious why women like these should be using contraception in ways that are counter to the Western logic of contraceptives as instruments of fertility reduction. They are trying to realize their God-given reproductive potential to the fullest extent possible by giving their body a rest—creating a space that is still one of potential but not yet fully committed—before resuming the demands of pregnancy, birth, and breastfeeding. When a woman's health and life are at stake, to say nothing of the health and lives of the children who depend on her, then economic and medical concerns, not simply child numbers, dominate thinking about reproduction. Our science has been well aware of bodily exhaustion as an outcome of repeated births. But our journals and textbooks treat the phenomenon almost exclusively as an outcome of uncontrolled fertility behaviors. The findings here, particularly on contraceptives as strategies of rest, show that worry about bodily expenditure is one of the most important factors influencing women's fertility behavior throughout their reproductive lives.

Encountering temporal patterns such as these brings back Gell's (1992) question of whether people like rural Gambians may simply be experiencing time differently than we do. Durkheim (1915) and others such as Gurvitch, G. H. Mead, and Geertz have seen time as differentially experienced and as a function of the sociocultural environment. Around such phenomenological perspectives, Gell argues, much needless mystique has grown up. Insisting that there must be "a distinction between time and the processes which happen in time" (315), he contends that all events can be related to each other through abstract linear schemes such as "dates" (159).

Gell claims that what he calls more objectivist "B-series" theories of time (constructs of mathematical reasoning) would encompass more subjective or phenomenological, culturally specific "A-series" representations of time. The former allows events that are subjectively experienced to be located onto a sequenced, universal template that can index all events relative to one another:

> [T]here is no contradiction between allowing that time can be studied in many different cultural and ethnographic contexts, and can be understood with the aid of many different analytical frameworks, while simultaneously maintaining that time is always one and the same, a familiar dimensional property of our experienced surroundings . . . the whole point of an abstract category such as "time" is precisely that it provides the means for the relative unification of otherwise diverse categories of processes. Time—which is intrinsically unitary and unifying—allows for the co-ordination of diverse processes; biological processes with social ones, psychological or subjective processes with objective, clock-timed ones, and so forth. (315–16)

Not only can B-series time be used to create commensurability among otherwise disarrayed events, writes Gell. The sociological analyst is in fact obligated to impose an objective template of "the real world" onto the ethnographic subject's temporalities, to hold them up to impartial scrutiny.

> The ethnographic subject's map of the world can only be evaluated (seen for what it is) in the light of the world to which it is supposed to refer, which is the real world, not an imaginary world which would be real were the ethnographic subject's map true. . . . It is merely patronizing to leave exotic ethnographic models of the world uncriticized, as if their possessors were children who could be left to play forever in an enchanted garden of their own devising. (324)

Taking what he recognizes will be an unpopular position among anthropologists, Gell argues that since cultural schemes of interpretation claim to describe objective reality, "the outside observer is never in a position to be more hard-nosed than his ethnographic subjects themselves" (325).

Gell assumes that B-series time can be used as an unquestioned universal measure of A-series time, and not vice versa. I have had to shift approaches, however. At first, I took chronological time as an unproblematic baseline, showing how age and birth intervals in rural Gambia might be mapped onto, and understood in terms of, chronology. As the findings began to unfold, the weight of the analysis shifted to culturally defined contingencies and temporalities as the more encompassing mode in which rural Gambians cast their reproductive lives. It is critical to note, however, that even in this mode, chronological time is by no means gone. It—or the temporalities that closely approximate it—can also be a form of subjectively perceived temporality. It can also be the background against which other temporalities are framed. But whether we use universalizing time or some subjectively experienced temporality as the baseline matters less than the fact that agency is exercised in making this shift. People strategically invoke different forms of temporality at different moments, sometimes foregrounding one and sometimes the other. The following section, returning to the world of conjugal relations, builds on precisely this point.

Contraceptive Use and the Conjugal Politics of Fecund Time

We have explored in detail the paradoxical logics of contraceptive use as enhancing fertility and of rest as time-neutral space for women.[35] What happens when women's temporalities of reproduction and aging are juxtaposed with those of men? In chapter 7 I take up male aging as a "straight-edge" comparison to women's more contingent trajectory. For now, I observe that nowhere are the paradoxical logics of contraceptive use and of rest played out more starkly than in conjugal debates over fecund time: the time during which a woman may be able to conceive, usually when she has resumed her menses after finishing breastfeeding a child or after a child's death or a nonlive birth. During these moments, husband-wife conversations, whether we establish their content through interviews or through surveys and numbers, validate and enrich the thesis that reproduction and aging rest most fundamentally on a principle other than that of linear time. They are the case par excellence of how the contingent life course is lived and interpreted.

Men throughout the African subcontinent have a reputation, as I noted before, as resolute opponents of their wives' desires to use contraceptives. Having a reputation like this pits men squarely against the weight of international opinion, both from forces that seek to curtail fertility and from

---

35. This section is based on a paper co-authored with William Hanks (Bledsoe and Hanks 1998).

those that would give women maximum control over their reproductive lives. This reputation appears to be well deserved. Everything from the Population Council's "Imam project" in The Gambia a few years ago, which sought to raise support among religious leaders for family planning programs, to efforts by the Ministry of Health to make contraceptives accessible to women who come to clinics for well-baby checks—all have come under attack by men for using the idiom of child spacing to limit child numbers. (Men are often joined in this resistance by female elders, however.) Few men are anxious to limit their children, and wives who show an interest in contraceptives are vulnerable to spousal accusations that they are trying to avoid a pregnancy that would testify to an affair. That a man might object to a wife's efforts to ensure his children's health through safe spacing was posed as a puzzle in chapter 5. Here we reach the point at which it is essential to ask what precisely husbands and wives are arguing about.

On the surface, men are a divided lot. Some seem to voice opposition to contraceptives; some do not. What *is* clear, as I showed in chapter 4, is that most men are supportive of women's efforts to "space" their births in order to protect their children from the early weaning that a new pregnancy would demand.[36] What is equally clear, though, is that most men are unenthusiastic about anything that would "limit" their children. As long as a wife expends her bodily resources in a devoted manner, her husband is usually quite sympathetic to her desire to use contraception well past weaning[37] or even to her desire to forego all further pregnancies, if necessary. Most men are even willing to allow a wife to rest after finishing breastfeeding but before starting a new pregnancy,[38] especially if she is sick or has suffered a miscarriage or a difficult delivery. A man may give a negative an-

---

36. A 1988 study in Malawi showed that the current rate of use of modern methods of contraception was only 8 percent (Kalipeni and Zulu 1993). Kalipeni (pers. comm.), however, attests that the overwhelming majority of respondents, both men and women, said they would be willing to use any method of contraception in order to space births: 84 percent for women and 89 percent for men. Such levels are substantially higher than those recorded in most of Africa on the general question of willingness to use contraception. Among those who responded positively, 70 percent of women and 64 percent of men said they would prefer to use modern methods. Ironically, the survey had resorted to the language of child spacing simply because the pronatalist government at the time forbade fertility surveys to use phrases that connoted the idea of reducing fertility: "population control," "family planning," "fertility reduction."

37. In a recent ethnographic study in rural Upper Egypt, Asdar Ali (2000) reports on a conversation that shows almost identical patterns of attitudes about contraception from the same man with regard to spacing versus "control" or "complete cessation."

38. There is a very possible parallel of this word in translation with that used by Orobaton (2000), who describes Nigerian men's "rest" from sexual exertion.

swer, vehemently expressed and intensely meant, to an abstract query about his objections to family planning. But when asked specifically about a wife who is unwell and is known to be at risk of resuming fecundity too early, he produces a quite different response. Still, although a husband wants to be sensitive to the rigors of pregnancy and childbirth, he may see the amount of rest his wife claims to need as excessive and therefore her use of contraceptives as suspect. Let us look closely at the logic by which he makes such a judgment in the context of birth intervals.

We have seen that there are distinctions between spacing and resting, and between different kinds of rest. There are also some critical elements of ambiguity in the notion of rest. This ambiguity is best captured in the distinction between fonyondiŋo, a rest that is deserved or legitimate, and *jaŋfaa,* a rest that is undeserved or nonlegitimate. The difference thus lies in how rest may be evaluated morally. In the case of birth intervals, *fonyondiŋo* implies an appropriate space, a genuinely needed opportunity to gain health and strength. Everyone approves of such a space. They may even urge a woman to create it if her situation appears grave. *Jaŋfaa,* however, is suspect. It connotes a space that is "too long" or "too far," a space that the speaker finds an unpleasant surprise. It implies an attempt to evade responsibility. With reference to birth intervals, *jaŋfaa* implies illicit stalling, creating an interval without the husband's approval. Its occurrence requires an explanation.

As these descriptions indicate, the meaning and morality of a space are determined not by the duration of the space but by the intentions with which it is created. For a man, as is true for a woman, both child numbers and the technologies of fertility control, though they are customarily treated as self-contained measures, have meaning only in relation to a certain conjugal partner with a certain reproductive history and circumstances. For a woman who has proven her loyalty to her husband and his compound by expending her reproductivity on their behalf, people are likely to accept on faith her assertion that she needs time to restore her health. For her, fonyondiŋo is whatever time she wants to take. The situation is entirely different for a subfertile woman who is at odds with her husband and others around her. Taking extra time before the next pregnancy provokes questions. If she has recovered her health, why is so much time now elapsing between her births? Is she secretly creating this space by using contraceptives?

These questions bring us face to face once again with the quandary of whether time or contingency governs the female life course. I pointed out in chapter 5 that it makes little sense that a man should object to contraceptive use if the woman is simply trying to ensure the survival of his child. But in reality, the larger puzzle lies with women. If reproduction hinges on time, then a woman has more to lose than her husband if she rests after weaning a child, for she is adding nonreproductive time to her birth intervals and subtracting time from her total span of fecundity. Whereas a man has the possibility of having more children by other wives, a woman who creates undue rest must be hurting herself more than she is her husband, because she alone can bear her own children. In this chronological logic, men should have no need to monitor their wives' use of contraceptives because women, who have the same high fertility goals that men do, should not want to limit children, which the use of post-weaning contraceptives would surely do. That a woman, valuing high fertility as much as her husband, might try to stall, and that he might suspect her of doing so, must stem from a very different logic of the life course than that which our fertility analyses have assumed.

The solution to the puzzle lies in the ambiguities surrounding rest: this nonpregnant, post-breastfeeding period. It is precisely at this point that men begin to waver at the prospect of contraceptive use. The reason is that they may see this period as jaŋfaa. If the woman were locked into a time-bound framework, her husband reasons, she would be depriving herself of children even more than she would him. But since everyone knows that contingency, not time, poses the limit on reproduction, they also know that the woman has much to gain if she withholds her reproductive potential from him, even if no alternative candidate is in sight. A woman seeking to stall—and a man suspecting her of doing so—is acting on the premise that her moderate resting after births will not limit her child numbers and may even increase them. This means that a woman's very logical strategy for keeping her future reproductive and conjugal options open is to manipulate this physical plasticity, to take advantage of its time-neutral character. That is, she is using contraceptives not only to delay births but to leave a difficult marriage.

Since men share these cultural premises, a man's hostility to contraceptive use is not only unsurprising: it is predictable.[39] To a man, the possibility that a wife, particularly if she is young and healthy, is using contraceptives past the point of weaning can only mean that she is trying to escape

---

39. McLaren (1990, 116), describing thirteenth-century England, writes: "Misogynists countered [women's claims to fear of pregnancy and childbirth by saying] that women were motivated by frivolous concerns. They were frequently accused of limiting their pregnancies to protect their beauty or reputation."

her marriage to him, and she is doing so by limiting fertility. The key point is that she is not limiting her *own* children; she is limiting *his*. He may end up with two of her children; she will have all eight. Whether the specific charge is one of infidelity, of being indifferent to the interests of his family, or of hoarding her reproductive resources—all are part of the same package of sins. Knowing that every woman wants all the children God gives her, a husband who decides that his wife is trying to suppress her pregnancies can draw only one conclusion: she must be saving the rest for someone else.

The intertwined male-female temporal logics proceed as follows. For men, the primary focus is the well-being of the last-born child. Men tend to reckon subsequent reproductive time from the point at which the child's health becomes established. Once the child is weaned and the woman appears to be healthy, the man will begin to suspect any extra time before a new pregnancy as stalling. The default male logic thus takes births as discrete events and reckons *forward*, progressively, from each. For a woman, the health of the last child is also important, as we saw in chapter 4. But as she begins to experience the cumulative toll of reproduction, she may begin to evaluate this same slice of the birth interval differently than her husband. For her, the previous birth begins to recede in importance as a marker, and the timing and circumstances of the next become more salient. As she contemplates in the present the prospects of becoming pregnant again in the future, she must calculate *backward* from a hypothesized end, that is, backward from the possible timing of the next birth. This she does in order to estimate when she will be recovered sufficiently from her present state, itself a function of the cumulative reproductive assaults she has experienced and the opportunities she has had to recover from them.

At the outset of reproductive life, these forces usually result in an uncontested linear logic. Women want to establish themselves in the compound quickly by having many children, and a man wants to be sympathetic with his wife's reproductive needs. But with the progressive physical degeneration of her body, a woman's logic increasingly becomes one of cumulative toll and of retrospective calculation from future events. Under ideal marital conditions, men and women tacitly agree on which logic should apply. Because their interests converge, the man trusts his wife and allows her to enact changes in her contraceptive behavior freely as they become necessary. This may result in little or no contraception at first and strong, effective contraception later if she needs more opportunity to rest after weaning.

If conjugal relations begin to erode, however, men and women may

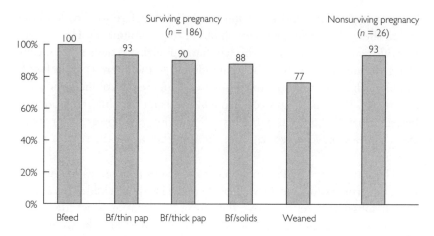

Fig. 6.2 Husbands knowledgeable about wife's Western contraceptive use, after various pregnancy outcomes

Source: Thirteen monthly rounds done in 1993–94, North Bank.

Note: Nonpregnant women using pills or Depo; husband in household.

begin to orient themselves differently to the critical segment of the birth interval: the part that begins after the child has been weaned and the woman appears to be recovered from the last cycle of reproduction. It is precisely at this point, where "rest" begins, that conjugal arguments most often arise and where the breach in the Gambian and Western understandings of time and reproduction emerges most starkly. Women, calculating backward from the next potential pregnancy, describe this time as fonyondiŋo: deserved rest. Men may charge that any further passage of time past the last child's weaning is jaŋfaa: suspect stalling. These exchanges provide an arresting instance of Mead's vision of individual pathways converging momentarily in a flat plane and diverging again as the character of their encounter and of their own temporal trajectories carry them on.

Evidence of such disputes about fecund time find strong backing in the monthly round findings on women's reports of their husband's knowledge of their contraceptive use. Taking women using Western contraceptives (pills or Depo Provera) whose previous pregnancy resulted in a surviving child, figure 6.2 shows a distinct relation between the child's stage of feeding and the husband's knowledge of contraceptive use. All of the women with infants on unsupplemented breastfeeding reported that their husbands knew about their contraception. Once a breastfeeding child began to eat thin pap, however, the percentage of women who reported that their husbands knew about their contraceptive use declined to 93 percent. The percentage of knowledgeable husbands (according to their wives) declined again, to 90 percent, among still-breastfeeding women whose children were eating thick pap and to 88 percent of breastfeeding mothers with children eating solid foods. Among mothers of weaned children, the percentage of women reporting knowledgeable husbands fell sharply to its lowest point of 77 percent. The safer a new pregnancy would be for the breastfeeding child, with weaning being the most decisive point, the less likely the man is to know about his wife's contraceptive use. Although the husbands' knowledge is almost certainly overreported, the pattern is consistent both internally and with other data.[40]

Of further interest in this graph is the bar on the right, which shows that a very high proportion of women who suffered a nonlive birth or a child's death reported that their husbands knew about their contraceptive use (93 percent of the cases). Thus, an extremely high percentage of men are approving of their wives' actions even though there is no child at all to space. Since such cases are often indicators of a woman's poor health, this is further evidence of consistency.

How do numbers like these play out in everyday life? Do men's misgivings about women's illicit rest have any real grounds? There is indeed evidence that men's mistrust of women's rest is sometimes well founded. Women report a well-developed corpus of strategies—a local techne—to create and legitimate illicit time. Some admitted in their commentary that they were continuing breastfeeding longer than necessary, perhaps claiming a child's illness, as an excuse to continue the contraceptive protection the husband had allowed for breastfeeding. Others feign tiredness or make more of an illness than its true severity warrants. Alternatively, they may use contraception secretly for several months after resuming fecundity in order to create the illusion that they have lengthy "natural" periods of postpartum infecundity. A woman may also visit an Islamic marabout healer claiming to seek treatment for a miscarriage after a pregnancy of some months when in fact she has been on contraceptives. Much rarer, but occasionally occurring, are cases of young women who were forced to marry men they did not want. Using contraceptives to feign sterility, they hope the husband will send them home or allow them to marry someone else. Said one young woman who had managed to extricate herself from an unwanted marriage:

40. It entirely possible, of course, that this chart may reflect women's misconstruals of their husbands' knowledge of their contraceptive use. Yet if this is true, then it only goes to support the logic of trying to stabilize health and not worries about time.

"Now my only strategy is to reserve myself until I get a husband I like and choose for myself because I was forced to marry him when he was not my choice" (R. 2). In all of this, efforts to create and account for illicit time are based on the premise that reproductivity is not bound to time. Indeed, time seems suspended.

What are the motives underlying such actions? A woman may feel that she is struggling as best she can for a miserly, shortsighted husband who has no sympathy for her plight. In response, she may begin to cut corners in domestic duties. She may refuse to come to her husband's house at night or to cook for him, the two activities being tightly linked symbolically, or to heat his bath water. She may even take a furtive detour from the market to the health clinic for a Depo Provera injection. Eventually, to make ends meet, she may even acquire an outside male "friend," an act that renders a husband's fears a self-fulfilling prophecy. Her own family members, since they will likely bear the brunt of the support for her children by an unsupportive man, are likely complicit if not instrumental in these actions. Getting old on behalf of an undeserving husband is both tragic and irresponsible. Scolding her for "delivering for nothing," of "wasting" herself, and of "growing toward old age" on behalf of a "useless man," her family members may demand that she stop having children. They do *not* mean, however, that she should stop altogether. Rather, she should stop temporarily. She should reserve her remaining endowment for someone else and resume it when she remarries. Because women have little to lose and everything to gain by stopping reproduction for a useless man, there is a very real possibility that their rest actually *is* illicit stalling. This fact men, in turn, know very well.

Whether we listen to survey numbers or interview transcripts, it is this "statistical noise" or these discordant voices that we tap when we attend to conjugal conversations about contraception in the later parts of the birth interval. Breastfeeding, contraception, and child health are hardly domains where one would think to look for politics. But ethnographically, these are charged moments. Men begin to accuse their wives of stalling, of the secret use of contraceptives, of wanting to leave for another man. Women begin to wonder whether this was the right man on whom to spend their youth, or whether it is in fact too late to defect from this marriage by using contraception further into the birth interval. The lives that came together for brief, deceptively commensurable moments now split wide open. At these points, where the noise becomes loudest, it becomes most clear that the pieces of common sense that have generated our fertility analyses have been wrong and that Western tendencies to privilege chronological time as determinant of fertility in high-fertility populations have been misguided.

What appear to be inconsistencies in both the male and the female orientation to these matters are now seen to be nothing of the kind. There is a clear cultural logic that unifies men and women and in which these inconsistencies are resolved. The shared cultural premises of a contingent life course, the physical effects of high fertility, a woman's desire to establish herself firmly in the compound, together with the common knowledge that a woman may withhold her reproductivity by "resting"—all generate a pattern of fertility whose logic lies beyond the grasp of a sheer calculation of linear chronological time.

The possibility that a woman may be creating illicit fecund time, and that her husband may well try to discover this, underscores the point that an irrevocably partitioned set of dualistic categories (Western versus Gambian, time versus contingency, men versus women), even though I had used these words as heuristics, only takes us so far. The rhythms and cycles associated with pregnancy and birth are based not only on social but also on physical plays of time. This observation leads to one of the most intriguing twists of all in the case of male resistance to contraceptive use: time as a chronological measuring stick is by no means gone from view. It is in fact a critical axis around which wifely devotion can be judged. Insofar as a wife's efforts to stall limit her husband's fertility, men's understandings are quite consonant with the Western time-based view of reproductivity: stalling reduces *male* fertility. It should not be surprising, therefore, that the key to discovering illicit stalling for a suspicious man (or his mother) lies in scrutinizing his wife's accounts of her reproductive temporalities to look for inconsistencies in chronology. With the previous child safely weaned and the woman apparently recovered from the birth, he will begin to suspect that a chronologically long space is the result of stalling and quite possibly a result of illicit contraceptive use. Time (or, more precisely, the physical events for which linear time is now the best index) is very likely to become the measure of the space for a woman who appears healthy enough to become pregnant again. The fact that time not only can but *must* be juxtaposed to contingency to gauge conjugal devotion makes a compelling case that a dualistic depiction of "rural Gambia" versus "the West" would miss entirely the dynamics of the scheme.

Summary and Discussion

Arguing against the conviction that reproductive capacity is bound to a time clock, this chapter has explored a cultural vision of reproductivity as a God-given endowment that must be realized within a life course of contingent physical tolls. At this point, it should be obvious why time is not seen as the limit on reproductivity for the majority of women in rural Gambia. Women living under precarious health and economic conditions, who nonetheless want all the children God gives them, will almost certainly run up against the anatomical and energy limits of the body before they encounter any presumed boundaries of chronological time, the matter with which contemporary Western culture is so concerned. A number of chronologically young women in the interviews and survey commentaries said that they could not bear more children because they were "too old"—by which I now know they meant "worn out." And few women asserted that they truly did not want any more pregnancies or children. But when their comments are examined closely, it is clear that these women saw circumstances as posing the limits, not time or some target number of children. (Not a single response in the 4,054 records from the monthly rounds gave chronological age as a reason to stop childbearing.) The overriding question a rural Gambian woman faces is rarely how long she will retain her capacity to conceive. It is instead how many of her child potentials she will be able to bear as living children and raise to healthy maturity. If a pressing need arises to continue bearing children (if, say, several children die, a rival co-wife appears, or a marriage to a new man becomes necessary), she may try to produce another child or two, even if her bodily resources are almost gone. A woman worries not about the time during which her reproductive events occur but about the conditions that bring her reproduction to an end. Since the time during which she can reproduce is itself a function of how well she can manage her social and bodily resources as she pursues a high-fertility life goal, measuring live births per total number of fecund years would be meaningless.

Both the Gambian and the Western logics recognize that there are limitations to reproduction. Both might even say that reproductivity is a limited good: in the West this limited good would consist of time; in The Gambia, it would be fetuses and muscles. How might these different conceptions shift the calculus of action? In the logic of linear time, a woman who wants as many children as God gives her will try to produce as many children as she can fit into her thirty or so years of fecundity, from age fifteen to age forty-five. Assuming that she has no problems with conceiving, she could have as many as thirty births or more simply by filling up her time with pregnancies and very brief periods of breastfeeding. In effect, the same assumptions about how child numbers are produced at the population level are applied to individual respondents. But in the contingency perspective, the question of a chronological duration of reproductivity would be irrelevant. Given the conditions a Gambian woman faces, she knows she could not have children at the pace of one per year in the manner that the Western emphasis on fecundity says is theoretically possible. Since reproduction can start when a woman is quite young, she is likely to become "spent" well before fecundity ends. What does determine the maximum number of healthy children she has is the care with which she manages her bodily resources. As a result, she often tries to *stretch out* the time between births. The economic, medical, and social conditions in these two circumstances shape reproductive logics that are radically different from one another.

Looking back, now, to the story in chapter 2 about the sixty-three-year-old woman in the United States who gave birth to a child, we can understand why the order in which the reproductively relevant clocks terminate is likely to be reversed in the Gambia. The fact that we lead an easy life in the West appears to allow us to eliminate anything but the clock governing eggs and ovaries as the limit on reproduction. An unused, undamaged muscular uterus is very likely to last far longer than the clock that regulates the production of viable eggs. The fact that the uterus is not bound to the same clock as the ability to conceive is now starkly apparent.

The nonchronological logic, so counterintuitive to us in one moment yet obviously commonsensical in the next, explains a number of puzzles. Among the most notable is the lack of concern, given the goal of high fertility in rural Gambia, with menopause. In the contingency logic, menopause does not cause the end of reproduction; it is if anything the result. Reproduction, in eroding bodily resources and aging the body, may precipitate menopause. The contingency logic also helps explain a woman's contraceptive efforts to create rest: the nonpregnant hiatus following the weaning of her most recent child. Whereas women in the West see time and contraceptives as ways to achieve *low* fertility, those in rural Gambia see them as allies of *high* fertility. In this region, where reproduction is so critical that temporal delays would seem to be its chief enemy, stretching birth intervals can create opportunities to recuperate from the cumulative ordeals of prior birth events and to forestall the ill health that would jeopardize the children who are still alive. Since the time spent in resting is considered largely irrelevant to ultimate child numbers, the most traumatic health assaults produce the strongest efforts to delay a new pregnancy.

The sense of a social and temporal calculus that a woman must enact for managing reproduction and a moral conjugal life is echoed in Bourdieu's (1990, 66–67) description of a ball player's spatial and temporal orientation to a field:[41] a landscape of positions, the agents in these positions, and the rules and materials by which competition among the positions is conducted. Ball players, he writes, attain an implied "feel" for the game: a sense of timing, an orientation toward a goal, a continual restructuring lines of force as moves transpire. They come to sense impending outcomes and develop their strategies in ways that are "lived" rather than understood overtly. Much as a ball player comes to sense a field and its temporalities, a woman in rural Gambia uses cues to triangulate on how her births are proceeding, when a new pregnancy is safe, and how much effort will be required to bear and raise further children. Just as she seeks to care for a child and cultivate its emerging character, she tries, through a mix of strategies of expenditure and containment, to cultivate her endowed potential in order to realize its best reward. Based on a sense of the cumulative past that led to the present state of depletion of her physical resources, and on a sense of the cumulative social capital available to her (including the support or enmity of her husband, mother-in-law, and co-wives), she tries to anticipate her limits. She may stretch out the time between her pregnancies to gain rest or may terminate them altogether before having more pregnancies becomes too dangerous. With an eye to the consequences of each action, she constantly weighs new courses of action and frames possibilities with an eye to modes of recourse, whether through hygiene, marital comportment, ritual, or connections to kin.[42]

Inevitably, a woman confronts forces that would seem to deplete her body and depreciate her value as a wife. But the possibility of guiding the trajectory of her reproductive career in the face of hardship, containing and buffering its unpredictable adversities, points to one of the most absorbing facets of the scheme: the tension between fate and action. As I have tried to emphasize, contingency is not experienced simply as uncontrolled adversity but also in terms of possible actions one might take to *contain* it. The question of destiny (or the will of a deity) is one that is echoed in every major religion, as is that of the individual's scope to influence this destiny. A reproductive endowment that is divinely bestowed, and in a quantity that cannot be known before it is finished, would seem to be an archetypal case of fate that renders action futile. Such an endowment, with its sacred fixity, might

41. Here he builds on Merleau-Ponty (1963, 198–99).

42. Bourdieu's view of the habitus as the "durably installed generative principle of regulated improvisations" (1977, 78) provides for choice. But individuals in his writings act within tightly constrained visions of what is possible, a critique that has been leveled at him on many occasions. The material documented here, much of it read through the codes and tables of surveys, also suggests far broader scope for action than Bourdieu conveys.

be expected to absorb unending ritual attention from diviners, who seek to intuit God's will concerning the reproductive potential of their male clients' prospective brides. Yet neither is the case. The logic of reproductive action described here reflects infinite scope for action, and there is no business at all in the divination of women's God-given reproductive endowments. How can these things be so?

The answer is that although the number of potential children is fixed, the number who are born and survive is not. Therefore, a woman must conduct her life as if the number of potential children were very high. For this reason, she sees success in realizing her predestined potential as living children, whatever the total number might be, as *entirely* determined by action. Although she might declare that she wants "as many children as God gives," she is not implying that accepting divine will renders action irrelevant, as such statements have often been interpreted. Quite the opposite. The fact that the most basic element of reproductive capacity is a divinely bestowed endowment paradoxically implies enormous scope for action. What determines how many fetuses out of her unknown allotment will be born as healthy, successful children or lost in reproductive mishaps is the care with which each reproductive opportunity is managed, whether by consulting the Islamic marabout or by obtaining antibiotics from a clinic. Such an action is taken both for its own sake and with an eye to its impact on future fertility.[43] The hapo itself, and the other fixed element, muscles, since their quantity can be neither known nor increased, are simply assumed. The more ephemeral elements of reproductivity, strength and blood, which hold the greatest potential to influence the ultimate numbers of children, draw the most attention in everyday reproductive life. Even if his ultimate will cannot be known, God's empirical ways are far less mysterious than a simple interpretation of "fate" might imply.

---

43. Amal Hassan Fadlalla (pers. comm.) reports similar patterns in The Sudan; see also Boddy 1989. In consonance with these emphases, Guyer's (1993, 1996) description of the cultivation of "singular" skills in children and of long-term investments in persons in equatorial Africa shows that people do not see identity as unfolding by itself in a kind of unfettered naturalism but rather as a product of an assiduous cultivation of emergent potentials.

CHAPTER 7

Time-Neutral Reproduction, Time-Neutral Aging

One of the most telling moments in all the research I have conducted in Africa occurred during an interview in June 1995 in the house of a village traditional birth attendant, an old woman with an extremely agile mind. It was she who had given me the motor vehicle metaphor, described in chapter 6, to explain the relation between strength and muscles. With Fatou translating, I explained that I was trying to understand the experience of high fertility because most people in the United States now have no more than two children.

As the conversation went on, it moved from how many children people want, which the TBA found an uninteresting question, to how many they end up with (a more interesting one), and finally to how pregnancies are spaced—a highly compelling one. I found myself pressing on some of the implications of non-time-dependent reproduction with which I had been struggling from the other side of the cultural divide. Thinking of time and menopause, I asked the TBA what could keep a woman from ending up with all the child potentials with which God had endowed her. "Sickness." Could Fatou, here—who is thirty years old and has had two children but is delaying more childbearing because she is working on this research project—continue expending her hapo (divine endowment of child potentials) whenever she is ready? "Yes."

Then, pressing the logic with an extreme case, I asked: Could a woman with a hapo of ten child potentials bear them all if she spaced her pregnancies every five years? This time the answer was surrounded by hesitation and confusion, something akin to "Well, . . . sort of . . . but. . . ."

As soon as we were out the door, Fatou (who had recognized the line of interrogation well) turned to me and exclaimed, "Did you see that?" Both of us had seen the cultural logjam the TBA encountered when she was forced to place the end of childbearing into a time frame. She showed no signs of being confused by the concept of age or of chronological time as measured in years *(sanjo)* that pass by. There was no problem, either, with the notion that bodily processes transpire at a certain average pace, as measured by time. In fact, her response to the last question seemed to assume this. She was confused instead by my determination to force the idea of reproductive capacity into a frame of time. To her, the question made no sense. Being boxed into a corner with two opposing logics, time and contingency, squared off so starkly against each other was precisely the problem I had had to confront from the other side of the cultural fence. Just as I had refused at first to acknowledge a non-time-based end point to fertility, the conviction voiced in rural Gambia that reproduction ages the body made the idea of a chronological reproductive boundary incomprehensible to the TBA.

Whereas Western precepts tell us that reproductive capability terminates with age, it is a fact of singular note that worries about age almost never appear in rural Gambian women's narratives of their fertility histories. This fact would seem to defy common sense in a society so desirous of children. Yet the emerging cultural logic explains this apparent anomaly quite well. Fertility and even senescence itself are seen as having almost nothing to do with what Western society refers to as age or time. Instead, people are playing with both biology and time.

In chapter 6 I laid out the critical relation of strength, blood, and muscles to reproduction, noting that chronological age is seen as related only tangentially. In this chapter I carry forward the thesis by turning to what should be, if the contingency thesis is right, the most critical part of a woman's reproductive life course: the end. In describing the character and pace of bodily decline, I confront the fact that chronological age does not necessarily coincide with physical senescence. More generally, I search for ways to describe life course events that can be plotted over time but are in no other way tied to time. I also search for ways to proceed when our disparate pockets of cultural knowledge are in such flagrant conflict with one another that we can no longer relegate their contradictions to the inconsequential "miscellaneous" pile. Emerging once more is the question of how we handle our science's objects.

This chapter and chapter 4 are the empirical linchpins of the book. Chapter 4, beginning squarely on the Western side of the fence in its assumptions about time and reproduction, opened to intense scrutiny concepts such as birth intervals and child spacing, which view chronological time as central to the life course. As the cases of blur and slippage began to increase, and in such systematic ways (chapter 5), the axis of exploration began to tilt away from measures of time toward alternative temporal vocabularies. What emerged most visibly were bodily temporalities of resting, recuperation, and health (chapter 6). Now, as I probe the aging phenomenon and the base rotates even farther away from time, there is a growing sense that the ethnographic subject's perspective must rise to the spirit of Gell's (1992) challenge of scrutiny. Conversely, the notion of time as a useful index of reproductive capacity must somehow stand up empirically to the principle of contingent physical expenditure.[1] Although I sometimes retain time as a base in the calculations, time can no longer sit as an unchallenged benchmark by which something else is tested. Time itself is now the subject of the tests.

Since, as I noted previously, the most convincing way to escape the strictures of time is to keep a firm grip on it, the present chapter follows suit. I examine the end of reproduction, a subject whose principal indicators (menopause, terminal abstinence, senility, and so on) are almost always expressed in terms of chronological time. Thus, I need some relativity tests. The scale that will offer the counter to time consists of the reproductive stages that are said to reflect life's contingent ordeals, particularly those of pregnancy and childbearing. Using this scale, I examine relations among body states, age, and the end of reproduction. Whereas in chapters 4 through 6 I began to move away from vocabularies of chronological time, the need for markers by which to detect relativities is even stronger than before. With time on trial, I refer to it constantly.

Of greatest interest is whether the end of reproduction comes about by time or by wear. The most important mark, therefore, will be the tipping point between reproductivity and the end of reproduction. In Gambian perceptions, this point, the sarifo ("spent") stage, is the physical moment

---

1. Gray (1994, 89) stresses that the value of the biomedical data used in his New Guinea study lies in validating indigenous observations that link premature aging to poor nutrition and maternal depletion.

at which women report that the limit of their childbearing capacity is well within view. Having just a bit of reproductivity left, they could continue or terminate childbearing. Such dilemmas—horizons—produce action, comment, and anxiety.[2] What induces women to stop childbearing or to try for another pregnancy? It is in these singularly awkward ethnographic and demographic moments, when time seems most to break down, that we find the greatest opportunity for experiment.

Sarifo is a critical juncture for theoretical reasons as well. Natural fertility theory, as it has been applied to high-fertility regimes, suggests that women do not change their fertility behaviors according to the number of children born, although they may stop sexual life at menopause if grand-motherhood status demands. The possibility we must now confront, however, is whether women actually do change their reproductive behavior over the life course. If so, what makes them do so? Changes in behavior may come about not because of numbers of children born but because of the cumulative bodily effects of their reproductive ordeals. If this view is right, the most dramatic changes in reported fertility goals and contraceptive behavior should occur abruptly, as women report that they are physically spent.

In devising tests for determining the end of reproductivity—time or physical state—the main dilemma is how to get a fix on the end of reproductivity. This point is usually identified by markers such as age, being menopausal, having a grandmother status, or desiring no more children. Yet each of these measures is flawed. Stated desire for no more children is a highly subjective issue and one on which women may change their minds later. As for grandmotherhood status, I have no data that systematically address this. Even so, the fact that older women have multiple duties as fictive and classificatory grandmothers would make it difficult to draw any convincing conclusions about the effects of grandmotherhood on a woman's fertility. Since I have only women's self-reports, the question of physical state is similarly problematic for estimating the end of reproduction. There are no measures of body mass, skin fold, muscle tension, or maternal depletion that Western science might regard as more objective.[3] Menopause is equally problematic as a marker in the rounds data, both because most of the women were selected because they had had a birth within the past three

2. For a very promising notion along these lines, that of "vital conjuncture," see Johnson-Kuhn 2000.

3. Contraceptive use, often used as a marker of desire to limit children, is of limited utility in a population that uses contraceptives systematically for spacing births.

years and since reproduction often ends by the woman's choice. As for using time or age to mark the end of reproductivity, this test is also flawed. Time is a measure that we have made to operate independent of events in the world, especially of social events. If we are to attempt to place age and physical state on a level playing field, we can no longer accord time its privileged abstract position outside the system. Because time is now part of the test, the ground must be allowed to shift.

Because no one external measure can solve all the problems surrounding the end of reproduction, I attempt to construct an argument of consistency and to do so by enlisting a variety of indices. The main measures include age, numbers of pregnancies, reported physical states, and number of further pregnancies desired for the husband.[4] Throughout the chapter, quotations, cases, and local terms explain and support the numerical tests. They also provide its central inspiration. Before moving to the tests, however, let us set a context by asking how rural Gambians describe the process of aging.

How Is Aging Described in Rural Gambia?

African ethnography has long established that local words such as *old* and *aged* bear little chronological significance. Far more important are their social connotations (see Stucki 1995 and Rasmussen 1997 for overviews). Being "old," whether one thinks of this state in terms of generation or kinship, is usually expressed in some form of relativity such as precedence. Being the first wife of a man, for example, gives a woman authority over the subsequent wives. The same is true for establishing rights to land or to political leadership. Being the descendants of the "firstcomers" who settled an area is said to accord privileges that the descendants of "latecomers" do not share.[5] Similarly, birth precedence gives children foundational knowledge of the history of the family and bolsters their future claims to leadership in the family. The importance of "history," therefore, is framed not in terms of the passage of time but of the record or memory of events. Yet we have not asked how physical senescence may have come about. The assumption

---

4. The question from Round 12 used here, "How many more pregnancies do you want for your husband?" is different from the questions used most often in fertility surveys for measuring fertility desires: "How many children do you want?" or "If you had it to do over again, how many children would you have?" Round 12's question was worded to reflect local emphasis on (1) pregnancies, rather than live births, as the most immediately important objects of reproductive attention and (2) the link between expenditure of bodily resources and a specific man.

5. See Beckerleg 1992–93 for the Mandinka in The Gambia, Murphy and Bledsoe 1987 for Liberia, and Kopytoff et al. 1987 for Africa more broadly.

apparently has been that this process occurs at a regular, predictable pace that lies outside the control of human action. The following descriptions suggest that the "normal" life trajectory of female senescence differs quite markedly from that with which most of us in the West are familiar. This possibility emerges both in the assertion that Gambian women may age more rapidly than do Western women and Gambian men and in the assertion that Gambian women see themselves as recovering key elements of their youth after they have finished childbearing. The most promising possibilities lie in comparing women of different types and different life stages and in comparing women to men.

Ideas of senescence that are articulated in rural Gambia bear little resemblance to what we find in contemporary Western scientific writings. Everyone knows that time passes, whether this passage is measured in years, seasons, or generations. Everyone also understands the meaning of chronological age. Yet people's responses to queries about their chronological age are very often wrong because they seldom bother to try to track their ages. The reason is that the most important connotation of bodily "age" or "oldness" is not one of time. It is instead one of being "worn out." This is the case especially for women. Becoming "old" implies that a person wears out in bodily forms and functions. Youth implies having firm body fat, taut muscles, and shining skin. By contrast, a woman who is "old" or "worn out" has wrinkled, sagging flesh, and flaccid muscles. She begins to complain of painful joints and dimming vision. Her abdomen sags with flabby creases, her breasts are limp and flat, her skin is dry and flaky, she is thin and weary. There is some fear that any children she bears at this point may be unhealthy because of the deficient maternal resources with which they are nourished before and after birth. Everyone knows that a subfertile woman will eventually reach menopause, grow old, and die. But they hold that a woman who has had multiple pregnancies will age faster. Since it is wearing out that effectively makes one old, and since bodily resources such as muscles will almost certainly wear out well before menopause occurs, then neither chronological age nor menopause is anything to worry about. Rather, it is the vagaries of life—sickness, hunger, injury, strenuous work—and the social world that produces them to which one is minutely attuned.

Although the ordeals of work, hunger, and illness have a general wearing and (hence) aging effect, certain events are seen as wearing the body more quickly than others. Among the most potent of all the forces that exact a toll on the body, as I noted chapter 6, is childbirth, particularly births that are closely spaced or difficult. Thus, the pace of a woman's aging picks up when she begins bearing children. One source of stress is the birth process itself. Another is the fact that a woman with the distraction of many children to care for fails to take care of herself. After she finishes bearing, the pace of her senescence may slow down again, especially if she has daughters-in-law and sons to take care of her and her younger children, eats good food, and so on. A miscarriage or a stillbirth, however, can entail a delivery that is far more traumatic than a normal birth. A young, energetic woman who experiences near-ruinous muscle loss after three days of obstructed labor may find herself catching up quickly in senescence to a woman who is chronologically older. Conversely, a barren woman may retain her youthful appearance far longer than her age peers who have had difficult childbearing careers. Since childbearing is far more wearing than any other event a person can experience, it is the woman who has lost all her muscles in childbearing, not necessarily the one with many years behind her, who is deemed, both by herself and by observers, to be old. This process, expressed in Fula, is "to dry" or "to become thin."[6] Such distinctions also emerge in the contrast between simply being old physically, which either a man or a woman can be, and being "old in delivery," sarifo (Mandinka), which only a woman can be.

Women recognize that their bodily resources will likely deteriorate in a nonlinear manner. They comment freely on the bodily changes that reproduction and other hardships produce in them. Pointing to the difficulties that rural women face, one thirty-five-year-old "spent" woman explained why she wanted only one more pregnancy even though she had only two surviving children:

> I came to this stage because of many pregnancies that are not spaced. I have lost most of my muscles and strength. Women in rural areas lose their strength also due to hard work because they are responsible for all their housework and also they join the men in farming. That is why we get old very easily. . . . The majority of my children died. Only two out of seven are alive. That is why I want another one, so that I have at least three children to take care of. If they were all alive I would not have need for any more because I am getting old now and I have little strength in me . . . because all my muscles are gone due to many pregnancies. (R. 12)

The challenges of a poor diet, strenuous work, and childbearing, particularly in a rural environment, all emerge in a twenty-eight-year-old woman's

---

6. From Senegal, Ousmane Sembène (1987), in a short story called "Her Three Days," describes his main character as follows: "She was not old, but one pregnancy after another—and she had five children—and her heart trouble had aged her before her time" (38–39).

description of her own rapid senescence after only four pregnancies. Comparing her lot to that of village men and of town-dwelling women who do not farm or struggle, she explained:

> Because of many pregnancies, I have lost most of my muscles. I eat adequate food but it is not a balanced diet. Women in the villages have more hard work than the men. I do all the housework, go to the bush to collect firewood and also join my husband when he goes to the farm during the rains. This hard work and the muscles I lost in deliveries make village women look older. (R. 12)

Recognition that there is in fact a chronological age (though it does not necessarily correspond to bodily age), that childbearing can accelerate bodily aging, and that contingency plans can be laid to try to shape the course of physical decline—all are captured succinctly in the following comment. After bearing four surviving children, a twenty-five-year-old woman explained why she wanted to rest after weaning the child she was currently breastfeeding: "I don't want to be very old [worn out] while I haven't reached the age [in years]" (R. 9). In the face of such descriptions of the decrement of bodily resources, strict linear interpretations of senescence somehow fall short.

Stages of Female Bodily Development and Decline

To lay the basis of the empirical tests for these cultural assertions about senescence, let us now turn to the major culturally recognized stages (s., *tɛmbo*) of a woman's life. They include, in rough translation, "virgin" *(sunkuto)*, "middle" woman *(foro musoo)*, "spent" woman *(sarifo)*, and "old woman" *(musu kɔtɔ)*. These phases each have social connotations that lend them certain meanings. But the principle that guides physical transformation to another stage is a wear-based deterioration of bodily resources. In the following discussion, which concentrates on the later phases, I examine what most people agree are the physical concomitants of these stages. Although there is no full agreement on these terms or on the characteristics they describe, the main classifying criteria revolve around the physical attributes associated with the production of young life.

Sunkuto refers to a virgin, a girl who is considered "ripe" for marriage. As a girl who is "young" or "fresh"—*nyinyaa*—she has appealing layers of rounded body fat. Her hips are narrow and her breasts, one of the most telling indicators of a woman's physical stage, are erect and firm; they are said to contain "stones." A new bride is referred to as having "fresh blood": she is someone in whom no muscles have yet been "cut" or "broken." Marriage negotiations for her may be under way, but she has never married and has never had sexual relations with a man.

Foro musoo ("middle woman") *didiŋo* ("beginning") refers to a young married woman. Usually she has had a child or two, though sometimes this term refers to a woman who is pregnant for the first time. The stones in such a woman's breasts have begun to "soften." *Foro musoo didiŋo*, however, can also be used in a negative sense to describe a young woman of anomalous conjugal standing, one whose imminent marriage was called off when some other man stepped into the picture. Despite her lack of fertility experience, such a woman has become devalued, and the bridewealth that her family is able to negotiate with the next man is likely to be considerably less than the first.

Foro musoo may refer to a woman of proven fertility who is located anywhere in the span of childbearing. Usually, however, such a woman has had two or more pregnancies. A foro musoo ("middle woman"), according to a man famed for his skills in brokering marriages for such women, is one "who has shown her nobleness as a woman." She is a woman of respect. Well beyond virginity, she is now steadily pursuing her primary task in life, that of bearing children. As further childbearing events transpire, the stones in her breasts become "crushed," and her hips open up. (These processes occur also in a woman who has had stillbirths, though not in a woman who has had only early miscarriages.)

At some point, a woman realizes that she is sarifo, with an understanding that childbearing is the cause of the condition. Throughout her body, her muscles are worn out, especially those in the region most involved in delivery, from the shoulders down through the abdomen and into the pelvis. She may have one or two pregnancy possibilities left. At this juncture, however, she senses a significant decline, and hints of health troubles and tiredness among women at this stage emerge repeatedly in both the survey numbers and the commentary. Everyone eventually gets old physically, but only childbearing makes a woman sarifo. Urban women, who have few children, are said, like men, to look fit for a long time. The same is true for white women, who, it is sometimes said, do not get "old." Local sentiment for both urbanites and white people, however, is one of pity, as far as fertility is concerned. A rural woman would much prefer to get old quickly by having many healthy, successful children.

Sarifo is the crucial tipping point between childbearing and entering retirement. As a woman approaches this point, the question arises of whether to stop childbearing and save her strength to take care of the children she already has or attempt another pregnancy. She might be able to conceive and bear another child or two. But if she has had many pregnancies and several of her children have survived, and especially if her conjugal status is secure, a sarifo may not hesitate to assert that she wants no more pregnancies. Because the risks of childbearing have risen sharply, a sarifo who continues to have more pregnancies may have few surviving children, whether because of child deaths, infertility, or divorce.[7]

Many sarifo women have experienced widowhood. Should such a woman remarry, any bridewealth that changes hands for her is symbolic. Any bridewealth paid for a sarifo is only a tiny fraction of that paid for a young woman who has not begun bearing. In fact, the tables are now turned completely. During her virginity she was the subject of competition and desire. Men came seeking her. Now, should she find herself unmarried, she must go looking for a man. Should she marry someone outside the compound, she will likely try to remain with her children and conduct her marital relationship by exchanging visits and by cooking an occasional meal for her husband. A sarifo is often said to be "married by the leg." That is, because the partners live away from each other, someone's leg must move, either hers or his, for the marriage to be operative. In most cases, a sarifo will choose to marry another man in the compound. Left with little reproductive capacity, she will almost certainly want to capitalize on her reproductive lifetime of struggle for the compound. As for a man, marrying a woman who is a sarifo can bring advantages of companionship and domestic services, insofar as she is experienced in conjugal life and has children from whom he may draw benefit. But if the children remain aloof and unaccepting of him (and such is very likely when their business and inheritance interests lie elsewhere), then the marriage may founder or remain one of distant ritual obligation.

Women who are "all finished" *(musu kɔtɔ tale)* have reached the termination of their reproductivity. The phrase *kɔtɔ ta* implies a permanent, irreversible stage. Particularly as it applies to childbearing, *kɔtɔ* means "worn out." A woman in this stage is "old in delivery." Her muscles are gone and

---

7. We see this suggested in the results of Round 12, in which women were asked to classify their physical state and how many pregnancies they wanted for their current husband. Of the sixty-nine women who reported themselves as sarifo, fifty-four gave a numerical answer, the answers ranging from zero to six. Of these fifty-four women, forty had had one husband and fourteen had had two. Not surprisingly, the women who reported having had two husbands were slightly older than those who had had one (age 37.6 versus 36.9). But they actually wanted more pregnancies for their particular husband than did women with one husband (.86 versus .65 pregnancies; the difference, however, was not significant: $p = .288$).

her abdomen is slack and folding, with distinct stretch marks. Weak and unable to carry heavy loads, she rarely picks up small children. When she does, she holds them on her lap while sitting or carries them only short distances. At the beginning of this phase, she will be quite literally spent: weak, thin, and haggard. She will also quite likely be anemic, the result of years of childbearing, work, and hunger, all compounded by endemic malaria. Because her reproductivity and her ability to perform hard work are gone, she is wholly dependent on her children and her husband and in-laws. They, however, are profoundly indebted to her for her devoted expenditure of her reproductivity on their behalf. In fact, being in such a physical state is a clear sign that she risked her life for the benefit of the compound. Whereas women in the earlier years of reproduction would like to appear abundantly fecund, most older women are eager to claim the prestige of being a *musu kɔtɔ:* a woman who has "finished" her reproductivity on behalf of her children and her husband's compound.

The critical point about this phase, though, is the difference between an individual's state as the phase begins and her state as time progresses. Contrary to our way of thinking about aging, a woman will become "younger" in some bodily elements at the end of the musu kɔtɔ phase than she was earlier. As she retires from childbearing, relieved from this duty by other women and fed and cared for by others, one of the most fascinating phases of female life is set to occur.[8] She becomes rejuvenated; she is fat and glowing again. She is nyinyaa—and note that this is the same word used to describe a young virgin: "young" or "fresh." A woman at this stage will not regain her muscles; she remains kɔtɔ. Her lack of muscles would make delivery difficult if not dangerous. As she weans her last child, however, and avoids further pregnancies, either through abstinence or through long-term contraception, she ceases heavy farm work and pounding of grain. Instead, she takes on small tasks around the compound, such as washing dishes, shelling groundnuts, and looking after small children. She will be sent by her sons to Mecca, returning to start a market business with capital they provide for her. In her new role, she can sit back, much as the older men do, and enjoy the choicest morsels from the family cooking pot. Her major tasks will consist of managing her younger co-wives and daughters-in-law, rationing the household's grain stores, and serving the compound as the voice of wisdom. She will eat and sleep well. Any ailments she contracts will be treated without delay. If necessary, her children (now young adults) will

---

8. For more on points related to retirement from childbearing, see Caldwell and Caldwell 1977; and Pearce 1995.

hire a taxi to take her to the clinic or even to Banjul, and they will purchase any necessary medicines. Honored and fed, she will begin to replete her body fat, and her skin will regain its premarital glow. "I am rejuvenating," she will say. Plump and fresh, her strength high, all signs of happiness, she will joke, "I am again in my twelve," referring to the stage of youthful vitality she left so long ago. Her actions may be slower than those of her subfertile age peers. But with many of her elements replenished, she can sit back and enjoy the fruits of her labor, basking in the gratitude of her husband and children. As this implies, much of elderhood can be a time of leisure, rest, and freedom for a woman. Certainly it can be a time of far better health than she suffered during the harsh tribulations of her childbearing years. Elderhood, even more profoundly than the ethnographers of Africa have realized, is a bodily achievement, especially for women.[9]

The most significant distinction among women at this point is not, therefore, between those who are chronologically old and those who are worn out. This is the distinction I tried for a long time to discern, to the great bafflement of the project staff, who (like most Gambians) had little interest in the question of chronological age. Rather, the key distinction is between kɔtɔ (or sarifo), and nyinyaa ("rejuvenated" or "renewed"). Paradoxically, to us at least, if we were to see a gaunt, sallow woman and a plump, healthy one with spent muscles, our best guess as to which was the older chronologically should be the latter. She has reached the point at which she could retire from childbearing. This does not mean, however, that she could bear any more children. Despite her renewed health and strength, her lack of muscles would make delivery difficult if not dangerous.

The points that should most draw our attention, then, about this scheme of aging for women are the following: (1) aging does not occur at a pace commensurate with time but with a woman's individuated reproductive history of hardships, (2) aging is not a singular process with elements moving in tandem but rather one whose elements can senesce at different paces, and (3) some elements of aging can reverse themselves.

The Exceptions That Prove the Rule

One of my strategies in exploring the contingencies that so challenge our ideas of the life course has been to find apparent "straight-edge" exceptions that prove the contingency rule. I mentioned the case of urban

---

9. For a related description of social elderhood as achievement, see also Stucki 1995 for Ghana.

women, who seldom become sarifo because they live an easy life, in contrast to rural sarifo women. Here are two additional instances.

Infertile or Subfertile Women

A key contrast with musu kɔtɔ is that of *musoo keba*. Both phrases allude to an "old" or "finished" woman. The word *kɔtɔ* implies (as did *sarifo*), however, that a woman has come to this condition specifically through childbearing. *Musoo keba*, by contrast, connotes a woman who has gotten old without having children or who was so unfortunate as to have very few children. Thus, a *kanyaleŋ* (barren, subfertile woman; see Skramstad 1997; Sundby 1997) eventually becomes a musoo keba because she has not undergone such reproductive travail. Like a "fresh" young woman, the kanyaleŋ will have firm flesh and noticeable body fat. As a widow or a divorcee, she is more likely to be linked to a man by "charity" marriage than is a musu kɔtɔ because she may not be offered an opportunity to remarry in a compound where she has no children. Close inspection of the terms for "old" reveals further linguistic differences. Whereas the term *kɔtɔ* implies a structural weakness because of the loss of substance, *keba* implies a state of hardness or firmness of a substance: something that the woman has never had an opportunity to lose. This kind of firmness is tragic—a stigma. Every woman wants to age in the way that *kɔtɔ* implies, not as a musoo keba. (One cannot help but wonder at the contrast between this ideal and that of women in the contemporary United States, who increasingly want to be firm and muscular in their elder years—taken by others to be young in age.)

The most tragic case of all is a woman who has never had a pregnancy or even a miscarriage. Suspended in an eerie state of agelessness, she knows that insinuations of supernatural interference hang over her. Nnu Ego, the young heroine of *The Joys of Motherhood* (1979), by the Nigerian novelist Buchi Emecheta, bemoans in the following terms her apparent infertility and the stigma that a youthful body implies at this stage of her life: "She would feel her body, young firm and like that of any other young woman. She knew that soft liquid feeling of motherhood was lacking. 'O my *chi* [spirit double], why do you have to bring me *so* low? Why must I be so punished . . . ?'" (32).

Although women in the contemporary West generally try to delay or disguise the physical process of aging, the African ethnography has shown that becoming a respected elder, a subject examined in more detail in chapter 8, is one of the most venerated social statuses a person can achieve. What we have not appreciated, though, is how the process of building social capital may leave such marked empirical traces on the body. If contemporary anthropology is right that the body is a collection of signs of the social world, then a woman's body in rural Gambia is nothing less than a moral archive.

Male Versus Female Aging

Besides the linear exception to the "normal" rule of contingent female decline that infertile women pose, the logic concerning men offers another straight-edge exception, with some key differences.

For men, health is a major theme of senescence, as it is for their wives, though in quite different ways. In their youth, men enjoy a surfeit of power. A young man may trouble his wife constantly while she is breastfeeding, and she, in acquiescing, may have to wean her child too early if pregnancy ensues. As a man grows older, losing strength and power, he begins to suffer problems of weakness and sexual function, and he becomes thin, dry, tired. He also becomes cautious about allocating his energies. Sex is said to be draining, and increasingly so as he ages. As his strength ebbs, he expects his older sons to retire him from all work except that of producing an occasional child to ensure continued esteem from his family and peers.[10] He tries to consolidate his expenditures of power, reserving them as much as possible for reproduction. But whereas a man would in theory like to have multiple wives in sequence and to continue to produce children up until the time he dies, the goal of an aging man is usually less one of producing seed per se than of proving to other men his continuing manhood. However long he lives, a man wants to be considered strong *(bambaŋɔ)*. If he is no longer producing children, he may be thought sick, weak: no longer a man (see also Fortes 1978, 141, on Ghana). With dwindling status, he will no longer be able to either maintain a young wife or to produce children by her. He becomes what Stenning (1958), studying the Fulani, referred to as an "old man in the yard." This implies an old man who lingers about the compound and whose opinions on weighty matters, despite his own declared status as an elder, receives only polite attention. In short, far less important to an older man than the number of children he has overall is whether he can have any more.

10. The Fula term *khahaldi*, which literally refers to a bull who is so old that he can do nothing else except reproduce, applies as well to old men (Adam Thiam, pers. comm.).

Whereas a man would like to maintain a series of young wives through-out his adult life by marrying a "fresh blood" each time his prior wife approaches the end of childbearing, such desires begin to yield to the reality of bodily depletion. Fears about wasting sexual energies appear unmistakably in the comments of older men. A man of about sixty-four reported that he refused to contact his wives sexually before their babies were eighteen months old. Sex, he declared, "troubles" the woman and exhausts the man, reducing his strength. It should thus be reserved for procreation. Once sex becomes a drain on his health, a man begins to regard marriage to further women with ambivalence. He feels pressure to marry in order to prove his manhood, yet should he do so, he will increasingly fall victim to his own success. Each new wife will want to produce as many children as God gives her, and in time she will want a junior wife, who will want her own children, and so on. As noted earlier, this implies that the twin peaks of male sexual activity in Africa, one before marriage and the other in the mid-to-late forties, reflect very different social pressures. The first peak reflects pressure to prove one's youthful manhood. The second, undertaken with private ambivalence if not consternation, stems almost entirely from pressure to prove an increasing untruth.

For an older man who does manage to marry a much younger woman, efforts to find mystical protection and medicinal stimulants begin to consume his attention (see, for example, Ousmane Sembène's novel *Xala*, 1976). Throughout West Africa, men feature prominently in advertisements for beer and Guiness Stout, which are alleged to stimulate sexual power (see, for example, Orobaton 2000 for Nigeria), and a man at this time of life is likely to be a regular client of those who sell potency medicines. With one eye on his ebbing strength, an aging man becomes a pious observer of religious scruples, lecturing younger men about the iniquities of "going outside" and of "stealing" from other men. Young wives, particularly if they are competing with each other, will wear out an aging husband with their demands for sex and children. Unless he turns a blind eye to their relationships with younger men, he may deteriorate rapidly. Even a young man finds it worrisome to have two young wives. Since they will almost certainly feel competition to establish themselves in the compound, young wives will be demanding their "legs" (sexual turns) frequently, and there will be no talk from either of resting between pregnancies. For an older man to have two young wives, a potentially fatal situation, is almost unknown.

How does all this play out with respect to the comparative pace of physical decline between men and women? By comparison to women, men are said to retain muscle longer and to have a pace of aging that is more linear.

Both patterns are attributed almost entirely to the fact that men do not bear children. Hence, women in general, and particularly those who have many pregnancies, are said to become "old" well before their male age peers. Gendered comparisons are often drawn explicitly. Complaining of fatigue and of difficulties during delivery, one thirty-six-year-old sarifo woman who had undergone seven pregnancies explained that she was using Depo Provera because of her forty-year-old husband's "youth": "It is only because of my health condition and my husband is also a young man" (R. 6). Perceptions of the relative paces of aging are reflected as well in men's comments about their wives. A seventy-year-old man, recounting why he married his second wife, explicitly linked the rigors of childbearing and hard work to women's rapid pace of aging: "At the time of my marrying her, my first wife was . . . going toward old age; you know women get old earlier than we men because of child bearing and hard work." And in one of the surveys of men, respondents were asked if they planned to take another wife. Yes, said a forty-eight-year-old man: "Because, you know, a woman and a man are different in getting old easily."[11] Yes also, said a forty-six-year-old man whose thirty-eight-year-old sarifo wife had had ten pregnancies: "Because she is getting old, and I am still young."

Among men, there is much variation in senescence, and once again the exceptions prove the rule of contingency, rather than autonomous linearity, as the basis of aging. The tolls taken by hard work and energy expenditure loom large in men's accounts of their aging, and men who work especially hard in their youth are said to get old quickly. Such deviations from a linear pace of aging among men, together with intrigue with their causes, are engaging themes in African literature. Images of a woman who "dries" the man's body and financial resources without compensating him with children appear in a short story from Nigeria (Kolon, 1980, 35). In this story, a mother upbraids her son with a series of scorching metaphors for keeping a wife who is growing fat at her husband's expense yet producing no babies for him.

Look at you. You are drying up. Your eyes have sunk into their sockets, the bones at your elbows are almost showing out. Look at your fingers like broom sticks. . . . The congregation is growing thin but the priest is

---

11. Similar anecdotal evidence appears on many fronts. Students in one of my classes noted that in a film from Sierra Leone, *The Mende*, in the "Disappearing Worlds" series, a husband appeared to be much younger in appearance than his elder-seeming wives. Reports Mariane Ferme, the anthropologist consultant for the series, however, the man was about sixty-seven when the film was made and his wives were about sixty-two and fifty-three.

growing fat. Which demon is sucking you, sucking your blood? Three years have passed and it is the same story, there is nothing on the [wife's] lap, nothing on the back, nothing on the hands and nothing in the belly.

In a region where the metaphor of eating implies economic exploitation, often at the commensurate expense of someone else, this case represents ominously aberrant declines by both a man and a woman. Not only does the woman retain her health and youth. Her increasing corpulence implies that she is preserving her reproductive potential, or at least withholding it from this husband, whose rapid decline is attributed to her greedy thriving. And despite the mention of the passage of time, the allusion to it is used not to mark the ticking of the biological clock's countdown toward menopause. Rather, the connotation is a social one: a lack of wifely devotion, or even the doings of a spirit or a witch.[12]

In another Nigerian story that alludes to the different paces of male and female aging (Kolon 1982), the plot hinges on a different anomaly: a man appears youthful *despite* his "usage," a word that appears to allude particularly to sexual activity. In this story, a forty-nine-year-old man named Aliu —and note that he is implied to be young—has a wife who, at age forty-four, is "old," having given herself in motherhood willingly and generously.

As a testimony she had been mother to five children. Her sin was that as she was only about five years younger than Aliu she was no longer young. It will be uncharitable to call a forty-four year woman 'old.' But by Aliu's standard his wife Mariam was getting 'old' and no longer agile." [As for Aliu himself] . . . time and usage seemed to have added fuel to the fire in him. And when he played the game he surpassed the younger men in peak form. (39)

Like the logic of infertility and the exception that it posed to the rule of contingency in the "normal" female life course, the logic of linear emergence and decline for men applies a similar straight-edge to the rule of contingency. But whereas the quality of linearity is usually undesired in the female life course, it is highly desired in men. It implies that a man was not obliged to do manual labor far into adulthood. Instead, he managed to amass the wealth that would allow him to have others work for him, to buy

---

12. See Clark 2001 for an extended description of the moral goodness of a slow, "little by little" erosion of bodily resources, as opposed to a sudden wasting, often an ominous sign of witchcraft.

potency aids, and so on, that would smooth out his trajectory into senescence. For a man, having a contingent life course would imply that he could not manage his life well enough to be able to devote his energies in elderhood to reproduction, something that most women would like to stop as soon as possible.

The cultural view of aging, or senescence, described here suggests several provocative conclusions. The first concerns the physical process of aging: its pace and what drives it. To rural Gambians, age is not the same thing as aging. Senescence is seen as having a character and a pace that are highly contingent on life's wearing hardships. Furthermore, the conduct of reproductive life is structured with this contingent character of senescence firmly in view. Aging certainly occurs through time, and physical status can be estimated and documented on a chronologically incremental scale. Yet any other relation between chronological age and senescence is incidental. Because the amount of fecund time a woman has is a function of how well she takes care of her body and avoids traumatic pregnancies, estimating the number of live births she could have in her total number of fecund years would be a meaningless exercise. (A discussion of the likely empirical concomitants of these possibilities in Western biogerontology appears in appendix B.)

Besides observations on the pace and cause of aging, a second set of key ideas about aging in the scheme presented here pertains to the character of aging. Whereas Western descriptions imply a uniform directionality, and a homogeneous pace of decline, for all elements of aging, the rural Gambian depiction of aging as having progressive as well as retrogressive elements marks a strong departure. Although some body components, once spent, cannot be replenished, others are expected to reverse as the woman retires from childbearing. Implied as well are distinct pathways along which aging occurs. Particularly significant is the difference between the pathway leading to being sarifo (spent through childbearing) and then to kɔtɔ (being finished with childbearing), and that leading to being keba (being "old" in ways other than childbearing). Indeed, the way a woman becomes old is a permanent physical emblem of her childbearing and marital history. The third conclusion that can drawn from these descriptions pertains to the cause of death or longevity. Here again we must distinguish between a universal, abstract concept of time itself and the processes that occur in time. Within the framework presented, all people eventually grow old and die, and time can index the pace at which this is likely to happen. But time does not "cause" aging or death. Nor is either chronological or biological aging necessarily related to longevity, the temporal duration of life, which draws as little interest as menopause. Finally, there is the relation between action and aging. Local people see many of their actions as bearing either directly or indirectly on the course of aging. A woman is said to be able to slow the pace of aging, if not to have more births with good outcomes, by allowing more opportunity to rest between births. That she takes such actions does *not* necessarily mean that she is trying to prolong her life. Her goal instead is to live well, and to earn, by her bodily sacrifices, honor from her children and family. In all of these cultural depictions of the decrement of body resources, our concepts of aging and senescence miss the mark.

Since many of these points run counter to the logic that our academic writings have reflected, I offer them merely as tantalizing empirical possibilities. I remain unclear on a number of facets of the logic of a contingent life course. Particularly unclear to me is how life is supposed to end. One line of the logic says that a person who is worn out, regardless of chronological age, will die sooner than one who is not. On the other hand, the commentaries give a strong impression that being "old" is a state that may be sustained for a long time. That is, a woman who survives to seventy could be "old" for more than half of her life. The only definitive conclusion I have reached on this point is that longevity itself evokes far less concern than how honorably one achieves senescence and lives thereafter (see chapter 8).

Age Versus Stage: Being Chronologically Old Versus Being Spent

Evidence supporting these assertions about managing the pace and character of female senescence through reproduction comes from many sources. It comes from women's behaviors and stated desires about future pregnancies. It comes from the actions and statements of men. Here I assess more empirical evidence for the contingent relations among age, physical state, and reproductive history. I take several tacks, slicing numerical and textual evidence in multiple ways. The principal comparisons are between age and the more time-neutral physical stage. Against these anchors, I play off numbers of pregnancies and nonlive births and expressed desires for further pregnancies. The experiments described below are neither exhaustive nor systematic. They are, however, highly suggestive and, in my view, eye-openers.

Table 7.1 Ages of women in various physical stages (self-reports)

Stage	N	Age	Range	Standard deviation
Sunkuto	5	18.6	16–22	2.4
Foro musoo didiŋo	55	20.8	15–30	2.8
Foro musoo	115	28.4	18–40	4.2
Sarifo	69	36.8	29–47	3.4
Musu kɔtɔ	5	41.0	37–45	2.9
	249			

Source: Round 12.

I begin with a descriptive table from Round 12, which incorporated elements of a conventional survey with a simulated survey form that Fatou brought to me on the evening when everything changed so completely for me. This round included a special set of questions designed to elicit the woman's view of her bodily stage and the events we guessed might best predict it. Table 7.1 lists the five stages described above, together with the mean ages of the women who occupy them and their age ranges. Note that the numbers of women in the first and last stages are very small because the women in the monthly rounds data were largely those who had borne a child within the three years prior to the inception of the rounds. In particular, the fact that many of the women who were filtered out of the sample were barren, sterilized, or moving out of reproduction makes the sample far from ideal for examining the numbers and the commentary in the ways that will now be required.

First we need to ask how women's desires to bear no more children for their present husband relate to our principal reference points of age and stage. As for age, women in Round 12 who stated this desire had a mean age of 35.4. And by stage, almost half of the women who reported that they were sarifo said they wanted no more pregnancies. For a more detailed look at how many more pregnancies women want for their husbands, given their self-reported physical states, I group the range of possible answers into three categories: zero, a numerical answer more than zero, and a nonnumerical answer such as "up to God" or no answer. This strategy of showing increment in the life course is parallel to figure 5.1. In contrast to figure 5.1, however, which showed responses according to age group, figure 7.1 shows responses by physical stage. Since there are only five women

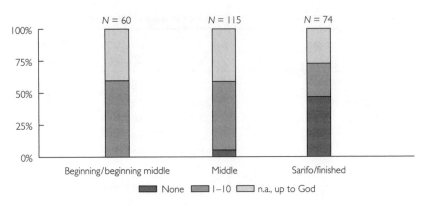

Fig. 7.1 Women wanting more pregnancies for husband, by physical stage

in each of the first and last stages, figure 7.1 combines the first two stages and the last two.[13]

Although questions about fertility desires should be interpreted cautiously (particularly the meaning of an "up to God" response), the results suggest that becoming spent, quite apart from chronological age, brings about a decisive change in reproductive outlook. Sarifo women declare that they want far fewer pregnancies for their husbands than do women who have not yet reached this stage. Among "beginning" (that is, physically "young") women, all want more pregnancies for their husbands (the smallest number wanted being two), and only 8 percent of the middle women say they want no more. For both groups, 40 percent either refuse to give a number or say they will bear as many as God gives them. Once women become spent, the proportion willing to leave the matter to God falls to 26 percent, and as many as 46 percent now say they want no more. The only change in desired pregnancies from the beginning of childbearing to middle woman status is a small rise, from 0 to 8 percent, in the proportion of women wanting more pregnancies for the husband and a corresponding fall in "up to God" responses. In the numbers that describe reproductive desires, then, much like what we saw in the verbal testimonies above, sarifo status marks a clear tipping point.

Let us now compare figure 7.1 with figure 5.1. Both use the same dependent variable, number of children desired. But whereas figure 5.1 used

13. Overall, the desire for more pregnancies varies according to the current physical stage of the woman, a difference that is significant at the .001 level.

age as the base, figure 7.1 uses physical stage. These are very different ways of depicting a life. Chronological age, the basis of figure 5.1, is an abstract, absolute measure, and one that we take as independent of local or subjective meaning. The smooth rise that figure 5.1 displayed from young to old in reported fertility desires is just what we might predict. The very fact of its linear smoothness is strong support for the notion that a chronological denominator is appropriate for describing the relation of age to fertility desires. But whereas using an age scale nicely smoothes out the change over time in children desired, using physical stage as the base reveals something quite different. Figure 7.1 shows a decisive shift in fertility desires at the precise moment when the woman reports that her body is spent. Until then, there is almost no change.

Much as was the case with the hapo (the divinely bestowed number of child potentials), these results reinforce the cultural conviction that a woman cannot know before she is spent what her bodily potential is. She may insist that she wants as many children as God gives her, a response connoting superstition or fatalism. But it is largely "young" women, ordinarily considered the enlightened wave of the future, who give such an answer. As such, it hardly makes sense to ask a woman, before her bodily capacity is spent, how many pregnancies she wants. This is an open question, the answer to which she can only begin to glimpse as the trajectory of her reproductive and work life takes more visible shape. It is possible, of course, that the abrupt shift in fertility desires with the transition to sarifo status simply reflects the possibility that being spent is an idiom for deciding that one wants no more pregnancies. Declaring oneself spent could thus simply reflect a determination to end childbearing. Indeed, this is quite plausibly the case. Let us turn, then, to some tests of the contingency thesis with a harder empirical edge—number of pregnancies and of nonlive births—and use them to set age and physical stage against each other.[14]

Two immediate problems arise, however. First, as much as I would like to, I cannot force chronological age into the status of a dependent variable. Since chronological time is a phenomenon that we have removed from the actual workings of the world. I cannot ask how the number of pregnancies affects age. The ultimate point, however, is not to understand why a person is getting older in time but why she is getting spent. Second, it would be difficult to make any definitive statistical claims regarding the temporal causes

---

14. Contraceptive use would in theory be useful in deciding to declare oneself spent, but since contraceptives are used so much for spacing children, the results would have less meaning here.

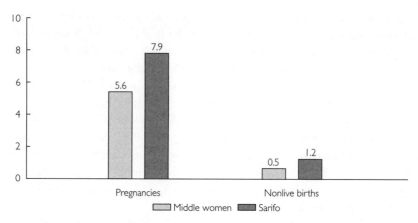

Fig. 7.2 Mean number of pregnancies by physical stage for women aged thirty-five to thirty-eight

of reaching a particular bodily stage. The data are cross-sectional, meaning that the likely causal effects of pregnancy events on individual women cannot be assessed as they occur over time. In any event, the key variables (body stage, age, and number of pregnancies) are highly correlated. Still, it is possible to look for systematic variation in the number of pregnancies and nonlive births to illuminate body stage by keeping chronological age as a constant. Age is not given the privileged status of an independent variable.

Figure 7.2 (again using data from Round 12) holds chronological age constant around the reproductive tipping point, or at least makes it as neutral as possible. By isolating the exact center of the age range between middle and sarifo women, it allows us to ask whether pregnancy experience affects women's decision to declare themselves either "middle" or "spent." In Round 12, it is the four-year span of thirty-five to thirty-eight that evenly straddles the point where age seems unrelated to whether women declare themselves to be middle women or sarifo.[15] In this group are forty-five women whose ages, despite their reported physical stages, are scattered randomly throughout the four years. Of these individuals, ten say they are middle women and thirty-five say they are spent (mean ages of 36.4 and 36.7, respectively).[16]

Since age has no relation to stage within this group, what makes the difference in whether a woman declares herself to be in one physical stage or

15. Since it would be misleading to use the x axis as an ordinally arrayed variable, I use it only to show body stages in comparison with one another.
16. I include also one woman, age thirty-seven, who declared herself "finished:" my stage 5.

the other? Figure 7.2 shows that the change from middle woman to sarifo is closely related to pregnancy history. Women who declared themselves spent had on average more than two pregnancies more than the middle women (7.9 versus 5.6).[17] They also had more than twice as many nonlive births as middle women (1.2 versus 0.5—not shown in the figure). These results, which I report in the time-neutral vocabulary that the structure demands, suggest that having many pregnancies and nonlive births makes chronologically young women "spent."

Another line of support for the argument that fertility experience is critical to women's physical condition is found in comparing variations in pregnancy histories among women who report that they are near the tipping point of reproductivity and who are of similar ages but different physical stages. For this, I take the chronologically young half of the sarifo group, a total of thirty-two women ranging in age from twenty-nine to thirty-six. The mean age of this group is 34.0. I then compare them to the closest group of age peers who report themselves as middle women. The closest match, a mean age of 34.3, occurs among sixteen middle women who fall within the age range of thirty-three to thirty-six. The mean ages of the two groups, then, are the same. But their pregnancy histories are significantly different. The women who declared themselves to be spent had two more pregnancies than their middle women age peers (7.6 versus 5.5) and three times as many nonlive births (1.2 versus 0.4).[18] (See fig. 7.3.) These results are similar to those shown in figure 7.2, although the composition of the groups is different. Again, pregnancy history, irrespective of age, appears to make a decisive difference in physical stage.

These relativity experiments have represented just a few pursuits of threads of logic in the manner that Epi Info's analysis mode encourages. Certainly the numbers in all cases are extremely small, making the question of statistical significance, although it exists, almost secondary. And there remain dangers of circular logic. In particular, the possibility that sarifo women who had reached this status might feel justified in refusing to have any more pregnancies would make the relation between fertility experience and physical status less convincing. Conversely, it is also possible that women who felt they were spent from fertility events may have been more likely to report being older in chronological terms than women who were

17. A *t*-test to see if the number of pregnancies varied by stage revealed a significant difference (<.001) in the number of pregnancies among women in the two stages.

18. A *t*-test comparison between the two groups shows that the differences in numbers of pregnancies and nonlive births were significant at the .001 and .05 levels, respectively.

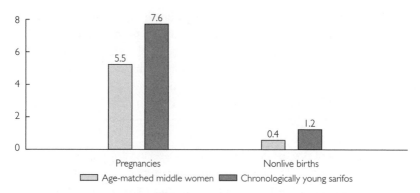

Fig. 7.3 Mean number of pregnancies for chronologically young sarifos and age-matched middle women

Note: Chronologically young = under thirty-seven.

not spent. Finally, the fact that this was a cross-sectional study makes it hard to disentangle various pathways to senescence. Ideally, one would follow women as their pregnancy events transpired.

But however the experiment is run, age loses ground as a privileged anchoring variable. Markedly different empirical histories underlie reported bodily states.[19] Although there has been no research, as far as I have been able to find, on reproduction as a lever for the process of aging, in chapter 9 and appendix B I piece together evidence that lends substantial credence to this possibility.

Cases and Quotations

In trying to understand the vision of aging with which these results confront us, let us thicken the numbers with some commentaries. Of greatest interest, once more, would be anomalies—cases of apparent disjunctures between chronological age and stage of senescence. Such disjunctures might include women whose body seems either "fresher" or more "worn out" than we would expect to see for their chronological age. A relevant case

---

19. The magnitude of the associations supporting the contingency thesis is, if anything, understated. Reports of ages and bodily states were checked and rechecked. All cases came under scrutiny, but especially those that were far out of line with chronological expectations. Thus, a report of a twenty-nine-year-old woman with six pregnancies who was spent would be checked two or three times, whereas that of a thirty-six-year-old spent woman with six pregnancies would receive less attention. Whereas women with a large number of pregnancies might simply have believed themselves to be chronologically old (or the interviewers recorded them as such), it is more likely that ages were over-estimated because the anomalous cases were checked so thoroughly. (On the problems of measuring chronological ages in rural Africa see van de Walle 1968; Pison 1997; Ohadike 1997.)

in point could also include that of a woman who had undergone a number of pregnancies that seems either excessive or understated for her age or body stage. Such analytical maneuvers are of course analogies to those above, except that verbal testimonies, rather than numbers, are the points of contrast that play off reports of age against those of bodily stage. With quotations as the data, we can scan a wide horizon of circumstance. In some cases I use minimal background information. In others, the importance of the case demands more depth. In addition to fertility desires, numbers of pregnancies, and nonlive births (as the quantitative portions of the questionnaires dictated), difficult pregnancy and work histories, and even the suggestions of an abusive conjugal life, are visible. What makes this exercise even more telling is that the women themselves recognize that they are extreme cases. The explanations they provide for their situations lend unmistakable support to the contingency thesis. Once again I concentrate on sarifos, the most critical group for the argument in this book.

Body "Younger" Than Chronological Age

The first set of cases represents women whose bodily states are "young" or "fresh" compared to their age peers. One twenty-seven-year-old woman with three pregnancy terminations reported herself to be only in the second stage of reproductive life: beginning middle woman. The fact that she was of a less advanced bodily state than either her chronological age or her number of pregnancies might suggest is one that she attributes to her diet and an undemanding work life: "I don't do hard work, but eat enough food and don't feel any strength loss yet. I am just as strong and healthy as I was before being married" (R. 12). Another woman who, despite her age (thirty-seven) and her seven pregnancies (including a stillbirth), still insists she is a middle woman. Why isn't she spent? Her life appears to be easy because her husband is working in Paris much of the time, a fact that has both allowed her to maintain wide birth intervals and provided her ample financial support:

I believe I look young because I am in good health since I take good care of myself. I eat a lot of good food to restore my strength and health. My births are not close to each other and I got a lot of financial support from my husband who is a hustler [one who makes money in various ways] in Paris. He sometimes goes for two or three years but before he comes I wean the child he left me breastfeeding. He sends money for me and to take care of myself and my kids.

Quite a different situation emerges in the case of a woman whose re-corded age, thirty-one, appeared far too high for the small number of preg-nancies she reported: two, both surviving as children. This configuration plus her stated eagerness to move on rapidly with more pregnancies made her sound so different from almost every other woman her age in Round 12 that I was tempted to alter her age de facto in the survey records. Close in-spection of her commentaries, however, revealed someone with both an ex-ceptionally subfertile record and a late start to childbearing. In her vivid de-scriptions of why her body and behaviors were so "young" for her age, she explained that she waited for ten anxious years before becoming pregnant, consulting numerous Islamic marabouts. Even then, once she bore her first child, she suffered another very long space of five years between her first and second children. Clearly, this was a case of overly long birth intervals. The maintenance of "youth" was the last thing she wanted. Every point this woman makes (and they appear choppy because of the interviewer's probes) conveys a desire to speed up the pace of fertility.

> I had only two children and they are all alive. . . . Any amount of children
> God gives me I am ready to take it. If I started having many children,
> I would then join family planning to delay births and not to avoid [them].
> . . . When I reach the age of sixty years I would then stop giving birth.
> I can be giving birth together with my daughter if I am not old then. My
> husband will not accept no contact because I am too young. (R. 6)

Of course, there remains the possibility that this woman's sense of age may not be chronologically accurate. Even if this were so, however, it would reflect an obvious lack of concern with keeping precise track of age and with using age to predict life events such as menopause. This as well I would take as support for the contingency theory.

Body "Older" Than Age

The cases above involved various circumstances that might explain why a woman has a "young" body relative to chronological age or to her age peers. Instances of undemanding work, good diet, lengthy pregnancies and (in the last case) subfertility were the principal reasons offered. The next set of cases takes the opposite question. What makes a woman "older" than her age peers in terms of bodily resources? In comparing themselves with their age mates, women commented readily on disparities between their chronological age and their appearance. They also speculated openly about the pathways through which these disparities may have developed. The following are two sarifo women who identified their number of pregnancies as the cause of their bodily stage. The first, age thirty, had eight pregnancies and seven surviving children: "I consider myself old because of the number of children I bore, not my number of years" (R. 12). The second, age thirty-six, had eight pregnancies (all surviving): "Childbearing cuts a woman's muscle; every delivery cuts a muscle. It makes her old. . . . I have eight pregnancies. My age mates who have not got as many as I have are not as old as I am" (R. 12).

Many women identify difficult births as a major precipitant of aging. One twenty-two-year-old woman described the impact of difficult births and a large number of pregnancies for her chronological age (five pregnancy terminations, only two children surviving), together with a hard domestic life: "I have come to marry and I cook and pound, all making me weak. I had delivery difficulties at my first birth [twins]. The second was obstructed. Really, childbearing has taken more of my power than inadequate food and hard work" (R. 12). Difficult deliveries (six pregnancies) are heavily implicated as well in one twenty-nine-year-old woman's description of the pathway by which she had aged: "I'm getting old now. I came to this stage because of childbearing. I had six pregnancies and I had difficulties in delivering all of my children. These made me look older than my age. I have lost all my strength now" (R. 12). Another woman, reporting herself to be a middle woman at the very young chronological age of eighteen, has had three pregnancies but expresses a desire for only three more. Her comments, sounding like those of a chronologically much older woman, hint at a conjugal life that may have made this the case: "[I came to this stage] because of hard work and inadequate food . . . having many children without support is useless" (R. 12).

As this quotation suggests, the aging or wearing phenomenon is often described as central to a woman whose life is beset by other adversities. Such a case emerges in this sobering statement from a woman with eight pregnancies (six children alive, two dead).

My first husband died when I was one month pregnant of my third child. I had my twins in my second marriage. [My husband] divorced me when I was eight months pregnant, and before he divorced me used to maltreat and beat me despite the fact that I was pregnant. I married the same man again. He is still maltreating me. . . . [He] beat me last month until I was

admitted to the hospital. I have weaned my last child now and I don't
want to have any more. I am not in good condition of health and, my
husband is not taking good care of me and my children. I am only
33 years old, but if you see me you will think that I am 100 years old.

Some of the most telling responses in matters of reproduction and its effects on aging came from sarifo women whose previous child was weaned
—women who might be expected, given conventional views of child spacing, to be attempting to become pregnant again. These women were trying
instead to rest. Such a case was that of a thirty-three-year-old sarifo with
eight pregnancies (six live births and two nonlive). Left with only three children, two boys and one girl, the last of which was weaned (she had actually
suffered a miscarriage recently), this woman nonetheless expressed a wish
for only one more pregnancy, and she was taking injections to preclude the
possibility of a new pregnancy starting too soon. "I am getting old now and
want to rest for eight pregnancies is too much now. My womb is deeper and
have no strength any longer. . . . I want only one child more but in two years
time for I want to rest for a while for bearing children is not easy, especially
after eight pregnancies" (R. 12).

Another woman, twenty-five years old, was one of a tiny handful of individuals using Depo one month after giving birth. She reported that she
was a middle woman, but there was considerable debate on this point
among the interviewers who knew her, some arguing that she should be re-
classified in the records by administrative fiat as a sarifo. Asserting that she
wanted no more pregnancies, she explained her situation: "I have been advised to take contraceptives to prevent pregnancy due to the system of how
I deliver my children. My pregnancies are very close together and I have six
children so the nurses advised me to stop because my womb is getting deep
and I might be at risk when I continue bearing children. This is why I don't
want to bear more" (R. 12).

And this from a sarifo, in her eighth pregnancy in Round 12; she had
had five live births and three miscarriages. Although she had only four surviving children, her account of sickness, difficult pregnancies, and miscarriage reveals why she wanted, at the young chronological age of thirty-
three, no more pregnancies. The following are two sets of comments:

> I have four children alive and one death and three abortions. During my
> pregnancy before the last one I felt sick. Later I was asked to look for iron
> tablets for my blood level was very low; also I was getting sick. I delivered
> that child at seven months and he died after birth. (R. 3)

Now [I have] my eighth child; very soon I'll come to my old stage, because I have lost so many muscles and strength just by bearing children. [I want no more pregnancies] because I've gone under lots of difficult pregnancies, especially three abortions I had before my live births. Now I want to stop bearing and take care of my alive children properly so that they can be good looking [healthy, well attired] in the future.[20] For me I will also be able to regain my health and strength and also retain my stage for a long period. But, if I continue bearing I will get old easily and might have other difficulties later. I have come across many difficulties during my former pregnancies by my husband. Now I want to rest forever in bearing so that I can regain my health and strength before getting to my old stage. To bear many children easily makes you old. (R. 12)

I end this section of cases and quotations from The Gambia with fiction from Nigeria: the novel *The Joys of Motherhood* by Buchi Emecheta (1979). An epic of maternal aging and reproduction, this novel chronicles the life of a woman for whom the trials and strains of reproduction take a tragic toll. She moves from a youth painfully prolonged by infertility, to the joys of beginning to age with reproduction, and finally to the tragedy of fatigue and sickness from unrequited reproductive efforts. Her children were too preoccupied with their lives in the outside world to help ease their mother's elder years. Eleven pregnancies after she began reproductive life

Nnu Ego . . . stretched out her work-worn hand to help Adim [her son], who noticed with horror how bony his mother's hand was and how all the veins that ought to have been covered with healthy flesh now stood crisscross in relief. And her teeth, those teeth that used to be her pride, had been badly neglected and were beginning to have black smudges round some of their edges. He knew his mother was not old in age, but she had never looked this old to Adim. She looked like a woman in her seventies. Oh, poor woman, he thought. (213)

U.S. Counterpoints

Given such abundant evidence, and from so many African sources, that reproductive wear under difficult economic and health conditions ages women, I cannot resist describing three cases that contrast the pace of aging

20. In Round 14, however, this woman seems to have changed her mind. She wanted to become pregnant again, but only after a substantial rest.

in Africa and in the United States. I take first the comments of two thirty-four-year-old women in rural Gambia, made over the course of the rounds. Both women reported that they were sarifo, their comments sounding very much like the others we have heard so far. The first, with nine pregnancies, six surviving, wanted no more, saying:

> "I am tired."
> "I am not well."
> "I am tired of bearing."
> "I am old now. I don't use any method because I trust God and I am sure I will not give birth again."

The second, with six pregnancies, all surviving, wanted no more:

> "I am elderly and tired of delivery."
> "I don't want a child anymore."
> "I don't want to get pregnant and I don't think I will again."
> "I am elderly now, and have even seen my grandsons. I have even stopped going to my husband's house because I don't want to get pregnant any more in life."
> "I want to stop. I am tired, my power is finished. I want to avoid my husband entirely. I don't know how he will cope with it. If he can get another woman, he will not worry [make demands on] me."

Compare these statements with media descriptions of an American age peer of theirs. In an article titled "Woman Ascending a Marble Staircase," the *New York Times Magazine* (11 January 1998) carried a story about thirty-four-year-old Cinderella figure Julia Flesher Koch, who had appeared suddenly on the New York social scene several years earlier by marrying fifty-seven-year-old billionaire David Koch. Describing her as "a young woman of manners and social ambition" (18), with "lanky good looks," the article quoted an editor of the magazine *Vogue* who described her as one of those "young, attractive women who look fantastic in clothes" (20). Never having had children, she was reported as wanting them, and hinted that she was pregnant for the first time. Given her sensational rise and her marriage to a man of such wealth, this woman was undoubtedly highly selected both for her youthful looks and because she had never been married or borne children. Still, the contrast with the Gambian women is striking.

Another U.S. counterpoint in support of the contingency view of the physical life course turns on the fact that African women in the United States say that they age more slowly here than they do in Africa.[21] What is more, Gambian women say that there are no sarifo women in the United States, neither Americans nor Africans. The explanation is that U.S. economic conditions make high fertility prohibitively expensive. Because no one can have many children, no one becomes worn out from childbearing. The fact that an entire segment of what rural West Africans see as the "normal" female physical life course simply does not exist in the United States is a remarkable commentary on the role of social life in shaping cultural perceptions of the body's "natural" temporalities.

The final set of observations, even more absorbing, turns on plays between African and U.S. temporalities on birth intervals and the end of reproduction. A common worry among women from Africa who live in the United States is that they will reach menopause having borne few children. This means that they will be at an irrevocable disadvantage should they return to Africa. The reason—and now I appear to contradict myself completely—is because of chronological time.

In the United States, where a youthful appearance is valued and high fertility, given the economic constraints of raising children in the West, is not, an African woman has an advantage over her counterparts living in Africa in that she ages more slowly. Once she and her husband return to Africa, however, a chronologically older woman's number of children, limited now by the menopausal clock, will be frozen at a level that is far lower than that of her age counterparts who have always lived in Africa. Here, her youth, or rather its underpinning of subfertility, is instantly converted to social and physical disadvantage. She is no longer attractively "young," as she thought of herself in the United States, but keba: anguishingly subfertile. Menopause, the factor that the contingency model of fertility could largely disregard, is now a matter of looming importance. The hapo, the divine endowment, has remained unused too long, and its potential can no longer be fulfilled before menopause occurs. Because of her low fertility, and because her husband was able to convert his earnings and remittances into status in Africa, a former U.S. resident is likely to find herself shortly with a young co-wife, a woman who has a clear field to forge ahead by realizing her full fertility potential. Having spent so long on "borrowed time" in the United States, she will now find that time is also against her when she returns to

21. I am grateful to Fatoumatta Banja, who collected the information on which these examples and those in the next set of cases are based.

Africa. Much as it defeats subfertile women in Africa, menopause will close the biological window of opportunity for the returnee before her fertility can catch up. For her, the end of reproduction is now a matter of time.

Conclusion

In this chapter I have explored the logic of contingent aging in social and cultural life in rural Gambia.[22] Several key points have arisen. The first is the enormous difference between these descriptions of aging and the life course and those voiced more commonly in the science and the lay discourse of the West. The view of an apparently "natural" timeline of chronological physical decline that is voiced more commonly in the West encounters a decisive challenge from the view of aging that we have seen here. Much as Plato's concept of the khóra (chapter 2) would suggest, there is considerable scope for the temporalities of a form to change in ways that are contingent on experience. The more traumatic the event, the greater the senescent effect. Second, the phenomenon of reversibility of some bodily elements but not others is one to which few of us might subscribe at first. The transition from being spent to being rejuvenated after retiring from childbearing in the more physiological elements of strength and blood but not in the more anatomical element of muscles marks a sharp departure from the notion that decline occurs at a uniform pace among all bodily functions. The third point that the analyses have brought to light is that although time may provide an index of the pace of senescence, nowhere has there been any evidence that time *causes* senescence. Instead, social action is seen as a key determinant of the pace and character of senescence, even though fertility, rather than worries about senescence and longevity, seem to be the foremost reasons why such actions are taken. Finally, we have seen once again that any effort to create a categorical dualism between the logic of contingency in rural Gambia and that of chronological time in Western society would miss entirely the intricacies that underlie both logics.

Both the abundance and the consistency of evidence in this chapter and in previous ones have suggested that these physical descriptions are very likely *not* simply reports of exotic cultural beliefs. Instead, they appear to be signaling highly empirical phenomena. In so decisively shifting the numerators and denominators of the life equation, Gambian descriptions open up to questioning qualities of physical existence that even the most committed

---

22. See Montgomery and Cohen 1997 for other demographic links between these domains.

constructionists among us have assumed to be natural. As I noted in chapter 2, we readily acknowledge that people can reach a certain physical stage before or after other people do. But we rarely ask why some people reach one physical stage of aging more quickly than another. The possibility that reproduction ages the body must be a pivotal social concern where fertility is high and living conditions are difficult. Let us recall now the confusing survey responses in chapter 5 from women in their mid-to-late thirties who reported that they were breastfeeding, having regular periods, and using long-term contraceptives—and yet they were "too old" to have more children. This response choice had been included in the survey on the assumption that it would indicate a woman who had reached or was reaching menopause. Clearly, however, it was tapping something else. Coming even from premenopausal, breastfeeding women, such responses should no longer be surprising.

As I have documented, aging, or senescence, is seen by women in rural Gambia as a process with immense plasticity and one that is highly dependent on one's circumstances and actions. The idea of any baseline of "normality" is a receding horizon. We now need to press harder on aging as a process over which people have some control as a social fact. Because women can take action with respect to the allocation or expenditure of their bodily resources, it should not be surprising that how they age is the subject of evaluation and debate. In chapter 8 I join these two domains, showing how the conduct of reproduction and senescence is linked to agency and morality.

CHAPTER 8

Reaping the Rewards of Reproduction:
Morality, Retirement, and Repletion

Having reached the tipping point between full reproductivity and decline, a woman living in rural Gambia is spent (sarifo). She is left thin and weary. Her exertions have "cut" or "finished" so many muscles that any further reproduction is perilous. The question is, what happens now? Becoming spent sets the stage for what is possibly the most important moment in a woman's life: her "retirement," or permanent rest, from the ordeals of childbearing.

In this chapter I describe some of the most fascinating implications of the contingency view of fertility: those that lie in the junctures between health and social morality. Turning to the social relations underlying reproduction, I show that a woman tries to expend her bodily resources for her husband's family in the expectation that its members will in turn begin to support her as she moves into elderhood. This effort rests on a set of tensions that are expressed in the language of struggle, sacrifice, obligations, and blessings. If (says the ideology) she has meticulously converted her physical capital into social and moral gain throughout a meritorious life of reproductive struggle, she should be able to watch all her travails come to fruition in blessings and comfort. What has ideally been a careful process of converting physical capital into social capital should bring about the singular moment when the rewards of a reproductive life of valued work and sacrifice can be reaped. All the tribulations undergone, all the pregnancies endured, all the school fees paid, all the demands from in-laws met, all the daughters successfully married to productive husbands—all of these efforts, if enacted carefully as God's will unfolds, should now be transactable toward the gain that retirement promises. To say that retirement is a key physical moment, therefore, is only a small part of the story. It is also a key social and moral moment: a moment of public acclaim and recompense for a worth accumulated throughout a lifetime of conjugal sacrifice.

I also describe efforts to convert bodily expenditure through sacrifice into social and moral capital, and the culmination of this process in retirement from childbearing. With the physical and the moral issues laid side by side, I compare a standard fertility questionnaire to the one that a Gambian woman might create, one that graphically depicts the convergence of physical expenditure and social significance in the temporalities of married life. I then use the insights gained from this very different vision of fertility and aging to forge new connections to the African ethnography of earlier eras, a corpus that carefully mapped out the social structures of life, yet systematically bypassed the significance of physical contingencies for social life.

Bodily Resource Conversion and the Moral Reproductive Life

The perception that a woman's bodily resources are seen as eroding not with time but with wearing experience raises an obvious question. How should she try to allocate her limited resources? Entailed in the overall West African answer to this question is a need to invest in social relations to build long-term value (see Guyer 1997). Let us explore some of the permutations that the connection between physicality and sociality brings to light, and some of the cultural idioms through which these connections are expressed.

The Conversion of Bodily Struggle and Sacrifice into Blessings

Bourdieu, among others, has been intrigued by the realization that values are set upon people as easily as upon things and that these values can be converted through exchange, bargaining, or manipulation (1990, 138–39). Conversion involves an exchange of one entity for another, often, as Mauss (1990) points out, in the act of giving to or on behalf of someone. For Mauss, the spirit with which gifts are given is critical. Apparently free and generously given, gifts are in fact incumbent and self-interested, he argues. In fact, the gift contains a moral "force"—even the "soul" of the giver (43)—that compels reciprocity. Describing gift-giving among the Maori, Mauss writes:

[T]he thing received is not inactive. Even when it has been abandoned by
the giver, it still possesses something of him. Through it the giver has a
hold over the beneficiary. . . . To retain that thing would be dangerous
and mortal, not only because it would be against law and morality, but
also because that thing coming from the person not only morally but
physically and spiritually, that essence, that food, those goods, whether
movable or immovable, those women or those descendants, those rituals
or those acts on communion—all exert a magical or religious hold over
you. (11–12)

The Gift continues to be read and quoted for its insights into exchange. But
Mauss wrote on other key topics as well. His work on the body (1973)
tapped a very different domain of theory, most notably, the concept of habitus that Bourdieu later developed as socially imbued, unconsciously performed actions. For example, the body's practices, said Mauss, are a mne-
monic: an encoded memory of the past (see also A. Strathern 1996). Mauss
also produced a collaborative book, much less known, on sacrifice (Hubert
and Mauss 1964). Surprisingly, however, Mauss, who wrote so insightfully
about these three topics—exchange, sacrifice, and bodily practice—wrote
little about their potential intersection. It is precisely this juncture, the conversion of bodily value from youth to elderhood through social acts of sacrifice in reproduction, that brings to life Gambian observations on reproduction and the life course.

In the West African view, life ideally consists of working on behalf of
benefactors (whether kin, in-laws, or patrons) in acts of sacrifice that convert physical effort into social and moral value. This emphasis is captured
in Mandinka by the notion of struggle (*kato/bataa;* alternative translations
are "suffer," "hustle"). By contrast with people such as migrant farm laborers or even office workers, who are said merely to engage in work *(dokuwo)*
for immediate cash remuneration, those who struggle are engaged in a
moral endeavor. They hope to exchange a hard life of exhaustion and privation, earning obligations from others, for long-term benefits.[1] In The
Gambia, a woman, on whom such expectations of struggle most palpably
fall, has values set upon her capacity for work and reproduction and upon

---

1. Isabel Garcia, the grants administrator for the University of Chicago's Population Research
Center, found an immediate translation equivalent, "effort," for me in the language of American human resources bureaucracy for the African concept of "struggle." Both concepts imply labor expended
by a subordinate on behalf of a superordinate, with the understanding of reciprocity toward a goal of
comfortable retirement.

her physical comeliness and character. For her, struggle ideally takes the form of converting, quite literally, her youth or "freshness" to gain through sacrifice and toil on behalf of her husband and his family. How she spends her bodily endowment determines her social worth at the end of her reproductive life.[2]

At the outset of adult life, a young woman's greatest physical resource is her body's divinely endowed capacity to reproduce. Over the struggle of her reproductive life, she loses this endowment and becomes "worn out" or "dry," a word connoting witheredness or barrenness. Yet her struggle has meaning only with reference to its intended beneficiaries: most notably, the husband and his relatives. In a way that parallels how men think of their reproduction not as an undifferentiated number of children but as children by their individual wives, a woman thinks of her reproduction as being in relation to a specific man. The main question for her is not how quickly she ages through the expenditure of her bodily resources but how, and on behalf of whom, she does so.

A woman seeks above all to realize her reproductive endowment in a manner that incurs obligation from her husband and his family and that enhances her value as a wife and future elder in his compound. In her marriage ceremony, a young wife is admonished to struggle in her husband's compound, to endure all hardship with resignation and humility. Besides toiling, enduring sickness, and undergoing the risk and pain of childbearing on her husband's behalf, she should remain virtuous and heed the wishes of his family elders. She should also speak demurely in their presence, avoiding even facial signs of disrespect. Wittrup (1990, 121) describes this value as *munya*, "to bear, to be patient, to endure," a value that "characterizes the female role from birth to the grave."

As this implies, the notion of value contains moral as well as social components. In West Africa, morality is most strongly reflected in the notion of blessings, which are bestowed by God and pass from him to people through long hierarchical chains of authority, from the ancestors who founded the family to living elders, from husbands to wives and children, from mothers to children (see also Kopytoff 1971 for sub-Saharan Africa more broadly). Success in any endeavor is contingent on blessings. Without them, a family as a collective cannot hope for bountiful harvests or good health. Nor can it produce children who do well in school, make good marriages, or grow

---

2. See Layne 1999 for an insightful examination of ideas of sacrifice among couples who lose a pregnancy or a child in the contemporary United States.

up to benefit the family and defend it from hostile forces (*baraka diŋo*—literally, "blessed child"). The same is true at the individual level. By working hard and adhering to a virtuous life, a woman hopes to earn or "buy" blessings from her husband and his kin. These blessings she bestows, in turn, on her children to ensure their success in life and, thus, her own future security.[3] In the words of an older man:

> A good wife who treats her husband well and works hard for her husband shall always have a child who will also look out for her at any time, especially during [senescence]. The first person in this world that a child learns to imitate is his mother so most of what he does has something to do with [can be attributed to] his mother. . . . All the women who struggled for and with their husbands always have children they can rely on. . . . [*baraka diŋo*, noted the interviewer, likely using the phrase the man himself used]

Referents to such tenets emerge in many cultural genres. Describing the symbolic meanings in the women's secret society helmet masks among the Mende people of Sierra Leone, Boone (1986, 171) notes that the masks, depicted as small and shut, reflect the ideal of a woman's image: silent and avoiding gossip and "palaver" (argument):

> A saintly mother accepts her troubles stoically and treats her child with kindness; her forbearance is a blessing to her child and is the assurance of a good future in life. Other women, overwhelmed by disappointments, lash out in their agony at the only possible victims, their children. In a spasm of fury a woman may curse her child, declaring he will never succeed, will never amount to anything. . . . Nothing is considered more harmful to a person than his or her mother's curse; it is sure to ruin a person's life. . . . When Mende observe a person who is a drunk, a brawler, or a thief, they conclude that the wretch was at one time cursed by his mother. No good can ever come of him. The community writes him off as a loss.

Boone's insightful observations about the Mende speak as well to The Gambia, where the blame for producing a bad child lays squarely on the mother's shoulders. A saying in Mandinka and Wolof suggests as much: "If the child is good, it belongs to everybody; if it is bad, it belongs to the

---

3. See Bledsoe 1990a for an analysis of the virtually identical cultural notions of struggle and earning blessings among older fostered children in Sierra Leone.

mother." The reasoning goes thus: because of the woman's churlish disre-spect toward her husband, he treats her badly, causing her, in turn, to mis-treat the children she has borne by him. Growing up with sour dispositions, they are disrespectful and do bad deeds, thus evoking their mother's curse. A woman who has the fortitude to bear with her troubles, on the other hand, will be able to raise children who are blessed. Such children will sup-port her, allowing her to retire—in effect, to "sit down" while they work for her. The blessings she earns in producing and raising children will reflect the degree to which she "throws her soul" or risks her life, a Fula expres-sion, in order to carry out this life duty, bearing for her husband all the child potentials that God has given her and raising them carefully for her hus-band. The greater the struggle, the more blessings she will earn. We see as much in an old man's remorseful recollection of his youthful disdain for the young woman his family chose for him and her undaunted efforts to win his respect and affection, efforts that eventually earned his devotion and blessings:

> Jainaba was my first wife . . . I use to hate her very much. When my uncle
> offered her to me, I rejected her. She said if I didn't marry her, she would
> leave me and she would not take any gift from me. My other relatives ad-
> vised me to accept her. Later I agreed and married her, but I maltreated
> her very seriously because I didn't love her. But I have never seen such a
> good wife as Jainaba. For many years I did not buy clothes for her, or
> soap to wash her clothes with, or clothes for her children. At times when
> she asked me for money I told her that I didn't have money, while I did
> have money, and she would manage and work. If she didn't have any-
> thing, she would not tell anyone about it but bear the hunger with her
> children. At last I would feel sympathy for my children and give her
> money to cook. . . . But now I regretted all that I was doing to her because
> God blesses all her children and they are the ones that are taking care of
> me and the rest of my family now.

Because of the close link between reproduction and conjugal morality, we can now see why posing an abstract question such as "How many chil-dren do you want?"—a question that could be put to a Western woman with the expectation of a clear numerical response—makes no sense. Such a query may produce not only confusion but even embarrassment. It im-plicitly challenges a woman's religious piety, suggesting that she is unwilling to accept all the children God might give her. It also alludes to the state of her marriage. Should she answer the question, and in particular, should she provide a numerical answer to it, she might imply that difficult marital circumstances (and therefore her low moral worth) have forced her to limit whatever number of child potentials God has given her, a number that may well have been larger than the answer she gave. "Up to God," a common response to such questions, may be the most diplomatic way to deflect such a presumptuous query.

Not only is reproduction a matter for evaluation. The process of aging is as well. In chapters 6 and 7 I showed how reproduction is depicted as aging a woman, draining her youth. But since reproduction is cast as something a woman can control, then how she ages becomes framed in evaluative terms. Whereas Westerners tend to view aging with distress, a Gambian woman considers it her duty, if not a privilege, to age on behalf of her husband and his family by producing worthy children for them. The complaints of a haggard wife may be dismissed with a proverb: "Water can't kill a frog." That is, the ordeals of childbearing are simply a woman's lot.[4] The achievements of a mother of many children are sometimes expressed in a striking phrase, "I have youth in my children." That is, she has become old by exchanging her youth for children, meaning that the process of aging can even be an index of moral worth, as long as the sacrifice it has entailed has brought very obvious rewards. Becoming old in conjugal service, through the visible struggle and sacrifice that childbearing entails, is one of life's most honored achievements. Alluding to the many pregnancies she has had and the sacrifices they have entailed, a woman will boast, "I am getting old." Addressing her as "old woman" is high praise. The subfertile age peers of the mother of many children may look and feel younger than she does. They may even live longer. Yet no one would choose the fate of a long, painful life of barrenness over the possibly shorter but far happier life of a woman who can bask in the love and gratitude of her husband and children.[5]

To the degree that she has exerted a sincere struggle during her life of reproductivity, those for whom she spent her financial and bodily resources should rally to make her post-childbearing years a time of resuscitation and repletion. The extra weight she can now put on and the health she can maintain are moral reflections of a life well lived, of wifely devotion and of responsible, industrious motherhood. As we saw in Mauss's point about the body as a reflection of society (1973), an older woman's body can be read as

4. Such convictions hold less, however, among urban people, many of whom are said to be willing to trade excess children for preserving their health.

5. In the light of these descriptions, we can now understand the opprobrium that J. K. Coker leveled at men for turning out the wife of their youth who struggled so hard for them (chapter 6).

a social text, a telltale indicator of a virtuous life. As the month of Ramadan begins, one can see a large influx of older people from the rural areas to the cities to be with urban children who have sent for them in order to care for them during this time. The children ensure that their parents eat good foods such as meat and fish. When the parents return, people will see their good bodies and healthy look, and they will deduce, "Ah, she (or he) has been to her son in Banjul. He is taking good care of her." In exchange, the child hopes for further parental blessings.

Additional clues to the magnitude of the sacrifice involved in the conversion of resources to moral gain as reproduction transpires are found in the differentiated language of "finishing," or getting old. Women are said to "finish" two kinds of bodily elements: replaceable and nonreplaceable. They express the expenditure of strength as *sɛmbo baŋtale* ("strength-finished"), the verb *baŋta* implying an act of temporarily depleting a renewable entity. Strength can be finished, as I explained in chapter 6, through hard work, hunger, sickness, and childbearing. By contrast, finishing muscles or the hapo (the divinely endowed "amount" of child potentials), *kuntu* or *kɔtɔ ta*, alludes to a permanent change, an irreversible expenditure of a finite resource or a fixed endowment. Whereas the expenditure of strength can earn a person moral credit, the expenditure of either muscles or the hapo connotes an extreme sacrifice. The fact that neither can be replenished implies an immense moral onus on the beneficiaries, whether they be children, husbands, or in-laws. The logic that connects reproduction and moral virtue is thus a seamless bundle of moral and physical causalities. Reproduction yields moral value, but the number of children a woman can have, together with how many of her pregnancies produce living children, reflects the degree to which her husband takes care of her, itself a reflection of her moral worth as a wife.

Childbearing is by far the most desirable way of demonstrating wifely virtue. But it is by no means the only way. A barren or subfertile woman may still earn conjugal credit by hard work and a dutiful life. By struggling for her husband's family and compound, becoming a devoted mother in name to all the compound's children, she may even rise above the fray of partisan domestic politics.[6] The logic of bodily struggle also reveals why

---

6. Some key exceptions prove the rule that the magnitude of a woman's struggle on behalf of the family bespeaks her worth. For example, there are occasional charges of efforts to deceive, to reap undeserved benefits from a body whose rights belonged to someone else. In a short story from Nigeria collected by Nita Kolon (1980), a woman named Rhoda, who bore five children by a previous husband, remarries but produces no children. Using a metaphor of international business corporations, the new husband's sisters are outraged by the wife's presumptive move on the family's benefits when

even child deaths and nonlive births, as tragic as they are, can earn conjugal credit. That such events have not only medical but conjugal significance, and are thus seen as reproductive effort, explains (as I implied in chapter 6) why a barren woman sometimes goes to the clinic seeking written medical documentation for a miscarriage. Whether her expenditure is reckoned in muscles lost or fetuses borne, the number of living children a woman has, though it comprises one measure of her worth, is ultimately less important than how she has spent herself. Simply getting pregnant periodically, even if some of these pregnancies eventually go wrong, is a sign that she acted in good faith.

Since so much is bound up in reproductive expenditure for a particular man and his family, a woman is expected to remain married, even if she ages quickly in her reproductive struggle, and to voice resentment only if the husband proves to be an egregious miser. Despite the ethic that women should bear their lives uncomplainingly, survey forms occasionally came back with unmistakable hints of bitterness at the gendered inequities of childbearing and aging. One thirty-nine-year-old woman with eight surviving children, three by her current husband, offered herself as a case in point:

> I can still produce more [children if] I want but I have a very useless husband now so I want to stop giving birth to be able to take great care of the children. My husband does not help me at all. Even when I got pregnant I found fire wood, and sold it to be able to pay for my antenatal card and also to buy good food. . . . My husband does not help me to have good food during pregnancy and [he puts] pressure on me; that makes me powerless [probably refers to lacking physical strength].

Among the most vivid examples of resentment was this one from a woman who described herself, at age thirty-seven, as completely finished:

> I am an old woman now, I had ten pregnancies and lost all my muscles due to child bearing. I have been doing hard work since I was married newly up to now. We don't have rest; women in the villages always do

---

she has invested nothing: "She worked for U.A.C. and she has come to draw her pensions at U.T.C. This one can't make a baby; all the children in her have been extracted by another man and she had brought the empty shell here. This one is a he-cat" (23). As Homiak (1995, 139) points out, bodily conditions, once they are public and visible, give rise to contending interpretations of the behaviors that produced them.

harder work than men. The men only work in the farms during the rainy season and that lasts for only three months. The rest of the year, they sit idling and chatting in the bantabas [shady sitting places] while women work throughout the year. Whenever we finish in the rice fields, we help men weeding in the farms before we go back to the fields for harvesting and during the dry season; we start gardening without good food. That is why we get old and weak easily. (R. 12)

"Legs Tied" and "Maternal Depreciation": The Double Edges of Conjugal Commitment

For a woman, then, realizing one's reproductive potential entails careful expenditure of social and bodily resources on behalf of a husband in the hope of long-term gain for herself and her children. To the degree that she "ages" or "finishes" for her husband, especially by producing sons for him, she finds that her "legs are tied" *(siŋɔ siti ta)*. "Tied by the placentas" is another way to express this commitment. Placentas, like the harijeos (fetuses) they contain, are considered to be limited in number, and the expenditure of each one in a reproductive event is an irrevocable act of sacrifice.[7] By metaphors like these, a woman refers to the commitment she has made, both moral and physical, to this man and his family to such an extent that she would now find it hard to divorce him and marry someone else. On her commitment hang not only her own security but that of her children as well.

Becoming tied ideally connotes success: bodily resources have been converted into enduring support and esteem on behalf of a worthy family. This kind of conversion, judiciously enacted, is the supreme marital goal to which she aspires. To the degree that she becomes tied in this positive sense, she will succeed in establishing roots (a Fula expression) that anchor her to the compound and its future. Explained a young Fula woman: "I have children here . . . who are part of the compound's future as my husband is a son to the compound head. A woman's children are her roots. . . . I am the only wife with male children so far; this assures me that the life after my husband will be one of my sons" (R. 13). The advantages of establishing roots, or becoming tied, have parallels in the ways in which the Bambara of Mali describe the life trajectories of their herding animals (Adam Thiam, pers.

---

7. Besides having many children, other things can tie a woman's legs. Two examples are having a large bridewealth paid for her or a kin relationship to her husband.

comm.). A cow is seen as having a limit of about six calves, after which she is "finished." No longer monitored or taken on long treks to graze, she is allowed, in her weakened state, to wander unsupervised, browsing close at hand on scraps of fodder. In a similar way, a woman who has spent her reproductive allotment can move in a more unfettered manner, freed from the stringent societal norms applied to younger women. If she has no interest in cooking for her husband or in contacting him sexually when he calls her to his house, she simply refuses. He cannot divorce her. And his death at this point would be irrelevant to her status. With an honorable history of serving her in-laws and producing sons who are now situated securely in their father's compound, her status is invincible.[8]

Yet being tied can also be a precarious state. A woman who has finished herself in a previous marriage can fool no one about the state of her body. A husband may, in fact, try to take advantage of this potential vulnerability. Knowing that her options for starting a new marital life outside the compound will be curtailed sharply once she is no longer fresh, he may try to tie his young wife's legs quickly by feigning geniality, inducing her to bear a number of children in rampant, depleting childbearing. Having a previous marriage and several pregnancies resulting from it would not only represent lost expenditure; it would also raise serious moral questions about her as a woman who failed as a wife. Should she try to divorce, she would have to leave the compound in shame, taking none of her children with her and having little capacity to bear any more. In some ways, however, taking her children with her would be worse than leaving them behind. It would imply that the husband denied connection to them; in other words, they could be taken to be illegitimate. Even if she remarried, having children with different surnames would be a slur on her character, for it would imply that she had failed to tie her legs securely for one compound. In a survey, she might well try to block this episode from view by denying that she had a prior marriage or pregnancies or by construing the surnames of her children as those of her current husband.

Aging through reproductive efforts for a worthy man is much preferred to aging slowly by having no children or children who prove ungrateful. It is certainly preferable to aging on behalf of a useless man. Getting old in

---

8. In an Ibibio story from Nigeria (Andreski 1970, 112), a widow reflects a similar sense of confidence: "I have four co-wives plus myself, making five. All of us are still here in the compound since my husband died. Though we were asked to choose any of my husband's relatives for marriage, none of us accepted to marry anyone because we all have got responsible children who can care for us."

ways that do not stem from legitimate struggle or in ways that fail to benefit the husband's family is a tragic waste of precious personal and family resources. Given the tension that becoming tied implies, a woman's life is locked into a paradoxical dilemma. She needs children and she expects to age through bearing them. Should her marriage go sour or her husband prove useless, her body will have been spent on a dead-end relationship and her income on its progeny. An educated woman with wide contacts in the international development world, but not-quite-perfect English, expressed the entire predicament as "maternal depreciation." This phrase is an obvious misreading of the international phrase "maternal depletion." Yet it signals a striking shortcoming in Western comprehensions of high fertility and its costs. It captures far better than the simple medical notion of depletion the combined economic, medical, and social plight of a woman who must watch each longed-for pregnancy result in a mishap or a child her husband does not support. In such a predicament, each pregnancy devalues her cumulatively and makes divorce increasingly infeasible.

The Social and Moral Nature of Retirement

Having sacrificed her youth for children, a woman faces one question with increasing intensity: when can she retire (*fɔnyɔɔ*, "rest, retire") from childbearing? That is, when can she stop bearing children and begin to replete physically?[9] Again, there is no age boundary. All depends on how she has conducted her life. If she has succeeded in converting her youth to blessings through her reproductive labors, she should have earned a secure place to spend her elderhood and earned the right to begin a wholly new phase of life, a permanent rest, from those to whom she brought life: her children and her husband's family. In fact, she should be surrounded by people eager to take care of her. Irrespective of her age in years or her menopausal status, she should be allowed to retire, and the beneficiaries of her reproductive struggles should hasten to replace her (*joosayo*, "replacement") with someone younger. Rallying on her behalf, they should recognize her achievements by giving her a young co-wife or a daughter-in-law to take over the reproductive role and heavy labor for the compound. As a thirty-five-year-old mother of six children explained, an early life of struggle, if

---

9. In this context, the practice of retirement seems to be a more appropriate term than "terminal abstinence," since the advent of contraceptives such as Depo Provera can now, in theory, make sexual abstinence a moot point.

converted into moral capital, can now pay off: "I want to bear more children in order to get a lot of assistance from them when I got old. In our society, we have the belief that the more children you have, the less labor you have to do in order to earn a living easily because you lost most of your muscles and strength in bearing" (R. 12).

Retirement from childbearing, then, is not simply the outcome of a hormonal process. Nor does it represent an individual decision to stop work or reproduction. Retirement is fundamentally social, so much so that this quality is reflected in the word itself. The verb *to retire* is understood to require an agent, as in "to retire someone" or "to be retired by someone."

Since retirement from childbearing for a woman requires an agent, who should this be? One very obvious person is her husband, who, recognizing her spent state, is expected to provide bridewealth to acquire a young co-wife for her. Even more than her husband, her sons are considered to be responsible for her. In particular, her oldest son is obligated to marry and bring his wife into the compound so that the generational tables can turn. His mother, who struggled so hard for him and his siblings, can begin a life of comfort and respect. So compelling are these expectations that a man, whether he is a husband or a son, describes a new marriage as less for himself than for an older wife or a mother, whether to retire her or simply to provide help for her.[10] One thirty-two-year-old monogamist reflected concerns for both his mother and his wife as he related the story of his current marriage and his reasons for beginning to consider marrying a second wife:

> I married this woman because I reached the stage of marriage. Without [my] marriage, my mother would continue to work for me. We Wolof, the first son should marry as soon as possible to help the mother. . . . [My wife] has no problem with my family; all the family likes her. I am planning to look for another wife so that this first wife can have less work to do.

The social impetus—and the financial resources—for a woman's retirement from childbearing would appear to come from men. But a woman may be so anxious to retire that she does not wait for a man, whether her husband or her son, to marry. Instead, she can bring social pressure to bear on a man (her son, for example) to enact a marriage that will allow her to retire. Facing growing rebukes for allowing his mother to toil on, her care-

---

10. Comments Andreski (1970, 57), "Traditionally, the only serious love relationship of the African man's life is that with his mother."

free bachelor son will be shamed into marriage. Alternatively, a woman seeking to retire may take matters into her own hands by fostering a girl, perhaps her brother's daughter, with the expectation that this girl will learn the ways of the household, and, when she reaches puberty in a few years, become either her co-wife or daughter-in-law. This kind of fostering is a very common way to lay the groundwork for a marriage. Andreski (1970), relating an Ibibio tale from Nigeria, describes a case of a mother who brings in a girl to relieve her of work and eventually to retire her by marrying her son. Bringing in a girl in this manner is done with an eye to establishing a proper relationship with the future mother-in-law. Andreski remarks: "For a comfortable old age, the Ibibio woman is dependent upon her daughters-in-law, and it would appear that she has rarely cause for complaint. Since they come often as mere infants into her house they are more like adopted daughters, and they have in any case been trained in filial duties and obedience almost from babyhood" (57–58). One might even speculate that a girl's good behavior, a strong theme in African ideology, may be the cause of her early marriage. In another Ibibio story, a woman recounts her early married life: "I was forced by my parents to marry a man who was even older than my father himself. Of course, it was not my husband who negotiated to marry me, but my mother-in-law, who was interested in the way I had been helping my mother and that feelings [*sic*] moved her to come and marry me to her son who had got four wives already" (ibid., 159). And whereas women are deeply invested in their own retirement possibilities, they also help each other in this crucial matter. A senior woman, herself retired, can use her authority to help the next wife retire by reallocating duties in the compound, placing increasing responsibility for the more arduous duties on the younger wives. Freeing up the next-oldest wife in this way is a clear statement to the husband that this woman also should be retired from reproduction.

Regardless of which person takes the initiative to retire an older woman, physical repletion can only occur if someone steps in to relieve her of her burden and replace her with another woman. This new woman will be younger, stronger, more fertile, someone who can step in to take over the hardest reproductive and domestic tasks.[11] Since this marriage is often enacted for the benefit of the older woman as much as for her husband or

---

11. The notion of "relieving" people of their heavy duties, whether permanently or temporarily, through social replacement, can be found widely in studies of Africa, whether this refers to collective work groups or financial support groups. An example is found in Herskovits's (1938, 74) descriptions of cooperative work groups in Dahomey in the 1930s.

son, the precise identity of this new woman, whether she is a co-wife or a daughter-in-law, matters less than the fact that someone young is entering the picture.[12] A woman's health and even her reproductivity, that is, are thus contingent on the fecundity, labor, and resources of the younger generation.

An older woman who seeks to retire perceives the transferral of the bride to her compound as a euphoric moment. For the mother of the departing bride, however, it is a decided setback. Losing her daughter means losing much-needed labor and even delaying her own retirement. The prospective husband and his mother (assume here that we are talking about the acquisition of a daughter-in-law and not a co-wife) want the bride urgently. Delays in transferring a new bride to her husband's compound, a subject of endless complaint, may represent quite intentional foot-dragging by mothers of brides. The mother of a bride tries to retain her daughter until the arrival of her own daughter-in-law, who is in turn being retained by her own mother for the same reasons. A delay in one marriage may set off an entire chain of delays.

The relations among health, aging, and morality thus play out in multiple permutations in the retirement process. The major questions that people pose about a woman are when, and under what conditions, her retirement occurs. What is the sequencing of a health trajectory relative to retirement? A woman who, even though she is spent, remains burdened with unrelenting work, continues childbearing long after she might have been retired by others, remains thin and drawn, with a light pallor and a listless fatigue, or suffers from repeated miscarriages, lack of food, or medical care—for such a woman, a large question about her morality hangs over her head. Why has she remained in this state for so long? Why is she not regaining her fat and sheen? If she was disobedient and disrespectful toward her husband and his family, her husband would not have blessed her and the blessings she tried to bestow on her children would have been empty. Having little

---

12. For the young woman in question, however, identity is critical. Either a daughter-in-law or a co-wife faces an exhausted older woman with a long list of assignments. If she is a co-wife, she begins from an almost insurmountable disadvantage. Unless the first wife was infertile, she will be forever behind in the fertility count, always having children who are junior in standing to most of the children of the first. The situation is quite different for a new daughter-in-law who marries the first son of the retiring woman. Marriage initially harnesses her to family interests and gives her little choice in a husband. And since some of his sisters likely left to marry already, she will likely be responsible for several of her husband's demanding brothers (her mother-in-law's sons). But ultimately she stands to gain more than the wives who will follow. It is she who will earn the credit for helping her husband build up his household and it is her children who will take precedence in their father's household.

success in life, she could not make her children succeed in life and thus they could not take care of her. They might even have no children of their own. For the rest of her life, she will remain kɔtɔ, "old" in the manner implied by permanent muscle loss. The suspicion is that she has brought this fate upon herself, perhaps by feuding with her co-wives or by allowing her romantic interests to stray. By contrast, a woman with successful children and a husband whose blessings she has earned does not mind growing "old" quickly. She much prefers an elderhood surrounded by grateful, productive children and grandchildren who take care of her than a long, lonely senescence clouded by suspicion.

For such reasons, a prospective husband is anxious to know the character of his prospective wife's family, especially that of her mother. Was she good to her own husband? If so, then her daughter is likely to be well trained and thus to have blessings. She may even have more children than will a woman with poor training and, consequently, few blessings.[13]

Recasting a Fertility Survey

We have examined in close detail the connections among sociality, morality, and physical status in the processes of reproduction and aging. So very different from Western thinking is this way of looking that it is useful to step back and stand the two schemes of fertility and aging up against each other as graphic representations of what I have been calling "linearity" and "contingency." The first is modeled on a standard fertility survey form. The second is based on the sketch of the fertility survey Fatou brought to me in April 1994: a fertility survey, as she phrased it, "the way an African woman might write it." I simplify the schemes to show the most basic points of difference, highlighting just a few of the attributes of each and the cultural assumptions they embody.

Figure 8.1 shows the first form, a stripped-down version of a standard Western fertility survey. It displays a series of rows and columns containing spaces to list all the woman's live births, together with details about each child that a birth produces. Each birth is listed in chronological order, and all events are indexed solely to the woman. The woman's present marital status is elicited to assess what is termed in demographic parlance as the

---

13. Riesman (1992), in *First Find Your Child a Good Mother*, seems to have missed an extraordinary opportunity in merely alluding to a man's desire to marry a woman from a good family.

Woman's name _____ Marital status _____ Age _____

For all children who were alive at birth:

Birth order	Name	Sex	Date of birth	Still alive?	Living here?	Date of death
1						
2						
3						
4						
5						

Boys born altogether   _____
Girls born altogether   _____
Total born   _____
Ideal number of children   _____

Fig. 8.1 Conventional survey form for history of childbearing

woman's likelihood or risk of childbearing in the immediate future. The same is true for age, which is used to gauge how fertile she has been relative to the number of children she might have had, and when she will likely stop bearing. This fertility history can be supplemented by any number of other background questions such as town or village of residence, age at marriage, number of marriages, number of co-wives, and current contraceptive use. Child deaths can be used to calculate proportion of surviving children, as well as to estimate further births a woman might try to have to replace the children who died. The question on ideal number of children, though considered not very relevant in a place where women want all the children God gives them, may be used if a woman has finished childbearing to estimate how many more children she had than the number she wanted or by how many she fell short of her ideal number. Names of children are used to keep

Name _____   Stage of muscle loss _____

For each man/husband:

	Present man	Previous man	The man before
Man's name			
Live births			
Abortions/miscarriages			
Stillbirths			
Total muscles cut			

Total muscles cut   _____
How many more pregnancies do you want for your husband? _____

Fig. 8.2 Survey form for history of muscle loss

the demographic events in her fertility career aligned with one another in the record.

The emphasis in this form is on the number of live births to an individual woman as a function of time. I could have displayed the survey in the form of a full fertility history, showing both nonlive and live births, although this has not been standard practice for recent years. Had I done so, I would have pointed out that the analysis was treating nonlive births as temporal placeholders to help account for the time between live births.

The second way of reckoning fertility is quite different. Based on the premise that the woman is a social being and that fertility events constitute a moral record of her life, it is transparently an accounting chart showing conjugal duty and sacrifice (fig. 8.2). Although some of the same questions could be asked in the two fertility frameworks, this second form entirely recasts how fertility and its relevant events are reckoned. No longer concerned with the time frame in which children are born, it bypasses chronological age and replaces it with the more contingent "stage of muscle loss" as a reflection of the number and severity of prior reproductive events. It also counts both live and nonlive births to estimate an overall bodily toll. Most important, marriage is no longer simply a social status or a risk category for a woman but the organizing principle of her entire reproductive life. Although fertility events occur to the woman, they are indexed to individual men, as is shown in their alignment into columns under the names of the men on whose behalf they occurred. The question on how many more pregnancies she wants for her husband, given her bodily state, can thus be used to assess not only how "old" she is physically but also how secure she feels in the present marriage, these two issues being tightly linked. This sense of bodily commitment is reflected in the number of pregnancies—the most basic unit of reproductive currency she would most like to claim—she has had per man.

Moral worth and the history of a woman's relationships, the implied themes of the chart and the end points of the calculations, are thus reflected in multiple ways. They also deeply cross-reference each other. Take the case of names. If the woman was divorced, with all the opprobrium this implies, her children may have different surnames because she will likely be anxious to regain some status by having children by the new husband. Even if she is spent, she may well declare a desire for more pregnancies for him. If she was widowed, on the other hand, we can tell by the surnames of the children whether she was worthy enough in the eyes of her in-laws to be asked to remain in the compound and marry one of her dead husband's relatives. If so, she may continue to bear children in the name of the family in which she invested her initial resources, and the surnames of both husbands and all the children will be the same. In any fertility record there is abundant material for cross-referencing. In this one, we may use some inconsistencies to discover an entirely different moral account than the one a woman seeks to convey. If she reports that she is spent and yet wants more pregnancies, even if the husband's and children's names appear to be the same, further probing may reveal a piece of her reproductive past that she may have tried to hide. The surnames of her children may in fact not be the same. There may have been two marriages, the first of which ended in divorce. Alternatively, the woman may have had more pregnancies and children than she reported at first, pregnancies that she omitted because they were for a man from whom she was later divorced. From such clues we may be able to reason backwards to make sense of a conjugal and reproductive life.

The physical state that figure 8.2 displays might at first appear to be an absolute attribute that she carries over from one marriage to another, independent of her marital history. But a woman's current physical state is still assessed with respect to moral conduct. The number and kinds of pregnancy outcomes she has had, and the toll that reproduction has taken, is a pathway that implies an evaluated history of her conjugal life.

In sum, Gambian women would construct a fertility history quite differently from the one we have come to take for granted. Our "commonsense" fertility protocols describe a record of live births and chronological time elements that make up the reproductive life span of an autonomous individual. In doing so, they mute if not erase traumatic reproductive events and reduce a conjugal relationship to a background variable or a risk factor for pregnancy. Gambian women, by contrast, would construct a chart that emphasizes not time or total numbers of births but the cumulative moral history of a woman's physical expenditure on behalf of a man. Such a chart, in its handling of fertility questions, would bring to light facets of reproduction that differ markedly from those in Western surveys. In joining contingent physicality with morality, the Gambian version would discard some very familiar variables (age, for example) and add some unfamiliar ones (muscles). It also would take some unaccustomed slices through familiar variables (marital status and fertility events) and place unfamiliar emphasis on information that we usually treat as marginal—placeholders, at best—or may not consider as variables at all (nonlive births, names).

New Connections to Classical Anthropology

Asking how a woman's reproductive endowment is enhanced by diligent care or destroyed by indifference alters entirely the way we think about two of the major processes in adult life: reproduction and aging. Social and bodily contingencies and the moralities they imply bring to life facets of the classical ethnography of Africa in ways that seem to have eluded even the architects of kinship theory. Drawing on material in this chapter as well as from previous ones, I re-describe several topics from the anthropological literature whose meaning now seems so transformed. The first example is that of polygyny.

Polygyny

Ethnographic descriptions often frame the phenomenon of polygyny in terms of whether its practice is detrimental or beneficial to women. Reframing the question in the light of a woman's bodily history suggests a number

of things. Starting first from the perspective of women, we can see that although having a young co-wife may pose a severe threat, a spent woman
who has produced many surviving children will not likely find a young co-
wife threatening, unless she is at odds with her husband in general. Indeed,
this young co-wife may be the key to her much-coveted retirement. Hints
of this possibility emerge in some of the quotations from a thirty-four-year-
old woman who reported being spent. After six pregnancies (all surviving),
she reported no sexual contact throughout the monthly rounds and no desire for more pregnancies because, in her words, she was "elderly and tired
of delivery" (R. 2). "I don't want a child anymore [she stressed]. I am elderly
now, and have even seen my grandsons" (R. 8). And more: "I am tired; my
strength is finished. I want to avoid my husband entirely; I don't know how
he will cope with it; if he can get another woman, he will not worry [de-
mand sex of] me" (R. 10).

Since most of the discussion has centered on women, however, let us
look at polygyny from the perspective of a man and his life cycle but with
respect to the changing reproductive and social statuses of his wives.[14] We
start with the vision of polygyny as our conventional anthropological diagrams have implied it: simultaneous co-residence — of a man and his wives,
each wife having her own children and forming the core of a matrilateral
segment of patrilineal descendants.

In reality, however, such a polygynous group almost never exists. A
more accurate depiction would show a man's diachronic *sequence* of wives. It
would also show the pace at which he acquires them and the "intensity"
with which he is married at any one moment. The configurations would
shift as each wife moved into the household and as she began and ended her
reproductivity. All of this would be shown in conjunction with the reproductive and residential activities of other wives. Although I cannot fully capture the dynamics of this set of factors, the base of such a chart would use
the man's life line, whether in time or more time-neutrally, and it would use
the life lines for each of his wives and the key points of their reproduction
and movement after his death at age sixty-five (figure 8.3). For illustrative
purposes, I oversimplify. I give everyone a similar duration of life (65 years)
and all the wives the same reproductive capacity. I also prevent divorce and
suppress discord. Despite these flattening efforts, the collective reproductive
and bodily dynamics that emerge are revealing.

For each woman in this figure, several items of information are appar-

14. For more recent demographic work on men in the same study area, see Ratcliffe 2000.

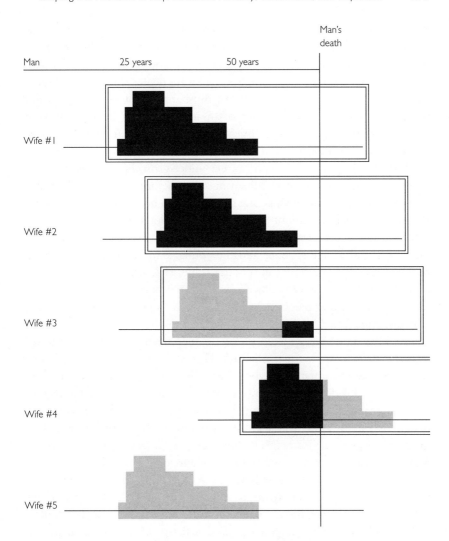

Fig. 8.3 The domestic career of a man and his sequence of wives

ent. The thin line shows her individual life line. The thick bars show the intensity and duration of her reproductivity, the latter reflected by the height of the bars. The dark color reflects the reproductivity each wife expends on behalf of our baseline man. Gray bars show the amount of reproductive capacity she spent for some other man, whether or not he is in the compound, and when during her own reproductive life this capacity is spent. Around some part of each woman's life is a double-lined box showing the period during which she actually lives in this compound, irrespective of her conjugal relationship to the man. All of the women are shown as living longer than the man because they were born later, and their "in-residence" boxes show them remaining in the compound after his death, since they are married as much to the compound as to the husband. Let us then follow what we might call the "domestic career" of this imagined man (in contrast to the usual description of a man's "political career") as we examine him in relation to his individual wives and their reproduction.

The man begins his domestic career under growing pressure from his mother to retire her from childbearing. Well before he reaches his mid-twenties, she has identified a young girl for him in her brother's household. By the time this girl is about fifteen, she is considered ready for marriage. After months of bridewealth negotiations, the young woman transfers into the compound at age sixteen, and the young man's busy sexual life as a bachelor abates as he settles into married life. His young wife's first child, born when she is around eighteen, is followed by several other children whose births occur at first in tight intervals, and, later, as she begins to age, at longer intervals.

Men say they marry a second wife to keep having children and to reduce the "loneliness" in the compound. They also explain their second marriages as an aid to a first wife, who is becoming spent. The man in our case thus couches his desire for a new wife not in terms of the sexual appeal of the young woman he has seen but of an attempt, enacted out of sympathy, to help his rapidly aging wife with the increasing burdens that work and reproduction now pose for her. The first wife, fully aware of the range of his motives, takes his tact as an auspicious sign and agrees to look into the matter of acquiring a new wife. At length, she finds a girl she likes and brings her in for training as bridewealth negotiations begin. Once this girl attains puberty, final bridewealth arrangements are made and she begins to have children. ("She is the youngest wife and is the producer," explained one man in the surveys, to distinguish this wife from the first.) Relations between the two wives are cordial because of the difference in their physical stage and status, because the first was enlisted to seek the second, and because the first wife closely trained the second in the details of practice and comportment in the compound. As the children of the new wife begin to arrive, the older wife retires, and her children begin to marry.

The first wife of a first son is said to be "for" her husband's mother and the second wife is for the first. The third wife, however, may have a very different profile. She can be a divorcee, a charity wife, or an infertile woman. If all has gone well with a man's fortunes, she can even be another young virgin. In this case, the third wife is the widow of the man's brother. Nearly finished herself, but having spent her reproductivity and youth in the compound, she elected, to no one's surprise, to stay on instead of moving out when she became a widow. Her new union produces nowhere near the fanfare of the first wife or even of the second, who had come as a mere girl. In fact, this third wife does not really "arrive" at all. Already living in the compound with her older children, she merely enters the cooking and sexual rotation with the second wife. Secure as she is, however, she eventually bears a child for the man just for good measure.

By now, the man is growing old, both physically and chronologically. His first wife, younger in years than he, is much older physically but commands considerable respect and authority in the compound. "She is our own family," as her husband's relatives say, implying that she is in some way becoming a senior agnate. Any further wives will be quite removed in status from her, and she can delegate authority on most domestic matters to the second wife, whom she trained personally. Therefore, when the man acquires a fourth wife, a young virgin, at a steep bridewealth fee, the new wife is placed immediately under the supervision of the second wife, herself a capable taskmaster and disciplinarian. The aging man now measures out his sexual energy cautiously. The other wives have retired, or are about to do so, and this new wife becomes the only one with whom he maintains regular sexual relations. Giddy with love for her, he plies her with gifts, attention, and food, to the exasperation of the senior wives, who see him as wasting household resources on a spoiled girl with little sense. Proof of her flightiness is seen in the fact that instead of trying to stall her childbearing to retain her appeal for a younger man in what will probably be the near future, she squanders her reproductivity on their old husband, bearing children who, because of their mother's late arrival in the compound, will be at the bottom of the household hierarchy.

The fifth wife (or perhaps she was fourth; everyone is rather vague on whether her marriage occurred before or after that of the very young woman) is a "charity wife." Acquired in the man's old age when her longtime husband died, she is very old, not only in the sense of being worn out from childbearing, but also old in time: almost as old as the man himself. Despite the religious mandate to limit wives to four, she is not counted as a real wife, and no one seems to worry about her whereabouts. An ephemeral presence, she lives in a distant village with one of her sons, appearing very occasionally with a symbolic meal for her symbolic husband. The fourth wife, in fact, has yet to meet her.

Having tracked the individual wives through a staged sequence, let us turn our attention to the man's physical life in ways that his relationships to women of different physical and reproductive statuses bring to light. Although I have cast the male life course as linear, at least by comparison to that of women, a closer inspection of the events in his marital life reveals far more contingency than we might have anticipated.

What a man sees as an escalating risk of sex has a strong bearing on how he allocates his ebbing life power. Figure 8.3 shows that there is a point, about age forty-five to fifty, when the man faces very high sexual demands.[15] His first wife, although she is slowing down, is still reproducing; he has ac- quired a second wife who rapidly came to the peak of her reproductivity; a third wife wants another child or two for him; and a new one is just starting her reproductive career. Thus, a man's most polygynous moment usually occurs when his own sexual strength has begun to decline. It is just, that is, when a polygynous man's multiple wives may be most demanding of chil- dren, that he begins to see sex as a risk to his ebbing bodily power. He must either allocate increasingly disproportionate amounts of his life strength to trying to give his wives children or ignore their efforts to seek outside help on this front. The man's problem is thus often one of spacing sex rather than one of spacing children. Indeed, there is some quiet speculation that this old and fragile man has sealed his own fate by acquiring such a young wife.

As this diagram demonstrates, it is a gross oversimplification to say that a man is a monogamist or a polygynist. Rather, virtually all men aspire to a polygynous life, and many will probably hold this status at one point or another. The wives' reproductivities may or may not overlap with one an- other. But such is the sequencing of women's physical and social stages that they are rarely placed in direct reproductive competition, and the older ones generally feel responsible for the younger ones. To "put one wife un- der the other wife" is a common way of expressing this layering effort.

The fact that wives are a highly differentiated lot in both their repro- ductive states and achieved moral statuses emerges even more sharply when we break out differences among men. Aside from differences posed by age, those of wealth and social standing are most important. A wealthy man like the one we have just followed is more likely than a poor one to maintain a continuous sequence of fertile young wives and to have multiple fertile wives simultaneously, with substantial overlap among their reproductivities. If he lives to age seventy, a wealthy man will probably end up having strung

---

15. See Blanc and Gage 2000 for demographic corroboration of this peak of expectation in Africa more widely.

together, or overlapped, the reproductive careers of several healthy women, and he may still have a relatively young wife when he dies.

Just as a man can make his way up the marital scale, however, he can also slide down it. A man with few resources will likely marry only one woman, and she will bear him, if he is fortunate, one set of children. Such a man may have been a high-birth-order son who had little money to marry and was forced, for much of his young adult life, to migrate for work or to remain in servitude to a marabout or a village chief. If he does marry several women, their characteristics will be entirely different from those of the man discussed above. The latter man's wives will never have much remaining reproductivity, either because they have reached the end of their reproductivity or they were subfertile. If they live with him at all, they will be in residence sporadically and consecutively, rather than simultaneously. He may start married life with a difficult divorcee: perhaps his marabout-patron's sister, whose husband became fed up with her arrogance and sent her back home. When this relationship ends, he will move on to a woman with a history of nonlive births, followed by a widow, a woman with ill health, a charity wife. Eventually he will have to move in with an older woman with grown children. Having limited tolerance for him, her children will make life so difficult that he must move on to yet another household and yet a more marginal union. As he becomes increasingly derailed from the preferred male pathway of marriage and reproduction, he will become a man of no consequence. If asked to recount his marriage history, he will recall these women painfully because they had no children for him, because the union was so ephemeral, or because they treated him so badly.

Looking through a sequence of conjugal events rather than through a frozen slice of time makes it possible to illuminate relativities in the male as well as the female life course and relationships among them. It also gives us a better understanding of the dynamics that both unite and divide other members of the conjugal unit. Rather than polygynous wives being a group of structurally equivalent co-residential individuals with uniform reproductive statuses, women who marry the same man are now seen as highly differentiated in their characteristics, their whereabouts, and the pathways that led them to this household. Indeed, women who leave because of divorce may move through a man's life not knowing each other at all.

Other Themes from the Ethnography of Africa

Besides its application to polygyny, a contingency framework brings to light quite different perspectives on a variety of other practices.

Cross-Cousin Marriage and Country Marriage

Among the most prominent of these practices is the classic anthropological topic of cross-cousin marriage, marriage to the mother's brother's daughter. Esoteric, exotic, arid—mother's brother's daughter marriage evoked the interest of only the most committed kinship enthusiasts, who usually described the practice in terms of jural mandates of kinship or of men's efforts to cement further ties with a wife's lineage (for example, Radcliffe-Brown 1950). Yet as we look at this practice through the eyes of an aging mother with a son nearing adulthood, the practice comes to life as the potential centerpiece of a woman's retirement strategy.

In the male marriage histories collected in the Gambian project, fully 65 percent of all first marriages for men (and many second marriages as well) were reported as being those to what is translated locally as a "cousin sister": a mother's brother's daughter.[16] Many of the male narratives about marriage reflect the prominent role of a man's mother in setting up this arrangement by acquiring a wife from her family for him. The impetus for the marriage seems to come from multiple sources, but especially from the mother and her son, the latter feeling under some obligation to retire his mother. In the following quotation, a forty-five-year-old man recounts how his mother obtained a daughter (Ramata) from her brother, trained her from an early age, and arranged the marriage, all, apparently, so that she could retire.

> Ramata was my uncle's daughter and since she was three years old my mother was . . . taking care of her because she wanted her to be my wife when she grew up, and then I was young too but I was older than her. Then when I reached 21 my father said I should get a wife now. But before that time they wanted me to marry Ramata because her father and mother wanted her to set a marriage time as soon as she was 15 years. She had been waiting for me and was getting older because as Fulas they marry at the age of eight or even before that. . . . Ramata is my uncle's daughter and she was cared for by my own mother; that is why my father chose her for me.

The acquisition of the young wife in this story appears to have been enacted more for an anxious, aging mother-in-law than for the son. In fact,

---

16. The term is often used in a classificatory sense in that it merges distant and close relatives into the same kinship category. Hence *mother's brother's daughter* may be the term being used to describe a more distant relative on the mother's side.

the only thing apparently keeping the mother from pressing for a yet earlier marriage was her son's immaturity.

Closely related to the theme of cross-cousin marriage is the practice wherein an established urban man who lives in the city with his educated wife may marry a second woman, a "country wife," who lives in the rural area where he was born. This union is less likely than an urban marriage to be sanctioned by a legal document. This new woman will likely have little or no schooling and she will be expected to have many children by the man, conceived when he returns periodically to visit. An elite man may thus lead a dual reproductive life. In the city or even abroad, with his educated cosmopolitan wife, he will have low fertility. In the countryside, where the costs of maintaining children are far lower, he may have high fertility with his rural wife. I saw such unions in Liberia primarily as the doings of an affluent man who sought to bolster his stake in his rural home where he might need political support, access to subsistence foods during periods of urban shortage, and the possibility of retirement (Bledsoe 1980). But if we focus also on the man's aging mother, a very different possibility arises. Feeling bereft of what she sees as adequate filial assistance, she may put pressure on her son to marry a local woman and keep her in the rural family compound. Her son is expected to increase his home visits and remittances because of the needs of his family there. (For a splendid novelistic treatment of the tensions from which such arrangements arise, and which they in turn generate, see Ba 1989.)

In sum, marriage for young people often occurs not simply because older men maneuver in ethnographically well-described patterns of alliance and descent. They also occur because aging women lay the groundwork for a comfortable retirement for themselves.

Widow Inheritance

A recognition of contingency as the principle on which women gauge their fitness for further childbearing also enriches our understanding of widow inheritance: the acquisition by a man of a wife of a kinsman who died. Another favorite anthropological topic during times past, widow inheritance was described almost solely in terms of the logical workings of kinship mandates: the family of a man who paid bridewealth for a woman was entitled to retain rights in her even after the man's death (for example, Radcliffe-Brown 1950). This practice was said to offer security to an aging widow and her children. Far less visible in these works, however, was the fact that a widow with substantial moral and bodily investment in her dead

husband's household would find it strongly in her interests to remain there
by marrying his agnate.

The Grandmother Rule, or Terminal Abstinence

Another practice that takes on new meaning in light of the Gambian
findings is one that has interested demographers more than it has anthropologists: the "grandmother rule," or "terminal abstinence," in which a
woman may cease sexuality and childbearing before her fecundity is finished, thus apparently contravening expectations that she would want to
keep having children as long as time allowed. This practice has been explained as the result of social norms of shame due to bearing children while
one's own children are bearing or of duties of nurturance toward one's
grandchildren. For a woman who has suffered many bodily ordeals, however, it may be misleading to say that becoming a grandmother compels
her to retire from childbearing. In most cases, it is more likely that a marriage of a son, not a birth to a daughter, precipitates her retirement. Furthermore, it may be a marriage that she herself helps to arrange. Instead
of waiting for grandchildren to arrive, that is, a woman may try to put in
place the structure that will make her a grandmother. Indeed, most women
seem to dismiss the idea that grandmother retirement is an iron-clad rule.
Instead, they see it as an excuse to fall back on if needed. A number of still-
reproductive women point out that their daughters are *already* giving birth.
Such a possibility can be sensed in the following quotation from a thirty-
eight-year-old woman who had had seven pregnancies: "I will have to stop
giving birth when my daughter gets married. She is now thirteen; in three
to four years' time she will be bearing children and I will stop to look after
my young ones. Then I will stay away from my husband" (R. 6).

Absorption of a Woman into Her Husband's Kin Group

The link between morality and the expenditure of contingent bodily resources casts a different light as well on the classic question of absorption
of a woman into her husband's kin group. Gluckman (1950), among others,
saw this matter through an entirely different lens. Comparing groups in
southern Africa, he argued that the degree to which a woman is assimilated
is a function of bridewealth: high bridewealth is associated with complete
assimilation, whereas low bridewealth goes with partial assimilation. In the
altered vision I have attempted to present, becoming part of the husband's
kin group has an entirely different connotation. It is something over which

a woman has a good deal of control. And for her the potential payoff is immense. The compensation for a reproductive lifetime of struggle and hardship on behalf of her husband's compound is the possibility of taking on the equivalence of senior agnatic authority over its younger generations. By comporting herself well, by respecting her husband's family elders, and particularly by struggling to produce children who are blessed by his family, she hopes to become accepted as a member of his family—in some classificatory sense, her husband's own sibling—in the compound that she has "dried" or "finished" herself to develop.[17] She maintains a bond with her natal family, but her primary affiliation has shifted.

The Sande Society

Apprehending the contingent character of the life course is revealing as well in the interpretation of some representational art in Africa. Among the most striking examples of such a possibility are the helmet masks from the Bundu (or Sande) society in Liberia and Sierra Leone, a society composed entirely of women. Delineating a number of key cultural values that the masks convey, Boone (1986, 57) draws attention to bodily plumpness, in contrast to being "dry." This plumpness, a symbol of fertility, youth, and wealth, is represented symbolically by abundant rings of fat in the neck. Citing the work of Rose Frische, who argued that a certain minimal proportion of body fat to weight was necessary to induce the onset of menstruation, Boone notes that "Encouraging the initiates to eat heartily of the abundant Sande *mèhè* [food] advances this growth spurt and the crucial minimum of weight needed to render a girl fertile" (57). Yet the question the Gambian findings raise is whether the focus has been too narrow. Who are these masks talking to, and what are they saying? Anthropological and art historical literature has focused almost exclusively on how they beckon to young uninitiated women (for example, MacCormack 1979; Boone 1986). Almost completely neglected (my own work is no exception, Bledsoe 1984) is the urgency of the society's appeal to the already recruited: women who have begun childbearing and may welcome its support in their efforts to avoid dangerous and depleting pregnancies during breastfeeding. As Mac-Cormack (1994) notes,

> Women's nutritional status and fecundity also depends [*sic*] upon patterns
> of birth spacing and lactation. Mende and Sherbo [*sic*] women breastfeed

17. For a parallel observation about the Tuareg of Niger, see Rasmussen 1997, xiv.

for about 12 to 18 months. The baby is carried on its mother's back by day and sleeps with her by night suckling on demand over the entire diurnal cycle. The Sande society also enforces a postpartum taboo on sexual intercourse while the mother lactates, and will publicly fine anyone who violated this ancestral law. (114) [18]

Schooling for Young Women

Whereas the preceding examples have come from the more "traditional" kinship genres of anthropology, a contingency lens can be applied also to imported social practices. Of these, Western-style education for girls is a critical example. The loss of adolescent labor, in particular that of girls, that schooling can entail is well known. Yet it should be apparent by now that the long-term "costs" of schooling for children are not only absorbed in national and household expenditures but in the bodies of mothers. Increases in the time required to educate a child can delay a mother's retirement by prolonging the period in which she must support her children (for novelistic hints of such effects on the older generation, see Emecheta 1979). It should not be surprising, then, that adults should be so ambivalent at times about education or that they might be willing to educate some daughters while routing others into the marriage market as quickly as possible.

Women and the Hajj

Finally, from Morocco comes an intriguing play on the ambiguities surrounding social, physical, and ritual aging that becomes highly significant in the light of the notion of contingency. This application concerns new strategies for making the hajj, the Muslim pilgrimage to Mecca. Moroccan women, in an account by Rosander (1991), relate religious piety, and hence their eligibility for making the hajj, to concerns about aging and retirement from childbearing. In this account, we see descriptions of life course changes that have occurred since the 1970s for women who begin to enter what she terms "old age," though the referent is obviously much broader.

As one of the sacred pillars of life for Muslims who can afford it, the hajj for Moroccan women is a trip closely associated with old age, because it "stands apart from the erotic or sexualized frame-work that encloses all other female activities" (151). Yet according to Rosander, "These women bring old age about" (156). To this end, they act like menopausal women,

18. See also Boone 1985, 58.

associating with elders and attending to religious values, in order to secure release from the taxing labors of reproduction. Even more intriguing
are the changes that have come about following the economic boom of
the 1970s in what can best be termed "aging strategies" among wealthy
women. Formerly the hajj, often postponed until late in life when all sins
could be atoned for shortly before death, was performed by a few old men
and widows and by old wives only thinly connected, by this point, to husbands. Now, women who are forty to fifty years old, a number of whom
are premenopausal and still married, have started to make the trip. These
changes have paved the way for a new breed of what Rosander describes as
"transgressors of social age borders": "women who choose to appear as
older women while still middle-aged" (155). In particular, a woman from a
relatively rich family may try to become a *haja* at a younger point than she
could before. As a result, a prospective middle-aged haja

> is deliberately and pointedly indifferent to concerns that generally attract
> women of her social age. She talks a great deal about Mecca. Her general
> behaviour reflects a greater devotion to spiritual values. She does not ap-
> pear too often in other women's houses, drinking tea and chatting. She
> stays at home and has other women visit her. This breach of the law of
> reciprocity is also a sign of her growing respectability and prestige; she
> does not have to repay every visit in order to keep the social bonds with
> other women alive. She ceases to use make-up at the big wedding and
> name-giving parties and begins to wear white clothes, like the older
> women. (155)

If, as the Gambian findings would suggest, the expenditure of one's bodily
resources is regarded as a moral act, then it should not be surprising that
(as Rosander's material suggests) women in such situations try to construe
themselves as old.

Conclusion

In searching for insight into patterns of reproduction and aging in rural
Gambia, we have moved from absolutes to contingencies, both social and
physical. We have also moved from a belief in time as nature in the body to
a multiplicity of temporalities. In previous chapters I emphasized the idea
that fertility, time, and aging are culturally shaped and embodied in the
physical contingencies of women's reproductive lives. Here we turned to the
moral meanings that pervade these contingencies. In doing so, we saw a

vision in which a woman's worth is read as a moral history that is related to a man and his family. What a woman loses physically in the sacrifice of bodily resources during reproduction, she hopes to convert to social gain and moral virtue in her conjugal life. What is important, in sum, is not how quickly a woman ages, or even how this occurs physically, the points that I addressed in chapter 7. Here we have seen that what most matters ultimately is the question of for whom she has done so and what she has gained as a result. Her chief desire is to convert her bodily resources to blessings and a comfortable life as an elder in a respected family that she has strengthened by her reproductive efforts. Economies of absolute time are irrelevant. Taking their place is a social and moral economy of the body.

Descriptions such as these evoke the vocabulary found in Mauss's collaborative essay on sacrifice with Hubert (Hubert and Mauss 1964), mentioned in the beginning of this chapter. Using the example of animal sacrifice in India, Hubert and Mauss note that through sacrifice, something passes from the common into the sacred domain through the mediation of something that is destroyed in the course of the ceremony (97). Sacrifice is thus a ritual act that, through consecrating and offering a victim, modifies the condition of the person who accomplishes it. By associating as closely as possible with the victim, the sacrifier (the person offering the sacrifice) is linked to the sacred. In this way, the act of sacrifice bestows upon the sacrifier a new power and a moral and spiritual rebirth. As a result, he may undergo a permanent metamorphosis and a new identity may be conferred upon him.

As to the motives for sacrifice, the theme that looms large in this work is abnegation, a selfless sacrificing of one's limited resources on behalf of a recipient that requires such an offering in order to perpetuate itself. This observation reflects almost precisely the explanations that women in rural Gambia offer for why they struggle on behalf of a husband in an activity that is so destructive to bodily resources and perilous to life. The pivotal insight that pervades *Sacrifice*—sacrifice as a mode of creating a moral obligation to generate a new identity—now can be seen to link this book unmistakably to the author of *The Gift*:

> In any sacrifice there is an act of abnegation since the sacrifier deprives himself and gives. Often this abnegation is even imposed upon him as a duty. . . . But this abnegation and submission are not without their selfish aspect. The sacrifier gives up something of himself but he does not give himself. Prudently, he sets himself aside. This is because if he gives, it is partly in order to receive. Thus sacrifice shows itself in a dual light; it is a

useful act and it is an obligation. Disinterestedness is mingled with self-interest. That is why it has so frequently been conceived of as a form of contract. . . . The two parties present exchange their services and each gets his due. For the gods too have need of the profane. . . . In order that the sacred may subsist, its share must be given to it, and it is from the share of the profane that this apportionment is made. (Hubert and Mauss 1964, 100)

In a striking parallel to the Fula expression of "throwing one's soul" with reference to the risks entailed in childbirth, *The Gift* argues that the things that are given in sacrifice contain a force of their own that compels those who have these things to return them. They may even contain the soul of the giver (43). In The Gambia, a woman's bodily resources, her finite God-given child potentials, and even, possibly, her life—these things she sacrifices for her husband and his family to create obligation on their part to accept her and support her as "one of them."

As many, including Bourdieu (1977) have argued, history is the residue of the past that is embodied in social relationships of the present. In this chapter I have shown that the moral character of a rural Gambian woman can be traced through signs of the bodily temporalities of her reproductive past. Indeed, much as Mauss's analysis in "Techniques of the body" (1973) might suggest, her body is mnemonically inscribed for all to see. The fact that she has regained good health after retiring from childbearing is a significant reflection of an exemplary life. (The state of a man's body is also a reflection of his character, as we saw in the Nigerian story of the hapless man whose gluttonous wife was "drying" him [see pp. 231–32].) To be sure, not everyone will agree on this reading of her past. Those who want to discredit her will interpret her bodily signs disparagingly. Nonetheless, if, as she would like people to believe, she has spent her bodily resources well on behalf of her grateful husband and his kin, she will be able to rebuild her strength. Also, she should have earned the blessings that will assure her a place to stay in comfort and respect until she dies.

Observations such as these bring us back to key examples elsewhere in this book. Among the most prominent is the Nigerian minister Jacob Coker's defense of polygyny to his fellow Christians in the early part of the twentieth century (chapter 6). His thesis rested on two major points. The first was a man's need to protect the health of his wife and children from the close birth spacing that monogamy could entail. The second justification for polygyny was a man's moral responsibility to care for the woman who had borne him many children when he acquired a new wife, rather than abandoning her, as monogamy would dictate. Now Coker's points return. To an early twenty-first-century Western audience, his statements may sound like little more than thinly veiled excuses offered by an older man who is lusting after younger women. Of course, they may sound no less questionable from our vantage point in the present than they did to an older Nigerian woman in Coker's time who found herself marginalized by the advent of a young woman into her husband's life (for a related discussion, see Mann 1994). Yet if we step back from the immediate controversy in which Coker's essay was embroiled, the tone of his treatise conveys an unmistakable sense of the moral obligation of a man toward the woman who had made such a physical sacrifice on his behalf. Even if Coker's primary motives could be demonstrated to lie in a wholly different direction, he was touching on a vein of experience that resonated deeply throughout the society.

The descriptions of the contingent life course and its social and cultural dynamics in an African setting contained in these chapters have laid the groundwork for looking afresh at our own cultural constructions of the life course—the theme from which we began and to which I return in chapter 9. What are the common circumstances that would lead women in other times or places to privilege a set of logical suppositions about time, temporalities, and bodily tolls that parallel those we have seen in The Gambia? As we will see, there are clear differences, and yet in the juxtapositional opportunities that these differences provide, we find striking confirmation of what the Gambian materials have turned up.

CHAPTER 9

Discovering Our Habitus: Contingency and Linearity in Western Obstetric Observations

Just after the turn of the twentieth century, Joseph B. De Lee (1869–1942), a professor of obstetrics at Northwestern University Medical School, published two books for physicians and medical students. The first, appearing in 1904, was a rough assemblage of his lecture notes. The second, a text called *The Principles and Practice of Obstetrics,* appeared in 1913. Written with eloquence and with a passion for what it called the "art" of obstetrics, it contained more than a thousand pages of carefully documented details on the anatomy, chemistry, and motion of pregnancy and labor. The latter book, a benchmark of technical mastery and medical illustration, became one of the most widely used obstetrics texts in the United States. As a document of state-of-the-art obstetrics in the early 1900s, it is a treasure chest of clues to the medical and social world we have left behind.

In addition to its more technical messages, the text advised physicians on the hygiene their patients should follow during both pregnancy and the puerperium (1913, 225–31),[1] the weeks following delivery. Among its recommendations were items such as the following: The patient should wear low-heeled shoes and clothes that hang from the shoulders or suspenders, eat fruits and vegetables, avoid alcohol and starchy foods fried in fat, drink ample

---

1. All references to De Lee's work come from this text, unless otherwise noted.

quantities of water, and attend unfailingly to emptying the bowel daily. Then, turning to the question of exercise and travel for the pregnant woman, De Lee expressed the following views:

> [V]iolent exercise, of course, is to be avoided. . . . To be avoided are jolts, running, sudden motions, lifting great weights, going up and down stairs quickly, horseback riding, cycling, riding over rough roads, golf, tennis, dancing, and swimming. . . . Railway travel, the automobile, and ocean voyages had better to be avoided, and if travel is necessary, the most comfortable accommodations must be secured. (227)

As for coitus, De Lee was unequivocal. This "pernicious practice" (227) should be banned throughout pregnancy, if possible, but especially during the latter phases. Then there was the unending controversy over bed rest in the puerperium. De Lee saw himself as more liberal than most physicians, especially those of times past, but not so irresponsible as those who allowed women to get up as soon as they felt fit. On no account, stressed De Lee, should a woman be allowed to get up before nine or ten days had passed, as much as she might plead to do so. Even in childbed, the pace of resuming activity should be slow and measured:

> For the first two or three hours the puerpera should lie quietly on her back, but after this she may be turned gently on the side, the nurse supporting the heavy uterus. Next day the position may be changed oftener, and by the third day only ordinary care is necessary, and the changes may be made as frequently as comfort demands. These changes facilitate drainage and better the pelvic circulation. The puerpera after the fourth day may be propped up with pillows or back-rest for her meals, bowel movements, and urinations, may sit up straight on the fifth or sixth days; but her perfect condition and her frequent requests to be let out of bed should not lead the physician to permit it until the ninth or tenth day. It is wise, too, to forbid too early resumption of household duties, responsibilities, and social functions. (326)

Finally, for the latter phases of pregnancy, there was a particular kind of maternity corset that supported the abdomen from below, unlike most maternity corsets on the market, which exerted a downward pressure on the uterus. This corset, De Lee explained, should be used during the latter months of pregnancy (see fig. 9.1).

For a while, we read smoothly, nodding our heads at De Lee's advice.

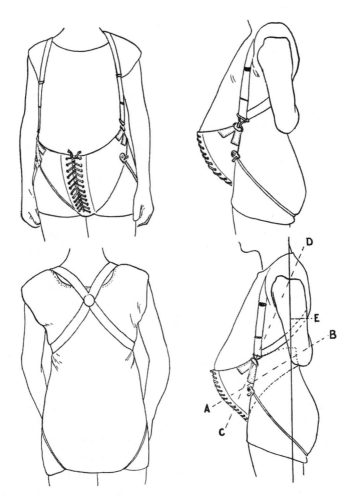

Fig. 9.1 Type of maternity corset preferred by Joseph B. De Lee
Source: De Lee 1913.

But as we move on to his views on bed rest, exercise, sex, and pregnancy corsets, our willingness to go along begins to evaporate. Most women and physicians today would scoff at his warnings about sex during the latter phases of pregnancy and at his bans on cycling, dancing, golf, and swimming and on land and ocean travel. And if confinement—meant literally— to bed for nine days after delivery sounds bizarre if not outright dangerous to a population that has come to expect only two or three days of insurance coverage for hospitalization following a normal birth, the idea of wearing a maternity corset would seem ludicrous. The question for us is how to understand De Lee's advice. Although we could easily dismiss it as an artifact of an archaic era, his advice yields critical clues to an empirical world that was very different from our own.

We have seen strong evidence to support the view that Africans describe: a woman's body changes irreversibly as a result of cumulative reproductive experience. Throughout, I have attempted to keep the time-based and the cumulative visions of fertility and aging within comparative reach of one another. Several of the empirical chapters pressed on the question of whether the cultural propositions uncovered in The Gambia have medical veracity in a wider set of disciplinary and world literatures. And throughout, I have described how West African social life is constructed with a contingent and cumulative life course firmly in view but set against the hypothetical backdrop of linearity. If we are encased in a growing international paradigm of low and safe fertility from whose confines we now peer out at the world, then at this point in the book the most convincing material to round out the task of destabilizing current Western scientific handling of reproduction through its own standards would come from Western society itself.

Apparent incongruities such as De Lee's advice on hygiene bring us back to larger issues of how we frame a problem and how we choose what to bring to the fore or relegate to the background. Taken in combination, the cases in this chapter demonstrate how rapidly the populations with respect to which we build a view of "normal" life can change. In much the way that Schutz argued for the taken-for-granted world of common sense, the cultural frames by reference to which we handle our science allow us to take at face value what we perceive as facts about the life course and to overlook both the internal contradictions they may contain and their departures from past conditions.

Gadamer, referring to ideas of knowledge, incites us to move beyond the limits of our own knowledge by transposing ourselves "into the historical horizon from which the traditionary text speaks" (1994, 302–3), to bring out the tensions between the text and the present. For probing issues of time and the body in ways that will sufficiently challenge a Western audience, De Lee's traditionary text is an exemplary device. It is close enough to us in time and context that we are led to follow it down an illusory path. It sounds like us. And yet the techniques and advice it describes diverge so markedly from our common sense that we are jarred to attention. Just as the Gambian findings did, the challenges that this text poses are so discordant from the way we conceptualize reproduction and the life course that they force us to reconsider some of our cardinal assumptions. Even what we find to be the most preposterous pieces of this advice, read in careful conjunction with other sections of De Lee's book and with other texts, can be seen to stem from a consummate empirical logic.

A key strategy throughout the book has been to alternate the conditionalities of childbearing to see if we can shift our view enough to bring to light alternative propositions about the world. In chapter 2 I brought out two notable incongruities from Western scholarship. One was the social science critiques of contraceptive distribution in the developing world on the grounds that using contraceptives must suppress total child numbers by reducing reproductive time. Another was the case of the sixty-three-year-old American woman who gave birth after an oocyte transfer. My interest in this case was the scientific inference that was drawn from it: that the reproductive capacity of the uterus outlasts the ability to conceive. From our standpoint in a society with fertility that is low and increasingly managed through technology, this conclusion makes perfect sense. A uterus undamaged by repeated acts of birth will retain its tone for a very long time. Yet material in subsequent chapters showed that rural Gambians see the matter from a very different standpoint. The average woman, who undergoes repeated pregnancy terminations, finds that her womb will wear out well before her ability to conceive is gone. Added to these cases of deceptive incongruities in chapter 2 was the story about reproduction that I described at the beginning of chapter 6, based on the assumption about conception as the heart of fertility.

We now need to move toward reconciling these two distinct descriptions of reproduction and the life course. Using the analytical leverage offered by Gambian women's descriptions of a contingent life course, I take a highly explicit juxtapositional form. I turn to the richness and variation of Western cultural models, as reported by two sets of chroniclers. In doing so, I continue the challenge of assumptions that seem to guide contemporary Western writings, both scientific and humanistic, of childbearing as an event of little physical consequence. The exercise suggests that contingency rather than linearity may have been the dominant model of the female life course even in our own past. Taking us back over time and circumstance, the examples highlight some of the various routes that a contingent life course can take. Central to the exercise is a close study of the images and texts that evoke the atmosphere surrounding the medical culture of childbearing in the settings. Here we find rich redundancy for experimentation. Here also entities that lie unnoticed in our peripheral vision may occupy center stage for an "other." In the spirit of Mauss, Bourdieu, and Foucault,

I dwell particularly on the techniques and technologies by which people sought to manage the course of reproductive events. Just as contraceptives and their use in contemporary rural Gambia provided a means to understanding the social and medical conditions that led to their use, so the techniques and technologies that come to light in Western obstetrical history give us means to infer the conditions that may have produced them.

In this chapter I seek temporal and geographical distance from West Africa: the turn of the twentieth century in the urban United States and in England. This was a critical moment in the demographic and medical history of the West. In both locales it was the last era of high fertility and of high mortality at childbirth, especially (in the United States) among certain immigrant groups and (in both countries) the poor.[2] New developments in medicine were moving into view as solutions to long-standing problems of infection and birth injuries. My principal source for reconstructing the medical habitus that this situation presented in the United States is De Lee's 1913 textbook. Although De Lee wrote a number of professional papers, the vast scope of the textbook opens up the possibility for the kind of open-ended exploration that one would undertake in an ethnographic study of a village. A close study of the maladies as well as the remedies and preventive measures in the book's images and text yields clues to the atmosphere surrounding the medical culture of childbearing at the time. Listening from our position in the present as he comments at length on problems that to him were commonsensical, we are brought up close against reproductive experiences (injury, sepsis, hemorrhage, disfigurement, lifelong debility, and death) that we have relegated to peripheral vision.

My choice of this work was serendipitous. I was searching for writings from the past that might give hint at what reproduction might have meant to those working with the best knowledge that medical science had at their time. Because of De Lee's history at Northwestern University and

2. Morgan et al. (1994) show that according to the 1910 U.S. census, the total fertility rate for native-born white women of native parentage was 3.56 live births. There was considerable variation, however. Regional differences, for example, were quite marked: 4.92 versus 2.85, respectively, for women in the South and those outside the South. Among foreign-born women, "old" immigrants (those who came in the first waves, from Britain, Germany, and Scandinavia) generally had lower fertility (2.95, 3.94, and 3.93, respectively) than "new" immigrants from eastern, central, and southern Europe. Particularly high rates were found among women from Italy (6.94) and Poland (6.97). Highest were the Slovaks, with 7.58. These levels tended to reflect those of the home country, and differences between the immigrant groups and the native population began to fade, usually quickly, in the succeeding generations.

As for maternal mortality, Leavitt (1986, 23, 25) estimates that early in the twentieth century in the United States, about one mother died for each 14 live births—about 65 times as high as the rate for 1980, in which there was one maternal death for each 10,000 live births.

in Chicago, a scan of the Northwestern library's electronic catalogue under the search term "obstetrics" quickly brought up several early books in his series of obstetrical works for physicians, including the first: the 1913 edition. Together with John Whitridge Williams at Johns Hopkins University, De Lee was one of the titans of obstetrics in early twentieth-century America. De Lee's papers have been placed in the archives of the Northwestern Memorial Hospital in Chicago,[3] making the case for selecting him even easier. Also from this era is a second source: a set of letters that were solicited from members of the Women's Guild in England (1916). In these descriptions of highly personal experiences, working-class women, some of them barely literate, document their childbearing ordeals. Like De Lee's text, these letters draw us in close to the sense of contingency in the life course. Framed more openly in the context of class reform in Britain, they convey, more than do De Lee's obstetrics books, a broad sense of the social contingencies that surrounded childbearing at the turn of the century. They also convey a highly subjective sense of women's experiences of childbirth and its sequelae.

Principles and Practice of Obstetrics, 1913

Joseph De Lee was an enthusiastic obstetrical educator, inventor, and clinical practitioner. Several editions of his main text, *Principles and Practice of Obstetrics,* were published while he was alive, and several thereafter in his name until 1965. De Lee also published a series of textbooks for nurses, invented more than forty obstetric instruments, trained scores of professionals, and pioneered medical filmmaking. He made forays into hospital architecture, both to plan his own hospital centers and to lay the basis for what he hoped would be a broader scheme for obstetrical care nationally. He even wrote scripts for two Hollywood films to try to support his medical center in Chicago, though they were never produced.

As Morris Fishbein, his student and biographer, recounted (1949), De Lee was a relentless "crusading obstetrician." Throughout his life, he voiced unreserved frustration about what he perceived as a paucity of public concern for childbearing women and their infants. As Speert (1958, 515) notes, "The [medical] school [De Lee attended] had only two full-time employees: the professor of chemistry and the janitor." One of the major influences on De Lee was his part-time work, undertaken to support his

---

3. I am grateful to Susan Sacharski, the head archivist at Northwestern Memorial Hospital, for help with gaining access to De Lee's papers.

studies. As a medical attendant at a farm for illegitimate and unwanted babies, he came to the grim realization that neonates in this setting suffered inexplicably high rates of mortality from cerebral hemorrhage. Whether this was due to brutal instrumental deliveries, to the child's repeated impacts with a young mother's slim, bony pelvis, or even from intentional attempts to end the babies' lives is not clear. What is clear is that the society of the time saw the lives of such children as largely dispensable. Chicago in the late nineteenth century was drawing in floods of workers from the rest of the country, especially blacks from the South and immigrants from Europe, bound for work in its booming lumber, grain-trading, and meatpacking industries. For workers at the bottom of the social and economic pyramid, life was highly precarious. Graft and corruption in city services were rampant, pay for laborers was negligible, foods were adulterated with toxic dyes and additives with no nutritional value, and housing and medical conditions were appalling. In particular, immigrants who came with little English or political savvy were drawn into the system and spewed out almost as quickly as replacements stepped off the trains.[4]

De Lee's technical writings contain occasional hints of this larger societal picture. He was clearly aroused, however, by the plight of the women and children who were suffering so badly. Choosing obstetrics as his medical specialty, he opened a free maternity clinic, the Maxwell Street Dispensary, in 1895, to deliver women in their homes under the supervision of his trainees. The dispensary, in the midst of the slums of Chicago, was less than a mile away from Hull House, the settlement house (a center for social "uplift") established by social reformer Jane Addams, whose population maps De Lee used to locate his clinic. Four years later, he built a hospital across the street from the dispensary to handle problematic deliveries. The Chicago Maternity Center's reputation for astonishingly low rates of maternal and child mortality grew quickly. Both the poor and the rich of the city began to seek out its services, and soon De Lee was able to support the free dispensary, which remained his lifelong interest, through the fees of wealthier clients.

Despite his professional enthusiasm and his philanthropic initiatives, he left a controversial legacy, in the judgment of many colleagues. "De Lee remained fundamentally a lonely, unhappy man, constantly plagued by his

---

4. For graphic descriptions of Chicago around this time, see the renowned proletarian novel *The Jungle* (Sinclair 1988) as well as writings by Jane Addams (1912) and other social reformers (e.g., Investigating Committee of the City Homes Association, Chicago, 1901).

excessive sensitivity and the compulsive tendencies of the perfectionist he was" (Speert, 1958, 516). Nor have subsequent generations held much reverence for him. His determination to elevate obstetrics beyond what he regarded as poorly informed midwifery evokes particular animosity in a contemporary readership concerned with the erosion of women's control over childbirth in an increasingly medicalized, and still largely-male-dominated, professional environment (for example, Davis-Floyd 1992; Rooks 1997).

Yet of all the statements De Lee made, those voicing his militant stance against the designation of labor as a "normal" or "natural" phenomenon have drawn the most rancor. In one of the most memorable pieces of medical writing in the twentieth century, he editorializes: "not until the pathogenic dignity of obstetrics is fully recognized may we hope for any considerable reduction of the mortality and morbidity of childbirth" (xiii). For statements such as this he is accused, with justification, of setting back the profession of midwifery in the United States to a point measurably behind the status it enjoys in many other industrialized countries and of handing over the experience of childbirth to the distant control of specialists (for example, Rooks 1997, 25–26).[5]

At the time, there was growing debate over how professional obstetric care should be administered. Many people lived far from lying-in hospitals, and more than half of all births occurred, whether by choice or by necessity, at home. Midwives were more available, and certainly more affordable, than physicians. Since most physicians who delivered babies were general practitioners, midwives were also easier to engage for the duration of labor. Midwives undoubtedly provided a safe birth for most of their clients and lent comfort to them as well.[6] Yet the fact that they were usually the first line of resort meant that physicians tended to be called in to handle more difficult cases in which the likelihood of injury or death was greater.

One very plausible explanation for De Lee's impatience with midwives and his effort to cast childbirth as a pathological process might be that he held a low regard for women. He referred in his 1913 textbook, for example, to the "mistakes and meddlesome interference" of unskilled obstet-

---

5. Although De Lee provoked acrimony for undermining midwifery in this country, his efforts undoubtedly raised national consciousness about the need for reform in obstetric care. See Leavitt 1988 for a perceptive analysis of De Lee's work, particularly his attempts to develop obstetrics as a preventive form of medicine.

6. See, however, Sinclair (1988, 126, 219–27), who depicts a very callous midwife using dangerous practices.

ric nurses (248) and "ignorant midwives" (565). But he also scolded "half-trained medical students" (565), all of whom would have been male, and he conveyed a constant compassion both for his patients and their infants in situations of jeopardy and for families and physicians faced with bleak choices in moments of crisis.

Yet if we try to move beyond the controversies De Lee sparked, a close reading of his book reveals a labor of great love and the work of a master. The text, a technical and scientific milestone, contains scrupulous attention to detail on state-of-the-art knowledge, whether of technology or pathology. It also bears the imprint of a pragmatist who is not too proud to try whatever might work, techniques sometimes bordering on kitchen remedies, in a desperate emergency. For a woman who became convulsed with the fevers of infection, De Lee advised the physician to prevent her from injuring herself by wrapping a large clothes pin in a thin handkerchief and clasping it on her tongue as an attack began (366). And in the event of hemorrhage, a doctor might stem the flow of blood by packing the patient's uterus with gauze mixed with two ounces of French gelatine; another way was to bind her waist and upper thighs tightly with cords (786–87). (Again see Castoriadis 1984 on the idea of the techne: what was at hand.)

Our larger concern with De Lee's text, therefore, is its historic value as a window into ways of knowing in a critical medical era. In the smallest of obstetric details, the text evokes facets of a physical experience that is now virtually gone from our cultural horizon. As Jane Guyer (personal communication) observed, reading the text brings back vague memories not of that moment or of times that we ourselves might have known, but of the world our parents were born into and therefore conveyed inadvertently, perhaps in the habitus of things, to us. We face a number of problems, obviously, in interpreting the text. Among them is the fact that De Lee writes as a clinician. This means that although he devotes a large proportion of the text to "normal" cases, it is difficult to tell from his treatment of "abnormal" cases how widespread each malady was. He refers occasionally to class differences with respect to the conduct and outcome of childbirth (for example, 249). But working in an era before the practice of statistics became so important, he gives us only an occasional sense of the representativeness of the pathologies described.[7]

---

7. Note as well that not all of De Lee's perceptions run in the expected direction. For example, puerperal infection in the immediate postpartum period "is more common among the delicately bred well-to-do than among the poor, who, through ages of squalor and filth, have developed immunities, which the other, in their protected lives, do not possess" (1913, 872).

Childbearing and Risk in Turn-of-the-Century America

Among the strongest senses we gain from De Lee's descriptions is that childbirth in America at the turn of the century was a dangerous undertaking. This sense suffuses everything from his architectural drawings of the ideal maternity hospital to his descriptions of the instruments and techniques a physician might have to use to extricate a baby. Some instruments, such as forceps, had benign purposes even though they could cause damage in unskilled hands or in situations allowing no other recourse. Other instruments—perforators, plungers, embryotomes, cranioclasts, and decapitating hooks—bespoke the grim sacrifice that, if all else failed, might save the mother's life (1006–12). During a maternal hemorrhage, the physician might turn a dead or dying baby into a plug, a "tampon," by pulling its leg out into the birth canal. By compressing the baby's body and (necessarily) the umbilical cord tightly against the hemorrhaging placenta (454), he might save the mother's life. Two of the most important examples of the sense of risk that De Lee's text conveys are those involving infection and the shape of the pelvis.

In contemporary obstetrical texts, discussions of infection focus on sexually transmitted diseases and urinary tract maladies.[8] They also specify antibiotics as the remedy, with little follow-up discussion. When the first edition of *Principles* was published, however, there were no antibiotics, and infection meant first and foremost "childbed fever": infection and inflammation caused during labor or the puerperium. Infection evoked terror among women because it was so contagious and it could be so deadly. In figures taken from the U.S. census, De Lee on page 870 notes that in 1909 and 1910, about half of the women who died in childbirth did so from puerperal septicemia.[9] The physician himself had been identified as a prime agent of infection, a phenomenon that had been brought to world attention in 1847 by Ignaz Semmelweis and openly lamented by De Lee (273) and many other physicians. Because the microbial nature of the problem was now fully in view but the ultimate cure was not (penicillin was not discovered until 1928, and antibiotics became widely used in obstetric care only in the 1940s and 1950s), professionals of the time lacked the measure that was so dramatically effective that contemporary readers can virtually

8. In a National Research Council report on reproduction in the developing world (1997b), a chapter titled "Infection-Free Sexuality and Reproduction" contains no mention of postpartum infection. Infection is instead discussed only in the context of sexually transmitted diseases.

9. This was an infection that became so virulent that it infected the bloodstream.

remove infection from view as a significant risk. De Lee's careful descriptions of hygienic strategies designed to mitigate what he saw as needless suffering from a known danger allow us to look in on the situation at a key moment.

Worries about infection strongly affected how a physician could conduct his work, not only in a hospital but especially in the tenements in which most of De Lee's deliveries occurred. They even affected his relationship with his patients. With an eye to the hazards of infection, he recommended extreme caution in considering any surgical procedures. He also advised physicians to work with a partner who could take over in case one of them came in contact with infection, and to avoid further patient contact for two days after exposure, frequently scrubbing the hands in carefully specified ways. Other evidence of worries about infection were reflected in the most routine details. Take, for example, the process of selecting and sterilizing new rubber gloves for medical procedures. In an appendix to the text (1021–22) De Lee instructs readers on how to test a new glove for holes by filling it with hot water and watching for leaks. Selecting only flawless gloves, the user is then to wash them thoroughly with soap and water, powder them with pure talcum powder, and suspend them in a low-pressure steam sterilizer for thirty minutes. Taking them out, the user is to wrap them in paper, put them back in the sterilizer for forty-five minutes, lay them out to dry on a steam radiator for six hours, and put them away, finally, in a covered box. Reading about such painstaking techniques, which now sound so rudimentary, throws into sharp relief the revolutionary changes in medicine that have so affected our reproductive lives. Among the most noticeable of these, we can now see, were the discovery and proliferation of antibiotics, which, in turn, facilitated the rapid rise in cesarean sections. These facts have decisively altered our presumptions of what "natural" childbirth can be about.

De Lee's text alludes to a turn-of-the-century patient population whose bodies bore the effects of far more injuries and chronic maladies than is true today. Some maladies more than others affected a woman's ability to sustain a pregnancy and bring it to successful termination. Among the most intense concerns for childbearing at this time was a contracted or deformed pelvis.

Problems of the shape of the pelvis that women in turn-of-the-century America and Europe encountered could arise from several factors: malnutrition, disease, or injury. (Far fewer cases seemed to stem from the risks posed by immaturity due to very low ages at marriage that continue to prevail in some parts of Africa.) Asserts De Lee, undoubtedly with some exaggeration, "Tramond of Paris, who studied many thousands of [pelves], found scarcely one in 5,000 that was nearly perfect" (651). Childhood diseases such as polio and rickets are a distant memory in America. Individuals who suffered from them are still among us, but their numbers are smaller each year. Especially in northern Europe and in the severely polluted cities of the northern United States, however, the vitamin D deficiency disease rickets was prevalent. Children who suffered from rickets had softened bones, which became deformed when the child walked and played. Women who had had rickets often died in childbirth, especially if they bore large babies. (Black women appear to have suffered ten times the risk that white women did from rickets [Leavitt 1986, 69] because of their skin's lesser ability to absorb the sun's rays.) Pelvic injuries also played a significant role in delivery problems. The Women's Cooperative Guild letters from England contain an arresting case of a woman whose strenuous farm tasks in her adolescent years damaged her pelvis. Reporting ten births, five males and five females, she related, with horrifying understatement:

> Through being left without a mother when a baby—[my] father was a
> very large farmer and girls were expected to do men's work—I, at the age
> of sixteen, lifted weights that deformed the pelvis bones, therefore making
> confinement a very difficult case. I have five fine healthy girls, but the
> boys have all had to have the skull-bones taken away to get them past the
> pelvis. (1916, 167)

With specters like this in view, De Lee's text constantly grapples for ways of knowing, of collecting and assembling a large enough corpus of knowledge to prevent tragedy. Concerning the obstetric complexities of the pelvic region, for example, he admonishes students: "It takes years of practice for the accoucheur to be able to form correct mind pictures of these things, but they must be learned" (240). Because surgical procedures that could obviate vaginal delivery could be undertaken only in the best of sterile conditions, and because there were so many cases of deformed pelvis, the use of the instrument to measure this complex structure, a pelvimeter, absorbed much of his attention (651–724).

A typical pelvimeter had two large curved blades that joined at a center point and expanded across a flat piece of metal marked with a numerical scale. A pelvimeter was obviously a more benign instrument than a perforator or a cranioclast. It was used not reactively, in crisis, but proactively, to create a wide repertoire of detailed information that could be integrated into existing knowledge and stored for possible future use in unforeseen situations.

De Lee recommended a thorough pelvimetry exam on the first prenatal visit (233–44). In using a pelvimeter, the operator had to assume certain bodily physics with respect to the woman and the unborn child, and the instrument and the technique had to be engaged in a set of maneuvers with specific questions in mind. De Lee showed how to locate potential risks (whether caused by heredity, disease, or previous childbirth) and to anticipate ways of handling them when the time of birth arrived. Readers learned when to suspect obstructions that may have altered the pelvic passage. Should the size or shape of the pelvis or the child's position in it forebode difficulty, preparations could be made for a surgical delivery. Student readers of the text were instructed at length on the planes of the pelvis, how to measure them, and which measures were more useful than others. Students were shown types of pelvimeters, each designed to measure a different plane and each taking its landmark from a different promontory (for example, 237). De Lee did everything he could to bring the descriptions close to home, even giving his own measurements as a comparison (238). Mingling sensory perceptions and instrumental measures at every step, he instructs the reader, in ways highly evocative of Mauss (1973), on the skill of charting an obstetric landscape: a skill that becomes so well learned that the instrument becomes almost a natural extension of the operator's body. In a section called "Technic of the internal examination" (239–44), he writes:

> The fingers now pass around the bony walls of the pelvis to obtain a mind picture of the capacity and configuration of the excavation. . . . Next the bispinous diameter is taken with the pelvimeter. The instrument is closed and passed, with the scale upward, along the finger until it has passed the group of the levator ani, then the blades are spread until one knob comes to rest on, or just in front of, the spine of the ischium. . . . Being assured that the patient's hips are horizontal, the blades are spread in the horizontal place until they are arrested by the bony walls of the pelvis, and at this instant the amount of separation is read off the scale. . . . (239–42)

From this meticulous mapping of invisible space,[10] we gain a rich sense of how a skilled practitioner of the times assembled and sifted the contents of his peripheral vision. In the process, we also learn about the larger soci-

---

10. After I had written this chapter, Wendy Griswold (pers. comm.) told me of a book bearing a title of striking similarity, though it dealt with an entirely different theme: *Mapping the Invisible Landscape: Folklore, Writing and the Sense of Place* (Ryden 1983).

ety, the techniques and resources available to its members, and the maladies and risks they routinely faced.

By contrast with this degree of attention, the technique of pelvimetry figures very little in contemporary texts. Beckmann et al. (1995, 106) dismiss pelvimetry as having no value for predicting whether a fetus can successfully negotiate the birth canal. Beischer et al. (1997, 511) mention examination of the pelvis as part of the general examination to which a pregnant woman is subjected but recommend radiographic pelvimetry, and this only in cases that forebode trouble. The dearth of interest in a subject that consumed such attention nearly a hundred years ago is astonishing.[11] Clearly the cesarean section, now a procedure of such ready resort (far too much so, in the views of many), which makes it possible to circumvent certain kinds of anticipated trouble, has also effectively removed from vision a wide span of human physical experience.

The Pathology of Childbirth

De Lee wrote during an era when childbirth was far more dangerous than it is today. Figures in his 1913 text show that whereas 8,500 women in the United States died from childbirth and 20,000 from the event or its aftermath (xii; the denominators to which he refers, however, are unclear), fully half of all women suffered significant aftereffects of labor at some point in their lives. Laceration of the pelvic floor and of the supports of the uterus, bladder, and vagina occurred in every labor, and women flocked to hospitals later in life, seeking treatment for injuries from and aftereffects of deliveries (xii). Moreover, women (especially the poor) were likely to have more births than they do now, each of which carried what we would judge to have inordinately high risk.

Worries about child and fetal death loomed large as well. De Lee writes of 3 to 5 percent of children dying in the birth process. In his unsparing prose:

[T]he highest mortality that befalls the human race in one day occurs on the day of birth. . . . 5 percent of children are still-born, dying during

11. In the series of obstetrics textbooks by John Whitridge Williams, which began in 1903 and has continued under his name until the present, the proportion of the text devoted to the pelvis declined over the years from 14.8 percent to 1.3 percent. The first edition devoted six of forty-five chapters to pathologies of the pelvis and its proximal bones; by the 1997 edition, the pelvis no longer occupied even a single chapter by itself.

labor, and 1.5 percent die shortly after birth, the result of the trauma of labor. . . . In Paris 9 percent die.[12] It is safe to say that in the United States 75,000 children die annually during delivery. . . . Besides this mortality, the children are frequently injured during delivery, either by the natural powers or, and more often, by operative procedure. Hemorrhages into the brain, tentorium tears, fracture of the skull, dislocation and fracture of the vertebrae, joints, and extremities, often result from the brutal deliveries rendered necessary in cases of mechanical disproportion. Milder injuries of brain, nerves, and bones are very frequent, but are often overlooked until their later effects become prominent. (147)

De Lee's statements evoke a world in which one of the most perilous ordeals in the human experience drew appallingly little public health concern. "Can a function so perilous, that in spite of the best care, it kills thousands of women every year, that leaves at least a quarter of the women more or less invalided, and a majority with permanent anatomic changes of structure, that is always attended by severe pain and tearing of tissues, and that kills 3 to 5 percent of children—can such a function be called normal?" (xii–xiii).

This statement gives us clues to what De Lee sought to accomplish in his campaign to "pathologize" labor. Obstetrics, he asserted, was the field of medicine wherein the most gains against malady and death stood to be won. Yet since it was the most difficult and arduous medical practice, the truly gifted physicians could not be recruited into it (565). Until society was willing to make the kinds of investments required in the medical and technical knowledge needed to stem tragedies of such proportions, significant gains would lie beyond reach. He acknowledged that among healthy women, pregnancy and labor may in fact proceed "physiologically," by which he meant a metabolic function that was occurring without undue harm. But because of the terrors of puerperal infection of the time, his Chicago Maternity Center trainees were forbidden to intervene or even to perform a vaginal examination in labors that were progressing uneventfully. At the same time, he expressed intense frustration with a society that seemed to regard high maternal and infant tolls as regrettable but "normal" or "natural." For example, he declared that injuries of the parturient canal "are generally considered normal, but why, the author cannot understand —no other function of the body is attended by injury" (725). Although such

12. The figure for the United States then was probably slightly higher than the Gambian rate today; the rate for Paris was higher still.

statements arouse antipathy when read today, De Lee clearly referred to a level of vulnerability to danger or damage—and perhaps even to a resignation to the course of events—that we would not accept today.

High Parity: Risks and Resources

De Lee knew very well that pregnancy and labor were likely to proceed uneventfully. Yet one of the most striking lines dividing our times from those that so thoroughly infused his descriptions a hundred years ago is that the female population was one on whom high fertility took a marked toll. Problems of disease and deformation often troubled women whose bodies, as they went into labor, already bore the effects of far more injury and disease than is the case today. In addition, he noted that the first pregnancy and birth brought about changes as tissues were stretched. Because women were likely to have more births than they do today, and each birth might carry greater risks, his descriptions of the physical changes wrought by high parity and traumatic births were infused with the sense that each successive birth, particularly if it was a difficult one, set a woman farther down a cumulative, non-recursive pathway: "[A] perfect restitutio ad integrum never occurs after labor. The woman carries the evidences of child-bearing all her life. . . . The process introduces pathogenic circumstances and precipitates structural changes, many of them consisting of increasing impairment; in many cases, the more the birth events, the greater the level of impairment" (204 ff.).

Modern texts often refer to primiparae (women who will give birth for the first time) and multiparae in terms of the differences these states can imply. But so different were the implications of births to high-parity and low-parity women that O'Connor et al., as late as 1966, asserted, "The obstetric population may be conveniently divided into two groups—primigravidas and multiparas" (210). De Lee's descriptions made it clear that he was dealing with a body that was altered by the birth event. Indeed, age rarely appeared at all in his discussions, an omission that might puzzle a contemporary student of obstetrics, whose texts almost routinely identify cases by both age and parity.

Also consonant with the Gambian findings is the fact that some of the most prominent physical changes wrought by high parity and traumatic births were those involving muscles. Among the signs of high parity and birthing traumas were the "rounding" of the hips over the course of multiple births, the slackening of muscle tone of the perineum and abdominal wall, and lacerations of the pelvic floor and supports of the uterus (230–31). Thus, "The [soft tissues of the perineum] are distensible to only a certain degree, after which they break like card-board. . . . The muscle-fibres [of the pelvic floor] are often torn and overstretched. Absorption of the blood and serum quickly takes place, but many minute and larger scars are left, which result in atrophy and a weakened pelvic floor" (210). Of the risk of ruptured uterus, almost inevitable fatal at the time because of massive hemorrhage, De Lee writes: "Multiparae are oftener thus injured than primiparae—about eight times as often—and the danger increases with the number of children. This is due to the structural changes, the weakness of the muscular fibers, the scars and inflammations, the residues from previous labors" (750). Even some cases of "abortion" (miscarriage) among multiparae were attributed to displacements of the uterus, themselves a function of muscle damage (1904, 310). And of the child's passage through the birth canal, he writes: "If the student wishes to study these movements, a multipara will offer better advantages than a primipara, because, in the latter, the head is already engaged [in the pelvis] when the labor begins" (181). One of the most mortifying afflictions a woman could suffer was prolapse, in which the uterus became detached from its ligaments and descended from the body like a balloon. Pessaries (metal, glass, or rubber inserts) might be used in an attempt to alleviate the problem, but they were imperfect and uncomfortable solutions.

A striking sign of the times among high-parity women in early twentieth-century America was the condition called anteversion, or "pendulous abdomen," in which a pregnant uterus might fall further forward with each pregnancy, even sagging down to the knees, owing to slackened muscle tissues (see fig. 9.2). De Lee traced the risk of pendulous abdomen to a contracted or deformed pelvis, congenital weakness of the abdominal plates, "improper habits" associated with "constipation, wearing ill-fitting corsets or high-heeled shoes, [or] carrying children or weights on the protuberant belly" (398). In his view, however, pendulous abdomen was particularly associated with an increased number and frequency of births.

A pendulous abdomen spelled grim prospects for labor. "The abdominal muscles," wrote De Lee, "are used to greater extent in pathological labor, and are very important in preventing the rupture of the uterus" (122). Weakened muscles and a flaccid uterus increased the risk of malpresentation and uterine rupture (179), and pendulous abdomen was often associated with problems of "dystocia" (literally, "difficult childbirth" but usually referring to malpresentation):

> During labor pendulous abdomen may cause serious dystocia. The uterus is thrown so far forward that its axis forms an acute angle with the pelvic

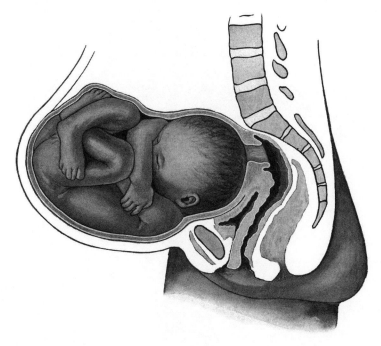

Fig. 9.2 Pathological pendulous abdomen as illustrated by Joseph B. De Lee
Source: De Lee 1913.

axis; the cervix is pulled up into the hollow of the sacrum, sometimes even
above the promontory; dilation is delayed, and the posterior uterine wall
is overstretched. This, together with obstructed labor because of malposi-
tion of the fetus and disturbed mechanism, invites rupture of the uterus.
Malpresentations, such as shoulder and breech, are common in these
cases, because the head, in spite of strong pains, cannot get down into the
pelvis. (398)

When the rectus muscles in the abdomen were widely separated, they were
sometimes unable to obtain a purchase on the uterus and its contents and
labor might cease. If forceps were not applied the uterus was in danger of
rupture.

Among the worst cases of dystocia were those in which the child's shoulder became the presenting part. This predicament, now circumvented entirely by prenatal detection and prophylactic cesarean section, spelled grave
risks during De Lee's time: "Shoulder presentations are always pathologic
. . . with rare exceptions the children all die, and often the mother, too"

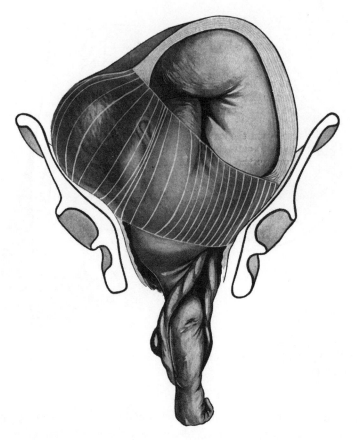

Fig. 9.3 Neglected shoulder presentation
    Source: De Lee 1913.

(618). Figure 9.3 shows a shoulder presentation, foreboding imminent uterine rupture and maternal death.

In De Lee's text, the fact that parity typically exerted such noticeable effects on the body is transparent at every step. Making an astute demographic observation, De Lee (1904, 149) warned students in his class notes that they might underestimate its effects at first because the patient population that high parity most affected was likely to remain invisible to them for some time: "as young physicians, you will get primiparae principally (the multiparae having a leaning toward the doctor who confined them before)."

Western women of today also worry about muscles. But as the books on pregnancy and childbirth in our popular bookstores reveal, we worry less about rupturing muscles than about "toning" them to regain a figure (on related points, see Reischer 1998), a discourse that exposes us immediately as a low- and safe-fertility society. In one of the few exceptions, *The Year after Childbirth* (Kitzinger 1994, 62), muscles appear in the discussion as a health issue. However, advice to tone the muscles after birth is not explained in terms of the risks of subsequent pregnancies or deliveries but with reference to the perineal muscles and the need to prevent incontinence in old age.

The Hygiene of High Fertility

Let us now return to some of the suggestions on hygiene for women that De Lee offered, which, in my view, constitute some of the most persuasive evidence that he believed that fertility produced cumulative changes in the body, and the more traumatic the event, the greater and more rapidly felt was the impact. Like the use of the pelvimeter, his recommendations on hygiene can be read as proactive measures to ward off ill effects. Since recommendations on what to ward off—certain kinds of contaminants, stresses, or injuries—reflect the problems by which members of a populace feel threatened, recommendations on hygiene provide key clues to the contents of the habitus. At the beginning of the chapter, I described the hygienic recommendations that I found most odd: his opinions on activity, travel, sex, maternity corsets, and postpartum bed rest. My intent in doing so was to use them to seize the more visible edges of a very different physical habitus than that which we assume today. The routines and daily practices they advocate hint at taken-for-granted, "naturalized" assumptions about how the body works that were quite different from what we have come to imagine the state of pregnancy to entail. Let us now return to see if we can make progress on resolving some of the puzzles they posed.

Bed Rest, Car Travel, and Intercourse

What about De Lee's advice to get nine days of bed rest? Extended bed rest was seen as essential to recuperating from the ordeals of childbirth, and the point at which a woman actually got up for the first time from bed was a critical marker of affluence. Women who could afford help to cover their domestic duties could lie in longer than those who could not. Although mandating nine days of bed rest seems to us very odd advice, it most seemed to reflect the fearful possibilities of unhealed lacerations in tissues that might burst open again or of displaced internal organs, especially in the wake of a difficult birth, given the state of surgery and suture techniques of his time.

De Lee in fact draws an explicit link between a premature rising from bed and possible repercussions for exacerbating the problem of a weakened pelvic structure, especially among poor women:

> [T]heoretic consideration of the condition of the pelvis postpartum will indicate the necessity for rest in the horizontal position. The bruised, suggillated condition of the pelvic floor has already been referred to. It stands to reason that such an impaired pelvic floor should not be given the task of supporting the large heavy puerperal uterus and the whole intra-abdominal pressure before it has regained, in a measure, its strength and elasticity. The ancient idea that too early getting up leads to prolapse of the vagina and uterus has anatomic foundation, and, further, clinical experience proves it. Prolapse is more common in the poor women who have to get up early after delivery and do heavy work. (326)

Fears of organ displacements, uterine prolapse, and miscarriage in high-fertility conditions also seemed to underlie De Lee's admonition to pregnant women to avoid auto travel. Given the abysmal condition of most roads (a problem he mentions specifically and a frequent theme in reformers' descriptions of the poor areas of Chicago) and the lack of shock protection on cars, auto travel may well have been treacherous, especially for women who had suffered multiple injurious births. His ban on intercourse is directly linked to the hazards of multiparous reproductive life among women with tissues that have been lacerated and poorly repaired during previous deliveries: dangers of infection are "greater in multiparae in whom the cervix is patulous [having exposed tissues]" (227).

Systematic Gymnastics and Maternity Corsets

So hazardous were the complications posed by anteversion under the conditions of the times that the puerperium was a period of special vigilance. In De Lee's view, a woman who had had an anteverted uterus during pregnancy should restore the muscle tone of her abdominal wall as fully as possible by preventing the accumulation of gas and feces in the bowel that would distend the muscles and by preventing infections that would inflame the intestinal wall. After remaining recumbent for some time, she should resume her household duties gradually, engaging in "systematic gymnastics" and massaging the abdominal muscles (399–400). The book's careful illustrations of the use of maternity corsets to mitigate this malady bring to our attention the problems that high fertility can entail.

De Lee's descriptions of the risks that childbirth posed, together with his stress on the hygienic vigilance required to cope with these risks, reflect the fact that he wrote from a different world than our own. Many of his views are unpalatable to us. But what is important about this text is that it goes against the grain of what we today treat as "natural" childbearing practices. Once we understand the context from which it arises, its meaning within the framework of the contingent life course becomes transparent. The world De Lee described is commensurate with, though not identical to, our own, yet its descriptions correspond closely to what we might expect to find under conditions of high fertility and poverty.

Whether they stem from "technics" of surgery or from the geometries of the pelvis, De Lee's efforts to impart anticipatory or curative knowledge about the cumulative damage that reproduction could wreak on the body yield remarkable clues to the obstetric habitus of the time. In the smallest of details—from the use of a clothes pin clasped on the tongue to prevent injury during convulsions to the painstaking mappings of invisible space through the use of pelvimeters—we are brought face to face with the risks that women of the time routinely faced. The contingencies of reproductive life and the intense vigilance required to cope with them are elaborated articulately through a wealth of images, techniques, and domains of knowledge. All are powerful testimony to the fact that the body, assuming it survived the process, changed cumulatively over the course of multiple pregnancies.

From our privileged temporal vantage point, we know that the development and proliferation of antibiotics were just on the horizon, as were techniques such as vacuum extraction and cesarean sections that have rendered the use of instruments such as forceps techniques of less urgent resort (Boston Women's Health Collective 1992, 458–59). Surgical measures to forestall or repair tears and prolapses are now uncomplicated. We also know that a fertility decline was under way. Our subject, however, in his lack of awareness of what lay ahead, elaborates for us the risks of childbirth under a set of conditions we can barely grasp.

The more general point turns on the empirical oddities that emerge when we shift the frame. Take the question of fetal delivery positions in labor. Hofmeyr, in a 1989 review article on fetopelvic disproportion, found statistical links between shoulder dystocia and high birth weight, maternal diabetes, and (possibly) body configuration—not of the mother but of the fetus (497). Sixty-eight years prior to this, the situation appeared to be quite different. Studying transverse presentation, a situation in which any other part than the head or the breech presents first (shoulder dystocia is the most common type of transverse presentation to which medical authors in the past seemed to refer), Oldfield (1921, 68–71) identified a premature or dead fetus as one of the chief predictors of the condition: one out of eight cases of transverse lie. That is, when the child is premature or its body is decaying, gravity does not favor the presentation of the head. Other common predictors for Oldfield were non-engagement of the head in the pelvis, defective uterine action, and lateral obliquity of the uterus. All of these conditions are common among multiparae, with their lax abdominal walls and their susceptibility to hydramnios, contracted pelvis, tumors, and placenta previa.[13] Yet only some of them are even tangentially related to Hofmeyr's list.

These two situations are not perfect comparables. Still, the lists of conditions that predict these two situations bear virtually no resemblance to one another. Oldfield's list is associated with shoulder dystocia or transverse lie: high fertility, contracted pelvis, and a decomposed fetus. Shoulder dystocia and other pathologies of fetal presentation draw little attention today both because there are fewer cases of them at delivery (thus, there are fewer high-parity births) and because cesarean sections can so readily obviate the entire process of vaginal delivery under such dangerous conditions. Sixty-eight years ago, obstetric events drew meaning from the view of reproduction as potential pathology and of high fertility as a strong contributing factor to this pathology. Today, obstetric events are read against the presumption that certain pathologies hardly exist at all, so easily can they be circumvented. Still, it is astonishing that these related anomalies of presentation can be attributed with such empirical confidence to such different causes.

Maternity: Letters from Working-Women, Collected by the Women's Co-operative Guild: Working-Class England at the Turn of the Century

In this juxtapositional exercise, my second source for exploring the dimensions of the contingent life course comes from the same historical time as De Lee's text. The place, however, is quite different, as are the authorial voices.

Shortly after De Lee's textbook appeared in 1913, a compilation of anonymous letters from working-class women was published in England. In 1914, the Women's Cooperative Guild contacted six hundred members of

---

13. Non-engagement may also occur among primiparae, but for an entirely different reason: the muscles may be so firm that they do not allow the child's head to descend into the pelvic cavity.

their organization and posed to each a series of questions: how many children she had borne, how soon after each other the children were born, whether any children had died under five years of age, whether any pregnancies ended in stillbirth or miscarriage, and how much she and her husband earned. In addition, the woman was asked to describe her childbearing experiences: what she "felt about the difficulty of taking care, the ignorance that has prevailed on the conditions of pregnancy, and how these conditions result in lack of health and energy, meaning that a woman cannot do justice to herself or give her best to her husband and children" (191). Of the responses received, 160 were published (Women's Guild 1916).[14] Since the middle classes in inner London had already begun to have smaller families in the late nineteenth and early twentieth centuries, "unrelenting childbearing" (Ross 1993, 92) was increasingly the fate of poor women. Vigorous campaigns to reform the bleak conditions in English work and factory life had been launched in the nineteenth century, but there had been little concern for the ordeals experienced by women in the less visible domestic domain. The guild's canvass of its members sought to bring these ordeals to light.

Considerable caution must be used when interpreting the letters. The women who chose to respond may have been those who had experienced the worst traumas and wanted to relate them. Similarly, the compilers of the volume may have used a biased hand in choosing letters to publish. Furthermore, the long-reply question to which women were asked to respond (that on childbirth experience) was a leading one, encouraging negative stories that could be used to aid in the fight for reform. However, the anonymous author of the introduction to the volume observes that the earnings and conditions of life of the respondents were probably above, rather than below, the level of their class as a whole. The author also asserts that the letters that were not published describe similar experiences (3). And some of the guild letters clearly contradict the thrust of the question by reporting uneventful pregnancies and benign reproductive lives, even if their responses appear to be exceptions to what everyone recognized as the rule. "I am by nature very active, and during pregnancy had very good health," said one woman, "and was able to look after my home and family up to the time of confinement. My confinements have not been what would be called bad

14. For a similar source, published more than a decade later, see the letters written to British reformer Marie Stopes (Stopes 1929). I rely on the guild letters, however, because they were published closer to the time of De Lee's text.

times" (92). Another wrote: "With the boys labour has only lasted twenty minutes, girls a little longer. I have never needed a doctor's help, and it has always been over before he came. I have never had an after-pain in my life, so the doctors don't know what I am made of" (42–43).

The overwhelming majority of the letters, though, are a moving indictment of the effects of poverty on childbearing women of the working class. Of "outcast" London, Ross (1993) observes: "Until after World War I, the women of London's miles of poor streets lived their adult lives undergoing numerous births, even more frequent pregnancies, and years of baby and child care. With their last child so often born in its mother's fifth decade, many women thus lived and died as full-time, active mothers of infants and small children" (97). The author of the introduction to the letters stressed, "[T]o bear children under such conditions is to bear an intolerable burden of suffering" (3).[15]

Among the maladies reported was "flooding" (hemorrhage), obstructed labor, a "fallen womb," varicose veins, invalidism, and greater susceptibility to contagious diseases.[16] Miscarriages and stillbirths in particular were often described in unmistakable tones of trauma: "[T]o me," said one woman, "the after-effects of the miscarriages have been worse than confinements, for it takes months to get over the weakness" (87). Childbed fever was a less frequently mentioned malady among guild women than De Lee's text might lead us to expect, possibly because De Lee was such a relentless crusader on this problem. Still, cases of it were present, as in this account:

> My last [confinement] was the worst; we had removed away to a strange
> place, and I happened to get a woman who did not know her work. I was

15. Speaking apparently of Scotland and England, Donald observed in 1955 that many of the medical problems of high parity seemed to stem from the economic problems brought on by having many children: "Sociological factors play a very important part, for the majority of these patients are poor, overworked and tired. Many of them have never fully regained a good blood picture, and anaemia may dog them from one pregnancy to the next without respite. They tend to feed their numerous children at the expense of their own nutrition, so that they are consequently often very short of vitamins and first-class protein. They are too busy to attend to their health, and in a rapid succession of pregnancies and periods of lactation they are likely to become seriously depleted of calcium. It is small wonder, then, that dental fitness is unusual and their mouths are often full of useless and infected stumps.

"With increasing weight and lumbar lordosis, the abdominal wall gives up the unequal struggle, and we have, therefore, the picture of a harassed woman who stands badly, walks badly, eats indifferently and cannot get enough sleep" (38–39).

16. To be sure, as Seccomb (1992) points out with regard to the Stopes letters, accounts such as these may have been phrased in the vocabulary learned from physicians. Still, the medical logic that unfolds is internally consistent among the cases.

very ill at the time, but everything was favourable until the third day I developed childbed fever. I went blind, sometimes unconscious, my breasts in slings, so large I could not see over the top, inflammation of the bowels, and blood-poisoning. I was almost beyond hope, and was seriously ill three weeks. Then took a turn for the better. We had to get a thoroughly efficient person in, the cost of which was £1 per week for seven weeks, and, God bless her, she deserved every farthing she got, although it was hard. We had to pay again for other housework to be done. I feel I owe much of my recovery to her. My husband was seriously reduced in means, but he would have sold anything to do good. (83–84)

Worry about a baby that was too large for a small, possibly distorted pelvis pervades the letters. As I noted in chapter 6, Gambian women sometimes described their efforts to keep the baby's weight down before birth, a strategy that the contemporary Western pregnancy advice books I have examined do not mention. So when I first encountered such descriptions in the Gambian field materials, I thought them a cultural oddity and put them aside. Since then I have discovered considerable evidence for these practices (what the maternal morbidity literature calls "eating down") elsewhere. Several of the guild letters contain allusions to babies who were too big for the pelvic passages of mothers with a history of malnourishment or injury, and they mention the possibility of undereating to keep the child's size small. In another variant of nutritional strategies, a guild woman who reported six unproblematic births advised her readers to avoid dangerous deliveries by keeping the unborn baby's bones soft: "A month before the time of birth, I left off all bone-making food such as bread, so that the birth should be easier, through the absence of very hard bones in the child." She goes on to chastise other women: "Women make a great mistake in feeding overmuch at this time, and bringing fat big babies into the world. Mine were designedly small, but they made up for it after birth, and will compare favourably with any now" (178).

As was the case with the Gambian women and De Lee's patients, afflictions seldom appeared singly in the guild letters. Causes often were inseparable from effects, and the cumulative tolls taken by reproductive assaults could spiral. Combined with this was a sense that high fertility, in conjunction with adverse nutritional, medical, and working circumstances, produced decisive bodily changes over the course of reproductive events. We see these convictions reflected in the following letter, in which the author links her fallen womb to her conjoined ills of increasing debility and vulnerability to miscarriage:

I have been a martyr to suffering through having children. . . . I was al-
ways sick, troubled with nausea and vomiting, which kept me very
weak. . . . After having three children born living I was unable to go the
full length of pregnancy. The last still-born child I had, during pregnancy
I was dropsical [had accumulated fluid] all the time I was carrying, and
I had to have two doctors chloroform me before the child could be born.
. . . Besides having two still-born children, I have had two miscarriages.
The last miscarriage I had I lost that [*sic*] much blood it completely
drained me. . . . Having all this to go through, it brought on falling of
the womb, and now that I am able to do for my family and attend to my
household duties, I have to wear a body-belt. . . . I am a ruined woman
through having children. (29)

One of the strongest themes is that of the dangers imposed by work and
of having to get up too soon from the desperately needed puerperium bed
rest. This passage from the introduction conveys such a sense:

[A pregnant woman] has to scrape and save to put by money for the inevitable expenses that lie before her. She often goes out to char or sits at
her sewing machine, to scrape together a few shillings. She puts by in
money-boxes; she lays in little stores of tea, soap, oatmeal and other dry
goods. At a time when she ought to be well fed she stints herself in order
to save; for in a working-class home if there is saving to be done, it is not
the husband and children, but the mother who makes her meal off the
scraps which remain over, or "plays with meat-less bones." (5)

Unmistakably visible in the commentary is the notion of cumulative assaults of childbearing and a wearing domestic and work life. In one of many
guild letters that convey this sense, a woman recalls the circumstances of her
mother's premature death:

My mother had thirteen children, and, as far as I can gather, suffered ter-
ribly at these times, because when a woman brings up ten children to full
age she has not much time to rest. . . . Mother died at the age of fifty-two
years from Bright's disease [an acute kidney disorder], brought on, I believe, from excessive childbearing, and the doctor said every organ in her
body was completely worn out. . . . I often wonder when I read of the
deaths of women, at from forty years of age upward, if, when they should

be having the best of their lives, that their early deaths are due to lack of
care and rest during the times they are having their babies. (103)

After giving birth to a large number of children, and suffering a variety
of physical assaults on the reproductive system, most women were simply
worn out by middle age.

> If there was any point in a childbearing life that was likely to plunge a
> woman into serious depression or other kinds of mental illness, it was not
> the birth of a *first* child. . . . Rather, for late Victorian and Edwardian
> mothers, trouble was more likely at the arrival of a fifth, seventh, or ninth
> child. Later births, especially those coming before any siblings reached
> working age, were the ones likely to keep an exhausted woman up at
> night worrying about how she would feed yet another child. (Ross
> 1993, 125)

In vocabulary bearing a striking similarity to the notion of being spent
in The Gambia (sarifo), many guild authors describe themselves as "ruined," "used up," "aged," "broken-down," a "wreck," "overdone," "worn
out," or "drained" in the wake of pregnancy and childbearing. Although
guild women were not asked their ages, whether from oversight or from a
lack of concern with this fact, those who did report their ages often did so
to mark how rapidly they had worn out under the strains of hunger, sickness, repetitive childbearing, obstructed labor, and miscarriages. Said one
woman, "I was married at the age of twenty-two (barely twenty-two years),
and by the time I had reached my thirty-second birthday was the mother of
seven children . . . at the end of ten years I was almost a mental and physical wreck" (60).

The ordeals of childbearing could inflict problems of such magnitude
that several of the guild writers, despite their increased age, expressed relief at reaching the point in their lives at which they could finish childbearing or create lengthy spaces between births. Reporting improved health,
they sounded remarkably like Gambian women who finally are able to retire from childbearing and care for the children who remain. Reported one
woman with four children:

> [I] suffered from nervousness, very bad legs, occasional neuralgia, and
> the usual miserable sickness, cough. . . . After having no more children . . .
> [m]y health improved, and people said I looked years younger, and I
> found life a happy place. I sometimes think that the Great Almighty has

heard the poor woman in travail, and shows her a way of rest. . . . I feel I
have better health to serve my husband and children. (93–94)

What about the children born into such circumstances? The possibility
that high rates of mortality in the first year of life and subsequent frailties
and disabilities among children were linked to the circumstances in which
working-class women had to bear children is reflected repeatedly in the letters. Much as we saw in the Gambian case, the child's health was widely believed to be inseparable from that of the mother, and the effects of the
mother's weakness on children, both before and after birth, drew frequent
comment (see Ross 1993, 125–26). Said one letter, "One does not wonder
at the sickly boys and girls one meets in the streets, especially when one
knows under what circumstances they were born, and how and what their
mothers had to bear before they came" (169). Another woman related a
friend's experience: "When the mother asked the doctor how it was her
children were so delicate [as well as deformed and retarded], he turned to
her and said in the kindest possible manner, 'Ask the mother,' showing that
it was due, in his opinion, to the weak state she was in previous to their
birth" (88).

Additional evidence from a physician, albeit indirect, is apparent in the
following letter from a mother who attributes her inability to have any more
healthy children to the cumulative effects of the lack of rest, both in the immediate postpartum period and thereafter:

> I had seven children and one miscarriage in ten years and three months.
> This left me at the age of thirty a complete wreck. . . . My last child was
> born a delicate, weak child, who suffered from malnutrition until she was
> eleven months old, and at her birth the doctor told me I should never
> have another strong and health baby, and that women should only have a
> child every three years, and rest at least a month after confinement. He
> knew I could not give myself the rest I needed, for I could not afford to
> pay anyone to look after my home and children. (128–29)

As I noted above, some women did manage to sustain good health
through their childbearing years. Yet those who did often sensed that they
were exceptions and seemed to feel obliged to explain their anomalous
condition.

One of the most important themes in the letters is that of social relations. Women who seemed to have weathered their childbearing well were
often those who had secure social and financial resources. Such a woman

may have lived close by her mother (if she were alive) or may have had a neighbor woman, a servant girl whose own parents were too poor to send her to school, an older daughter, or a competent midwife or doctor. As in the Gambian case, most important factor of all was a fortunate marriage. To have a husband who held a secure job, brought home all his earnings, and did not drink, beat his wife, or squander his income on an outside woman was every woman's hope. One woman summed up this bundle of contingencies succinctly: "Much depends on what kind of a husband the wife has" (171). In many cases, a wife reported on the kindness and concern displayed by her husband despite his own pitiable health, working under the grind of a job as a laborer in a coal mine or as a mason. The times when the family had no income at all, as when the man was laid off or went without wages to support a strike, were the worst of all. Having no money to hire help, the woman might have to get up almost immediately after birth and begin washing, cleaning, and cooking for what could be several small children and a new baby.

The cases examined in this chapter have gone back in time, examining populations that were at far greater risk of malnutrition, disease, and injury than is true of today's world. Still, the reported ordeals of childbearing among working-class English women after the turn of the century and American women at the turn of the century reveal striking parallels with Gambian women's reports. They are all highly consistent with a contingency vision of a physical life course. Worries about obstructed labor, blood loss, loss of strength, closely spaced pregnancies, the importance of support to obtain rest—these themes run throughout the sources. The sense that child numbers per se are less important in people's views of reproduction than the well-being of the mother and her surviving children is also common to the populations studied. It is not clear that the guild women want all the children God might give them, as Gambian women claim to do, but they never mention a target number of children. Age, when it is mentioned, is alluded to as a baseline against which to understand the ordeals of a reproductive lifetime. Social and economic circumstances rather than time seem to pose the limits on their reproductivity. It is striking that the concept of nature comes up repeatedly in the guild letters and, as was the case in De Lee's writings, seldom in a benign way. In a conspicuous parallel to De Lee's assault on society's dismissal of women's childbearing travails as "natural," the introduction to the letters observes: "Too poor to obtain medical advice during the months of pregnancy, [a woman] 'learns by experience and ignorance,' comforting herself with the belief that however ill she be it is only 'natural'" (5). Yet, despite the frequent referents to the term *natural*, it is clear that no one was resigning herself to nature or to fate. Like Gambian women, all were trying to take action to contain the damage if not to guide the course of events.

Of course, there are differences between the populations examined here and Gambian women. Guild women convey a far more urgent sense of being on the edge nutritionally than do Gambian women, who seem to have more access to food. In addition, the mix of fertility-related maladies seems different. Although I have little systematic information on problems of disproportion between a maternal pelvis and a fetal head in The Gambia, rickets is an unknown disease in The Gambia, and cesarean section, while highly undesirable, is an option well known to everyone, though it is not necessarily easily obtainable in moments of unexpected crisis. Finally, Gambian women's responses reflect far less worry about maternal death from infection following a birth than we see in De Lee's text or even in the guild letters. Infection is by no means out of the picture, however. As the descriptions in chapter 6 showed, "dirty blood," which is frequently associated with infertility, is often attributed to infection.[17] Still, one might speculate that the spread of antibiotics throughout West Africa may have lessened fears of death from infection. Important as well might be the strides that governments have taken to train midwives in antiseptic techniques. In any case, the risks and uncertainties converge in surprising ways.[18]

Framing Observations of the Life Course

By now it should be evident that the embeddedness of scientific inquiry in particular times, places, and social arenas powerfully shapes the frames through which we view the empirical landscape of fertility and the body. In

17. Along different lines, Inhorn (1994, 19–20), describing the plights of infertile women, shows that for Egypt, infection is not only a prevalent gynecological problem among infertile women; it is often caused by repeated biomedical treatment.

18. There are some important exceptions to the rule about the risks of high-parity childbearing. On one hand, a vast, though shrinking, literature from developing countries with high fertility emphasizes the practice's great risks. A 1992 study among women from lower socioeconomic classes in the Nigeria Teaching Hospital, for example, links grandmultiparity to a high incidence of anemia, hypertension, abruptio placentae, breech presentation, abnormal lie, multiple pregnancy, low birth weight, cesarian section deliveries, and perinatal deaths (Oxumba and Igwegbe 1992). (See also studies from South Africa [Skelley et al. 1976] and Latin America [Puffer and Serrano 1976].) But in Saudi Arabia, where, until a few decades ago, childbearing would have occurred under difficult socioeconomic circumstances, Fayed et al. (1993) conclude that high socioeconomic status and high standards of prenatal care mean that "extreme grand multiparity" (parity 10 or more) carries no more obstetric or perinatal risk than among women of parities 2–5. (See also Hughes and Morrison 1994 on the United Arab

this chapter I have asked how we can systematically misread the social and medical logic of a contingent life course even in societies apparently familiar to us by assimilating a profusion of changes in technology, resources, and knowledge. I have argued that as we build common sense, the assumptions of minimal risk and trauma that infuse our habitus smooth out the contingent nature of a woman's reproductive life and stretch it into a trajectory that can be described quite satisfactorily by chronological time. In this reading, the body is the same from one birth to the next, varying only, perhaps, with the linear effects of age. The social and economic conditions that affect physicality are removed from sight.

Of course, the idea that what is seen as "normal" or "commonsensical" is embedded in particular times, places, and social arenas has been an enduring theme in anthropology. We can naturalize beliefs gained through any avenue, whether Islamic ritual or scientific procedure. I have argued that a tremendous amount of scientific energy hinges on the assumption that there is a normal or natural linear baseline along which the life course

---

Emirates.) And a 1992 study in Sweden in a socioeconomically "stable" community with free access to medical care (Brunner et al.) concluded that with good health care, there was little increased risk in multiparous births to mothers and no effects on neonatal outcomes (see also a study from Massachusetts: Williams and Mittendorf 1993). Clearly the caveat "given good medical care and nutrition" must be held in view. Preventive knowledge, sanitation, nutritional regimes, and medical professionalization vary immensely across time and place, as do risks of disabilities and infectious disease. Most Gambian women have diets that are both seasonally stressful and less adequate than do the women where these studies were conducted. And the Gambian national medical system, as good as it is for the African context, cannot compare to those of Scandinavia, Massachusetts, or United Arab Emirates. Similarly, English women in the Co-operative Guild would have encountered far more risks than do those in present-day Scandinavia, the United States, and the United Arab Emirates.

A different example of how strongly culture frames the way we look at medicine and the body (Newman's *Fetal Positions*, 1996) emerges from contemporary literary critique: concerns about women's rights to abortion in the tense legal and political climate of late twentieth-century America. Using a series of Western paintings, engravings, and photographs dating as early as the ninth century, Newman asks how the female body has been subjected to scientific study and technologies. She argues that post-Enlightenment Western obstetrics has treated the fetus as a baby or an unborn child, a person with inalienable rights that cannot be lost, sold, or given away (18). Among the illustrations are those from a 1513 German midwifery manual, which in later English editions showed fetuses that were "plump and cherubic, jumping, dancing, diving, tumbling in unfettered freedom in a uterus" (29). Through the course of the seventeenth century, relates Newman, artists depicted fully formed fetuses cut off from the maternal body and actively negotiating a uterine environment (29–33). (Indeed, before the eighteenth century, there was a popular belief in some circles in Europe that the fetus played an active role in labor, struggling its way out of the womb [e.g., Lieberman 1976, 41].) Such critiques of science's controlling gaze are compelling themes to an early twenty-first-century academic audience in America. But what most of these images much more unambiguously portray are delivery positions that, given the technologies of the seventeenth and eighteenth centuries, would have been fatal or highly injurious for mother or child or both: transverse lie, shoulder dystocia, breech presentation, prolapsed and anteverted uteri, prolapsed umbilical cord, and so on (see my appendix A). Furthermore, against the backdrop of enormous variation in time, place, and polities, women are held as a universalized group, regardless of health, youth, disease, or parity, or cultural or historical nexus.

flows. But the material presented in this book has suggested that this is not so. Most salient in making this case has been evidence of the social and physical contingencies that women experience in rural West Africa, a region with strong expectations of high fertility yet difficult conditions for achieving it. In this chapter, turning to early twentieth-century America and England, I have explored cases that manifested some striking parallels with the African case. All have presented evidence of patterns that vary substantially from commonsense assumptions about the body that now seem to prevail in the West. But whether we consider demographic findings from contemporary rural West Africa or, at a greater temporal and geographical distance, Joseph De Lee's obstetric patients in the United States or members of the Women's Guild in England, it is clear that what is considered natural or normal becomes embodied in the disciplinary concepts we use and in the ways in which we collect, analyze, and interpret data.

Given the cultural assumptions that inevitably direct our gaze, how do we create, remember, and forget knowledge about naturalisms and risk, particularly those surrounding the female body? It is impossible to do full justice to this question. It is possible to observe, however, that what we might call a natural or benign experience frame, stemming usually from a low-and-safe fertility experience, would posit no differences in risk levels between low- and high-parity births. All birth risks would be the same, and childbirth could be read as a natural function, in the sense in which we have come to understand it: free from medications, instruments, and a controlling medical gaze. We sense a very different framing of nature, refracted through a long historical and linguistic lens, in De Lee's campaign to shift the public image of birth from "normal" or "natural" to "pathological." Surely one piece of the answer to the question of how knowledge about nature and risk arises, then, lies in the fact that a lifetime package of preventive or proactive measures—vitamin supplementation to food, the development of antibiotics and transfusion technologies, and so on—has led to the near-elimination of many injurious, deforming, and life-threatening maladies (see also Shorter 1997). Our wealth plus the medical "fixes" at our disposal—surgery, drugs, technologies, knowledge—can support the body on a scale that was unimaginable a hundred years ago.

Another example of how assumptions about the health of a population can slip almost invisibly into our understanding is that of social forces, of which triages and the contingency plans they can put into play are classic cases. Agents and sources as diverse as midwives, physicians, neighbors, and popular media can route women and their projected ailments into diverse pathways of risk and protection, whether to home births handled by a midwife or to a specialty hospital miles away. Developments that make childbirth safe may consist of a scheduled cesarean section for a threatened case of shoulder dystocia or simply a watchful eye on a home birth, with a knowledge of the full range of options if things go wrong. Indeed, women try actively to position themselves in these pathways to circumvent or forestall certain anticipated problems. The reproductive life course of a woman thus evolves within a specific configuration of precautions, interventions, and social relations. As cases are shuttled pre-emptively into particular pathways of risk, a distinct set of bifurcating experiences of risk constantly unfolds for each individual. Although most cases of childbearing end well, with the woman's body uncompromised by disease, injury, or parity,[19] therefore, it is the memories that are created alongside them that make this seem like a "natural" process. The problem for the analyst is that as the outcomes of such processes become sedimented into our understanding, the factors that weigh heavily in other times and places become invisible to us as we construct our cultural generalizations about a human physical baseline. As I have emphasized, our disciplinary backgrounds are largely irrelevant. We all face the challenge, in one way or another, of discriminating between deceptively commensurate logics.

If this is an accurate depiction of the process of life course emergence, then it raises a critical question: If the bodily "baseline" shifts as medical and public health measures alter the human constitution, how valid is it to claim to detect the effects of some particular factor on the body or its health? Brought to light is a set of tightly clustered paradoxes surrounding the question of what is natural. That is, the more benign the experience of childbirth, the more likely it is that low fertility, enhanced medical care, and better economic resources have made such a reading possible, and the less necessary the forms of backup and surveillance seem to be for producing safe outcomes. Beliefs about the natural capacities of the body thus influence the development and proliferation of particular sets of ideas, technologies, training regimes, hygienic practices, and social positions: the "field" (as Bourdieu might call this broader landscape) of reproduction. The result is an odd dialectic in which ideas about what is natural are used to press for the development of certain kinds of medical practices, including (in our own society) those that are seen as minimally intrusive. In turn,

---

19. See, however, Murphy-Lawless 1998 and Davis-Floyd 1992, among others, for insightful discussions of perceptions of risk in the United States.

medicine, in attempting to accommodate these demands, shapes new ideas about what is natural.[20]

20. See, e.g., some of the contributions to Chalmers et al. 1989 for this perspective. DeVries, for example, observes that the new development of "controlled care" at alternative birth centers "is something of an irony. It uses technology to reduce technology; the technology of monitoring and risk management allows some women to have less technological, less medical births" (147). More generally, there is a rich literature in studies of science that asks how culture shapes science and vice versa (e.g., Keller 1985; Martin 1987, 1998; Strathern 1992b; and Franklin 1997).

CHAPTER 10

Rethinking Fertility, Time, and Aging

Using ethnographic and demographic data from rural Gambia, this book has worked through a number of propositions about reproduction, aging, and social life that span disciplines in the social sciences, medical sciences, and humanities. These propositions, centering on what I have called contingent lives, shift the ground on which most Western writings have come to describe the relations among these subjects. The resulting perspective may have seemed at first counterintuitive, if not wrong: something to be dismissed as folk belief. Yet the more intensely it was subjected to scrutiny, the more puzzles it solved and the more it drew in pieces of the classical African ethnography with richness and depth. The farther we went down this road, the clearer it became that the major conventions by which our analyses of fertility and aging have been handled, especially in societies with high fertility, have been deceptively commensurate with the view that descriptions from rural Gambia convey. The possibility that our analytical conventions are artifacts of our own times and circumstances should not surprise scholars who engage in the study of science. Nor should anthropologists be surprised to hear that a local cultural perspective makes a great deal of sense. The surprise is that this alternative view makes more coherent sense of Western science's own empirical objects—the data that science itself has generated—than do the dominant frameworks themselves.

Seeking to escape the traps of commensurability that arose, I pursued two related strategies. First, I scrutinized a broad range of numerical and narrative data from rural Gambia on how women and men manage their conjugal and reproductive lives. To describe the local mindsets surrounding such practices, Bourdieu might have used the concept of habitus. Yet I have argued that this concept can—indeed, should—be applied to our own analytic practices. Doing so reveals that the conventions by which we handle analyses of reproduction and aging have equated time with bodily experience. To solve the anomalies that began to surface as the logic of time was pressed, therefore, I also sought to exploit the edges of several disciplines, anthropology and demography in particular, forcing each to confront the other's logic. I now summarize the findings in terms of these themes.

The Case against Time

Each chapter has made the case against contemporary Western assumptions of a woman's ability to produce and maintain young life as a function of chronological time. In the vision we have explored, life is built on the premise that the pace and character of senescence are contingent on cumulative wearing events such as reproduction that erode life's sustaining forces, with harsh experiences causing disproportionate loss. In the situations rural Gambians face, a woman does not assume a life trajectory of smooth, linear decline. Bodily resources erode in a highly saltatory manner, punctuated by dips, surges, and lags. Periods of tribulation interspersed with periods of rest and replenishment make the progression toward senescence one of relativities and contingencies. Senescence is not linear. Rather, the hardships of life inscribe themselves on the body at a pace that is contingent on external events. This means that women who care intensely about high fertility manifest little apparent concern for the passage of reproductive time because for them the question is not one of time—"When does senescence shut down reproductive capacity?" Rather, it is "How do the toils and struggles of reproduction bring on senescence?" Such a causal sequence is now "just common sense." These conclusions suggest that although the front end of the reproductive span has commanded the most demographic attention, the end of reproductive life is equally telling. There is far more variation in the age at which women cease childbearing than in the age when they begin.[1] It is now that the health effects of high

---

1. See Wood (1994, 422), who points out that "variation in menopause is likely to be a more important cause of interpopulation variation in the length of the reproductive span than is variation in menarche."

fertility—anemia, depletion of fat reserves, injuries incurred in childbirth, and so on—are most visible. And individuals approach the end of reproduction after very different childbearing careers and with very different prospects for the future. One woman of thirty-eight may have had six easy deliveries and be left with six surviving children who will retire her in comfort. Another woman of thirty-eight, after six traumatic miscarriages, and no living children at all, may face the specter of having to attempt more pregnancies.

Once we recast the emphasis from linearity to contingency, it is clear why women who want all the children God gives them should view the anatomical and energy limitations on the body as more important than a menopausal end to reproductivity. The contingency perspective also explains why people use contraceptives in ways that seem counterintuitive to us. Because the ability to reproduce is not seen as tied to time, women see the effort to create interstitial calendar time between births as largely inconsequential to their overall goals of high fertility. Contraceptives can thus preserve one's ability to sustain a pregnancy and give birth—to enhance high fertility goals. Thus, *bodily* younger women—those who are "fresh" or "new," regardless of chronological age, and who are able to withstand the ordeals of frequent childbearing—use contraceptives infrequently. Young women who do use Western contraceptives are usually those whose children had to be weaned too quickly or whose fecundity resumed before the child reached a point of stable health. Older women, those who are bodily "worn out" by the strains of childbearing, are also likely to use contraceptives if they resume fecundity too soon. But for them, "too soon" refers as much to themselves as to the child, to the time before which they have recovered from the strains and trauma of childbearing. The logic of contingency also explains why women who have suffered a nonlive birth often use contraceptives—to regain their health after what may have been a traumatic ordeal—and it explains why men (as well as mothers-in-law and retired senior wives) often oppose family planning. In this logic, a husband may suspect that a wife with inexplicably long spaces between her births may be trying to withhold her reproductive potential from him, perhaps saving it for another man.

To be sure, any woman (whether she lives in the United States or in The Gambia) who is healthy, eats well, bears only two children, and retires on a pension will likely experience a more linear decline. For her, the ability to conceive becomes the limit on reproduction.[2] Yet the contingency perspec-

2. The analysis presented here has been looking through the lens of fertility, which stands paramount in women's descriptions of their lives. Yet as Ellen Ross and Christine Oppong (pers. comm.)

tive would incorporate this as one end of the spectrum of its possibilities. There are thus not two discrete logics but one.

Investing broadly and deeply in social relations is the cornerstone of the contingency scheme. Predominant in women's descriptions of husbanding their bodily resources are metaphors of economy: in wealth and bodily endowment (of muscles, strength, or an endowed number of child potentials), in the saving and expenditure of moral capital (exchanging youth for children and for moral esteem from affines), and so on. Fragility and unpredictability, whether they are experienced as infertility, sickness, the risk of death, crop failure, a child's failure in school, or a husband's dismissal from an urban job, pervade life. Such worries provoke women to cultivate diversity among children—to send some to school and others to gain skills in a trade—to arrange advantageous marriages for their children, or to withhold children from an unsupportive husband. The more intensely we subject the contingency framework to scrutiny, the more important social life becomes.

If the cultural logics of contingency and linearity are now juxtaposed, the grounds of the disagreement become clear. Those of us who are brought up in Western countries would likely see the notion of God's will, or of reproductive outcomes whose numbers cannot be known until they are finished, as superstition. It is also circular. Thus, the belief that the number of children a woman will produce depends on her God-given reproductive potential is fallacious because it is not independent of the assumptions underlying the question. And yet Gambian women would find equally fallacious Western beliefs about time as the determinant of how many children a woman could have. To people who see the capacity to produce all the children God might give as a function of health, the length of fecund time itself is a function of how well a woman takes care of her body—if necessary, through contraceptives. People are not confused by the concepts of age or chronological time. Nor are they unaware that bodily processes transpire at a pace that can be estimated by an average chronological duration. Under the conditions that they experience, attempting to force the notion of a contingent reproductive life into a fixed chronological frame makes no sense at all.

---

have emphasized, women living under conditions such as those I have described do many other things that must exert wearing effects, especially hard work; they also endure illness and hunger. Conversely, although most of the women for whom pregnancies have become dangerous in the wake of such events are likely to cease or slow the pace of active reproduction, multiparity and events such as miscarriages and stillbirths are not invariably harmful and depleting.

The resulting paradoxes are multiple. The most notable is that women in rural Gambia are using high-technology contraceptives to construct through careful cultural strategies what appear, in statistical analysis, to be birth spacing patterns created by "nature," producing what demographic analyses term "natural fertility." They are using Western contraceptives for very "African" purposes: to ensure the survival of many children by spacing their births carefully. Thus, as I noted in chapter 4, it is not that births are spaced because of the simple passage of biological time. Rather, someone skillfully creates a biological space that can then be described by time. In effect, the same contraceptive technologies can yield opposite results, depending on how they are used. Used for short periods and to protect health, a birth-preventing measure can result in many living children. I do not know the effect these actions may have had on actual numbers of children. But certainly the intents with which contraceptives are used subvert the intentions of family planning programs.

Another paradox of the contingency perspective is the fact that a woman's success in realizing her full reproductive potential—what we might call fate—is highly consonant with action-oriented frames of social life. In the linear frame, variation in child numbers and birth intervals would be largely a function of inherent, unalterable differences, whether they were conferred by genes or by fate. In the contingency framework, given the premise of a set of bodily resources that must be protected from wearing experiences under harsh conditions, a woman must constantly protect her health during and after pregnancy. She must be able to rest and replenish her body after adverse events, a strategy that might produce birth intervals that are uneven by intention. The contingency perspective also has action-related implications for the process of aging. By adjusting the pace of childbearing and by the careful management of bodily resources, women may attempt to contain the pace and character of their physical decline. Slowing the pace of aging itself, however, is of less concern than mitigating trauma. Indeed, a cumulative decrement of youth ideally brings social gain by building moral commitments among a husband's family.

As I noted earlier, the resulting perspective opens to question facets of social and physical life that the most committed constructionists among us have assumed to be natural. The observation that there is such wide scope for maneuver surrounding a phenomenon that contemporary Western culture has relegated largely to nature means that women become active shapers of their biological destinies, even to the point of trying to influence not only how but for whom they age. The result is not an economy of chronological time but a socially meaningful expenditure of a bodily endowment. So although an emphasis on the pace of aging in social life might be construed as biological determinism, the reverse is the case: bodily time bends according to the lines of force in a social universe.

Time, Contingency, and the Disciplines

If notions of reproduction and aging that are voiced in rural Gambia are not simply exotic reports but are signaling highly empirical phenomena, we confront some perplexing questions. Why have we collectively come to imagine that time and hormones are the essence of reproductivity? Why do we enumerate vital events in the ways that we do? These questions remain perhaps the most intriguing of all, but they are the ones least easily answered within the scope of this book. Most of the evidence, however, suggests that our increasing personal distance from the high-and-risky end of the experiential spectrum of fertility, combined with our unprecedented levels of preventive care and copious backup in case of emergencies, has sharply truncated our vision of the bodily tolls that reproduction can take. A fast-dwindling number of us have experienced sickness, insecurity, and poverty on the scale that much of the world still experiences. Few of us know women who endured an adult life of exhaustion from reproduction, women who, although they survived multiple acts of childbirth, may have died an early death from their cumulative effects. An easy explanation is not in sight.

Whatever the reasons, the population science that has resulted from this mix of experience and vision has made two related mistakes. First, it has extrapolated a set of assumptions about our own low-and-safe fertility conditions and applied them to high-fertility conditions in which reproductive life is precarious. Setting aside the perils of childbearing, we can isolate brief slices of the contingent life course and shape them into a smooth trajectory of physical decline. In doing so, we can entertain highly schematic visions. We can imagine that fertility is a set of biological absolutes in a social vacuum, or that the reproductive process reflects simply desire, whether for children, sex, or identity fulfillment. We can imagine that conception (or, at increasingly smaller levels, the replication of the genetic code) is the crux of fertility and that the costs of children are limited to economics. The clock and the calendar are the pivot points of our theories and hence the bases of our graphs.

Second, and related to this, our population science has assumed that synthetic models of a population, most prominently the total fertility rate, apply as well to the reproductive life course of individual women. The TFR uses slices of time—the fertility rates of sets of women separated into age groups—in a population to describe the rate at which it is reproducing. No one individual necessarily fits the overall pattern, a fact that is fully recognized in theory. Nonetheless, the TFR is almost invariably the model that underlies statements about individual women's fertility practices and desires, effectively erasing their particular experiences and, moreover, their connections to people whose lives have intersected with their own. Individuals do not behave in the same ways populations do, even if their actions collectively make up the population. Nor do they have identical experiences. Each reproductive event will have unique effects on an individual's life, and the effects of all these events, in tandem with her social situation, will shape her future options, a vision that a more developmental or experiential model would accommodate. If individuals are taking action to slow the pace of cumulative damage and buffer the contingent harms, their efforts to manage both births and reproductive trauma would be invisible with a measure such as this. What we need, in sum, are better ways to connect the experiential histories and circumstances of individual lives—vital events—with the larger population perspective. Contingency and cumulativity are not simply interesting observations. They are the principles with which theory about the life course and the social life that shapes it should begin.

The paradoxes not only extend to which variables we choose for our statistical analyses, the meanings we assign to these variables, and even the statistical tests that we run on them. They also pervade our political agendas. Thus, worries about political reactions to suggestions about fertility limitation policies have led family planning programs throughout the world to de-emphasize the ideal of limiting numbers of children in favor of a more neutral-sounding goal of spacing births.[3] Indeed, if the stated goal of child spacing by means of which contraceptives are promoted in Africa is to be taken at face value, then contraceptives represent one of the largest international investments in maternal and child health that has ever been made in the region. But although the need to space children has become the ideological cornerstone for vast international efforts, my search to date of the

---

3. In *Child Spacing in Tropical Africa* (1983), for example, none of the numerous tables or graphs used the child's or the mother's health or the child's phases of development as a variable, either independent or dependent, even though almost all the articles drew attention to these factors as critical reasons why child spacing is important. Most instead used some measure of time as the independent variable and abstinence, breastfeeding, amenorrhea, and contraception as the dependent variables.

available bibliographic sources in *Population Index* turned up almost no quantitative analyses of the effects of contraceptive use on maternal or child health through child spacing in the high-fertility regions of Africa.[4] Indeed, works that conclude that women are spacing births usually treat such findings as troubling. That women are not using contraception for limiting numbers of children, as those who promoted contraception implicitly intended them to do, but for spacing births—what the promoters actually urged them to do[5]—places us, the population-conscious West, in an awkward situation. African women are adopting contraceptives for the public reasons we urged them to, yet their purposes—and quite possibly their achieved empirical outcomes—contravene entirely our private intentions.

What is most striking about this, however, is how clearly the essence of a concern such as the need to space births to justify vast policy efforts can be grasped, and yet how completely the analytical implications of these efforts can be overlooked.[6] Work on the deleterious effects of high fertility on health are read as an almost entirely separate literature from that on the use of contraceptives for reducing fertility. The fact that there is no demonstrated numerical attention to the central rationale for promoting contraceptives in Africa (the effects on the health of child and mother) is a striking case of how tightly we can seal off our own cultural frameworks from one another. By allowing the Gambian material to question Western scientific conceptualizations, we may be able to identify the cultural specificity of Euro-American naturalizations of fertility, time, and aging that underlie scientific studies.[7]

4. See, however, Montgomery and Lloyd 1996. Another key exception, a study by Kirk and Pillet (1998), does provide statistical analyses of the relation between contraceptive use and improved maternal and child mortality in sub-Saharan African countries, but it does so in the context of fertility decline. It argues that increased levels of female education increases contraceptive use, leading to lower fertility and hence improving women's and children's mortality risks. The next question, one might imagine, is whether—*irrespective* of fertility decline—contraceptive use improves health and lowers mortality risks. An article that moves in this direction and also draws attention to the contradictions in population ideology is Margolis 1997.

5. This is not to say that African women would not have recognized this potential independently; I strongly suspect that they would have.

6. Similar observations were made more than two decades ago by the United Nations Secretariat in the introduction to its *Manual IX* (1979, 1). Although this document noted that one of the ultimate objectives of a family planning program was the "reduction of infant and maternal mortality and improvements in the general well-being of mothers and children," it conceded, "Relatively little has been done to ascertain, reliably, what the planning programmes established for various health-related purposes have accomplished." Conversely, much effort had been devoted to perfecting methodologies for assessing the impact of programs on fertility. Furthermore, most programs of up to three years' duration have been evaluated for fertility impact, even where the programs did not have fertility decline as an objective. Little appears to have changed in two decades.

7. I am grateful to Susan McKinnon for helping to draw out the implications of this point.

As I have stressed throughout, however, a blanket indictment of population science, or of any of the other sciences whose subject matter has come under scrutiny, would be quite wrong. The reasons are twofold. First, since completing the Gambian fieldwork, convinced that Western science was wrong about the dynamics of reproduction and aging, I have discovered that our science does indeed contain sharply articulated pieces of the contingency perspective. Many of these pieces are tucked away on obscure shelves, where they are forgotten or mislabeled. Those that remain we hold out as exoticisms in contrast to what we believe that our more enlightened science has shown, or as fragments of a life we believe we no longer live. This means that if what Gambian women are saying is neither wrong nor new, there is an enormous irony at work. Gambian theory has restrung our science. It has seized facets of reality from domains that contemporary Western science rarely analyzes, arranged them into an entirely different configuration, and pointed causal arrows in different directions. What seemed at one moment so exotic was in the next moment completely commonsensical. It is less the case, therefore, that our science has its facts wrong than that the "right" facts have lain in scattered pieces throughout Western science's vast storehouses. Once we extract these facts from their conventional locations and try them out in this alternative configuration, a different picture emerges with force and clarity.

Which facts would we retrieve in order to understand reproduction and aging in places such as The Gambia, and through what lenses would we view them? Since no field offers the perfect solution, different perspectives can be brought to bear in reconstituting a vision like that which we have seen. Here is one set of possibilities.

To sociocultural anthropology, we would add broad empiricisms of biology and bodily temporalities, and we would speculate boldly about people's intentions in these domains. To demography and reproductive biology, we would add strong doses of obstetrics and gerontology. We would also devise some finer measures of cumulativity and contingency. We would keep linear time within view but use it judiciously, not as the presumed cause of aging but as the background against which to examine a vast set of relativities. With regard to the contemporary medical fields of fertility (which in the United States now refers to the specialty field of "infertility") and obstetrics, we would emphasize the risks to a woman of infection and hemorrhage, but especially the effects of high fertility and closely spaced births on organs such as the uterus. We would thus be more wary of claims such as that voiced in the case of the sixty-three-year-old California woman who was said to have been able to give birth because the ability of a uterus to perform its reproductive task outlasts the ability to conceive. Organs and tissues other than ovaries and eggs are involved in reproduction. The actions of chemicals moving tiny entities through tiny tubes to implantation, followed by an uneventful pregnancy and delivery, are only part of the story. In gerontology we would, in addition to genetics, attend to contingent events that might drive senescence. Added to the mix might be fields such as orthopedics and occupational health, which, although they have been little concerned with reproduction, recognize the wearing effects of repetitive stress injuries, independent of time. All of our fields would have to be turned inside out, and our texts would have to be written with more conditionalities.

Most important, we would turn to cultural insights about social forces that shape the trajectory of physical life. Here we would search for ethnographic sensitivities that could shed new light on understandings of finely honed contingencies in the timing, pacing, and mutual constitution of life events and agendas. One of the strengths of the new genre of studies of the body, for example, is their emphasis on the physical side of reproduction, a theme that engaged almost none of the older kinship studies. In the stream of anthropology scholarship on the political economy of the body, the fact that women are managing their own bodies as resources, in essence "realizing" themselves, sometimes to benefit them but sometimes to leave them, has implications for utterly new existential feminist agendas.

The second reason why a blanket indictment of Western science would be wrong is that there are some deep cracks in the core of contemporary Western culture that affect how *all* of us, despite our vast disciplinary differences, believe in certain chronological naturalisms in the body. These deeply resonant cultural understandings, stemming from our experience of low and safe fertility, pervade our understanding of "the natural." In doing so, they flatten the saltatory and cumulative character of what both African women and our own forbears would recognize as the "normal" course of senescence. So accustomed are we to this vision that we export it into our divergent disciplines and use it to construct our analytical concepts, define our variables, and write our textbooks. In reproducing "in their own terms the logic from which that coherence is generated" (Bourdieu 1990, 92), our models fashion the image of the life course into something that is described quite satisfactorily by chronological time. In constructing, from our vast historical, cultural and scientific repertoires, a set of academic models of a linear life course, we have all participated in universalizing something that is not a universal at all. To us, quite irrespective of our disciplines, time *is* nature in matters of the body.

Getting a fix on the habitus that so thoroughly enshrouds us is no easy task. We all can somehow relate to a more contingent view of the life course, whether from our readings or from our life experience. Yet traces of the extraordinary plasticity that rural Gambians describe have all but disappeared from our medical journals, our demographic formulas, our ethnographies. In demography, anomalies, the most visible edges of alternatives to linear time, are smoothed over in survey recodes of awkward translations or classified into categories of "other." A universal linear grid of chronological time is not always wrong. Like any other absolute measure, time highlights facets of the empirical world that we might overlook otherwise. It also yields both simplicity and comparability. And it comprises one vein of logic that actors themselves exploit in debates about reproductivity and aging. The reproductive concerns of men in rural Gambia showed this abundantly well. Certainly time is an anchor for those of us conditioned to reach for its security. As a place to start, chronological time is a reasonable estimate of the pace at which the body and its reproductivity will likely decline. Yet the more we flatten observations about reproduction and aging into abstract, universal measures such as time, the harder we must work to fit them back into the world. We privilege time at the risk of erasing evidence of other temporalities and of forces such as medical trauma that may be more relevant.

The fact that our academic descriptions of experienced temporalities tend to overlook a more contingent and cumulative vision of life course events has particular significance for sociocultural anthropology. Our descriptions of both nature and time as products of cultural construction would seem to help us to avoid the universalizing sins of the harder sciences in handling reproductive events. Yet the discomfort that many of us now express about science places us in an awkward position. If the people we study seem to have better science than our own scientists, are we to dismiss theirs as readily as we sometimes do our own? Paul Riesman's reproach to his profession, although written when anthropological concerns about exoticizing drew less attention than they do now, still strikes close to home: "In their studies of the cultures of other people, even those anthropologists who sincerely love the other people they study almost never think that they are learning something about the way the world really is. Rather they conceive of themselves as finding out what other people's conceptions of the world are" (1976, 53).[8]

All this is to say that demography merely lays bare a version of common

8. See also Lock (1993c, 331), and Keller (1985, 6) on science more broadly.

sense that we all share. In much the way that Schutz would have predicted, our disciplinary practices allow us, irrespective of the political sympathies that may otherwise divide us, to take certain knowledge and practice as natural and to pass over the contradictions they may pose. Even the concept of natural fertility is arguably a simple distillate of our collective logic of time in the body: formalized, crystallized, and played back at us through the precision instruments of our specialists.[9]

Although there are critical empirical differences between low-fertility and high-fertility reproductive regimes, models of linearity and contingency operate in many contexts in both the West and The Gambia.[10] Our lives, like those of rural Gambians, reflect the coalescence of multiple rhythms and challenges. The fact that few of us face such extremes of hardship may explain why we underplay the tolls that hardship can take and why linear narratives dominate our discourse about reproduction and aging. But to assume that experience alone determines how we perceive the world is too simple. Gambian women may live more by the contingency view than we do. Certainly they articulate it more clearly with reference to reproduction. But as nearly as I can tell, we all, irrespective of our disciplines, our nationalities, or our stations in life, entertain both logics. We interweave chronological and contingent elements in different blends and in different contexts. Under certain conditions, we assume certain elements and causal sequences and overlook others.

The fact that contingency perspectives are found in the West (and the likelihood that many other examples could be uncovered, were the question to be undertaken systematically) raises further questions. How do we selectively attend to different life temporalities at particular historical or personal moments? What are the logics of these temporalities? What power relations might underlie the privileging of one or the other? Western women probably see and feel far more contingency than our disciplines recognize. Some of us may want to avoid further births not just because of economic con-

9. The fact that our models of experience overlook a more contingent and cumulative vision of life course events might suggest that a more predictable, linear life is preferred to one of uncertainty and contingencies. Hence, what rural African women need to smooth out the afflictions that create an uncertain life trajectory is economic development, in order to improve their standards of living. This question is too complicated to resolve here, even if it were taken on its own terms. Furthermore, what, specifically, development is—how, for whom, and at what costs it is to be achieved—are longstanding questions that show no signs of going away. My concern here has simply been to point out that Western scholars need different ways to understand reproduction.

10. The cultural terms in which they are expressed are different, with some striking exceptions: for example, both the letters to the Women's Guild in England and a traditional birth attendant in rural Gambia described metaphors of childbearing and miscarriage in which fruit may drop with little damage to a maternal tree as long as the fruit is ripe.

cerns with child numbers but because of the bodily toll that childbearing has taken on us. When used in studies of high-fertility societies, therefore, the language of contingency tends to be a justifying one: the contingency idiom of maternal depletion is enlisted to urge women to limit births. And so Western scholars can indeed view the world in terms of maternal depletion. But when addressing rates of fertility and contraceptive use in those societies, analyses usually shift to a mode that implies pressures to reduce population. Depending on which hat we are wearing, we can see contraception as a tool of political domination, the mark of an ecologically responsible citizenry, or a feminist salvation.

Similar observations can be applied to rural Africans, who do not always see the world in terms of contingency. The clock and the calendar are very much in play in rural Gambia. Farming families may live their working days by the rising and setting of the sun, but at least some of their members also listen to chronologically scheduled radio programs, wear watches, attend weekly markets, and send their children to school on a daily schedule and a yearly calendar. Women use monthly cycles of birth control pills, and they know that injections are effective for only three months (at least in theory). Subfertile women even worry about a chronologically estimated menopause deadline. Men orient themselves to time as the best index for gauging when a healthy young wife should begin a new pregnancy, as long as the last-born child's health appears secure. On every front, the boundaries between linearity and contingency are blurred. Even Africans who are trained in demography in Western universities speak of the life trajectory in terms of linearity. They use it in their analyses just as skillfully and consistently as would any Westerner. Yet when thinking back to women's reproductive experience in their rural homelands, they shift mentally to a very different life world than the one their text books portray. We all use assumptions of linearity and contingency, and we all switch frames. So although it might seem that the great struggles are those between the technical terms of science and idioms of common sense, the highly quantifying versus the culturally specifying disciplines, or Africans versus Westerners, the lines of logic diverge in every domain.

The findings of this study have brought into alignment a wide range of data on social organization, demography, biology, and culture. Many of the specific findings are not new. What is new is the synthesis that arises from the reconfiguration of such apparently divergent facts. To highly quantitative disciplines such as demography, cultural attempts by contemporary anthropology to deconstruct definitions of family, gender, and reproduction can hardly sound like promising turf on which to join forces. To sociocultural anthropologists, on the other hand, the use of universalizing measures such as number of live births and chronological time seems to breach some of our discipline's most sacred tenets about the irreducibles of culture. Yet there should be considerable appeal to both disciplines in mapping out new domains of physical existence and the social life that is constituted around them. Culturally constituted quantifications of the sequencing and pacing of physical expenditure should comprise a mutually compelling, richer explanatory base for discovery in multiple fields. Taking on time and reproduction in this way has the potential to integrate the disciplines in ways that do not reduce any to the terms of another but capitalize on their differences.

Evidence for the Gambian Results
in Western Medical Research

In this appendix, I pursue two strategies to bring empirical Gambian postulates about fertility into alignment with the tenets of Western science for assessment. First, I examine some overall demographic and medical statistics on maternal and child risks in difficult environmental conditions and in particular on the risks of high fertility for women under such conditions. Second, I look at fertility through the lenses of the science of obstetrics, focusing on the categories that seem to be closest in meaning to the Gambian analogues of muscles, strength, and blood. The aim is to evaluate the notions that rural Gambian women see as so key to the course of reproduction and its end. I focus especially on the question of the cumulative effects of reproductive events in terms that may be independent of age, and on whether these consequences may raise the risks of childbearing. These strategies are not meant to be comprehensive. Yet given the inevitable difficulties in translation and in interpreting the metaphorical quality of some of the vocabulary, the pieces of evidence to which they point make Gambian cultural tenets all the more convincing.

Maternal Morbidity and Mortality Risks
under High-Fertility Conditions

Even the most superficial scans of demographic and health figures on infant and maternal mortality from around the world yield support for Gambian women's views that childbirth poses great risks for both mothers and children in difficult economic and medical circumstances. Analyses of the DHS have shown that risks to neonates (children in the first week of life) are appreciably higher for Africa than for other parts of the world (Govindasamy et al. 1993, 16), and sub-Saharan Africa has an overall mortality rate for infants (children in their first year of life) that is fourteen times as high as that in the United States: 96/1000 and 7/1000, respectively (Population Reference Bureau 1996). Higher risks for children are also associated with high birth order and maternal age. According to Sullivan et al. (1994, 28), risks are greater at all stages up to age five for firstborn children and children of birth order seven and above. Those born to women age thirty-five and older encounter high risks, especially in the neonatal period.

Risks of maternal mortality mirror patterns of child mortality. According to Koblinsky et al. (1993, 34), 500,000 women die each year in childbirth, 99 percent of them in developing countries. The major causes are hemorrhage, obstructed labor, infection, hypertensive disorders of pregnancy, and septic abortion. (In the eleven months spanning pregnancy and the postpartum period, the greatest risk of death occurs from the onset of labor through the first forty-eight hours following delivery [Stanton et al. 1997, 21]). Women in developing countries have eighteen times the risk of maternal mortality—and Africa thirty-two times—of those in developed countries, both because women in these areas have more births than women in developed countries and because each delivery is riskier. The lifetime risks of maternal mortality are one in forty-eight for developing countries and one in eighteen hundred for developed countries; for Africa, they are one in sixteen (National Research Council 1997b, 116–17). Maternal mortality risks are especially stark for African women. According to 1990 WHO/UNICEF figures (1996), the lifetime chances of dying from maternity-related causes range from zero in countries such as Iceland, Malta, and Luxembourg to one in seven in countries such as Afghanistan, Somalia, Guinea, and Sierra Leone. For The Gambia, the lifetime risk of maternal mortality is one in thirteen. (See fig. A.1 for examples.)

Gambian women's view that there is great maternal risk in high-order births is widely shared in Western obstetric medicine. A National Research Council report summarized the risks in developing countries as being high for the first birth, declining at the second and third, and then increasing again with each successive birth. Women of parity 5 or more have 1.5 to 3 times the risk of maternal mortality than do those of parity 2 and 3, who have the lowest risk (1989, 30, 32); this is just the point, of course, at which

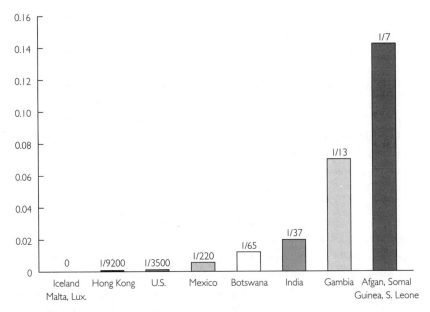

Fig. A.1 Lifetime chances of death from maternity-related causes for various
countries
Source: WHO/UNICEF 1990.

most women in developed countries stop bearing. According to the report,
this pattern exists universally although poverty, poor medical conditions,
extremes of age, and some infectious diseases increase the risk (ibid., 30,
32–33).[1]

The picture is similar for maternal morbidity. Jacobson (1993, 19–20)
describes the risks for many women in developing countries:

> As girls grow into adulthood, their nutritional status often worsens due to
> the combined demands of childbearing, an increasingly heavy workload,
> and loss of iron stores through menstruation. . . . These nutritional defi-
> cits contribute to what may become lifelong handicaps, such as stunted
> growth and chronic anemia, two of the main factors behind complications
> of pregnancy and childbirth. . . . Ironically, women's needs—for adequate
> rest, good nutrition, and health care—are often ignored even when they

1. Risks of maternal mortality and morbidity of high-parity women are difficult to disentangle
from risks to older women. Although there are increased risks with higher parity, women age thirty-five
and older have higher risks of death at all parities (Govindasamy et al. 1993, 23).

are engaged in the one activity in which they have an undisputed monopoly: pregnancy. Poverty pressures both rural women and those in the informal urban economies to work through the final stages of pregnancy, putting enormous demands on their physical energy and allowing them little time for the rest they so badly need. . . . The lifelong drain on physical stamina experienced by women and girls is magnified during pregnancy, further compromising the health of both mother and child. The United Nations Children's Fund (UNICEF) has found that many African women gain minimal weight even in the last trimester of pregnancy, which, coupled with anemia, increases the chances of premature birth and a low-birth-weight baby.

In addition to these incidents, "[t]here are over one hundred acute morbidity episodes for every maternal death—an estimated sixty-two million women suffer maternal problems annually" (Koblinsky et al. 1993, 34), with a spectrum of ailments and injuries ranging from uterine prolapse to vesico-vaginal fistula, wherein the pressures exerted during labor perforate the vaginal wall and create a cavity through which urine or feces will leak thereafter (National Research Council 1997b, 121).

The tendency to wear out from childbearing and the life-threatening conditions it can pose can be discerned as well in descriptions of efforts to control fertility from historical Europe. Flandrin (1979, 217), for example, records women's descriptions of the demands of perpetual pregnancies and childbearing as fatiguing and painful. Extremely suggestive material can also be found in analyses of fourteenth-century Tuscany (Herlihy 1985, 146) and Ottonian Saxony (Leyser 1979, 55), in Seccomb (1992), and, more generally, McLaren (1990, 13–14). Beyond doubt, however, the most riveting sources are original ones such as Stopes (1929) and Women's Cooperative Guild (1916), examples of which appear most prominently in chapter 9. There is predictable variation as well among contemporary high-fertility populations that are under far less physical or nutritional stress. One is that of the contemporary Hutterites. Reproductive biologist Carole Ober (personal communication) speculates that Hutterite women are able to have as many children as they do because they have abundant diets of meat, milk, fat, and starch. They have gardens and do domestic work but do not do heavy farm work. Still, Hutterite women look worn out after having several children, Ober reports, and although fears of religious transgression make women reluctant to discuss their own maternal exhaustion, they do talk at length about worn-out friends and sisters. Despite religious bans on contraception and on limiting births, most women now use contraception—

especially tubal ligation—after a number of births. The excuse is often that the doctor told them to do so because of "varicose veins" or "migraines." And, according to Ober's description, Hutterite women stop breastfeeding once they become pregnant, just as Gambian women do, though, unlike Gambian women, they often turn to bottles. Moreover, like Gambian women, they pay little attention to menopause.

Evidence that nonlive births can inflict or signal trauma comes from several studies far apart in time and distance. Writing on Tokugawa, Japan, Skinner (1993, 252) infers that infanticide was preferred to abortion because it was safer for the mother and because it created more space between children who were allowed to live. Gregson (personal communication; Gregson et al. 1998) finds in his data from rural Zimbabwe that women who experienced a miscarriage, abortion, or stillbirth in the previous five years were more likely to be current users of modern contraceptives than those who did not, and people often try to delay a new birth after the death of a young child. In North India, Jeffery and Jeffery (1996, 27) report, women who suffer repeated miscarriages are seen as needing to seek treatment for medical problems associated with pregnancy and are likely to be granted more rest from work and pregnancy and better diets.[2]

It is much more difficult to glean outside evidence of women's efforts to recover from mishaps through contraceptive actions. As I showed in chapter 6, all the core Demographic and Health Surveys questionnaires for countries with low levels of contraceptive use systematically screen out questions about nonlive births.

Full fertility surveys that included nonlive births were, however, collected more than twenty years ago (from 1977 to 1980) by the World Fertility Surveys. With the help of Sangeetha Madhavan, I examined six African countries (Cameroon, Sudan, Senegal, Kenya, Lesotho, and Ghana) to

2. Patricia Woollcott (pers. comm.), a nurse-midwife in Evanston, Illinois, finds the Gambian descriptions of the birth of a stillborn child at odds with her experience in the contemporary United States, where a stillbirth usually causes no more difficulty than a normal birth. She speculates that a stillbirth may produce a hard labor when the fetus may have been dead for some time, and the head, which may have begun to decompose, has become pliant, making it difficult to deliver the shoulders. A woman writing in the early part of the twentieth century to the Women's Guild (1916, 85) describes an event that lends support: "the birth . . . was harder than usual, as a live baby helps in its own way. The baby had gradually died after the flooding [bleeding or hemorrhage], and had been dead more than a week at birth." It should be pointed out, however, that such events rarely occur now in developed countries because of revolutionary technologies that can quickly detect when a fetus has died and because of the ability to perform a pre-emptive cesarian section. On the whole, readings on obstetrics in the nineteenth and early twentieth centuries support Gambian women's descriptions of the trauma of many stillbirths.

I am grateful to M.R.C. physician Elizabeth Poskitt in The Gambia and to Patricia Woollcott for other insights on materials in this section.

see if any "new" discoveries might emerge from data like these, which are now relegated to the back shelf. Measuring the use of what the WFS called "efficient" contraceptives (pills, condoms, injections, IUDs, sterilization, and "other female science"), we focused on women who were ever-married, uneducated, and rural: the group most comparable to the women in the Gambian study and those least likely to want to limit fertility. The number of users in all the surveys together was tiny: only 109 in all six countries. Still, we found that cases that very obviously consisted of some reason other than fertility limitation—women with problematic fertility records or who were still breastfeeding—account for at least 38 percent of cases of these most unlikely users. At least 21 percent of all uneducated ever-married rural WFS women using "efficient" contraceptives had highly problematic fertility records, including 13 percent who were using them after a nonlive birth or a child death. Furthermore, several had multiple fertility problems, and at least seven of the nineteen breastfeeding users had a history of fertility problems or what appeared to be closely spaced pregnancies. If numbers such as these can talk to us through such vast cultural, linguistic, and temporal distances, they are declaring that many of these women went out of their way to obtain what during this period must have been an exceptionally rare "treatment" for their health or fertility problems. (See Bledsoe et al. 1998 for details of this analysis.)

Western Analogues to Gambian Obstetric Concepts

We now turn to obstetrics, where another strategy by which to assess Gambian views of reproductivity, especially under conditions of high fertility, lies in looking at some of the most likely empirical analogues in Western obstetric science for the salient elements I have described in Gambian theory. For blood I focus on anemia, hemorrhage, and placenta previa; for strength, maternal depletion; and for muscles, fetal malpresentation, cephalopelvic disproportion, and uterine and abdominal musculature.

Blood: Western obstetric medicine widely supports the Gambian view that some severe blood-related problems can be associated with high-parity childbearing. The cumulative effects of multiple pregnancies increase mortality risks from blood-related diseases such as hepatitis and malaria (National Research Council 1989, 32), and high-parity women are susceptible to anemia, which increases risks for the fetus of prematurity, nonlive birth, and perinatal and neonatal mortality (National Research Council 1997, 122). Besides these maladies, the risks of hemorrhage during pregnancy and especially during labor increase with parity. According to Nigerian physician Ben Olalaye (personal communication), high-parity women are more likely to experience conditions in which the uterus and the placenta become thickly congested with blood vessels; as a result, delivery often precipitates severe loss of blood and a high risk of hemorrhage. Similarly, placenta previa (a condition wherein the placenta overlies the cervical opening of the uterus), which carries immense risks from hemorrhage to both mother and child, is much more common in multiparae than in primiparae because the slackened uterus is weaker than before.

Strength: In Western medicine, problems related to what Gambians translate into English as a lack of "strength" has one obvious analogue in the Western notion of maternal depletion syndrome (for example, Jelliffe and Jelliffe 1964), in which a woman who has finished breastfeeding is unable to replenish her nutritional reserves to pre-pregnancy levels. In this situation soft tissue reserves are reduced because of negative energy balance during pregnancy and lactation.

There is considerable evidence linking maternal morbidity to repetitive births and short birth intervals (National Research Council 1989). Under normal conditions, as Miller et al. (1993) explain, pregnant women put on weight that stems from growth of the fetus and placenta and also from uterine expansion and fat deposition. After birth, maternal weight remains above average for several months, followed by a decline to below-pregnancy level and, finally, by a weight "repletion" achieved by building energy stores, back to normal. The longer the recuperative interval before the next birth, the greater the weight gain. According to Merchant et al. (1990), women with six months or more between weaning and the next conception experience the smallest declines in weight loss; women who overlap lactation with the next pregnancy experience the greatest loss of fat stores.

Maternal depletion is exacerbated when work, hunger, or disease imposes seasonal hardships (see, for example, Miller et al. 1993; Miller and Huss-Ashmore 1989; Winkvist et al. 1992) and extra stress is placed on already strained maternal nutritional reserves.[3] The energy requirements of producing food and clothing, collecting fuel, and caring for children and the elderly pose significant complications during pregnancy and lactation (for example, Townsend and McElroy 1992; Jackson 1997). In a malnourished population, a woman who becomes pregnant before repletion begins,

---

3. Among the large number of works on this subject are Jelliffe and Maddocks 1964; Prentice et al. 1981; Merchant et al. 1990; Winikoff 1983; Miller and Huss-Ashmore 1989; Merchant et al. 1990; Tracer 1991; Winkvist et al. 1992; Miller et al. 1993; and McDade and Worthman 1998. I have not found discussions of the somatic costs of miscarriages or stillbirths. For reviews of the field in general, see Wood 1994; Ellison 1994; and Leidy 1994.

that is, whose births are closely spaced, will be at a significant nutritional disadvantage. According to Winkvist et al. (1992), women who are chronically malnourished are most susceptible to weight loss through "non-repletable" cycles, although Miller et al. (1993) find evidence of metabolic adaptation under such conditions, implying that the potential for maternal repletion is more dependent on spacing of pregnancies. Further complications arise from sharp seasonal patterns of work demands and illness in regions such as the Sahel. A woman who is engaged in unsupplemented breastfeeding during seasonal food shortages may lose more weight than one who gives birth several months later. (On many occasions, women in the Gambian surveys expressed a desire to delay both pregnancy, for their own sake, and weaning, for the child's sake, until the dry season, after the harvest.) Such problems are often intensified under conditions of seasonal food shortages (Miller et al. 1993).

As for the relation of child mortality and morbidity to maternal depletion and its presumed correlates, Hobcraft (1992), among others, has shown clear associations between short birth intervals and child morbidity and mortality. Using WFS data for developing countries, Hobcraft et al. (1985, 370) found that any birth occurring within two years of an index birth is associated with "considerable excess mortality for the index child" even when controlling for factors such as birth order and the age and education of the mother (see also Hobcraft et al. 1983). According to Boerma and Bicego (1992), preceding birth intervals of less than twenty-four months were also linked to higher mortality for the neonate (see also Sullivan et al. 1994, 21–28). An even more apposite study from Bhutan traces faltering growth among children to what I have called "overlapped pregnancies"; children who were weaned during their mothers' subsequent pregnancy grew more slowly than did either age peers weaned from nonpregnant mothers or children who continued breastfeeding (Bohler and Bergstrom 1996). The Gambian data, however, might suggest a different causal sequence in some instances: pregnant mothers may wean children with faltering growth, attributing the children's failure to thrive to the new pregnancy.

Geronimus's (1987, 1992) provocative findings—that African American adolescents have better birth outcomes than do African Americans of other age groups—lends further perspective. Geronimus argued that post-teenage mothers have poorer birth outcomes than do mothers aged fifteen to nineteen because black women's health begins to deteriorate as early as the mid-twenties—a process she called "weathering." To be sure, she was not dealing with high fertility; nonetheless, it is interesting that the effects of childbearing begin to appear so rapidly under difficult conditions. Although

Geronimus (1992) relates weathering to hypertension, smoking, and high blood levels of lead, we might also posit that weathering is related to the strains of having additional children to care for. Many African American women, although they do not undergo the kinds of successive childbearing ordeals that rural Gambian women do, may endure enormous physical hardship in raising a series of dependent children under difficult circumstances: their own and their children's. We have turned over innumerable stones on the welfare of the adolescent mother and child but almost none on the welfare of the young mother's *own* mother, who effectively becomes responsible for *two* children, one a young teen and the other an infant. Similarly, it would be helpful to know what role parity plays in weathering among African American women.

Muscles: Among populations where fertility is high, the uterus, a thick-walled, muscular organ, is a frequent locus of medical problems in pregnancy and childbirth. The uterus and the ligaments holding it in place are comprised of muscle cells, which are incapable of replacement, and the wearing and injury that uterine muscles may sustain during pregnancy and childbirth can create permanent changes if not damage. The muscles and ligaments associated with the uterus and its immediate surroundings (the abdominal wall, the rectal sphincter, and the anterior vaginal wall) are tight at the outset of reproductive life but can become increasingly slack as they are stretched or torn irreversibly during successive pregnancies and births (Patricia Woollcott, personal communication). Several possible analogues of Gambian descriptions of the problems associated with muscles in multiparous women can be identified. Among the most obvious are fetal malpresentation, uterine rupture, uterine prolapse, and cephalopelvic disproportion (for example, Donald, 1979, 404, 412, on uterine rupture).

The slackening of the uterine muscles is associated with a number of risks. Because the primigravida muscles and tissues are so firm, the primigravida uterus is virtually immune to rupture, although primigravidas are most prone to develop difficult and prolonged labor (O'Connor et al. 1966, 217). By contrast, multiparae are susceptible to uterine rupture or placenta previa (ibid., 238) and, because the fetus seldom "engages" with the pelvis until delivery, to the dangers of "unstable lie." In multiparous labor, uterine contractions tend to be forceful to the point of being dangerous, although, as Ben Olalaye (personal communication) points out, the opposite problem can occur: the cervix and the uterine muscles and ligaments can become stretched or damaged and lose their tension, making it harder to produce contractions and increasing the risks of prolonged labor, of hemorrhage, and of postpartum infection from a retained placenta. Lack of muscle tone in the uterus and surrounding tissues makes high-parity women vulnerable to a number of risks such as increased amniotic fluid volume (polyhydramnios), long labor, and stillbirth and the sepsis it may foster (National Research Council 1997b, 130). In addition, having uterine muscles that become dangerously worn after multiple pregnancies increases the risks of prolapsed cord, wherein the umbilical cord drops into the vagina and is compressed, cutting off oxygen to the baby. According to Patricia Woollcott, there may be some genetic component underlying vulnerability to muscle stretching in the area of the uterus, although repeated pregnancies, exertion, and poor nutrition are the precipitating causes.

Attached in the center of the pelvic cavity like a sling, the uterus can become displaced downward into the space between the bladder and the bowel, a condition known as prolapse of the uterus, an outcome of damage during childbirth to the muscles and ligaments that support the uterus and the vagina. In extreme cases it may actually protrude from the vagina, a condition sometimes alleviated in times past by the use of a supportive internal pessary. Further pregnancies undergone in this condition can lead to fetal loss and intensify risks to the mother (see Macpherson 1992, 613). (According to a National Research Council report [1997b, 123–24], prolapse is considered a normal consequence of high-parity childbearing in many developing countries.)

Stretching and injury to the muscles and ligaments of the uterus and the abdominal wall are known to present risks to multiparae of malpresentation, a delivery position in which something other than the head is set to emerge first (for example, Donald 1979, 404). In a primipara, the baby usually lies upright, well-supported by taut muscles. In a multipara, and particularly a grand multipara, the uterine muscles have slackened and the baby tilts forward, increasing the risk of a breech presentation or the initial emergence of a limb. The laxity of the abdominal wall and the lack of uterine tone mean that "the child is free to move, and the factors making for a longitudinal presentation are absent" (De Lee 1913, 616). This condition can result in uterine rupture and hemorrhage (National Research Council 1989, 30–31; see also Gillmer et al. 1991, 76). Particularly if there is hydramnios involving excess amniotic fluid, the fetal position may shift frequently, although it can be corrected at each prenatal visit by external version in the hope of forestalling a transverse position at delivery (Donald 1979, 414–15).

An oblique or "transverse" lie may produce labor in which an arm or a shoulder is closest to the cervical opening and the head may occupy one or the other iliac fossa—a condition called shoulder dystocia. Shoulder dystocia is the most fearsome delivery position; once the umbilical cord becomes compressed, there are only three to five minutes to extract the baby. Worries about the risks of transverse lie are so great even in the contemporary United States that *The New Our Bodies, Ourselves* states flatly, despite its overall wariness of medical interventions, that babies in such delivery positions "must be born by cesarean" (Boston Women's Health Collective 1992, 452).

According to Donald (1979, 405), multiparae—and particularly grand multiparae—are more likely than others to contract placenta previa, which prevents engagement of a "fetal pole" (the head or feet) as a presenting part, causing transverse lie and risking hemorrhage. Also associated with multiparity is prolapse of the cord, which may occur with malpresentation, when something prevents the presenting fetal part from fitting closely into the lower uterine segment, thus shutting off the forewaters from the hindwaters (Donald 1979, 417).[4]

---

4. Although multiparity is on the whole a dangerous condition, the fact that the birth canal has been widened by numerous births led Donald (1979, 405) to remark on "the treacherous brow presentation," a situation in which the largest of the fetal head diameters attempts to engage, and descent is impossible with an average baby and pelvis: "from time to time one sees some remarkable spontaneous deliveries in the experienced multipara who has a cavernous pelvic cavity and a baby of no more than normal size" (411).

Gerontology and the Plasticity of Aging

In chapter 7, I examined the Gambian view that high fertility exerts such stress on the body that it precipitates what Western science terms "aging" or "senescence"—a possibility of obvious significance not only for high-fertility societies but also for general theories of the life course. I have no direct empirical evidence that Gambians are right in this, although a striking consonance among their behaviors and statements supports this possibility. If we turn to findings arising more broadly from Western empirical science, what evidence can we muster to assess these assertions? The possibility that childbearing (or other stressful experiences) takes a toll on the body is a notion with intriguing parallels in the history of our own culture. Today, such ideas are seldom discussed outside the field of gerontology, let alone in demography, a field in which the locus of attention for women is heavily concentrated in the first half of the life span. Although the entire reconfiguration was unfamiliar to two gerontology specialists (Linda Martin and Jay Olshansky, personal communication), both found the overall scheme plausible. As explained in appendix A, much evidence from obstetric medicine suggests that muscles can undergo considerable stretching and damage over multiple pregnancy terminations. Here I examine some research from gerontology that suggests that reproduction can age women. I restrict the discussion to the organic level; I omit work on cellular metabolism and genetics.

The Gambian view of human development emphasizes a fundamental plasticity of the physical life course in which aging is contingent on wearing life events such as pregnancy and labor. I look for support for this proposition in Western scientific writings concerning aging effects of reproduction on the body overall. In particular, I seek descriptions of decline that may be reversible or repletable, or in which the body components specifically associated with female reproduction undergo deterioration more rapidly than others. Subsidiary support would consist of evidence of "episodic" or "saltatory" aging—aging that is evenly paced at times but rapid and dramatic at others.

Aging: Causes, Speed, and Modifiability

Trying to get a grip on the notion of aging is a confusing undertaking. The notion of chronological age itself is straightforward: measuring how many years have elapsed since birth. Yet the assumption that physical age is closely related to, if not caused in some way, by chronological age clouds our progress at every step in the literature.

The word *aging* itself is often defined in highly tautologous ways. According to Spence (1989, 8), for example, aging is "the process of growing old, regardless of chronological age." In this definition, the state of growing old is not described independently from the term it seeks to define. Even the strategy of defining aging as "losses in normal function that occur after sexual maturation and continue up to the time of maximum longevity for members of a species" (Hayflick 1994, 15) begs the critical question, What is "normal"? On the other hand, this definition would accommodate the fact that in The Gambia, the normal loss of reproductivity occurs well before the time at which Western women lose it. Similar problems arise with the term *senescence*, following a definition by Spence (1989, 8), who refers more narrowly to the deterioration of efficient functioning of an organism with increasing age, a process leading to an increased probability of death. Here again, though, the notions of increasing age and efficient functioning are incorporated closely with the term they are intended to define. Although many of the problems inherent in these definitions—particularly those of equating chronological age with biological age—are well known in the field of gerontology, the Gambian view, which clearly separates the physical trajectories of bodily elements, brings them into sharp focus.

Given the problems of trying to pin down concepts such as "old" and "normal," a common procedure to describe the individual's overall rate of aging or to predict longevity—duration of life—is to try to distill from various measures of senescence one indexical "biological age" that can be compared to a temporal scale. The fact that some individuals "look young" and some look "old" for their age has been long recognized in the field of gerontology, and terms such as *senescence* and *biological age* have been used to draw attention to the disparity between physical or biological status and chronological age. Yet because there is no universal template against which aging can be assessed, subjective images of normality—ways the "average" person is imagined to appear and function at certain chronological ages—are often employed. Hence, even these strategies run into teleological problems.

The final problem in investigating aging is that the end point of the analysis in both technical demography and popular culture is usually the chronological measure of longevity and not senescence, because the former is seen as a close proxy for senescence. Being aged is almost invariably linked to temporal proximity to death, but the pace or even the pattern of physical decline is not necessarily related to longevity (as Hayflick notes, "Death may not be related to aging at all" [1994, 15]). Still, in practice, both aging and senescence are routinely linked to longevity, a practice that may stem from the actuarial procedure of calculating age-related death and disability rates for insurance and Social Security purposes.

Leaving aside, for the moment, the problem of what aging is, we can ask what causes it. For most Americans, the most immediate answer to this question is the passage of time. Hayflick (1994, 12), however, decisively lays this tenet to rest: "Time itself produces no biological effects. Events occur *in* time but not *because of* its passage. The biological events that follow birth happen at different times and occur at different rates in each of us" (emphasis in original). Time and age can be used, with caution, as indices of senescence. But they are not seen as its cause; that is, aging is not a function of age.

Although there is general agreement among gerontologists that time does not cause aging, there is no clear agreement on what does cause it.[1] Rowe and Kahn (1997, 434), summarizing a rapidly developing body of recent information, emphasize instead the role of "lifestyle and other factors that may be age-related . . . but are not age-dependent." "Wear and tear" theories of aging see senescence as a reduction in efficiency as a function of

---

1. Views on the possible evolutionary roots of aging and its functionality can be found in, e.g., National Research Council 1997a. And Olshansky et al. (1998) see senescence as an "inadvertent consequence" of survival extended into the postreproductive period, when the individual becomes disposable. That is, whereas growth and development are genetically programmed, aging is a side effect of survival.

repeated use or stress, with an emphasis on the centrality of one system or another, such as the heart or even cellular systems (Bittles 1996, 10). This observation would be especially important in the case of an organ such as the uterus, which undergoes enormous stress in giving birth. The loss of muscles, which are composed of tissue that is *postmytotic* (incapable of replication), figures strongly in scientific descriptions of aging. This fact would be exceptionally important with respect to the uterus, an organ composed largely of muscles.

The wear-and-tear view has been somewhat marginalized as the target of research. This trend has occurred in part because, as Hayflick (1994, 23) points out, the effect on the body of an external stressor does not necessarily cause senescence or lead to a life-threatening state. It has also occurred because issues of genetics and longevity have been absorbing the interests of gerontologists in recent years. Even though cutting-edge research lies elsewhere, credence in the basic proposition appears to be widespread among gerontologists. Variants include a "rate of living" hypothesis and nongenetic or stochastic theories, which posit a cumulation of minor, adverse changes that "ultimately overwhelm the capacity of an organism to survive" (Bittles 1997, 10). In another variant, Rowe and Kahn (1997) follow contemporary lines of logic of the wear-and-tear theory in casting doubt on beliefs that increased risk of diseases and disability with advancing age results from inevitable, genetically determined aging processes. Describing what they call "successful aging," they point to "altered within-individual variability in physiologic functions" that may underlie much of what we consider the usual aging syndrome: "the capacity for positive change, sometimes called plasticity, persists in old age; appropriate interventions can often bring older people back to (or above) some earlier level of function" (436–37). Focusing on the impact of short-term variability in physiological change, physical capacity, and cognitive function, they argue that

> intrinsic factors alone, while highly significant, do not dominate the deter-
> mination of risk in advancing age. Extrinsic environmental factors, in-
> cluding elements of lifestyle, play a very important role in determining
> risk for disease. [Moreover], with advancing age the relative contribution
> of genetic factors decreases and the force of nongenetic factors increases.
> Third, usual aging characteristics are modifiable. These findings under-
> line the importance of environmental and behavioral factors in determin-
> ing the risk of disease late in life. (435–36)

By contrast to a model of the life course as continuous or linear, a "wear" view implies that aging may occur episodically or even in a saltatory (abrupt, random) manner. It may even occur precipitously (see, for example, Bittles and Brightwell 1997, 5). In this view, aging appears to occur in a manner that is to some extent contingent on the state of other body elements, a likelihood that is particularly important in the case of reproduction under conditions of nutritional stress.

What about the possibility that body systems age at different paces? According to Spence (1989, 8), "All organs in an individual do not age at the same rate; and any specific organ does not necessarily age at the same rate in different individuals. Consequently, different individuals undergo aging at different rates." Indeed, in reviewing a number of indices—stature, neurocranial height, neuroendocrine function, triceps skinfold thickness, bone mineral content, bone tissue, total body water, muscle mass, and muscle fatigue (for example, hand grip strength and muscle specific force)—Bittles and Brightwell (1997) point out that such measures are not independent of one another. Although this fact may be used to create an average or composite "biological age," overexpenditures in one system that generate compensatory actions in related systems can distort the overall biological age. In any case, composite measures of aging are often flawed because of the "multifactorial" nature of aging: "There is . . . considerable individuality in terms of the timing and trajectory for many of the commonly measured variables which comprise the overall ageing phenotype" (ibid., 3). Moreover, according to Bittles and Brightwell, there is little comparative information on how people in a range of societies actually rank on these scales at various chronological ages, or on how men compare with women on either measures of individual elements or composite scales.

That some of these effects may be saltatory if not reversible opens the further possibility that they are modifiable and, indeed, are very likely the subject of intentional action. In their work on anticipating and preventing diseases and disorders that are expressed at older ages, Rowe and Kahn (1997, 439) stress, "Many of the predictors of risk and of both functional and activity levels appear to be potentially modifiable, either by individuals or by changes in their immediate environments." Similarly, Olshansky et al. (1998) argue that the manifestations of senescence are inherently modifiable by "manufacturing survival time": moderating genetic expression through, for example, buffering environmental assaults, developing medical technologies to treat diseases of old age, and changing dietary patterns.

All this leads to the question of which processes of senescence a society might attempt to modify and how it does so. Whereas most citizens of the

West seem to fear the process of aging, it is not clear that African men and women have the same values or (therefore) whether they try to modify senescence or any of its permutations in the ways that we might. Indeed, given the value of aging in the context of achieving maternal status, African women may even try, under certain circumstances, to intensify certain aspects of the aging process (see, for example, the discussion of Rosander 1991, in chapter 8, for hints that women seek to enhance views of themselves as aged).

Clearly there are many unexplored mysteries of the plasticity of the human body under varying conditions of reproductive, work, and dietary stress. One might even speculate that the enormous research efforts being directed to genetics, as opposed to variation in expression of physiology and the saltatory dynamics of the physical life course, are in part a reflection of our belief in the linear life course.

The Wearing or Aging Effects of Reproduction

Gambian women describe the overall effect of the loss of muscle in childbirth through damage and stretching as one of "aging." Entailed as well, they say, are the effects of repeated stressful labor on uterine and abdominal muscles, differences that can be observed in the vicinity of the uterus and abdomen, where muscles may become visibly flaccid after several births. Contained in this implied theory of reproduction and aging, to the extent that these components individually undergo senescence, are various possibilities of plasticity, repletion, and reversibility.

In chapter 6, I mentioned Western scientific evidence that pelvic relaxation and uterine prolapse are associated with the slackening of the muscles of the pelvic floor, such that they no longer adequately support the pelvic organs, especially after a history of difficult births (Boston Women's Health Collective 1992).[2] It is notable, of course, that the wearing effects that Gambian women (and Western obstetricians) describe imply that reproductive events may exact differential tolls on different women and on different body regions and systems in the same woman. Such assertions seems to combine observations of the irreversible wearing effects of pregnancy and childbirth

---

2. The kinds of wearing effects that rural Gambian women describe with respect to muscles apply more broadly to the depleting effects of fat loss, resulting in thinning of the skin and in wrinkling. Most scholarly sources describe an average trajectory of aging in a Western country—first as a replacement of muscle cells by fat and eventually as the absorption of fat and the formation of collagenous fibers in a final thinning phase, leaving wrinkled skin (e.g., Macpherson 1992, 13). Gambian theory, however, draws attention to differentiated possibilities, with some people growing thin and others fat.

on muscles, which undergo extraordinary stress in pregnancy terminations, with the effects of energy expenditure to compensate for the incremental loss of muscles. And the Gambian assertion that some of these resources can be regained at the end of childbearing appears to have a parallel in the Western notion of a middle-age fat deposition prior to the final thinning phase of old age. Clearly the parallel cannot be taken too far, however. In The Gambia, women are moving from a draining phase of life, childbearing, into a recuperative mode, and most Western women are not.

Leslie Lieberman (personal communication) speculates that childbearing very likely does produce saltatory aging effects, in part because nutritional status before, during, and after pregnancy affects all systems, particularly those governing the acquisition of cutaneous wrinkles and the loss of subcutaneous fat. And Patricia Woollcott (personal communication) lends observational support to the possibility that childbearing exerts wearing effects on women based on her experience with high-parity Orthodox Jewish women in Illinois. Support is also found in some ethnographic accounts. Patricia Jeffery et al. (1988, 196) quote a woman in northern India as follows:

> You see how we must deal with babies' pee and shit. Babies cause a lot of worries. Last night my new baby was sleeping on my bed but my two-year-old refused to sleep with anyone else, so he was on my bed too. My sleep is always broken, never complete. My head aches. Having too many children has brought weakness to my body. With every child I lose a bit more of my spirit. Bearing a child every two years does not let us remain young for long. We are not as old as we look: women here become old quickly.

Similar observations come from western Kenya, where Susan Watkins and Steve Green (field notes, 1994) recorded interviews with women concerned with aging, anemia, and worn-out uteri. All were mentioned frequently by women as rationales for contraceptive use. A study from Papua New Guinea (Setel 2000, 249–50) reveals virtually identical ideas, even in a society with lower fertility thresholds: "[R]epeated births exacted a cumulative toll on the constitutions of their wives; they were thought to become prematurely aged and unable to work. Once they had borne three or four children, women were entitled to express their desire to cease childbearing and even to opt out of sex."

Corroboration of the possibility that reproduction precipitates aging is a particularly prominent theme in the work of Gray (1994, 89, 90), who links premature aging from reproduction in particular to poor nutrition among Enga women of Papua New Guinea. For example, "the Enga stressed their belief that women's reproductive powers made them age early, and be thin and weak and short-lived relative to men. . . . There is considerable evidence from New Guinea and other societies with poor nutrition that the menopause occurs at a relatively early age." Very much in line with the Gambian emphasis on muscles, Gray cites Sinnett (1977, 80), who reports that "muscle loss, which is a major factor accounting for the age-related decrease in body weight experienced by the Enga, reflects their low protein intake."

In addition to their intrinsic importance for studies of reproduction, such possibilities support assertions that it is less useful to think of aging as a global process than to recognize different kinds of senescence. Some of these forms can lead to death quickly; others may have more benign if not reversible effects. Muscle deterioration does indeed appear to be unidirectional and irreversible in the assessments of both Western scientists and Gambian women, and the logic of reversibility quickly runs aground on the fact that there are no cases of wholly successful attempts to reverse senescence. But the possibility that certain effects can be reversed in other body systems—supplies of strength and fat and skin tone, according to Gambian women—is supported in the work of Rowe and Kahn (1997), who employ the notion of "resilience" to describe the capacity to recover from adverse physical states usually associated with aging: "Under the most fortunate circumstances, aging brings with it some repetitive experience of chronic or recurrent stresses, the "daily hassles" of life . . . and their cumulative effects. . . . We propose the concept of *resilience* to describe the rapidity and completeness with which people recover from such episodes and return to meeting the criteria of success" (439).

Note: Although Mandinka is a tonal language, I have not attempted to represent tones here.

bambaŋɔ:	strong; referring to a male ideal
baŋta:	to finish temporarily a replenishable resource such as strength
baraka diŋo:	lit., "blessed children"
buruu:	weaning a child too soon, usually because of the mother's new pregnancy
dokuwo:	work for immediate cash remuneration (contrast *kato/bataa*)
faso:	lit., "sinew"; fig., "muscle," commonly referring to a woman's reproductive capacity, which she expends
fonyondiŋo:	an appropriate or acceptable space, as in rest from pregnancy and childbearing, that is deserved or legitimate (the opposite of *jaŋfaa*)
foro musoo:	"middle woman"; usually a woman of proven fertility who has had two or more pregnancies; a woman of respect
foro musoo didiŋo:	"just-beginning middle woman"; a young married woman, usually one who has had a child or two or who is pregnant for the first time. Alternatively, a young woman who had relations with an outside man before her marriage could take place, bringing about a devaluation of her worth.
fɔnyɔɔ:	permanent or earned rest; retirement from childbearing
hajj:	the pilgrimage to Mecca
hapo:	divinely endowed total number of "child potentials"
harijeo:	fetus, "child potential"

jaŋfaa: an inappropriate or unacceptable space (the opposite of *fonyon-diŋo*); rest from pregnancy and childbearing that is undeserved or illegitimate

joosayo: to replace someone with someone younger; an act of appreciation after work or reproductive struggles have finished

juruma: "overlap:" a situation in which a woman becomes pregnant while her young child is still breastfeeding. The result can be births that occur in rapid succession.

kato/bataa: work, in the sense of short-term sacrifice for long-term benefit; exchanging a hard life of exhaustion and privation for benefits such as obligations, blessings, and development (contrast *dokuwo*)

kuntu: cut or finished; refers to the permanent loss of something like a reproductive muscle

kɔtɔ: permanently "cut," finished, or worn out, as in *musu kɔtɔ*, the permanent expenditure of muscles or the divinely endowed hapo

musoo keba: a woman who has grown old without bearing children

munya: to be patient or to endure, the value that women in particular are expected to have

musu keba: a woman who has become worn out by things other than pregnancy and birth; an infertile or subfertile woman (contrast *musu kɔtɔ*)

musu kɔtɔ or *kɔtɔ tale:*   "all finished"; having one's reproductive potential finished permanently; women who have reached the irreversible end of their reproductivity (contrast *musu keba*)

nyinaa: young; fresh; ripe for marriage

sanjo: year

sarifo: "spent," usually referring to the effects of childbearing; the crucial tipping point between childbearing and retirement from it

sɛmbo: strength; power; energy. Expenditure of strength: *sɛmbo baŋtale* ("strength-finished"), the verb *baŋta* implying an act of temporarily depleting a renewable entity, by contrast to *kuntu*, an irreversible expenditure.

süriŋo: stillborn child

siŋɔ siti ta: having one's "legs tied"; becoming committed to a man and his family, usually through expending one's reproductive potential on their behalf

sunkuto: a virgin

tɛmbo: stages of life

toubab: Western, modern, or white person

wulu: a pregnancy termination

wulu kurɔŋ: extremely bad or painful pregnancy termination; miscarriage

yeloo: blood

REFERENCES

Abu-Lughod, Lila. 1986. *Veiled Sentiments: Honor and Poetry in a Bedoin Society.* Berkeley: University of California Press.

———. 1991. Writing against culture. In *Recapturing Anthropology: Working in the Present,* edited by Richard G. Fox, 137–62. Santa Fe, N.M.: School of American Research Press.

———. 1993. *Writing Women's Worlds: Bedouin Stories.* Berkeley: University of California Press.

Adamchak, D., and P. Gabo Ntseane. 1992. Gender, education and fertility: A cross-national analysis of Sub-Saharan nations. *Sociological Spectrum* 12:167–82.

Addams, Jane, 1912. *New Conscience and an Ancient Evil.* New York: Macmillan.

Adeokun, Lawrence A. 1983. Early child development and the next child decision. *Genus* 39:115–40.

Ainsworth, M., K. Beegle, and A. Nyamete. 1996. The impact of women's schooling on fertility and contraceptive use: A study of 14 Sub-Saharan African countries. *World Bank Economic Review* 10:85–122.

Ajayi, J. F. Ade, and Michael Crowder, eds. 1976. *History of West Africa.* New York: Columbia University Press.

Anarfi, John K., and Clara Korkor Fayorsey. 2000. Male protagonists in the "commercialization" of aspects of the female life-cycle in Ghana. In *Fertility and the Male Life Cycle in the Era of Fertility Decline,* edited by Caroline Bledsoe, Susana Lerner, and Jane I. Guyer, 144–60. Oxford: Oxford University Press.

Andreski, Iris. 1970. *Old Wives' Tales: Life-Stories from Ibibioland.* New York: Schocken.

Appadurai, Arjun. 1986. *The Social Life of Things: Commodities in Cultural Perspective.* Cambridge: Cambridge University Press.

———. 1990. Disjuncture and difference in the global cultural economy. *Public Culture* 2:1–24.

Arens, W., and Ivan Karp. 1989. Introduction to *Creativity of Power: Cosmology and Action in African Societies,* edited by W. Arens and I. Karp, xi–xxix. Washington, D.C.: Smithsonian Institution Press.

Asdar Ali, Kamran. 2000. Making "responsible" men: Planning the family in Egypt. In *Fertility and the Male Life Cycle in the Era of Fertility Decline,* edited by Caroline Bledsoe, Susana Lerner, and Jane I. Guyer, 119–43. Oxford: Oxford University Press.

Askew, I., S. F. Njie, and A. Tall. 1992. Overcoming religious barriers to family planning in rural Gambia. Paper presented at the 19th Annual NCIH International Health Conference, Arlington, Va.

Ba, Mariama. 1989. *So Long a Letter.* Oxford: Heinemann.

Barth, Fredrik. 1959. *Political Leadership Among Swat Pathans.* London: University of London, Athlone Press.

———. 1965. *Nomads of South Persia: The Baseri Tribe of the Khamseh Confederacy.* New York: Humanities.

Baruch, E. H., et al., eds. 1988. *Embryos, Ethics, and Women's Rights.* New York: Harrington Park.

Becker, G. S. 1976. *The Economic Approach to Human Behavior.* Chicago: University of Chicago Press.

Beckerleg, Susan. 1992–1993. The interplay of precedence and patronage in Mandinka village politics, *Cambridge Anthropology* 16 (1): 45–60.

Beckmann, Charles R. B., F. W. Ling, W. N. Herbert, D. W. Laube, R. P. Smith, and B. M. Barzansky. 1995. *Obstetrics and Gynecology.* Baltimore: Williams and Wilkins.

Beinart, Jennifer. 1989. The inner world of imperial sickness: The MRC and research in tropical medicine. In *Historical Perspectives on the Role of the MRC: Essays in the History of the Medical Research Council of the United Kingdom and Its Predecessor, the Medical Committee, 1913–1953,* edited by Joan Austoker and Linda Bryder, 109–35. Oxford: Oxford University Press.

Beischer, N. A., E. V. Mackay, and P. B. Colditz. 1997. *Obstetrics and the Newborn: An Illustrated Textbook.* London: W. B. Saunders.

Bell, Rudolph M. 1979. *Fate and Honor, Family and Village: Demographic and Cultural Change in Rural Italy Since 1800.* Chicago: University of Chicago Press.

Berry, Sara. 1985. *Fathers Work for Their Sons: Accumulation, Mobility, and Class Formation in an Extended Yoruba Community.* Berkeley: University of California Press.

Bittles, Alan H. 1996. The biology of human ageing. In *Psychiatry in the Elderly,* edited by R. Jacoby and C. Oppenheimer, 3–23. London: Oxford University Press.

Bittles, A. H., and R. F. Brightwell. 1997. Defining biological age. Paper presented at the International Union for the Scientific Study of Population seminar "Age—between Nature and Culture," Rostock, Germany.

Blanc, Ann K., and Anastasia J. Gage. 2000. Men, polygyny, and fertility over the life course in sub-Saharan Africa. In *Fertility and the Male Life Cycle in the Era of Fertility Decline*, edited by Caroline Bledsoe, Susana Lerner, and Jane I. Guyer, 163–87. Oxford: Oxford University Press.

Blanc, Ann K., Brent Wolff, Anastasia J. Gage, Alex C. Ezeh, Stella Neema, and John Ssekamatte-Ssebuliba. 1996. Negotiating reproductive outcomes in Uganda. Calverton, Md.: Institute of Statistics and Applied Economics [Uganda] and Macro International.

Bledsoe, Caroline H. 1980. *Women and Marriage in Kpelle Society*. Stanford, Calif.: Stanford University Press.

———. 1984. The political uses of Sande ideology and symbolism. *American Ethnologist* 11:455–72.

———. 1990a. "No success without struggle": Social mobility and hardship for foster-children in Sierra Leone. *Man* (n.s.) 25:70–88.

———. 1990b. The politics of AIDS, condoms, and heterosexual relations in Africa: Recent evidence from the local print media. In *Births and Power: Social Change and the Politics of Reproduction*, edited by W. Penn Handwerker, 197–223. Boulder, Colo.: Westview.

———. 1990c. The politics of children: Fosterage and the social management of fertility among the Mende of Sierra Leone. In *Births and Power: Social Change and the Politics of Reproduction*, edited by W. Penn Handwerker, 81–100. Boulder, Colo: Westview.

———. 1991. The trickle-down model within households: Foster children and the phenomenon of scrounging. In *The Health Transition: Methods and Measures*, edited by John Cleland and Allan G. Hill, 115–132. Health Transition Series, vol. 3. Canberra: Australian National University.

———. 1992. The cultural transformation of Western education in Sierra Leone. *Africa* 62 (2): 182–202.

———. 1994. "Children are like young bamboo trees": Potentiality and reproduction in sub-Saharan Africa. In *Population, Economic Development, and the Environment: The Making of Our Common Future*, edited by K. Lindahl-Kiessling and H. Londberg, 105–38. New York: Oxford University Press.

———. 1996. Contraception and "natural" fertility in America. *Population and Development Review*, special supplement to vol. 22, edited by John Casterline, Ronald D. Lee, and Karen A. Foote, 297–324.

Bledsoe, Caroline, with Fatoumatta Banja. 1997. Numerators and denominators in the study of high fertility populations: Past and potential contributions from cultural anthropology. In *The Continuing Demographic Transition*, edited by G. W. Jones, R. M. Douglas, J. C. Caldwell, and R. M. D'Souza, 246–67. Oxford: Oxford University Press.

Bledsoe, Caroline, Fatoumatta Banja, and Allan G. Hill. 1998. Reproductive mishaps and Western contraception: An African challenge to fertility theory. *Population and Development Review* 24:15–57.

Bledsoe, Caroline, and Monica F. Goubaud. 1985. The reinterpretation of Western pharmaceuticals among the Mende of Sierra Leone. *Social Science and Medicine* 21 (3): 275–82.

Bledsoe, Caroline, Jane I. Guyer, Barthélémy Kuate Defo, and Shobha Shagle. 1999. An anthropological vision and research logic: An Epi Info primer. Program of African Studies, Northwestern University, Evanston, Ill: Working Paper No. 7.

Bledsoe, Caroline, Jane I. Guyer, and Susana Lerner. 2000b. Introduction to *Fertility and the Male Life Cycle in the Era of Fertility Decline,* edited by Caroline Bledsoe, Susana Lerner, and Jane I. Guyer, 1–26. Oxford: Oxford University Press.

Bledsoe, Caroline, and William F. Hanks. 1998. Legitimate recuperation or illicit stalling: Time, contraceptive use, and the divided man in rural Gambia. Paper presented at the 1998 meeting of the Population Association of America, Chicago.

Bledsoe, Caroline, and Allan G. Hill. 1998. Social norms, natural fertility, and the resumption of postpartum "contact" in The Gambia. In *The Methods and Uses of Anthropological Demography,* edited by Alaka Malwade Basu and Peter Aaby, 268–97. Oxford: Oxford University Press.

Bledsoe, Caroline, Allan G. Hill, Umberto d'Alessandro, and Patricia Langerock. 1994. Constructing natural fertility: The use of Western contraceptive technologies in rural Gambia. *Population and Development Review* 20:81–113.

Bledsoe, Caroline, and Uche C. Isiugo-Abanihe. 1989. Strategies of child-fosterage among Mende "grannies" in Sierra Leone. In *Reproduction and Social Organization in Sub-Saharan Africa,* edited by R. Lesthaeghe, 442–74. Berkeley: University of California Press.

Bledsoe, Caroline, Susana Lerner, and Jane I. Guyer, eds. 2000a. *Fertility and the Male Life Cycle in the Era of Fertility Decline.* Oxford: Oxford University Press.

Boddy, Janice. 1989. *Wombs and Alien Spirits: Women, Men, and the Zar Cult in Northern Sudan.* Madison: University of Wisconsin Press.

———. 1995. The body nearer the self. *American Anthropologist* 97:134–37.

Boerma, J. T., and G. T. Bicego. 1992. Preceding birth intervals and child survival: Searching for pathways of influence. *Studies in Family Planning* 23:243–56.

Bohler, E., and S. Bergstrom. 1996. Child growth during weaning depends on whether mother is pregnant again. *Journal of Tropical Pediatrics* 42:104–9.

Bongaarts, John. 1978. A framework for analyzing the proximate determinants of fertility. *Population and Development Review* 4:105–32.

———. 1983. Introduction and overview to *Fertility, Biology, and Behavior: An Analysis of the Proximate Determinates of Behavior,* edited by John Bongaarts and Robert G. Potter, 1–20. New York: Academic.

Bongaarts, John, and Robert G. Potter. 1983. *Fertility, Biology, and Behavior: An Analysis of the Proximate Determinants.* New York: Academic.

Boone, Sylvia A. 1986. *Radiance from the Waters: Ideals of Feminine Beauty in Mende Art.* New Haven, Conn.: Yale University Press.

Boston Women's Health Collective. 1992. *The New Our Bodies, Ourselves: A Book by and for Women.* New York: Touchstone.

Bourdieu, Pierre. 1977. *Outline of a Theory of Practice,* trans. Richard Nice. Cambridge: Cambridge University Press.

———. 1984. *Distinction: A Social Critique of the Judgment of Taste,* trans. Richard Nice. Cambridge, Mass.: Harvard University Press.

————. 1990. *The Logic of Practice,* trans. Richard Nice. Stanford, Calif.: Stanford University Press.

Bourguinon, Erika, ed. 1980. *A World of Women: Anthropological Studies of Women in the Societies of the World.* New York: Praeger.

Bracher, M. D., and G. Santow. 1982. Breast-feeding in Central Java. *Population Studies* 36:413–29.

Brass, William. 1985. P-F synthesis and parity progression ratios. In *Advances in Methods for Estimating Fertility and Mortality from Limited and Defective Data.* London: Centre for Population Studies, London School of Hygiene and Tropical Medicine, University of London.

Brems, Susan, and Alan Berg. 1988. Eating down during pregnancy: Nutrition, obstetric, and cultural considerations in the third world. UN Advisory Group on Nutrition Discussion Paper, Sub-Committee on Nutrition, New York.

Bruce, Judith. 1987. Users' perspectives on contraceptive technology and delivery systems: Highlighting some feminist issues. *Technology in Society* 9 (3–4): 359–83.

Brunner, Jochen, Eva Melander, Margareta Krook-Brandt, and Peter A. Thomassen. 1992. Grand multiparity as an obstetric risk factor: A prospective case-conrol study. *European Journal of Obstetrics, Gynecology, and Reproductive Biology* 47:201–5.

Buckley, T., and A. Gottlieb. 1988. A critical appraisal of theories of menstrual symbolism. In *Blood Magic: The Anthropology of Menstruation,* edited by T. Buckley and A. Gottlieb, 1–53. Berkeley: University of California Press.

Caldwell, J. C. 1980. Mass education as a determinant of the timing of fertility decline. *Population and Development Review* 6:225–55.

————. 1982. *Theory of Fertility Decline.* London: Academic.

Caldwell, J. C., and P. Caldwell. 1977. The role of marital sexual abstinence in determining fertility: A study of the Yoruba in Nigeria. *Population Studies* 31:193–217.

————. 1981. The function of child-spacing in traditional societies and the direction of change. In *Child-Spacing in Tropical Africa: Traditions and Change,* edited by Hilary J. Page and Ron Lesthaeghe, 73–92. New York: Academic.

Caldwell, J. C., I. O. Orobuloye, and Pat Caldwell. 1992. Fertility decline in Africa: A new type of transition? *Population and Development Review* 18:211–42.

Campbell, K. L., and J. W. Wood. 1988. Fertility in traditional societies. In *Natural Human Fertility: Social and Biological Determinants,* edited by Peter Diggory, Malcolm Potts, and Sue Teper, 39–69. London: Macmillan.

Cantrelle, Pierre, and Henri Leridon. 1971. "Breast-feeding, mortality in childhood and fertility in a rural zone of Senegal. *Population Studies* 25:505–33.

Carney, Judith A. 1992. Peasant women and economic transformation in The Gambia. *Development and Change* 23 (2): 67–90.

Carney, Judith A., and Michael Watts. 1991. Disciplining women? Rice, mechanization, and the evolution of Mandinka gender relations in Senegambia. *Signs* 16:651–81.

Carr-Saunders, A. 1922. *The Population Problem: A Study in Human Evolution.* Oxford: Clarendon.

Carter, Anthony. 1995. Agency and fertility: For an ethnography of practice. In *Situat-*

ing Fertility: Anthropology and Demographic Analysis, edited by Susan Greenhalgh, 55–85. Cambridge: Cambridge University Press.

Casterline, John B. 1989a. Collecting data on pregnancy loss: A review of evidence from the World Fertility Survey. *Studies in Family Planning* 20:81–95.

———. 1989b. Maternal age, gravidity, and pregnancy spacing effects on spontaneous fetal mortality. *Social Biology* 36 (3–4): 186–212.

Castoriadis, Cornelius. 1984. *Crossroads in the Labyrinth.* Cambridge, Mass.: MIT Press.

Cecil, Rosanne, ed. 1996. *The Anthropology of Pregnancy Loss: Comparative Studies in Miscarriage, Stillbirth, and Neonatal Death.* Oxford and Washington, D.C.: Berg.

Chalmers, Iain, Murray Enkin, and Marc J. N. C. Keirse, eds. 1989. *Effective Care in Pregnancy and Childbirth,* vol. 1: *Pregnancy.* Oxford: Oxford Medical Publications.

Chan, K. C. 1982. Application of methods of measuring the impact of family planning programmes on fertility: The case of Hong Kong. In *Evaluation of the Impact of Family Planning Programmes on Fertility: Sources of Variance.* United Nations Dept. of International Economic and Social Affairs, Population Studies, No. 76, 41–64. ST/ESA/SER.A/76.

Chapman, Rachel. 2001. Endangering safe motherhood: Prenatal care as reproductive threat when medical norms exclude screening for social risks. Paper presented at the conference Discovering "Normality" in Health and the Reproductive Body. Program of African Studies, Northwestern University.

Chomsky, Noam. 1965. *Aspects of the Theory of Syntax.* Cambridge, Mass.: MIT Press.

Chudacoff, Howard P. 1989. *How Old are You? Age Consciousness in American Culture.* Princeton, N.J.: Princeton University Press.

Clark, Gracia. 1989. Money, sex, and cooking: Manipulation of the paid/unpaid boundary by Asante Market Women. In *The Social Economy of Consumption,* edited by Henry J. Rutz and Benjamin S. Orlove, 323–48. Monographs in Economic Anthropology, vol. 6. Lanham, Md.: University Press of America, Society for Economic Anthropology.

———. 2001. "Little by little": Models of legitimate and illegitimate accumulation for Kumasi market women. Paper presented at a workshop titled "Women and Work in Africa." Northwestern University.

Coale, Ansley. 1973. The demographic transition. In *International Union for the Scientific Study of Population,* vol. 1, *International Population Conference,* 53–72. Liège: International Union for the Scientific Study of Population.

———. 1986. The decline of fertility in Europe since the eighteenth century as a chapter in human demographic history. In *The Decline of Fertility in Europe,* edited by A. J. Coale and S. C. Watkins, 1–30. Princeton, N.J.: Princeton University Press.

Cohen, Barney. 1993. Fertility levels, differentials, and trends. In *Demographic Change in Sub-Saharan Africa,* edited by Karen A. Foote, Kenneth H. Hill, and Linda G. Martin, 1–67. Washington: National Research Council, National Academy Press.

———. 1998. The emerging fertility transition in Sub-Saharan Africa. *World Development* 26:1431–61.

Cohen, Lawrence. 1998. *No Aging in India: Alzheimer's, the Bad Family, and Other Modern Things*. Berkeley: University of California Press.

Coker, Jacob K. 1913. Polygamy defended. Lagos: pamphlet published by the author.

———. 1986a. Native marriage. [1915?] In *Jacob Kehinde Coker: Father of African Independent Churches*, edited by S. A. Dada, 109–16. Ibadan, Nigeria: AOWA Printers.

———. 1986b. The future of polygamy. [1936?] In *Jacob Kehinde Coker: Father of African Independent Churches*, edited by S. A. Dada, 170–76. Ibadan, Nigeria: AOWA Printers and Publishers. Printed and bound in Nigeria by The Mustard Printers, Idaban.

Collier, Jane Fishburne. 1974. Women in politics. In *Woman, Culture, and Society*, edited by Michelle Z. Rosaldo and Louise Lamphere, 89–96. Stanford, Calif.: Stanford University Press.

Collier, Jane Fishburne, and Sylvia Junko Yanagisako, eds. 1987. *Gender and Kinship: Essays Toward a Unified Analysis*. Stanford, Calif.: Stanford University Press.

Comaroff, Jean. 1985. *Body of Power, Spirit of Resistance: The Culture and History of a South African People*. Chicago: University of Chicago Press.

Comaroff, John L., and Jean Comaroff. 1992. *Ethnography and the Historical Imagination*. Boulder, Colo.: Westview.

Comaroff, John L., and Simon Roberts. 1981. *Rules and Processes: The Cultural Logic of Dispute in an African Context*, Chicago: University of Chicago Press.

Cooley, Charles H. 1902. *Human Nature and the Social Order*. New York: C. Scribner's Sons.

Cordell, D., and J. Gregory, eds. 1994. *African Population and Capitalism: Historical Perspectives*. Madison: University of Wisconsin Press.

Crowder, Michael. 1968. *West Africa Under Colonial Rule*. Evanston, Ill.: Northwestern University Press.

Csordas, Thomas. 1990. Embodiment as a paradigm for anthropology. *Ethos* 18: 5–47.

Dada, S. A., comp. 1986. *Jacob Kehinde Coker: Father of African Independent Churches*. Ibadan, Nigeria: Mustard Printers.

Davey Smith, George, Carole Hart, David Blane, Charles Gillis, and Victor Hawthorne. 1997. Lifetime socioeconomic position and mortality: A prospective observational study. *British Medical Journal* 314:547–52.

Davidson, Basil. 1987. *African Nationalism and the Problems of Nation-Building*. Lagos: Nigerian Institute of International Affairs.

Davis, Kingsley. 1986. Low fertility in evolutionary perspective. *Population and Development Review*, special supplement to vol. 12: *Below-Replacement Fertility in Industrialized Societies: Causes, Consequences, Policies*. Pp. 48–65.

Davis, Kingsley, and Judith Blake. 1956. Social structure and fertility: An analytic framework. *Economic Development and Cultural Change* 4:211–35.

Davis-Floyd, Robbie E. 1992. *Birth as an American Rite of Passage*. Berkeley: University of California Press.

Davis-Floyd, Robbie E., and Carolyn F. Sargent, eds. 1997. *Childbirth and Authoritative Knowledge: Cross-Cultural Perspectives.* Berkeley: University of California Press.

De Lee, Joseph B. 1904. *Notes on Obstetrics for the Junior and Senior Classes.* Chicago: Kentfield.

————. 1913. *The Principles and Practice of Obstetrics.* Philadelphia: W. B. Saunders.

Devisch, Renaat. 1993. *Weaving the Threads of Life: The Khita Gyn-Eco-Logical Healing Cult Among the Yaka.* Chicago: University of Chicago Press.

DeVries, Raymond G. 1989. Caregivers in pregnancy and childbirth. In *Effective Care in Pregnancy and Childbirth,* vol. 1: *Pregnancy,* edited by Iain Chalmers, Murray Enkin, and Marc J. N. C. Keirse, 143–61. Oxford: Oxford Medical Publications.

Diamond, Ian, Margaret Newby, and Sarah Varle. 1999. Female education and fertility: examining the links. In *Critical Perspectives on Schooling and Fertility in the Developing World,* edited by Caroline H. Bledsoe, John Casterline, Jennifer A. Johnson-Kuhn, and John Haaga, 23–48. Washington, D.C.: National Academy Press.

Di Leonardo, Micaela. 1987. The female world of cards and holidays: Women, families, and the work of kinship. *Signs* 12:440–53.

Donald, Ian. 1955. *Practical Obstetric Problems.* London: Lloyd-Luke.

————. 1979. *Practical Obstetric Problems.* 5th ed. London: Lloyd-Luke.

Douglas, Mary. 1966. *Purity and Danger: An Analysis of Concepts of Pollution and Taboo.* London: Routledge and Kegan Paul.

————. 1970. *Natural Symbols: Explorations in Cosmology.* London: Barrie and Rockliff.

Duden, Barbara. 1991. *The Woman beneath the Skin: A Doctor's Patients in Eighteenth-Century Germany.* Cambridge, Mass.: Harvard University Press.

Durkheim, Emile. 1915. *The Elementary Forms of the Religious Life.* London: Allen & Unwin.

————. 1951. *Suicide: A Study in Sociology,* trans. John A. Spaulding and George Simpson. New York: Free.

Easterlin, Richard A. 1978. The economics and sociology of fertility: A synthesis. In *Historical Studies of Changing Fertility,* edited by C. Tilly, 57–133. Princeton, N.J.: Princeton University Press.

Easterlin, Richard A., and Eileen M. Crimmins. 1985. *The Fertility Revolution: A Supply-Demand Analysis.* Chicago: University of Chicago Press.

Ebron, Paulla A. 1993. Negotiating the meaning of Africa: Mandinka praisesingers in transnational context. Ph.D. diss., University of Massachusetts at Amherst.

————. 1999. Tourists as pilgrims: Commercial fashioning of transatlantic politics. *American Ethnologist* 26 (4): 910–32.

Edholm, Felicity, Olivia Harris, and Kate Young. 1977. Conceptualising women. *Critique of Anthropology* 3:101–30.

Edwards, J., S. Franklin, E. Hirsch, F. Price, and M. Strathern. 1993. *Technologies of Procreation: Kinship in the Age of Assisted Conception.* Manchester: Manchester University Press.

Ellison, P. T. 1994. Advances in human reproductive ecology. *Annual Reviews of Anthropology* 23:255–75.

Emecheta, Buchi. 1979. *The Joys of Motherhood: A Novel*. New York: George Braziller.

Enel, Catherine, Gilles Pison, and Monique Lefebvre. 1994. Migration and social change: A case study of Mlomp, a Joola village in southern Senegal. In *Nuptiality in Sub-Saharan Africa: Contemporary Anthropological and Demographic Perspectives*, edited by Caroline Bledsoe and Gilles Pison, 92–113. Oxford: Clarendon.

Epple, Carolyn Anne. 1994. Inseparable and distinct: An understanding of Navajo Nadleehi in a traditional Navajo worldview. Ph.D. diss., Northwestern University.

Etienne, Mona, and Eleanor Leacock. 1980. Introduction to *Women and Colonization: Anthropological Perspectives*, edited by Mona Etienne and Eleanor Leacock, 1–24. New York: Praeger.

———, eds. 1980. *Women and Colonization: Anthropological Perspectives*. New York: Praeger.

Evans-Pritchard, E. E. 1940. *The Nuer: A Description of the Modes of Livelihood and Political Institutions of a Nilotic People*. Oxford: Clarendon.

Ezeh, Alex C., Michka Seroussi, and Hendrik Raggers. 1996. Men's fertility, contraceptive use, and reproductive preferences. DHS Comparative Studies, No. 18. Calverton, Md.: Macro International.

Fage, J. D., and Roland Oliver, eds. 1982. *The Cambridge History of Africa*. Cambridge: Cambridge University Press.

Fayed, H. M., S. F. Abid, and B. Stevens. 1993. Risk factors in extreme grand multiparity. *International Journal of Gynaecology and Obstetrics* 41 : 17–22.

Feierman, S., and J. Janzen, eds. 1992. *The Social Basis of Health and Healing in Africa*. Berkeley: University of California Press.

Feldman-Savelsburg, Pamela. 1999. *Plundered Kitchens, Empty Wombs: Threatened Reproduction and Identity in the Cameroon Grassfields*. Ann Arbor: University of Michigan Press.

Ferme, Mariane. 2001. *The Underneath of Things: Violence, History, and the Everyday in Sierra Leone*. Berkeley: University of California Press.

Fishbein, Morris, with Sol Theron De Lee. 1949. *Joseph Bolivar De Lee: Crusading Obstetrician*. New York: E. P. Dutton.

Flandrin, Jean Louis. 1979. *Families in Former Times: Kinship, Household, and Sexuality*. Cambridge: Cambridge University Press.

Fortes, Meyer. 1958. Introduction to *The Developmental Cycle in Domestic Groups*, edited by Jack Goody, 1–14. Cambridge: Cambridge University Press.

———. 1970. *Time and Social Structure and Other Essays*. London: University of London, Athlone Press.

———. 1978. Parenthood, marriage, and fertility in West Africa. In *Population and Development: High and Low Fertility in Poorer Countries*, edited by Geoffrey Hawthorne, 121–49. London: Frank Cass.

———, ed. 1962. *Marriage in Tribal Societies*. Cambridge: Published for the Dept. of Archaeology and Anthropology at the University Press.

Foucault, Michel. 1972. The formation of enunciated modalities. In *The Archaeology of Knowledge and the Discourse on Language*, trans. A. M. Sheridan Smith, 50–55. London: Tavistock.

———. 1979. *Discipline and Punish: The Birth of a Prison.* New York: Vintage.

———. 1980. Body/power. In *Power/Knowledge: Selected Interviews and Other Writings 1972–77,* edited and translated by C. Gordon, 55–62. New York: Pantheon.

Fox, Nicholas J. 1994. *Postmodernism, Sociology, and Health.* Toronto: University of Toronto Press.

Fox, Robin. 1967. *Kinship and Marriage: An Anthropological Perspective.* Harmondsworth: Penguin.

Frank, Odile, P. Grace Bianchi, and Aldo Campana. 1994. The end of fertility: Age, fecundity, and fecundability in women. *Journal of Biosocial Science* 26:349–68.

Franklin, Sarah. 1997. *Embodied Progress: A Cultural Account of Assisted Conception.* New York: Routledge.

———. 1998. Making miracles: Scientific progress and the facts of life. In *Reproducing Reproduction: Kinship, Power, and Technological Innovation,* edited by Sarah Franklin and Helena Ragoné, 102–17. Philadelphia: University of Pennsylvania Press.

Franklin, Sarah, and Helena Ragoné, eds. 1998. *Reproducing Reproduction: Kinship, Power, and Technological Innovation.* Philadelphia: University of Pennsylvania Press.

Freedman, Ronald, and Deborah Freedman. 1992. The role of family planning programmes as a fertility determinant. In *Family Planning Programmes and Fertility,* edited by J. F. Phillips and J. A. Ross, 10–27. Oxford: Clarendon.

Friedl, Ernestine. 1962. *Vasilika: A Village in Modern Greece.* New York: Holt, Rinehart and Winston.

Frische, R. E., and R. Revelle. 1970. Height and weight at menarche and a hypothesis of critical body weights and adolescent events. *Science* 169:397–99.

Gadamer, Hans-Georg. 1994. *Truth and Method.* New York: Continuum.

Gamble, David. 1955. *Economic Conditions in Two Mandinka Villages: Kerewan and Keneba.* London: Colonial Office.

Geertz, Clifford. 1973. Ethos, world view, and the analysis of sacred symbols. In *The Interpretation of Cultures,* 128–41. New York: Basic.

———. 1975. Common sense as a cultural system. *Antioch Review* 33:5–26.

Geertz, Hildred, and Clifford Geertz. 1975. *Kinship in Bali.* Chicago: University of Chicago Press.

Gell, Alfred. 1992. *The Anthropology of Time: Cultural Constructions of Temporal Maps and Images.* Oxford: Berg.

Geronimus, Arline. 1987. On teenage childbearing and neonatal mortality in the United States. *Population and Development Review* 13:245–79.

———. 1992. The weathering hypothesis and the health of African American women and infants: Evidence and speculations. *Ethnicity and Disease* 2:207–21.

Giddens, Anthony. 1977. *Central Problems in Social Theory: Action, Structure, and Contradictions in Social Analysis.* Berkeley: University of California Press.

Gillmer, Michael D. G., Philip J. Steer, and Julian Woolfson. 1991. *100 Case Histories in Obstetrics and Gynaecology.* Edinburgh: Churchill Livingstone.

Ginsburg, Faye, and Rayna Rapp. 1991. The politics of reproduction. *Annual Review of Anthropology* 20:311–43.

————. 1995. Introduction: Conceiving the new world order. In *Conceiving the New World Order: The Global Politics of Reproduction,* eds. Faye D. Ginsburg and Rayna Rapp, 1–17. Berkeley: University of California Press.

Gluckman, Max. 1950. Kinship and marriage among the Lozi of Northern Rhodesia and the Zulu of Natal. In *African Systems of Kinship and Marriage,* edited by A. R. Radcliffe-Brown and Daryll Forde, 166–206. London: Oxford University Press.

Goldman, N., and A. Pebley. 1989. The demography of polygyny in sub-Saharan Africa. In *Reproduction and Social Organization in Sub-Saharan Africa,* edited by Ron Lesthaeghe, 212–37. Berkeley: University of California Press.

Goodenough, W. H. 1955. A problem in Malayo-Polynesian social organization. *American Anthropologist* 57:71–83.

Goody, Jack, ed. 1958. *The Developmental Cycle in Domestic Groups.* Cambridge: Cambridge University Press.

Gordon, Linda. 1976. *Woman's Body, Woman's Rights: A Social History of Birth Control in America.* New York: Grossman.

Gottlieb, Alma. 1998. Do infants have religion? The spiritual lives of Beng babies. *American Anthropologist* 100 (1): 122–35.

Govindasamy, Pavalavalli, M. Kathryn Stewart, Shea O. Rutstein, J. Ties Boerma, and A. Elisabeth Sommerfelt. 1993. High-risk births and maternity care. Demographic and Health Surveys Comparative Studies, No. 8. Columbia, Md.: Macro International.

Gramsci, Antonio. 1971. *Selections from the Prison Notebooks.* London: Lawrence & Wishart.

Gray, B. M. 1994. Enga birth, maturation, and survival: Physiological characteristics of the life cycle in the New Guinea Highlands. In *Ethnography of Fertility and Birth,* edited by C. MacCormack, 65–103. Prospect Heights, Ill.: Waveland.

Greene, Diana, Akin Bankole, and Charles Westoff. 1997. The effect of contraceptive use for spacing on the length of the birth interval. Paper presented at the Population Association of America annual meeting, Washington, D.C.

Greenhalgh, Susan. 1994. Controlling births and bodies in village China. *American Ethnologist* 21:3–30.

————. 1996. The social construction of population science: An intellectual, institutional, and political history of twentieth-century demography. *Comparative Studies in Society and History* 38 (1): 26–66.

Gregson, Simon, Tom Zhuwau, Roy M. Anderson, and Stephen K. Chandiwana. 1998. Is there evidence for behaviour change in response to AIDS in rural Zimbabwe? *Social Science and Medicine* 46:321–30.

Guyer, Jane I. 1993. Wealth in people and self-realization in equatorial Africa. *Man* (n.s.) 28:243–65.

————. 1996. Traditions of invention in Equatorial Africa. *African Studies Review* 39:1–28.

————. 1997. *Thresholds and Conversions: The Social Life of Money in Africa.* Evanston, Ill.: Northwestern University. Typescript.

————. 1998. Anthropology: The study of social and cultural originality. Paper prepared for the International Symposium on Social Sciences and the Challenges of Globalization in Africa. University of Witswatersrand, Johannesburg.

———. 2000. Traditions of studying paternity in social anthropology. In *Fertility and the Male Life Cycle in the Era of Fertility Decline,* edited by Caroline Bledsoe, Susana Lerner, and Jane I. Guyer, 61–90. Oxford: Oxford University Press.

Hafkin, Nancy, and Edna Bay, eds. 1976. *Women in Africa: Studies in Social and Economic Change.* Stanford, Calif.: Stanford University Press.

Halbwachs, Maurice. 1980. *The Collective Memory,* trans. F. J. Ditter Jr. and V. Y. Ditter. New York: Harper & Row.

Hammel, Eugene. 1990. A theory of culture for demography. *Population and Development Review* 16 : 433–85.

Hanks, William F. 1996. *Language and Communicative Practices.* Boulder, Colo.: Westview.

Hannerz, Ulf. 1996. *Transnational Connections: Culture, People, Places.* London: Routledge.

Hansen, Karen Tranberg, ed. 1992. *African Encounters with Domesticity.* New Brunswick, N.J.: Rutgers University Press.

Hardin, K. L. 1993. *The Aesthetics of Action: Continuity and Change in a West African Town.* Washington, D.C.: Smithsonian Institution Press.

Hareven, Tamara. 1994. Aging and generational relations: A historical and life course perspective. *Annual Review of Sociology* 20 : 437–61.

Hartmann, Betsy. 1987 *Reproductive Rights and Wrongs: The Global Politics of Population Control and Contraceptive Choice.* New York: Harper & Row.

Haswell, Margaret R. 1975. *The Nature of Poverty: A Case-History of the First Quarter-Century After World War II.* London: Macmillan.

Hayflick, Leonard. 1994. *How and Why We Age.* New York: Ballantine Books.

Henry, Louis. 1961. Some data on natural fertility. *Eugenics Quarterly* 8 : 81–91.

Herlihy, David. 1985. *Medieval Households.* Cambridge, Mass.: Harvard University Press.

Herskovits, Melville. 1938. *Dahomey, an Ancient West African Kingdom,* vol. 1. New York: J. J. Augustin.

Hill, Allan G. 1993. Breaking free: Alternatives to the Lexis diagram. Paper for the International Union for the Scientific Study of Population meeting New Approaches to Anthropological Demography, Barcelona, 10–13 November 1993.

———. 1997. "Truth lies in the eye of the beholder": The nature of evidence in demography and anthropology. In *Anthropological Demography: Toward a New Synthesis,* edited by David I. Kertzer and Tom Fricke, 223–47. Chicago: University of Chicago Press.

Hill, Allan G., Caroline H. Bledsoe, Umberto d'Allessandro, and Patricia Langerock. 1992. Report on the demographic survey of the MRC Main Study Area (the North Bank Villages Surrounding Farafenni). Boston: Department of Population and International Health, Harvard School of Public Health.

Hill, Allan G., Mary C. Hill, Pierre Gomez, and Gijs Walraven. 1996. Report on the living standards survey conducted in the villages of the MRC Main Study Area,

North Bank Division, Republic of The Gambia in June–July 1996. Banjul, The Gambia: Medical Research Council.

Hill, Catherine A. 1994. An investigation into family building patterns and fertility determinants in the Gambia, West Africa. Master's thesis, University of London.

Hobcraft, John. 1992. Fertility patterns and child survival: A comparative analysis. *Population Bulletin of the United Nations* 33 : 1–31.

Hobcraft, John, John W. McDonald, and Shea Rutstein. 1983. Child-spacing effects on infant and early child mortality. *Population Index* 49 : 585–618.

———. 1985. Demographic determinants of infant and early child mortality: A comparative analysis. *Population Studies* 39 : 363–85.

Hodgson, Dennis. 1991. The ideological origins of the Population Association of America. *Population and Development Review* 17 (1): 1–34.

Hoëm, Jan M. 1990. Social policy and recent fertility change in Sweden. *Population and Development Review* 16 : 735–48.

Hofmeyr, G. Justus. 1989. Suspected fetopelvic disproportion. In *Effective Care in Pregnancy and Childbirth*, vol. 1: *Pregnancy*, edited by Iain Chalmers, Murray Enkin, and Marc J. N. C. Keirse, 493–98. Oxford: Oxford Medical Publications.

Holmes, H. B., ed. 1992. *Issues in Reproductive Technology: An Anthology*. New York: Garland.

Homiak, John. 1995. The Jamaican body social. Review of *One Blood: The Jamaican Body*, by Elisa J. Sobo. *American Anthropologist* 97 : 138–39.

Hopkins, Nicholas S. 1971. Maninka [*sic*] social organization. In *Papers on the Manding*, edited by Carleton T. Hodge, 99–128. Bloomington: Indiana University Press.

Hoskins, Janet. 1994. Review of *The Anthropology of Time: Cultural Constructions of Temporal Maps and Images*, by Alfred Gell. *Man* 29 (3): 766–67.

Howell, Nancy. 1979. *Demography of the Dobe !Kung*. New York: Academic.

Hrdy, Sarah Blaffer. 1999. *Mother Nature: A History of Mothers, Infants, and Natural Selection*. New York: Pantheon.

Hubert, Henri, and Marcel Mauss. 1964. *Sacrifice: Its Nature and Function*, trans. W. D. Halls. Chicago: University of Chicago Press.

Hughes, P. F., and J. Morrison. 1994. Grandmultiparity—not to be feared? An analysis of grandmultiparous women receiving modern antenatal care. *International Journal of Gynaecology and Obstetrics* 44 : 211–17.

Husserl, Edmund. 1964. *The Idea of Phenomenology*, trans. William P. Alston and George Nakhnikian. The Hague: M. Nijhoff.

Iliffe, J. 1989. The origins of African population growth. Review of *African Population and Capitalism: Historical Perspective*, edited by D. Cordell and J. Gregory. *Journal of African History* 30 : 165–69.

Inhorn, Marcia. 1994. *Quest for Conception: Gender, Infertility, and Egyptian Medical Tradition*. Philadelphia: University of Pennsylvania Press.

Interviewer's Manual For Use with Model "A" Questionnaire for High Contraceptive Prevalence Countries. 2000. Measure DHS+ Basic Documentation—3. Calverton, Md: Macro International.

Interviewer's Manual For Use with Model "B" Questionnaire For Low Contraceptive Prevalence Countries. 1997. Measure DHS+ Basic Documentation—3. Calverton, Md: Macro International.

Investigating Committee of the City Homes Association (Chicago), 1901. *Tenement Conditions in Chicago.* Text by Robert Hunter.

Isichei, P. A. C. 1978. The basic meaning of a child through Asaba personal names. In *Marriage, Fertility, and Parenthood in West Africa,* vol. 1, edited by C. Oppong, G. Adaba, M. Bekombo-Priso, and J. Mogey, 325–41. Canberra: Australian National University Press.

Jackson, Cecile. 1997. "Working bodies and gender divisions of labour." Paper presented at the Development Studies Association Annual Conference, University of East Anglia, Norwich.

Jacobson, Jodi. 1993. Women's health: The price of poverty. In *The Health of Women: A Global Perspective,* edited by Marge Koblinsky, Judith Timyan, and Jill Gay, 3–31. Boulder, Colo.: Westview.

Jacobson-Widding, Anita, ed. 1991. *Body and Space: Symbolic Models of Unity and Division in African Cosmology and Experience.* Uppsala Studies in Cultural Anthropology, vol. 16. Uppsala: Academiae Ubsaliensis.

Jacobson-Widding, Anita, and Roger Jeffery. 1996. Delayed periods and falling babies: The ethnophysiology and politics of pregnancy loss in rural North India. In *The Anthropology of Pregnancy Loss: Comparative Studies in Miscarriage, Stillbirth, and Neonatal Loss,* edited by Rosanne Cecil, 11–37. Oxford: Berg.

Jeffery, Patricia, Roger Jeffery, and Andrew Lyon. 1988. *Labour Pains and Labour Power: Women and Childbearing in India.* London: Zed.

Jejeebhoy, S. J. 1995. *Women's Education, Autonomy, and Reproductive Behavior: Experience from Developing Countries.* Oxford: Clarendon.

Jelliffe, Derrick B., and E. F. Patrice Jelliffe. 1978. *Human Milk in the Modern World: Psychosocial, Nutritional, and Economic Significance.* Oxford: Oxford University Press.

Jelliffe, Derrick B., and I. Maddocks. 1964. Notes on ecologic malnutrition in the New Guinea Highlands. *Clinical Pediatrics* 3:432–38.

Johnson-Kuhn, Jennifer. 2000. An uncertain honor: Schooling and family formation in Catholic Cameroon. Ph.D. diss., Northwestern University.

Jordan, Brigette. 1983. *Birth in Four Cultures: A Cross-Cultural Investigation of Childbirth in Yucatan, Holland, Sweden, and the United States.* Montreal: Eden.

Kalipeni, Ezekiel, and Eliya M. Zulu. 1993. Gender differences in knowledge and attitudes toward modern and traditional methods of child spacing in Malawi. *Population Research and Policy Review* 12:103–22.

Karp, Ivan. 1980. Beer drinking and social experience in an African society: An essay in formal sociology. In *Explorations in African Systems of Thought,* edited by Ivan Karp and Charles S. Bird, 83–119. Bloomington: Indiana University Press.

Keller, Evelyn Fox. 1985. *Reflections on Gender and Science.* New Haven, Conn.: Yale University Press.

Kenya Demographic and Health Survey, Final Report. 1993. Calverton, Md.: Macro International.

Kertzer, David I., and Jennie Keith, eds. 1984. *Age and Anthropological Theory*. Ithaca, N.Y.: Cornell University Press.

Kirk, Dudley, and Bernard Pillet. 1998. Fertility levels, trends, and differentials in sub-Saharan Africa in the 1980s and 1990s. *Studies in Family Planning* 29 (1): 1–22.

Kitzinger, Sheila. 1994. *The Year After Childbirth: Surviving and Enjoying the First Year of Motherhood*. New York: Charles Scribner's Sons.

Knodel, John. 1983. Natural fertility: Age patterns, levels, and trends. In *Determinants of Fertility in Developing Countries*, vol. 1: *Supply and Demand for Children*, edited by Rodolfo A. Bulatao and Ronald D. Lee, 61–102. New York: Academic.

Knodel, John, Peerasit Kamnuansilpa, and Apichat Chamratrithirong. 1985. Infant feeding practices, postpartum amenorrhea, and contraceptive use in Thailand. *Studies in Family Planning* 16:302–11.

Koblinsky, M. A., Oona M. R. Campbell, and Sioban D. Harlow. 1993. Mother and more: A broader perspective on women's health. In *The Health of Women: A Global Perspective*, edited by Marge Koblinsky, Judith Timyan, and Jill Gay, 33–62. Boulder, Colo.: Westview.

Kolon, Nita. 1980. *Mothers-in-Law*. Ijebu-Ode, Nigeria: Natona.

———. 1982. *The Other Woman*. Ijebu-Ode, Nigeria: Natona.

Kopytoff, Igor. 1971. Ancestors as elders in Africa. *Africa* 4:129–42.

———, ed. 1987. *The African Frontier: The Reproduction of Traditional African Societies*. Bloomington: Indiana University Press.

Kratz, Corinne A. 1994. *Affecting Performance: Meaning, Movement, and Experience in Okiek Women's Initiation*. Washington, D.C.: Smithsonian Institution Press.

Kreiter, Shelley R., Robert P. Schwartz, Henry N. Kirkman Jr., Philippa A. Charlton, Ali S. Calikoglu, and Marsha L. Davenport. 2000. Nutritional rickets in African American breast-fed infants. *Journal of Pediatrics* 137 (2): 153–57.

Latour, Bruno. 1986. Visualization and cognition: Thinking with eyes and hands. In *Knowledge and Society: Studies in the Sociology of Culture Past and Present*, vol. 6, edited by Henrika Kuklick and Elizabeth Long, 1–40, Greenwich, Conn: JAI.

Laumann, Edward O., John H. Gagnon, Robert T. Michael, and Stuart Michaels. 1994. *The Social Organization of Sexuality: Sexual Practices in the United States*. Chicago: University of Chicago Press.

Layne, Linda L. 1996. "Never such innocence again": Irony, nature and technoscience in narratives of pregnancy loss. In *The Anthropology of Pregnancy Loss: Comparative Studies in Miscarriage, Stillbirth, and Neonatal Death*, edited by Rosanne Cecil, 131–52. Oxford: Berg.

———. 1999. *Transformative Motherhood: On Giving and Getting in a Consumer Culture*. New York: New York University Press.

Leavitt, Judith Walzer. 1986. *Brought to Bed: 1750–1950*. New York: Oxford University Press.

———. 1988. Joseph B. De Lee and the practice of preventive obstetrics. *American Journal of Public Health* 78:1353–59.

Leidy, L. E. 1994. Biological aspects of menopause: Across the lifespan. *Annual Review of Anthropology* 23:231–53.

Leridon, Henri. 1975. Biostatistics of human reproduction. In *Measuring the Effect of Family Planning Programs on Fertility*, edited by C. Chandrasekaran and A. I. Hermalin, 93–131. Dolhain, Belgium: Ordina Editions.

Lesthaeghe, Ron. 1989. Production and reproduction in Sub-Saharan Africa: An overview of organizing principles. In *Reproduction and Social Organization in Sub-Saharan Africa*, edited by Ron Lesthaeghe, 13–59. Berkeley: University of California Press.

Lesthaeghe, Ron, P. O. Ohadike, J. Kocher, and H. J. Page. 1981. Child-spacing and fertility in sub-Saharan Africa: An overview of issues. In *Child-Spacing in Tropical Africa: Traditions and Change*, edited by Hilary J. Page and Ron Lesthaeghe, 3–23. London: Academic.

Lesthaeghe, Ron, Camille Vanderhoeft, Samuel Gaisie, and Ghislaine Delaine. 1989. Regional variation in components of child-spacing: The role of women's education. In *African Reproduction and Social Organization*, edited by Ron Lesthaeghe, 122–66. Berkeley: University of California Press.

Levin, Elise C. 2001. The meaning of menstrual management in a high fertility society—Guinea, West Africa. In *Regulating Menstruation: Beliefs, Practices, Interpretations*, edited by Etienne van de Walle and Elisha P. Renne. Chicago: University of Chicago Press.

Lévi-Strauss, Claude. 1969a. *The Elementary Structures of Kinship*, trans. James Harle Bell, John Richard von Sturmer, and Rodney Needham, editor. Boston: Beacon.

———. 1969b. *The Raw and the Cooked*, trans. John and Doreen Weightman. New York: Harper & Row.

Leyser, K. J. 1979. *Rule and Conflict in Early Medieval Society: Ottonian Saxony*. London: Edward Arnold.

Lieberman, Janet Joseph. 1976. Childbirth practices: From darkness into light. *Journal of Gynecologic and Neonatal Nursing* 5 (3): 41–45.

Lightman, Alan. 1993. *Einstein's Dreams: A Novel*. New York: Werner.

Linares, Olga F. 1992. *Power, Prayer, and Production: The Jola of Casamance, Senegal*. Cambridge: Cambridge University Press.

Lindenbaum, Shirley, and Margaret Lock, eds. 1993. *Knowledge, Power and Practice: The Anthropology of Medicine and Everyday Life*. Berkeley: University of California Press.

Livi-Bacci, Massimo. 1992. *A Concise History of World Population*, trans. Carl Ipsen. Cambridge, Mass.: Blackwell.

Lock, Margaret. 1993a. Cultivating the body: Anthropology and epistemologies of bodily practice and knowledge. *Annual Review of Anthropology* 22 : 133–55.

———. 1993b. *Encounters with Aging: Mythologies of Menopause in Japan and North America*. Berkeley: University of California Press.

———. 1993c. The politics of mid-life and menopause: Ideologies for the second sex in North America and Japan. In *Knowledge, Power, and Practice: The Anthropology of Medicine and Everyday Life*, edited by Shirley Lindenbaum and Margaret Lock, 330–63. Berkeley: University of California Press.

Lockwood, Matthew. 1995. Structure and behavior in the social demography of Africa. *Population and Development Review* 21 : 1–32.

————. 1996. Contrast and continuity in the African fertility transition: A cultural hypothesis. Research Paper 28, Geography Laboratory, University of Sussex.

Lorimer, Frank. 1954. *Culture and Human Fertility: A Study of the Relation of Cultural Conditions to Fertility in Non-Industrial and Transitional Societies.* Paris: UNESCO.

Luck, Margaret. 1997. Effects of a Family Planning Intervention in Rural Gambia. Ph.D. diss., Harvard University.

MacCormack, Carol P. 1979. Sande: The public face of a secret society. In *The New Religions of Africa,* edited by B. Jules-Rosette, 27–37. Norwood, N.J.: Ablex.

————. 1994. Health, fertility and birth in Moyamba District, Sierra Leone. In *Ethnography of Fertility and Birth,* 105–29. Prospect Heights, Ill.: Waveland.

MacCormack, Carol P., and Marilyn Strathern, eds. 1994. *Nature, Culture, and Gender.* Cambridge: Cambridge University Press.

Macpherson, Gordon. 1992. *Black's Medical Dictionary.* Lanham, Md.: Barnes and Noble Books.

Madhavan, Sangeetha, and Caroline H. Bledsoe. 2001. The compound as locus of fertility management: The case of The Gambia. *Journal of Culture, Health, and Sexuality* 3 (4): 451–68.

Malthus, T. R. 1926. *First Essay on Population, 1798.* With notes by James Bonar. London: Macmillan.

Mann, Kristin. 1994. The historical roots and cultural logic of outside marriage in colonial Lagos. In *Nuptiality in sub-Saharan Africa: Contemporary Anthropological and Demographic Perspectives,* edited by Caroline Bledsoe and Gilles Pison. Oxford: Clarendon Press. Pp. 167–93.

Margolis, Sara Pacqué. 1997. Population policy, research and the Cairo Plan of Action: New direction for the Sahel? *International Family Planning Perspectives* 23 (2): 86–89.

Martin, Emily. 1987. *The Woman in the Body: A Cultural Analysis of Reproduction.* Boston: Beacon.

————. 1991. The egg and the sperm: How science has constructed a romance based on stereotypical male-female roles. *Signs* 16 (3): 485–501.

————. 1998. Anthropology and the cultural study of science. *Science, Technology, & Human Values* 23 (1): 24–44.

Mason, Karen Oppenheim. 1997. Explaining fertility transitions. *Demography* 34: 443–54.

Mason, Karen Oppenheim, and Anju M. Taj. 1987. Differences between women's and men's reproductive goals in developing countries. *Population and Development Review* 13:611–38.

Maupassant, Guy de. 1969. The necklace. In *Short Stories: An Anthology,* edited by Norman Nathan, 200–7. Indianapolis: Bobbs-Merrill.

Mauss, Marcel. 1973. Techniques of the body. *Economy and Society* 2:70–88.

————. 1990. *The Gift: The Form and Reason for Exchange in Archaic Societies.* London: Routledge.

McDade, Thomas W., and Carol M. Worthman. 1998. The weanling's dilemma reconsidered: A biocultural analysis of breastfeeding ecology. *Journal of Developmental and Behavioral Pediatrics* 19:286–99.

McKaughan, Molly. 1989. *The Biological Clock: Balancing Marriage, Motherhood, and Career.* Harmondsworth: Penguin.

McKenna, James. 2000. Cultural influences on infant and childhood sleep biology, and the science that studies it: toward a more inclusive paradigm. In *Sleep and Breathing in Children,* edited by Gerald M. Loughlin, John Carroll, and Carol M. Marcos, 99–130. New York: Marcel Dekker.

McKeon, Richard. 1994. *On Knowing — The Natural Sciences,* compiled by David B. Owen; edited by David B. Owen and Zahava K. McKeon. Chicago: University of Chicago Press.

McLaren, Angus. 1990. *A History of Contraception: From Antiquity to the Present.* Oxford: B. Blackwell.

McLennan, John Ferguson. 1886. *Studies in Ancient History: Comprising a Reprint of Primitive Marriage: An Inquiry into the Origin of the Form of Capture in Marriage Ceremonies.* London: Macmillan.

McNeil, Maureen, Ian Varcoe, and Steven Yearley, eds. 1990. *The New Reproductive Technologies.* New York: St. Martin's.

Mead, George H. 1934. *Mind, Self, and Society from the Standpoint of a Social Behaviorist.* Chicago: University of Chicago Press.

———. 1980. *The Philosophy of the Present.* Chicago: University of Chicago Press.

Mead, Margaret. 1928. *Coming of Age in Samoa: A Psychological Study of Primitive Youth for Western Civilisation.* Foreword by Franz Boas. New York: W. Morrow.

Medical Research Council. 1995. Annual Report. Banjul, The Gambia: MRC Laboratories.

Meillassoux, Claude. 1981. *Maidens, Meal, and Money: Capitalism and the Domestic Community.* Cambridge: Cambridge University Press.

Merchant, Kathleen, Raynaldo Martorell, and Jere D. Hass. 1990. Consequences for maternal nutrition of reproductive stress across consecutive pregnancies. *American Journal of Clinical Nutrition* 52:616–20.

Merleau-Ponty, Maurice. 1963. *The Structure of Behavior,* trans. Alden L. Fisher, Boston: Beacon.

Miller, Jane E., and Rebecca Huss-Ashmore. 1989. Do reproductive patterns affect maternal nutritional status? An analysis of maternal depletion in Lesotho. *American Journal of Human Biology* 1:409–19.

Moberg, Vilhelm. 1951. *The Emigrants: A Novel,* trans. Gustaf Lannestock. New York: Simon & Schuster.

Montgomery, Mark R., and Barney Cohen, eds. 1998. *From Death to Birth: Mortality Decline and Reproductive Change.* Washington, D.C.: National Academy Press.

Montgomery, Mark R., and Cynthia B. Lloyd. 1996. Fertility and maternal and child health. In *The Impact of Population Growth on Well-Being in Developing Countries,* edited by Dennis A. Ahlburg, Allen C. Kelley, and Karen O. Mason. 37–65. New York: Springer-Verlag.

Moore, Henrietta L. 1994. *A Passion for Difference: Essays in Anthropology and Gender.* Bloomington: Indiana University Press.

Morgan, Lewis Henry. 1970. *Systems of Consanguinity and Affinity of the Human Family.* Lincoln: University of Nebraska Press.

Morgan, S. Philip, Susan Cotts Watkins, and Douglas Ewbank. Generating Americans: Ethnic differences in fertility. In *After Ellis Island: Newcomers and Natives in the 1910 Census,* edited by Susan Cotts Watkins, 83–124. New York: Russell Sage Foundation.

Morsy, Soheir A. 1995. Deadly reproduction among Egyptian women: Maternal mortality and the medicalization of population control. In *Conceiving the New World Order: The Global Politics of Reproduction,* edited by Faye D. Ginsburg and Rayna Rapp, 162–76. Berkeley: University of California Press.

Munn, Nancy D. 1986. *The Fame of Gawa: A Symbolic Study of Value Transformation in a Massim (Papua, New Guinea) Society.* Cambridge: Cambridge University Press.

———. 1992. The cultural anthropology of time: A critical essay. *Annual Review of Anthropology* 21:93–123.

Murdock, George P. 1975. *Outline of World Cultures.* 5th ed. New Haven, Conn.: Human Relations Area Files.

Murphy, William P., and Caroline H. Bledsoe. 1987. Kinship and territory in the history of a Kpelle chiefdom (Liberia). In *The African Frontier: The Reproduction of Traditional African Societies,* edited by Igor Kopytoff, 121–47. Bloomington: Indiana University Press.

Murphy-Lawless, Jo. 1998. *Reading Birth and Death: A History of Obstetric Thinking.* Bloomington: Indiana University Press.

Mussalam, B. F. 1983. *Sex and Society in Islam: Birth Control Before the Nineteenth Century.* Cambridge: Cambridge University Press.

National Research Council. 1989. *Contraception and Reproduction: Health Consequences for Women and Children in the Developing World.* Working Group on the Health Consequences of Contraceptive Use and Controlled Fertility. Washington, D.C.: National Academy Press.

———. 1993a. *Factors Affecting Contraceptive Use in Sub-Saharan Africa.* Working Group on Factors Affecting Contraceptive Use, Panel on the Population Dynamics of Africa. Washington, D.C.: National Academy Press.

———. 1993b. *The Social Dynamics of Adolescent Fertility in Sub-Saharan Africa,* edited by Caroline H. Bledsoe and Barney Cohen. Washington, D.C.: National Academy Press.

———. 1997a. *Between Zeus and the Salmon: The Biodemography of Longevity,* edited by Kenneth W. Wachter and Caleb E. Finch. Washington, D.C.: National Academy Press.

———. 1997b. *Reproductive Health in Developing Countries: Expanding Dimensions, Building Solutions,* edited by Amy O. Tsui, Judith Wasserheit, and John G. Haaga, Washington, D.C.: National Academy Press.

Needham, Rodney. 1974. *Remarks and Inventions: Skeptical Essays About Kinship.* London: Tavistock.

Newman, Karen. 1996. *Fetal Positions: Individualism, Science, Visuality.* Stanford, Calif.: Stanford University Press.

Nichter, Mark. 1989. *Anthropology and International Health: South Asian Case Studies.* Boston: Kluwer.

Nigeria Demographic and Health Survey, Final Report. 1990. Calverton, Md.: Macro International.

Nord, D. E. 1994. Review of *Love and Toil: Motherhood in Outcast London, 1870–1918,* by Ellen Ross. *The Nation,* 8/15 August.

Notestein, Frank W. 1953. Economic problems of population change. In *Proceedings of the International Conference of Agricultural Economists, Eighth Conference, 1952.* 13–31. London: Oxford University Press.

Nyabally, Lamin, and Sheriff Sonko. 1997. An assessment of the influence of sex preference on fertility in The Gambia. Program of African Studies, Evanston, Ill.: Northwestern University. Typescript.

Obermeyer, Carla Makhlouf. 1992. Islam, women, and politics: The demography of Arab countries. *Population and Development Review* 18:33–60.

O'Connor, Timothy C. F., Denis Cavanagh, and Robert A. Knuppel. 1966. Intrapartum emergencies. In *Obstetric Emergencies,* edited by Denis Cavanagh, Ralph E. Woods, Timothy C. F. O'Connor, and Robert A. Knuppel, 210–69. Philadelphia: Harper & Row.

Ohadike, Patrick O. 1997. Attributions of age in African censuses and surveys. Paper presented at the IUSSP seminar "Age—between nature and culture." Max Planck Institute, Rostock, Germany.

Okri, Ben. 1992. *The Famished Road.* New York: N. A. Talese.

Oldfield, Carlton. 1921. *Herman's Difficult Labour: A Guide for Students and Practitioners.* London: Cassel.

Oliver, Roland Anthony, ed. 1967. *The Middle Age of African History.* London: Oxford University Press.

Oliver, Roland Anthony, and Anthony Atmore. 1981. *Africa Since 1800.* 3d ed. Cambridge: Cambridge University Press.

Olshansky, S. J., B. A. Carnes, and D. Grahn. 1998. Confronting the boundaries of human longevity. *American Scientist* 86:52–61.

Olusanya, P. O. 1969. Modernisation and the level of fertility in Western Nigeria. In *International Union for the Scientific Study of Population,* 1:812–25. London: International Population Conference.

Oppong, C., and W. Bleek. 1982. Economic models and having children: Some evidence from Kwahu, Ghana. *Africa* 52:15–33.

Orobaton, Nosa. 2000. Dimensions of sexuality among Nigerian men: Perspectives for fertility and reproductive health. In *Fertility and the Male Life Cycle in the Era of Fertility Decline,* edited by Caroline Bledsoe, Susana Lerner, and Jane I. Guyer, 207–30. Oxford: Oxford University Press.

Ortner, Sherry B. 1974. Is female to male as nature is to culture? In *Women, Culture, and Society,* edited by Michelle Z. Rosaldo and Louise Lamphere, 67–87. Stanford, Calif.: Stanford University Press.

Ortner, Sherry B., and Harriet Whitehead, eds. 1981. *Sexual Meanings: The Cultural Construction of Gender and Sexuality.* Cambridge: Cambridge University Press.

Oxumba, B. C., and A. O. Igwegbe. 1992. The challenge of grandmultiparity in Nigerian obstetric practice. *International Journal of Gynaecology and Obstetrics* 37: 259–64.

Page, Hilary J., and Ron Lesthaeghe, eds. 1981. *Child-Spacing in Tropical Africa: Traditions and Change.* London: Academic.

Paulson, Richard J., Melvin H. Thornton, Mary M. Francis, and Herminia S. Salvador. 1997. Successful pregnancy in a 63-year-old woman. *Fertility and Sterility* 67:949–51.

Pavelka, Mary S. M., and Linda Marie Fedigan. 1991. Menopause: A comparative life-history perspective. *Yearbook of Physical Anthropology* 34:13–38.

Pearce, Tola Olu. 1995. Women's reproductive practices and biomedicine: Cultural conflicts and transformations in Nigeria. In *Conceiving the New World Order: The Global Politics of Reproduction,* edited by Faye D. Ginsburg and Rayna Rapp, 195–208. Berkeley: University of California Press.

Pickering, H. J., J. Todd, D. Dunn, J. Pepin, and W. Wilkins. 1992. Prostitutes and their clients: A Gambian survey. *Social Science and Medicine* 34:75–88.

Pison, Gilles. 1997. Manipulations and errors in age assessment. Paper presented at the IUSSP seminar "Age—between nature and culture." Max Planck Institute, Rostock, Germany.

Plato. 1949. *Timaeus,* trans. Benjamin Jowett. New York: Macmillan.

Poovey, M. 1986. Scenes of an indelicate character: The medical treatment of Victorian women. *Representations* 14:137–68.

Prentice, Andrew M., Roger G. Whitehead, Susan B. Roberts, and Alison A. Paul. 1981. Long-term energy balance in child-bearing Gambian women. *American Journal of Clinical Nutrition* 34:2790–99.

Puffer, R. R., and C. V. Serrano. 1976. Results of the inter-American investigations of mortality relating to reproduction. *Bulletin of the Pan American Health Organization* 10:131–42.

Quinn, Charlotte A. 1972. *Mandingo Kingdoms of the Senegambia: Traditionalism, Islam, and European Expansion.* Evanston, Ill.: Northwestern University Press.

Radcliffe-Brown, A. R. 1950. Introduction to *African Systems of Kinship and Marriage,* edited by A. R. Radcliffe-Brown and Daryll Forde, 1–85. London: Oxford University Press.

Ragoné, Helena. 1994. *Surrogate Motherhood: Conception in the Heart.* Boulder, Colo.: Westview.

Rapp, Rayna. 1999. *Testing Women, Testing the Fetus: The Social Impact of Amniocentesis in America.* New York: Routledge.

Rasmussen, Susan J., 1997. *The Poetics and Politics of Tuareg Aging: Life Course and Personal Destiny in Niger.* De Kalb: Northern Illinois University Press.

Ratcliffe, Amy. 2000. Men's fertility and marriages: Male reproductive strategies in rural Gambia. D.Sc. diss., Harvard School of Public Health.

Reischer, Erica. 1998. Muscling in: the changing female body aesthetic and women's work in contemporary America. Research proposal. Committee on Human Development, University of Chicago.

Republic of The Gambia. 1993. *Gambian Contraceptive Prevalence and Fertility Determinants Survey.* Medical and Health Services Directorate, Ministry of Health and Social Welfare, Human Resources Unit; CERPOD, Bamako; and The Population Council.

Richards, A. 1956. *Chisungu: A Girl's Initiation Ceremony among the Bemba of Northern Rhodesia.* London: Faber and Faber.

Ridley, Jeanne Clare. 1979. Introduction to *Manual IX: The Methodology of Measuring the Impact of Family Planning Programmes on Fertility,* Population Studies, no. 66, 112–25. New York: United Nations Secretariat, Department of International Economic and Social Affairs. ST/ESA/SER.A/66.

Riesman, Paul. 1976. A comprehensible anthropological assessment. In *Seeing Castaneda: Reactions to the "Don Juan" Writings of Carlos Castaneda,* edited by Daniel C. Noel, 46–53. New York: Capricorn.

———. 1986. The person and the life cycle in African social life and thought. *African Studies Review* 29:71–138.

———. 1992. *First Find Your Child a Good Mother: The Construction of Self in Two African Communities.* New Brunswick, N.J.: Rutgers University Press.

Robertson, A. F. 1991. *Beyond the Family: The Social Organization of Human Reproduction.* Berkeley: University of California Press.

Rooks, Judith Pence. 1997. *Midwifery and Childbirth in America.* Philadelphia: Temple University Press.

Rosander, Eva Evers. 1991. *Women in a Borderland: Managing Muslim Identity Where Morocco Meets Spain.* Stockholm University, Department of Anthropology.

Rose, Geoffrey. 1992. *The Strategy of Preventive Medicine.* Oxford: Oxford University Press.

Ross, Ellen. 1993. *Love and Toil: Motherhood in Outcast London, 1870–1918.* New York: Oxford University Press.

Ross, John A., and Elizabeth Frankenburg. 1993. *Findings from Two Decades of Family Planning Research.* New York: Population Council.

Rowe, John W., and Robert L. Kahn. 1997. Successful aging. *Gerontologist* 37:433–40.

Russell, Andrew, Elisa J. Sobo, and Mary S. Thompson, eds. 2000. *Contraception Across Cultures: Technologies, Choices, Constraints.* Oxford: Berg.

Ryden, Kent. 1993. *Mapping the Invisible Landscape: Folklore, Writing, and the Sense of Place.* Iowa City: University of Iowa Press.

Ryder, Norman B. 1965. The cohort as a concept in the study of social change. *American Sociological Review.* 30:843–61.

———. 1992. The centrality of time in the study of the family. In *Family Systems and Cultural Change,* edited by Elza Berquo and Peter Xenos, 161–75. Oxford: Clarendon.

Sahlins, Marshall D. 1976. *The Use and Abuse of Biology: An Anthropological Critique of Sociobiology.* Ann Arbor: University of Michigan Press.

Said, Edward. 1978. *Orientalism.* New York: Random House.

Sallis, John. 1999. *Chorology: On Beginning in Plato's* Timaeus. Bloomington: Indiana University Press.

Sambisa, William, and Sian Curtis. 1997. Contraceptive use dynamics in Zimbabwe: Postpartum contraceptive behavior. Calverton, Md.: Macro International.

Santow, Gigi. 1995. *Coitus interruptus* and the control of natural fertility. *Population Studies* 49:19–43.

Santow, Gigi, and Michael Bracher. 1989. Do gravidity and age affect pregnancy outcome? *Social Biology* 36:9–22.

Sargent, Carolyn Fishel. 1982. *The Cultural Context of Therapeutic Choice: Obstetrical Care Decisions among the Bariba of Benin.* Dordrecht: D. Reidel.

Sargent, Carolyn Fishel, and Dennis Cordell. 1998. Representations of family among Malian migrants to France. Paper presented at the meeting of the American Anthropological Association, Philadelphia.

Saucier, J.-F. Correlates of the long postpartum taboo: A cross-cultural study. *Current Anthropology* 13:238–49.

Scheffler, Harold W. 1978. *Australian Kin Classification.* Cambridge: Cambridge University Press.

Schneider, David Murray. 1968. *American Kinship: A Cultural Account.* Englewood Cliffs, N.J.: Prentice-Hall.

Schoenmaeckers, Ronny, Iqbal H. Shah, Ron Lesthaeghe, and Oleko Tambashe. 1981. The child-spacing tradition and the postpartum taboo in tropical Africa: Anthropological evidence. In *Child-Spacing in Tropical Africa*, edited by Hilary J. Page and Ron Lesthaeghe, 25–71. London: Academic.

Schroeder, Richard A. 1999. *Shady Practices: Agroforestry and Gender Politics in The Gambia.* Berkeley: University of California Press.

Schutz, Alfred. 1973. *Collected Papers: The Problem of Social Reality*, vol. 1. The Hague: Martinus Nijhoff.

Schutz, Alfred, and Thomas Luckmann. 1973. *The Structures of the Life-World*, trans. Richard M. Zaner and H. Tristram Engelhardt Jr. Evanston, Ill.: Northwestern University Press.

Scott, James C. 1985. *The Weapons of the Weak: Everyday Forms of Peasant Resistance.* New Haven, Conn.: Yale University Press.

Seccomb, Wally. 1992. Men's "marital rights" and women's "wifely duties": Changing conjugal relations in the fertility decline. In *The European Experience of Declining Fertility, 1850–1970: The Quiet Revolution*, edited by J. R. Gillis, L. A. Tilly, and D. Levine, 66–84. Cambridge, Mass.: Blackwell.

Sembène, Ousmane. 1976. *Xala*, trans. Clive Wake. Westport, Conn.: L. Hill.

———. 1987. Her three days. In *Tribal Scars and Other Stories*, 38–53. Portsmouth, N.H.: Heinemann.

Setel, Philip. 2000. "Someone to take my place": Fertility and the male life-course among Coastal Boiken, East Sepik Province, Papua New Guinea. In *Fertility and the Male Life Cycle in the Era of Fertility Decline*, edited by Caroline Bledsoe, Susana Lerner, and Jane I. Guyer, 233–56. Oxford: Oxford University Press.

Shipton, Parker. 1992. The rope and the box: Group savings in The Gambia. In *Informal Finance in Low-Income Countries,* edited by Dale W. Adams and Delbert A. Fitchett, 25–41. Boulder, Colo.: Westview.

Shore, Bradd. 1996. *Culture in Mind: Cognition, Culture, and the Problem of Meaning.* Oxford: Oxford University Press.

Shorter, Edward. 1997. *Women's Bodies: A Social History of Women's Encounter with Health, Ill-Health, and Medicine.* New Brunswick, N.J.: Transaction Publishers.

Shweder, Richard A. 1990. Cultural psychology—what is it? In *Cultural Psychology: Essays on Comparative Human Development,* 1–43. Chicago: University of Chicago Press.

———. 1991. Post-Nietzschean anthropology: The idea of multiple objective worlds. In *Thinking Through Cultures: Expeditions in Cultural Psychology,* 27–72. Cambridge, Mass.: Harvard University Press.

Siegemund, Justine Dittrich. 1691. *Spiegel der Vroed-Vrouwen,* pl. 2. Amsterdam: National Library of Medicine.

Simmel, Georg. 1971a. How is society possible? In *On Individuality and Social Forms: Selected Writings,* edited by Donald N. Levine, 6–22. Chicago: University of Chicago Press.

———. 1971b. The transcendant character of life. In *On Individuality and Social Forms: Selected Writings,* edited by Donald N. Levine, 353–74. Chicago: University of Chicago Press.

Sinclair, Upton. 1988. *The Jungle.* Urbana: University of Illinois Press.

Sinnett, P. F. 1977. Nutrition adaptation among the Enga. In *Subsistence and Survival: Rural Ecology in the Pacific,* edited by T. P. Bayliss-Smith and Richard G. Feachman, 63–90. London: Academic.

Skelley, H. R., A. M. Duthie, and R. H. Philpott. 1976. Rupture of the uterus: The preventable factors. *South African Medical Journal* 50 (13): 505–9.

Skinner, G. William. 1964. Marketing and social structure in rural China, Part I. *Journal of Asian Studies* 24:3–43.

———. 1993. Conjugal power in Tokugawa Japanese families: A matter of life or death. In *Sex and Gender Hierarchies,* edited by B. D. Miller, 236–70. Cambridge: Cambridge University Press.

———. 1997. Family systems and demographic processes. In *Anthropological Demography: Toward a New Synthesis,* edited by David I. Kertzer and Tom Fricke, 53–95. Chicago: University of Chicago Press.

Skramstad, Heidi. 1997. Coping with childlessness: The Kanyaleng kafos in Gambia. Paper for the IUSSP seminar Cultural Perspectives on Reproductive Health, Rustenburg, South Africa.

Sobo, Elisa J. 1993. *One Blood: The Jamaican Body.* New York: State University of New York Press.

Sonko, Sheriff. 1995. National fertility analysis. Population and housing census 1993. Banjul, The Gambia: Central Statistics Department, Ministry of Finance and Economic Affairs.

Speert, Harold. 1958. *Obstetric and Gynecologic Milestones: Essays in Eponymy.* New York: Macmillan.

Spence, Alexander P. 1989. *Biology of Human Aging*. Englewood Cliffs, N.J.: Prentice-Hall.

Stanton, Cynthia, Noureddine Abderrahim, and Kenneth Hill. 1997. DHS maternal mortality indicators: An assessment of data quality and implications for data use. Demographic and Health Surveys Analytical Report No. 4. Calverton, Md.: Macro International.

Stenning, Derrick J. 1958. Household viability among the pastoral Fulani. In *The Developmental Cycle in Domestic Groups*, edited by Jack Goody, 92–119. Cambridge: Cambridge University Press.

Stichter, Sharon B., and Jane L. Parpart. 1988. Introduction: towards a materialist perspective on African women. In *Patriarchy and Class: African Women in the Home and the Workforce*, edited by Sharon B. Stichter and Jane L. Parpart, 1–26. Boulder, Colo.: Westview.

Stopes, M. C. 1929. *Mother England: A Contemporary History. Self-written by Those Who Have Had No Historian*. London: Bale & Danielsson.

Strathern, Andrew J. 1996. *Body Thoughts*. Ann Arbor: University of Michigan Press.

Strathern, Marilyn. 1992a. *After Nature: English Kinship in the Late Twentieth Century*. Cambridge: Cambridge University Press.

———. 1992b. *Reproducing the Future: Essays on Anthropology, Kinship, and the New Reproductive Technologies*. New York: Routledge.

———. 1994. No nature, no culture: The Hagen case. In *Nature, Culture and Gender*, edited by Carol P. MacCormack and Marilyn Strathern, 174–222. Cambridge: Cambridge University Press.

Strauss, Anselm. 1964. Introduction to *On Social Psychology: Selected Papers*, by George Herbert Mead, vii–xxv. Chicago: University of Chicago Press.

Stucki, Barbara, R. 1995. Managing the social clock: The negotiation of elderhood among rural Asante of Ghana. Ph.D. diss., Northwestern University.

Sullivan, Jeremiah, M. Shea, Oscar Rutstein, and George T. Bicego. 1994. Infant and child mortality. Comparative Studies No. 15. Calverton, Md.: Macro International.

Sundby, Johanne. 1997. Infertility in The Gambia: Traditional and modern health care. *Patient Education and Counseling* 31: 29–37.

Sundby, Johanne, Sheriff Sonko, and Reuben Mboge. 1998. Infertility in the Gambia: Frequency and health care seeking. *Social Science and Medicine* 46:891–99.

Szreter, Simon. 1993. The idea of demographic transition and the study of fertility: A critical intellectual history. *Population and Development Review* 19 (4): 659–701.

Townsend, Nicholas. 1997. Reproduction in anthropology and demography. In *Anthropological Demography: Toward a New Synthesis*, edited by David I. Kertzer and Tom Fricke, 96–114. Chicago: University of Chicago Press.

Townsend, Patricia K., and Ann McElroy. 1992. Toward an ecology of women's reproductive health. *Medical Anthropology* 14:9–34.

Tracer, D. P. 1991. Fertility-related changes in maternal body composition among the Au of Papua New Guinea. *American Journal of Physical Anthropology* 85:393–405.

Turner, Terence. 1994. Bodies and anti-bodies: Flesh and fetish in contemporary social theory. In *Embodiment and Experience: The Existential Ground of Culture and Self,* edited by T. Csordas, 27–47. Cambridge: Cambridge University Press.

Turner, Victor 1969. *The Ritual Process: Structure and Anti-Structure.* Chicago: Aldine.

United Nations. 1959. *Multilingual Demographic Dictionary.* Population Studies No. 29. New York: United Nations.

———. 1994. Report of the International Conference on Population and Development (Cairo, 5–13 September 1994). No. A/Conf.171/13, Oct. 18, 1994. New York: United Nations.

———. 1995. *Women's Education and Fertility Behaviour: Recent Evidence from the Demographic and Health Surveys.* New York. United Nations.

United Nations Secretariat. 1979. Introduction to *Manual IX: The Methodology of Measuring the Impact of Family Planning Programmes on Fertility.* New York: United Nations Dept. of International Economic and Social Affairs. Population Studies, No. 66. ST/ESA/SER.A/66. Pp. 1–5.

van Deventer, H. 1701. *Operationes Chirurgicae Novum Lumen Exhibentes Obstetricantibus.* Lugduni Batavorum: Apud Andream Dyckhuisen.

van de Walle, Etienne. 1968. Marriage in African censuses and inquiries. In *The Demography of Tropical Africa,* edited by W. Brass et al., 183–238. Princeton, N.J.: Princeton University Press.

———. 1992. Fertility transition, conscious choice, and numeracy. *Demography* 29:487–502.

van de Walle, Etienne, and John Kekovole. 1984. The recent evolution of African marriage and polygyny. Paper presented at the annual meetings of the Population Association of America, Minneapolis.

van de Walle, Etienne, and Elisha P. Renne, eds. 2001. *Regulating Menstruation: Beliefs, Practices, Interpretations.* Chicago: University of Chicago Press.

van de Walle, Etienne, and Francine van de Walle. 1991. Breastfeeding and popular aetiology in the Sahel. *Health Transition Review* 1 (1): 69–81.

———. 1993. Post-partum sexual abstinence in tropical Africa. In *Biomedical and Demographic Determinants of Reproduction,* edited by Ronald Gray, Henri Leridon, and Alfred Spira, 446–60. Oxford: Clarendon.

Ware, Helen. 1976. Motivations for the use of birth control: Evidence from West Africa. *Demography* 13:479–94.

Watkins, Susan Cotts. 2000. Local and foreign models of reproduction in Nyanza Province, Kenya. *Population and Development Review* 26 (4): 725–59.

Watkins, Susan, Naomi Rutenberg, and David Wilkinson. 1997. Disorderly theories, disorderly women. In *The Continuing Demographic Transition,* edited by G. W. Jones, R. M. Douglas, J. C. Caldwell, and R. M. D'Souza, 213–45. Oxford: Oxford University Press.

Watts, Michael J. 1993. Idioms of land and labor: Producing politics and rice in Senegambia. In *Land in African Agrarian Systems,* edited by Thomas J. Bassett and Donald E. Crummey, 157–93. Madison: University of Wisconsin Press.

Weeks, John R. 1999. *Population: An Introduction to Concepts and Issues.* 7th ed. Belmont, Calif.: Wadsworth.

Weil, Peter. 1968. Mandinka Mansaya: The role of the Mandinka in the political system of The Gambia. Ph.D. diss., University of Oregon. Ann Arbor, Mich.: University Microfilms International.

―――. 1971. Political structure and process among The Gambia Mandinka: The village parapolitical system. In *Papers on the Manding*, edited by Carleton T. Hodge, 249–72. Bloomington: Indiana University Press.

―――. 1986. Agricultural intensification and fertility in The Gambia. In *Culture and Reproduction: An Anthropological Critique of Demographic Transition Theory*, edited by W. Penn Handwerker, 294–320. Boulder, Colo.: Westview.

Welch, Thomas R., William H. Bergstrom, and Reginald C. Tsang. 2000. Vitamin-D-deficient rickets: The reemergence of a once-conquered disease. *Journal of Pedriatics* 137 (2): 143–45.

Whitehead, Harriet B. 1981. *Sexual Meanings: The Cultural Construction of Gender and Sexuality*. Cambridge: Cambridge University Press.

Whiting, J. W. M., Richard Kluckhohn, and Albert S. Anthony. 1958. The function of male initiation ceremonies at puberty. In *Readings in Social Psychology*, edited by Eleanor E. Maccoby, T. Newcomb, and E. Hartley, 359–70. New York: Henry Holt.

Whittemore, Robert Dunster. 1989. Child caregiving and socialization to the Mandinka way: Toward an ethnography of childhood. Ph.D. diss., University of California at Los Angeles.

WHO/UNICEF. 1996. *Revised 1990 Estimates of Maternal Mortality: A New Approach by WHO and UNICEF*. WHO/FRH/MSM/96.11. UNICEF/PLN96.1.

Whyte, Susan Reynolds. 1997. *Questioning Misfortune: The Pragmatics of Uncertainty of Eastern Uganda*. Cambridge: Cambridge University Press.

Williams, M. A., and R. Mittendorf. 1993. Increasing maternal age as a determinant of placenta previa: More important than increasing parity? *Journal of Reproductive Medicine* 38:425–28.

Winikoff, Beverly. 1983. The effects of birth spacing on child and maternal health. *Studies in Family Planning* 14:231–45.

Winkvist, A., K. M. Rasmussen, and J.-P. Habicht. 1992. A new definition of maternal depletion syndrome. *American Journal of Public Health* 82:691–94.

Winterbottom, T. 1803. *An Account of the Native Africans in the Neighborhood of Sierra Leone; to which Is Added, an Account of the Present State of Medicine among Them*. Vol. 1. London: C. Whittingham.

Wittrup, Inge. 1990. Me and my husband's wife: An analysis of polygyny among Mandinka in the Gambia. *Folk* 32:117–42.

Women's Co-operative Guild. 1916. *Maternity: Letters from Working-Women, Collected by the Women's Co-operative Guild*. London: G. Bell and Sons.

Wood, James W. 1994. *Dynamics of Human Reproduction: Biology, Biometry, Demography*. New York: Aldine De Gruyter.

Wrigley, E. A. 1969. *Population and History*. New York: McGraw-Hill.

Yanagisako, Sylvia, and Carol Delaney, eds. 1994. *Naturalizing Power: Essays in Feminist Cultural Analysis*. New York: Routledge.

Note: Page numbers followed by *f*, *t*, or *n* indicate figures, tables, or note numbers, respectively.